LIBRARY OF NEW TESTAMENT STUDIES

629

formerly the Journal for the Study of the New Testament Supplement series

Editor
Chris Keith

Editorial Board
Dale C. Allison, John M. G. Barclay, Lynn H. Cohick, R. Alan Culpepper,
Craig A. Evans, Robert Fowler, Simon J. Gathercole, Juan Hernández Jr.,
John S. Kloppenborg, Michael Labahn, Matthew V. Novenson, Love L. Sechrest,
Robert Wall, Catrin H. Williams, Brittany Wilson

Paul's Emotional Regime

The Social Function of Emotion in Philippians and 1 Thessalonians

Ian Y. S. Jew

LONDON • NEW YORK • OXFORD • NEW DELHI • SYDNEY

T&T CLARK
Bloomsbury Publishing Plc
50 Bedford Square, London, WC1B 3DP, UK
1385 Broadway, New York, NY 10018, USA
29 Earlsfort Terrace, Dublin 2, Ireland

BLOOMSBURY, T&T CLARK and the T&T Clark logo are trademarks of
Bloomsbury Publishing Plc

First published in Great Britain 2021
This paperback edition published in 2022

Copyright © Ian Y. S. Jew, 2021

Ian Y. S. Jew has asserted his right under the Copyright, Designs and Patents Act, 1988,
to be identified as Author of this work.

For legal purposes the Acknowledgements on pp. xiii–xiv constitute an extension
of this copyright page.

All rights reserved. No part of this publication may be reproduced or
transmitted in any form or by any means, electronic or mechanical,
including photocopying, recording, or any information storage or retrieval
system, without prior permission in writing from the publishers.

Bloomsbury Publishing Plc does not have any control over, or responsibility for, any
third-party websites referred to or in this book. All internet addresses given in this
book were correct at the time of going to press. The author and publisher regret any
inconvenience caused if addresses have changed or sites have ceased to exist, but can
accept no responsibility for any such changes.

A catalogue record for this book is available from the British Library.

Library of Congress Cataloging-in-Publication Data
Names: Jew, Ian Y. S., author.
Title: Paul's emotional regime : the social function of emotion in
Philippians and 1 Thessalonians / Ian Y.S. Jew. Description: London ; New York : T&T Clark,
2020. | Series: Library of New Testament studies, 2513–8790 ; 629 | Revision of author's
thesis (doctoral)–Durham University, 2017. | Includes bibliographical references and index. |
Summary: "This book is the first full-length treatment of emotion in the Pauline corpus.
In his letters, Paul speaks often of his emotions, and also promotes certain feelings while
banishing others. This indicates that for Paul, emotion is vital. However, in New Testament
studies, the study of emotions is still nascent; current research in the social sciences
highlights its cognitive and social dimensions. Ian Y. S. Jew combines rigorous
social-scientific analysis and exegetical enquiry to argue that emotions are intrinsic to the
formation of the Pauline communities, as they encode belief structures and influence
patterns of social experience"–Provided by publisher. Identifiers: LCCN 2020025162 (print) |
LCCN 2020025163 (ebook) | ISBN 9780567694126 (hardback) |
ISBN 9780567694133 (pdf) | ISBN 9780567694157 (epub)
Subjects: LCSH: Bible. Thessalonians, 1st–Criticism, interpretation, etc. |
Bible. Philippians–Criticism, interpretation, etc. |
Emotions–Biblical teaching. | Emotions–Religious aspects–Christianity.
Classification: LCC BS2655.E46 J49 2020 (print) |
LCC BS2655.E46 (ebook) | DDC 227/.06–dc23
LC record available at https://lccn.loc.gov/2020025162
LC ebook record available at https://lccn.loc.gov/2020025163

Series: Library of New Testament Studies, ISSN 2513-8790, volume 629

ISBN: HB: 978-0-5676-9412-6
PB: 978-0-5676-9644-1
ePDF: 978-0-5676-9413-3
ePUB: 978-0-5676-9415-7

Typeset by Newgen KnowledgeWorks Pvt. Ltd., Chennai, India

To find out more about our authors and books visit www.bloomsbury.com
and sign up for our newsletters.

Contents

List of Illustrations	x
Foreword	xi
Acknowledgements	xiii
List of Abbreviations	xv

1. Introduction — 1
   - 1.1. Introductory Comments — 1
   - 1.2. Emotion and Early Christianity: Survey of Research — 1
     - 1.2.1. Studies of Emotion in the Wider New Testament — 1
       - 1.2.1.a. Recent Studies — 1
       - 1.2.1.b. Stephen Barton — 3
       - 1.2.1.c. Katherine M. Hockey — 4
     - 1.2.2. Studies of Emotion in Paul — 5
       - 1.2.2.a. Paul's Rhetorical Use of Emotional Appeal — 5
       - 1.2.2.b. Paul's Treatment of Grief — 7
       - 1.2.2.c. Paul's Notion of Joy — 8
     - 1.2.3. Summary — 10
   - 1.3. Contemporary Emotions Research: Selected Aspects — 11
     - 1.3.1. Overview — 11
     - 1.3.2. Emotions Research in the Social Sciences and Humanities — 12
     - 1.3.3. Emotion: Nature and Terminology — 14
       - 1.3.3.a. The Nature of Emotion and Its Conceptual History — 14
       - 1.3.3.b. Emotion and Cognition — 17
       - 1.3.3.c. 'Emotion' as a Portmanteau Term — 17
   - 1.4. Aims of the Study — 18
   - 1.5. Methodological Approach — 19

2. Emotion in Stoicism — 23
   - 2.1. Introduction — 23
     - 2.1.1. Translating πάθος — 23
   - 2.2. The Broader Philosophical Background — 24

	2.2.1.	Rationality, Virtue, and *Eudaimonia*	24
	2.2.2.	Stoic Physics and the *Pneuma*	26
	2.2.3.	Stoic Psychology of Knowledge and Action	28
		2.2.3.a. Knowledge	28
		2.2.3.b. Action	31
2.3.	The Stoic Understanding of Emotion		32
	2.3.1.	The Passions as 'Excessive' Impulses	32
	2.3.2.	The Passions as Value Judgements	35
	2.3.3.	The Taxonomy of the Emotions	37
		2.3.3.a. The Passions	37
		2.3.3.b. The *Eupatheiai*	38
		2.3.3.c. The *Propatheiai*	39
		2.3.3.d. 'Moral Emotions'	42
2.4.	The Stoic Therapy of Emotion		44
	2.4.1.	Reason, Nature, and *Oikeiōsis*	44
	2.4.2.	Philosophy as Therapy	46
	2.4.3.	The Case for Stoic Therapy	47
	2.4.4.	Stoic Therapy in Practice	50
2.5.	The Early Roman Empire Stoics on Grief and Joy		51
	2.5.1.	Grief	52
		2.5.1.a. Consolation in Antiquity	52
		2.5.1.b. Seneca on Grief	53
		2.5.1.c. Epictetus on Grief	59
	2.5.2.	Joy	61
		2.5.2.a. Joy as a Eupathic Response	61
		2.5.2.b. Seneca on Joy	61
2.6.	Conclusion		64
3. Joy in Philippians			65
3.1.	The Background to Philippians		65
	3.1.1.	Overview	65
	3.1.2.	Literary Integrity	66
	3.1.3.	Genre	68
		3.1.3.a. A Hortatory Letter of Friendship	68
		3.1.3.b. A Letter of Consolation	70
		3.1.3.c. Other Proposals and Conclusion	70

		3.1.4. Distinctives	71
		3.1.4.a. Lexical Distinctives	71
		3.1.4.b. Thematic Distinctives	71
	3.2. Suffering in Philippians		73
		3.2.1. Paul's Suffering	73
		3.2.1.a. Paul in Prison (Phil. 1.7, 13-14, 17)	73
		3.2.1.b. The Actions of Paul's Rivals (Phil. 1.15-17)	74
		3.2.1.c. Paul's Common Suffering with the Philippians (Phil. 2.17-18)	74
		3.2.2. The Philippians' Suffering (Phil. 1.27-30)	76
		3.2.3. Christ's Suffering (Phil. 2.5-11)	78
		3.2.4. The Examples of Paul's Co-workers (Phil. 2.19-30)	79
		3.2.5. Conclusion	80
	3.3. Joy: Exegetical Considerations		81
		3.3.1. Joy in Partnership in the Gospel (Phil. 1.3-5; 2.28-30; 4.10-19)	81
		3.3.2. Joy in the Gospel's Advancement	86
		3.3.2.a. Joy and the Progress of the Gospel in Rome (Phil. 1.15-18)	86
		3.3.2.b. Joy and the Progress of the Gospel in the Philippians' Lives (Phil. 1.18-26; 2.1-4; 4.1)	87
		3.3.2.c. Mutual Joy in the Face of Suffering (Phil. 2.17-18)	88
		3.3.3. Joy 'in the Lord': The Eschatological Horizon (Phil. 3.1; 4.4-9)	89
	3.4. The Basis and Function of Joy		92
		3.4.1. The Theological Basis of Joy	92
		3.4.2. The Social Character and Function of Joy	95
	3.5. Conclusion		97
4.	Grief in 1 Thessalonians		101
	4.1. The Background to 1 Thessalonians		101
		4.1.1. Overview	101
		4.1.2. Literary Integrity	102
		4.1.3. Genre	103
		4.1.3.a. A Paraenetic Letter	103
		4.1.3.b. A Letter of Consolation	104
		4.1.3.c. Other Proposals and Conclusion	105
		4.1.4. Distinctives	106

4.2.	Conflict and Suffering in 1 Thessalonians	108
	4.2.1. Introduction	108
	4.2.2. The Nature of the Thessalonians' Suffering (1 Thess. 1.6)	108
	4.2.3. The Cause of the Thessalonians' Suffering (1 Thess. 2.14)	109
4.3.	Grief in 1 Thessalonians 4.13-18	111
	4.3.1. Extent of the Passage	111
	4.3.2. The Disclosure Formula	112
	4.3.3. The Circumstances of the Thessalonians' Grief	112
	4.3.3.a. The Martyrdom of Fellow Believers?	113
	4.3.3.b. Major Hypotheses Concerning the Thessalonians' Grief	114
	4.3.4. A Prohibition against Grief?	117
4.4.	Consolation in 1 Thessalonians	120
	4.4.1. The Theological Basis of Consolation	120
	4.4.1.a. The Confession of the Church (1 Thess. 4.14)	120
	4.4.1.b. The 'Word of the Lord' (1 Thess. 4.15-17)	121
	4.4.1.c. Comfort One Another with These Words (1 Thess. 4.18)	124
	4.4.2. The Social Character and Function of Consolation	125
	4.4.2.a. The Social Regulation of Grief	125
	4.4.2.b. The Thessalonians' Grief	126
	4.4.2.c. The Social Character of Consolation	127
	4.4.2.d. The Function of Consolation	131
4.5.	Conclusion	136
5.	**The Pauline Emotional Regime**	**139**
5.1.	Introduction	139
5.2.	The Early Christians and Emotion	141
	5.2.1. Wayne Meeks's *The First Urban Christians*	141
	5.2.2. Moving beyond Meeks: The Social Function of Emotion	143
5.3.	The Sociological Concept of the 'Emotional Regime'	145
	5.3.1. The Emotional Regime	145
	5.3.2. Religious Emotional Regimes	146
	5.3.3. Key Characteristics of Religious Emotion	146
	5.3.3.a. Emotional Ordering	147
	5.3.3.b. Emotional Transcendence-Transition	147
	5.3.3.c. Inspiration-Orientation	147

	5.3.4. Dialectical Relationships within an Emotional Regime	148
	5.3.5. The Power of Religious Emotion	150
	5.3.6. Conclusion	151
5.4.	The Function of Emotion in the Pauline Congregations	151
	5.4.1. Introduction	151
	5.4.2. The Integrating and Differentiating Functions of Emotion	151
5.5.	Exploring the Pauline Emotional Regime	153
	5.5.1. Emotional Ordering	153
	5.5.2. Symbols and Emotional Ordering	154
	5.5.3. Instruction, Imitation, and Emotional Ordering	157
	5.5.4. Ritual and Emotional Ordering	161
	5.5.5. Language and Emotional Ordering	168
	5.5.6. Letters and Emotional Ordering	170
	5.5.7. Conclusion	173
5.6.	Comparing the Pauline and Stoic Emotional Regimes	175
	5.6.1. Paul on Joy and Grief	175
	5.6.2. The Stoics on Joy and Grief	176
	5.6.3. Similarities	176
	5.6.4. Differences	178
5.7.	Conclusion	182
	5.7.1. Suggestions for Further Research	183
Bibliography		185
Index of Ancient Sources		203
Index of Subjects		213

Illustrations

Figure

1. Dialectical Relationships within an Emotional Regime   148

Tables

1. Impression and Assent in the Formation of Belief   30
2. The Passions   38
3. The *Eupatheiai*   39
4. The 'Moral Emotions'   43

Foreword

In recent decades, the multidisciplinary study of emotions has become prominent across all academic disciplines, although in biblical studies emotions research has been largely limited to analysis of the interface between emotion and rhetoric. It is therefore a particular joy to welcome Ian Jew's fresh, deeply researched, and interdisciplinary study of emotion in the letters of Paul. This book arises out of conversations at Durham University, led by Stephen Barton, which also inspired Katherine Hockey's *The Role of Emotion in 1 Peter* (2019), but it charts its own unique path and provides a wholly fresh approach to the study of emotions in Paul's letters. Emotion has often been taken to be irrational; here, in line with research in the psychology of emotions, it is rightly interpreted as a form of cognition and evaluation, integral to the embodiment of belief. It is generally assumed that emotion is purely individual, inner, subjective, and therefore inaccessible; here, following significant research in sociology, it is shown to be also communal, and therefore readily learned, ordered, even managed. Far from being merely episodic, emotions can be long-lasting, habituated, and therefore formative, both for the individual and for a community. For such reasons, it turns out that the study of emotions can take us deep into Paul's theology and into his attempts to shape the life and thought of his communities, and no one could read this book without gaining a significantly new understanding of joy and grief and their pivotal role in Philippians and 1 Thessalonians.

The field of emotion studies is now so vast and complex that it is easy to lose one's way. Fortunately, Ian Jew chooses and clears his way along two paths that lead in particularly fruitful directions. First, he situates Paul's letters in their ancient context, and conducts an extensive comparison with the influential theory of emotions developed in Stoicism. He is scrupulous in presenting Stoic views on their own terms (not through Christian lenses) and thus offers a balanced comparison that brings out both the similarities and the differences between Paul and the Stoics. Second, he brings to the analysis of Paul's letters the sociological notion of an 'emotional regime', as developed by Ole Riis and Linda Woodhead, again with careful attention to its conceptual nuances. By integrating ancient and modern theories on emotion, he is able to shed a flood of new light on familiar Pauline texts, and clarifies, for instance, how the emotions inculcated by Paul serve not only to integrate his communities but also to differentiate them from their environment.

From now on, no one can read the New Testament references to joy, anger, grief, comfort, or fear, and dismiss these phenomena as 'mere emotions'. Here we are alerted to the fact that all such emotions serve as windows onto whole patterns of thought and play a crucial role in the long-term formation of communities. Ian Jew's results are clear and convincing, and his work will surely stimulate further studies of other emotions and other texts, using these and other tools of analysis. Slowly, we will learn how to reintegrate this essential feature of the human condition into the web of early Christian thought, experience, and social expression. In this regard, this book takes us to a new scholarly frontier. Once we have got the measure of the new territory here explored, I am confident we will find there is plenty more to discover.

John M. G. Barclay
Lightfoot Professor of Divinity
Durham University

Acknowledgements

This volume is a slightly revised version of my Durham University PhD thesis, which was successfully defended in April 2017.

First and foremost, I thank God for his hand of guidance and provision upon this project, from start to finish. While this work is offered to the scholarly community for its consideration, it is, more importantly, offered to God as an act of devotion. There were many days when I felt totally unequal to the task before me; but God's grace sustained me through it all.

It was as a student at Trinity Theological College, Singapore, that I made my first giddy foray into biblical studies. I am grateful especially to Dr Tan Kim Huat, whose passion for the New Testament was utterly infectious, and Dr Chris Dippenaar, who adroitly inducted me into the joyful rigours of Koine Greek.

The initial ideas for this work emerged during several master's courses at Durham University. It is no coincidence that my approach reflects the influence of my teachers: from Prof. Francis Watson, I learnt how to be a more attentive reader of Paul; Dr Stephen Barton showed me the value of social-scientific criticism; and I was inspired by Prof. Walter Moberly's perspectives on theological hermeneutics.

I am deeply thankful to my doktorvater, Prof. John Barclay, who supervised my thesis with extraordinary perspicacity and was always generous with his encouragement and time. I have learnt so much from him and his own work on Paul. While almost every page bears his influence, any infelicities that remain are entirely my responsibility. I am also thankful for the feedback of my examiners, Prof. Louise Lawrence and Prof. Francis Watson; their insights have only improved this work.

At Bloomsbury T&T Clark, I thank Prof. Chris Keith for accepting this work into such a distinguished monograph series, Dominic Mattos and Sarah Blake for ably guiding me through the publication process, and Nathan Shedd for his kind help.

In Durham, it was a special blessing to have had friends for the journey: I am so grateful to Nathanael and Charmaine Goh, James and Beng Kwee Lim, Lam Swee Sum, Kyle Yeo, Kelley Wong, Isabel Lim, and Izabella Chia for their vivifying camaraderie. St Nics was a spiritual refuge for me; David and Rosemary Day, Tony and Joan Prested, and Jack and Carol Winskill were constantly looking out for us.

This book and the thesis on which it is based would not be what they are without the prayers of friends who are too many to name. I am thankful for all of them. However, I want to specially mention those brothers who were often in touch to cheer me on: Jasper Sim, Jasper Ngoh, Goh Ser Guan, Chua Swee Tuck, Joshua Lim, Eric Wong, Aaron Tan, Amos Lau, Jason Lim, Alfred Tan, Raveen Mannar, Timothy Pang, See Hao Jun, Titus Tng, Hoi Kok Fu, Andrew Yap, Andy Chong, Mervin Tee, Ivan Liew, Larry Lim, Albert Yim, Reuben Ong, Wilson Tan, Andrew Peh, and Sim Hwee Hong. I also want to thank Andy Goh, my colleagues, and the church leadership at Grace Methodist

Church, Singapore, as well as my fellow pastors in the Chinese Annual Conference of the Methodist Church in Singapore, for their support. I am grateful also for the special kindness of Julian and Lai Fun Thumboo. And as always, my family and relations were unique blessings.

Finally, I acknowledge my indebtedness to the three amazing people without whose unstinting encouragement and prayers all this could not have happened. I thank my parents, Sin Cheng and Fook Min Chia, for believing in me and supporting me with such loving largesse. And I thank my wife, Angela, who has selflessly shared this journey with me and never failed to point me to God; this work is as much hers as it is mine. Angie, Dad, and Mum – this book is dedicated to you.

To God alone be the glory.

Abbreviations

AASF	Annales Academiae Scientarum Fennicae
AB	Anchor Bible
ANRW	Hildegard Temporini and Wolfgang Haase (eds), *Aufstieg und Niedergang der römischen Welt: Geschichte und Kultur Roms im Spiegel der neueren Forschung* (Berlin: W. de Gruyter, 1972–)
ANTC	Abingdon New Testament Commentaries
ATANT	Abhandlungen zur Theologie des Alten und Neuen Testaments
BDAG	Walter Bauer, Frederick W. Danker, William F. Arndt, and F. Wilbur Gingrich, *Greek-English Lexicon of the New Testament and Other Early Christian Literature* (Chicago: University of Chicago Press, 3rd ed., 2000)
BDF	Friedrich Blass, Albert Debrunner, and Robert W. Funk, *A Greek Grammar of the New Testament and Other Early Christian Literature* (Chicago: University of Chicago Press, 1961)
BECNT	Baker Exegetical Commentary on the New Testament
BETL	Bibliotheca ephemeridum theologicarum lovaniensium
BEvT	Beiträge zur evangelischen Theologie
BFCT	Beiträge zur Förderung christlicher Theologie
BJRL	*Bulletin of the John Rylands University Library of Manchester*
BNTC	Black's New Testament Commentaries
BWANT	Beiträge zur Wissenschaft vom Alten und Neuen Testament
CBQ	*Catholic Biblical Quarterly*
CBR	*Currents in Biblical Research*
ConBNT	Coniectanea Biblica, New Testament Series
DPL	Gerald F. Hawthorne and Ralph P. Martin (eds), *Dictionary of Paul and His Letters* (Downers Grove, IL: Intervarsity, 1993)
EGGNT	Exegetical Guide to the Greek New Testament
EKKNT	Evangelische-katholischer Kommentar zum Neuen Testament
FRLANT	Forschungen zur Religion und Literatur des Alten und Neuen Testaments
HTKNT	Herders theologischer Kommentar zum Neuen Testament
HTR	*Harvard Theological Review*
JBL	*Journal of Biblical Literature*
JSNT	*Journal for the Study of the New Testament*
JSNTSup	Journal for the Study of the New Testament, Supplement Series
KEK	Kritisch-exegetischer Kommentar über das Neue Testament
LEC	Library of Early Christianity
LNTS	Library of New Testament Studies

LS	Long, Anthony A., and David N. Sedley, *The Hellenistic Philosophers* (2 vols; Cambridge: Cambridge University Press, 1987)
NCB	New Century Bible
NIBCNT	New International Biblical Commentary on the New Testament
NICNT	New International Commentary on the New Testament
NIDNTT	Colin Brown (ed.), *New International Dictionary of New Testament Theology* (4 vols; Grand Rapids, MI: Zondervan, 1975–8)
NIGTC	New International Greek Testament Commentary
NovTSup	Novum Testamentum, Supplements
NTAbh	Neutestamentliche Abhandlungen
NTOA/SUNT	Novum Testamentum et orbis antiquus/Studien zur Umwelt des Neuen Testaments
NTS	*New Testament Studies*
OSAP	*Oxford Studies in Ancient Philosophy*
PHP	*Galen: On the Doctrines of Hippocrates and Plato* [= *De Placitis Hippocratis et Platonis*] (trans. Philip De Lacy; 3 vols; Berlin: Akademie-Verlag, 1978–80)
PilNTC	Pillar New Testament Commentary
RevExp	*Review and Expositor*
RNT	Regensburger Neues Testament
RSPT	*Revue des sciences philosophiques et théologiques*
SBL	Society of Biblical Literature
SBLDS	Society of Biblical Literature Dissertation Series
SBLSBS	Society of Biblical Literature Sources for Biblical Study
SGBC	Story of God Biblical Commentary
SHAW	Sitzungsberichte der Heidelberger Akademie der Wissenschaften
SNTSMS	Society for New Testament Studies Monograph Series
SR	*Studies in Religion*
SVF	H. von Arnim (ed.), *Stoicorum Veterum Fragmenta* (4 vols; Leipzig: Teubner, 1903–24)
TDNT	Gerhard Kittel and Gerhard Friedrich (eds), *Theological Dictionary of the New Testament* (trans. Geoffrey W. Bromiley; 10 vols; Grand Rapids, MI: Eerdmans, 1964–76)
THKNT	Theologisher Handkommentar zum Neuen Testament
TynBul	*Tyndale Bulletin*
WBC	Word Biblical Commentary
WUNT	Wissenschaftliche Untersuchungen zum Neuen Testament
ZCINT	Zondervan Critical Introductions to the New Testament
ZECNT	Zondervan Exegetical Commentary on the New Testament
ZST	*Zeitschrift für systematische Theologie*
ZTK	*Zeitschrift für Theologie und Kirche*

1

Introduction

1.1. Introductory Comments

The New Testament attests strongly to the fact that Paul displayed a wide range of emotions in his life and ministry, and expected the same from his converts in the churches that he had founded. However, the study of emotion in the Pauline letters is still in its infancy; and to my knowledge, there is, as yet, no monograph-length treatment of Paul and emotion. To date, scholarly work has focused largely on Paul's rhetorical use of *pathos*, though in recent years there has been a nascent interest in probing the relationship between his construals of emotion and early Christian eschatological faith. However, more fundamental questions regarding the role of emotion in Paul's writings have not been addressed.

Accordingly, this present investigation aims to get at the heart of what Paul is doing with emotion in his letters. Through historical analysis and exegetical study, and in dialogue with present-day social-scientific approaches to emotion, I will offer an account of the function of emotion in Paul's letters that engages deeply with his theological discourse and pastoral agenda, while also taking careful account of the complexes of sociality, symbolic meanings, and cultural influences that shape the sociocultural milieu in which his churches are set.

1.2. Emotion and Early Christianity: Survey of Research

1.2.1. Studies of Emotion in the Wider New Testament

1.2.1.a. Recent Studies

There are several older studies in the New Testament that have a specific emotion such as love or joy as their focus, but they are targeted at a non-specialist readership.[1] As far as I am able to discover, there have been in recent years only a handful of monographs

---

[1] James Moffatt, *Love in the New Testament* (London: Hodder and Stoughton, 1929); William G. Morrice, *Joy in the New Testament* (Exeter: Paternoster, 1984).

that have emotion as the main focus; however, they are generally wanting in theoretical and analytical depth.

Stephen Voorwinde's two monographs both deal with the significance of Jesus's emotions for aspects of Christology: in the first of them, Voorwinde seeks to establish that the emotions of the Johannine Jesus throw significant light on the ongoing debate surrounding his humanity/divinity, and in its sequel Voorwinde extends his scope to include the synoptic gospels in order to ascertain if they together with John's gospel present a coherent picture of Jesus's emotions.[2] However, Voorwinde offers only a cursory appraisal of what emotions are: for him, they are experiences of feeling that activate action.[3] Voorwinde's interest in Jesus's emotions lies in how they confirm his identity rather than in their function in the gospel narratives. While there is some recognition that emotions emerge from situational reasoning, Voorwinde's discussion is somewhat lacking in theoretical rigour.

In a wide-ranging study, Matthew Elliott applies current research in psychology to emotion in the New Testament writings.[4] Elliott's expressed desire to interpret emotion in the light of both modern studies of emotion and its ancient context is certainly laudable.[5] Unfortunately, his exegetical approach is somewhat facile, and there is minimal engagement with the Greco-Roman sociocultural setting for emotional life. Furthermore, though Elliott stresses that emotion is connected to ethics,[6] he does not adequately explore its implications for the early Christian communities. While Elliott's efforts to utilize a cognitive approach to understanding emotion have certain echoes in my approach, any indebtedness to his work is negligible.

In a recent, groundbreaking volume of theoretically sophisticated case studies of emotions displayed by divine and human figures in the biblical texts, a team of biblical scholars investigate emotions such as joy, hate, grief, and disgust.[7] The approaches that are employed in these essays come from varied disciplines such as cultural psychology, literary theory, linguistic science, ancient and modern philosophy, and cognitive science, and the essays demonstrate how such resources can be fruitfully applied to the exploration of emotions across a range of biblical genres. However, while the essay collection provides evidence of a burgeoning scholarly interest in the emotional terrain of the Bible, unfortunately it hardly interacts with emotion in the Pauline letter corpus and shows only a limited engagement with specifically *early Christian* emotional life.[8]

---

[2] Stephen Voorwinde, *Jesus' Emotions in the Fourth Gospel: Human or Divine?*, LNTS 284 (London: T&T Clark, 2005); Stephen Voorwinde, *Jesus' Emotions in the Gospels* (London: T&T Clark, 2011).

[3] Voorwinde, *Gospels*, 3.

[4] Matthew Elliott, *Faithful Feelings: Emotion in the New Testament* (Leicester: Inter-Varsity, 2005).

[5] Elliott, *Faithful Feelings*, 124–5.

[6] Elliott, *Faithful Feelings*, 252–64.

[7] F. Scott Spencer, ed., *Mixed Feelings and Vexed Emotions: Exploring Emotions in Biblical Literature* (Atlanta, GA: SBL Press, 2017).

[8] Only in the final two essays – which are both engaged with 1 Peter to different degrees, in relation to desire and the absence of anger, respectively – is there any sustained exploration of early Christianity emotional life: see David E. Frederickson, 'When Enough Is Never Enough: Philosophers, Poets, Peter, and Paul on Insatiable Desire', in *Mixed Feelings and Vexed Emotions: Exploring Emotions in Biblical Literature*, ed. F. Scott Spencer (Atlanta, GA: SBL Press, 2017), 311–30; and in the same volume (331–53), Katherine M. Hockey, 'The Missing Emotion: The Absence of Anger and the Promotion of Nonretaliation in 1 Peter'.

1.2.1.b. Stephen Barton

One scholar whose short studies are helping to advance the study of emotion in early Christianity is Stephen Barton. In 2011, the first of his explorations of emotion in the New Testament was published;[9] this article has become a seminal contribution to this emerging area of scholarly interest. Barton's approach is exemplary: after surveying recent developments in emotions research in the social sciences and judiciously using these theories to open up the question of early Christian emotions,[10] he brings key interpretative perspectives to bear on the issue of grief in 1 Thessalonians, situating such grief alongside wider sociocultural views of grief in the Greco-Roman world.[11] Using grief as a case study, Barton argues convincingly that early Christian eschatological faith and emotional life are intimately connected to each other.[12] In not insignificant ways, my own theoretical stance takes its cue from some of Barton's proposals: first, that emotions, being cognitive and evaluative, are a form of rationality that may offer another avenue towards understanding early Christian rationality as a whole; second, that emotions play a role in expressing identity and marking social boundaries and points of transition, for example, through 'feeling rules'; and third, that emotions arise in the course of social relations and are integral to processes of social engagement.[13] Important for Barton as an analytical tool is the concept of the 'emotional regime', the import of which is the capacity to locate emotions within wider social-symbolic realities.[14]

Barton continues to probe emotion in early Christianity in a subsequent study, adopting again a multidisciplinary and broadly constructionist approach; this time he focuses on joy in Luke-Acts and Philippians, taking note also of how joy is inflected in earlier biblical tradition.[15] Several of Barton's conclusions are especially noteworthy. He argues that while the basis of joy is eschatological, 'its expression is *social*, bound up with the quality of ecclesial sociality'.[16] Moreover, joy is the individual and corporate manifestation of what really matters – the progress of the gospel and the progress in faith of those who accept this gospel.[17] Furthermore, since joy has to do with an entirely new and countercultural way of classifying, and being in, the world, it has to be inculcated. Thus, for Barton, Philippians is 'both a display of joy and a pedagogy in joy'.[18]

In a recent essay, Barton explores the relationship between anger and sin in Ephesians, concluding that anger has to be understood in the light of the letter's

---

[9] Stephen C. Barton, 'Eschatology and the Emotions in Early Christianity', *JBL* 130 (2011): 571–91.
[10] Barton, 'Eschatology', 574–81.
[11] Barton, 'Eschatology', 581–9.
[12] Barton, 'Eschatology', 573, 591.
[13] See especially Barton, 'Eschatology', 575–81.
[14] Barton, 'Eschatology', 577–8, 589–91. On the 'emotional regime', see Section 1.3.2 of my study.
[15] Stephen C. Barton, 'Spirituality and the Emotions in Early Christianity: The Case of Joy', in *The Bible and Spirituality: Exploratory Essays in Reading Scripture Spiritually*, ed. Andrew T. Lincoln, J. Gordon McConville, and Lloyd K. Pietersen (Eugene, OR: Cascade Books, 2013), 171–93.
[16] Barton, 'Spirituality', 185–7 (quote from 187, emphasis original), 190; see also 183.
[17] Barton, 'Spirituality', 187–8, 191.
[18] Barton, 'Spirituality', 187.

overall moral-theological vision of unity in the Church.[19] Again, Barton's approach is instructive: he brings perspectives on anger in Jewish thought and in Greco-Roman philosophy into conversation with a careful reading of Eph. 4.26a, while being even-handed in his use of modern theories of emotion. Useful too is Barton's highlighting of 'the potential for the emotions, as a form of cognition, to be in alignment with, and an expression of, *the truth*',[20] that is, the realities associated with Paul's notions of divine redemption; and the fact that new ways of feeling, along with new ways of thinking and behaving, have to be learnt – which underlines the important role that processes of moral instruction and discipleship play in the Church.[21]

1.2.1.c. Katherine M. Hockey

In her very recent monograph – which is the first full-length exploration of emotion in a New Testament epistle – Katherine Hockey examines the role of emotion in the rhetorical discourse of 1 Peter.[22] Using Stephen Barton's work as a springboard for her own approach,[23] Hockey ably mobilizes analytical tools from modern emotion theories and Greco-Roman philosophical teaching on emotions to establish a methodological framework for her inquiry that is both theoretically informed and historically sensitive. She argues in her incisive analysis of key emotions such as joy, suffering, fear, hope, and shame in 1 Peter that as evaluative judgements they are used in particular contexts to rhetorically shape the recipients' interpretation of the world, and thus construct and enforce a new worldview.[24] As Hockey maintains, 'The positive or negative presentation of each emotion creates an emotional regime for the believers, which subsequently produces the boundaries for their understanding of self and other.'[25] By drawing connections between emotion, worldview, and action, Hockey demonstrates persuasively that the emotional reinforcement of the believers' new realities has profound effects: ethically, it helps to drive the believers collectively towards the achievement of desired outcomes; sociologically, it repositions them in relation to objects in their revised worldview, which strengthens in-group bonds and weakens previous societal ties, thereby bolstering their community identity; and therapeutically, it helps to concretize a stable and confident outlook on their present circumstances of persecution and suffering.[26]

---

[19] Stephen C. Barton, '"Be Angry But Do Not Sin" (Ephesians 4:26a): Sin and the Emotions in the New Testament with Special Reference to Anger', *Studies in Christian Ethics* 28 (2015): 21–34. See also Stephen C. Barton, 'Why Do Things Move People?: The Jerusalem Temple as Emotional Repository', *JSNT* 37 (2015): 351–80, which explores the relationship between material-symbolic objects and emotion.
[20] Barton, 'Be Angry', 33 (emphasis original), citing Eph. 1.13; 4.25; 5.9; 6.14.
[21] Barton, 'Be Angry', 33–4.
[22] Katherine M. Hockey, *The Role of Emotion in 1 Peter*, SNTSMS 173 (Cambridge: Cambridge University Press, 2019).
[23] Hockey, *Role*, 9, 18.
[24] Hockey, *Role*, 253; see also 139–41, 175–6, 225, 249–50.
[25] Hockey, *Role*, 253.
[26] See especially Hockey, *Role*, 257–9.

1.2.2. Studies of Emotion in Paul

For much of the twentieth century, discussions by New Testament scholars surrounding Paul's use of passion language traditionally portrayed him as strenuously rejecting the perspectives of Hellenistic philosophy.[27] However, this view has been refined in more recent scholarship; in the past four decades a growing number of scholars have argued that Paul's references to emotion are best understood in conversation with contemporaneous philosophical and literary perspectives on emotion in the Greco-Roman world. David Aune observes that four areas have received the most attention: (1) Paul's rhetorical use of emotional appeal; (2) Paul's descriptions of his own sufferings and emotional endurance; (3) Paul's treatment of grief, anxiety, and anger in his communities; and (4) Paul's negative assessment of sexual passions.[28] To this list I would add a fifth category to account for a discernible though still modest measure of scholarly interest in very recent years: (5) Paul's notion of joy.

In the interests of space, the following discussion of current research is necessarily selective. I will limit my attention to categories (1), (3) (with a focus on grief), and (5): (1) is the area that has been studied the most and is of some relevance to the questions that I am bringing to Paul's letters; (3) and (5) have to do with grief and joy, which form the twin affective foci of my study. Those aspects of research into Paul and emotion that I do not cover are addressed in Aune's instructive and still useful survey (cited above).

1.2.2.a. Paul's Rhetorical Use of Emotional Appeal

In recent decades, many scholars have mined categories from ancient rhetoric for data to bring to the study of Paul's language of persuasion, though there is still little consensus on how best to go about analysing πάθος, or discursive emotional appeal, in rhetorical criticism. Examples of studies that investigate Paul's rhetorical use of πάθος include Edgar Krentz on 1 Thessalonians, Larry Welborn on 2 Corinthians, Lauri Thurén on Galatians, and, more recently, Oda Wischmeyer on 1 Corinthians.[29]

In 2001, the Society of Biblical Literature published a collection of essays entitled *Paul and Pathos* that sought to address the question of how to develop systematic

---

[27] See the overview in David Charles Aune, 'Passions in the Pauline Epistles: The Current State of Research', in *Passions and Moral Progress in Greco-Roman Thought*, ed. John T. Fitzgerald (Abingdon: Routledge, 2008), 222–31.
[28] Aune, 'Passions', 224.
[29] Edgar M. Krentz, '1 Thessalonians: Rhetorical Flourishes and Formal Constraints', in *The Thessalonians Debate: Methodological Discord or Methodological Synthesis?*, ed. Karl P. Donfried and Johannes Beutler (Grand Rapids, MI: Eerdmans, 2000), 287–318; Larry L. Welborn, 'Paul's Appeal to the Emotions in 2 Corinthians 1.1–2.13; 7.5–16', *JSNT* 82 (2001): 31–60; Lauri Thurén, 'Was Paul Angry? Derhetorizing Galatians', in *The Rhetorical Interpretation of Scripture: Essays from the 1996 Malibu Conference*, ed. Stanley E. Porter and Dennis L. Stamps (Sheffield: Sheffield Academic Press, 1999), 302–20; Oda Wischmeyer, '1Korinther 13. Das Hohelied der Liebe zwischen Emotion und Ethos', in *Deuterocanonical and Cognate Literature Yearbook 2011*, ed. Renate Egger-Wenzel and Jeremy Corley (Berlin: De Gruyter, 2012), 343–59. See further Aune, 'Passions', 224–5.

guidelines for πάθος that would be most apropos for biblical criticism.³⁰ I shall highlight features of certain essays that are especially pertinent to my study.

Steven Kraftchick argues in his nuanced approach that Paul's letters reveal that his use of πάθος is a hybrid of Aristotle and the Roman tradition.³¹ On the one hand, with the Roman tradition, Paul's appeals are directed to the emotions rather than being arguments from them. On the other hand, Paul's sensibility for building a community's ethic and well-being puts him closer to Aristotle in the logic behind his arguments: Paul is not merely persuading his audience, but using emotional argumentation to provide reasons why it is appropriate for a community to take a specific action.³² Kraftchick thus seems to recognize the presence of distinctly noetic as well as social elements to emotional appeal in Paul; and in his analysis of Galatians he seeks to demonstrate that Paul is a pragmatic, innovative rhetor who uses arguments based on emotion in order to persuade his readers, and that these arguments are made because the matters under deliberation are vital for their continued communal existence.³³

Jerry Sumney concludes from his investigation of Paul's argumentative strategy in 2 Corinthians that he seems to regard emotions as intelligent and discriminating aspects of the human personality.³⁴ From the evidence in the letter, Paul probably understood as rational his own emotive arguments both for perceiving his actions as he wanted the Corinthians to and for their seeing his opponents' actions as being objectionable.³⁵ Sumney finds that Paul uses widely known rhetorical conventions to affect the πάθος of his hearers; these conventions drew largely on Aristotelian categories of affect in which emotions were regarded not as irrational but as being 'based to some degree on beliefs arrived at through the use of reason'.³⁶ A broadly similar approach is adopted by James Thompson, who reads Paul's argument from πάθος in 2 Corinthians against an Aristotelian view of affect and thus connects Paul's rhetorical strategy to an understanding that emotional response is 'intelligent behaviour open to reasoned persuasion'.³⁷

Overall, while the essays in the collection arrive at slightly different conclusions concerning the extent to which the theories of classical rhetoricians are relevant for assessing πάθος in the Pauline epistles, they all highlight the affective dimensions of Paul's thought and thus represent an effort to understand it in more holistic terms.

---

[30] Thomas H. Olbricht and Jerry L. Sumney, eds, *Paul and Pathos*, SBL Symposium Series 16 (Atlanta, GA: Society of Biblical Literature, 2001). On emotional appeal in the creation of discourse, see Jakob Wisse, *Ethos and Pathos from Aristotle and Cicero* (Amsterdam: Hakkert, 1989).

[31] Steven J. Kraftchick, 'Πάθη in Paul: The Emotional Logic of "Original Argument"', in *Paul and Pathos*, ed. Thomas H. Olbricht and Jerry L. Sumney, SBL Symposium Series 16 (Atlanta, GA: Society of Biblical Literature, 2001), 39–68.

[32] Kraftchick, 'Πάθη', 56.

[33] Kraftchick, 'Πάθη', 57–68.

[34] Jerry L. Sumney, 'Paul's Use of Πάθος in His Argument against the Opponents of 2 Corinthians', in *Paul and Pathos*, ed. Thomas H. Olbricht and Jerry L. Sumney, SBL Symposium Series 16 (Atlanta, GA: Society of Biblical Literature, 2001), 147–60.

[35] Sumney, 'Paul's Use', 160.

[36] Sumney, 'Paul's Use', 148; referencing the work of Martha C. Nussbaum, 'Aristotle on Emotions and Rational Persuasion', in *Essays on Aristotle's Rhetoric*, ed. Amélie O. Rorty (Berkeley: University of California Press, 1996), 303–4.

[37] James W. Thompson, 'Paul's Argument from Pathos in 2 Corinthians', in *Paul and Pathos*, ed. Thomas H. Olbricht and Jerry L. Sumney, SBL Symposium Series 16 (Atlanta, GA: Society of Biblical Literature, 2001), 129–30 (quote from 130).

In addition, the authors seem to detect and thus implicitly promote a cognitive basis for emotion, in so far as they place Paul's use of πάθος within broadly Aristotelian categories, which argue for the intelligibility of emotional response. However, more work needs to be done to move the discussion of πάθος in the biblical documents beyond Aristotle;[38] and a deliberate engagement with modern theories of emotion may prove to be helpful. My study, which is not primarily interested in the rhetorical dimensions of Paul's pathetic discourse, nevertheless seeks both to broaden the discussion of Paul's use of emotion and to take it forward using insights from current developments in emotions theory.

1.2.2.b. Paul's Treatment of Grief

The scholar who has probably done the most work in this area is Abraham Malherbe, who has demonstrated convincingly that Paul's approach to the assuaging of grief has its parallels in the therapeutic strategies of many of the moral philosophers of the day.[39] Malherbe focuses in particular on the paraenetic character of Paul's language of consolation in 1 Thessalonians,[40] and shows that Paul's treatment of grief in 1 Thess. 4.13-18 shares many of the features of ancient consolation,[41] which was widely practised and well attested throughout the Greco-Roman world.[42] Malherbe concludes that Paul's consolatory instructions regarding appropriate grief have their basis in his understanding of the eschatological events surrounding the Parousia of Christ.[43]

Several other scholars have also investigated the topos of Paul's treatment of grief in 1 Thessalonians.[44] A particularly thought-provoking contribution comes from John Barclay, who argues that in 1 Thess. 4.13 Paul is not merely trying to moderate the Thessalonians' grief on the occasion of the deaths of some of their brethren but is literally instructing them not to grieve at all.[45] As Barclay sees it, for Paul it was crucial that the way that the early believers dealt with death and bereavement marked them out clearly from the world around them, since they were, after all, 'a community who made a special point of being destined to salvation'.[46] By specifying how the Thessalonian

---

[38] As indeed Thomas H. Olbricht, one of the editors of the essay collection, recognizes, see 'Introduction', in *Paul and Pathos*, ed. Thomas H. Olbricht and Jerry L. Sumney, SBL Symposium Series 16 (Atlanta, GA: Society of Biblical Literature, 2001), 1-3.

[39] On Hellenistic philosophy as therapy, see the survey of literature in Abraham J. Malherbe, 'Hellenistic Moralists and the New Testament', *ANRW* 2.26.1 (1992): 301-4; see Martha C. Nussbaum, *The Therapy of Desire: Theory and Practice in Hellenistic Ethics* (Princeton, NJ: Princeton University Press, 1994), for an extensive discussion.

[40] Abraham J. Malherbe, 'Exhortation in 1 Thessalonians', in *Paul and the Popular Philosophers* (Minneapolis, MN: Fortress, 1989), 49-66; Abraham J. Malherbe, *Paul and the Thessalonians: The Philosophic Tradition of Pastoral Care* (Philadelphia, PA: Fortress, 1987), 57-60, 68-81.

[41] Malherbe, 'Exhortation', 64-5; Abraham J. Malherbe, *The Letters to the Thessalonians*, AB 32B (New Haven, CT: Yale University Press, 2000), 264.

[42] I survey the topos of consolation in antiquity in Section 2.5.1.a.

[43] Malherbe, 'Exhortation', 65-6.

[44] See also Barton, 'Eschatology', which I discussed earlier in Section 1.2.1.b.

[45] John M. G. Barclay, '"That You May Not Grieve, Like the Rest Who Have No Hope" (1 Thess. 4.13): Death and Early Christian Identity', in *Pauline Churches and Diaspora Jews*, WUNT 275 (Tübingen: Mohr Siebeck, 2011), 217-35.

[46] Barclay, 'Death', 234.

believers were to view and mark death, Paul was taking the first momentous steps towards 'making the death of a Christian a Christian death', or, in other words, making death itself a central symbol of Christian distinction – a distinction that had everything to do with the believers' theological convictions concerning their eschatological destiny and confidence for the future.[47] Even if one is not convinced by Barclay's argument that Paul is here completely prohibiting the expressing of grief,[48] his primary thesis concerning the 'christianizing' of death, which he grounds in a careful reading of Paul's theological strategy to quell the Thessalonians' grief, still holds in the main.[49]

In a recent article, Larry Welborn explores λύπη in 2 Corinthians from the perspective of Greco-Roman psychagogy.[50] He contrasts Paul's treatment of emotional pain with the therapeutic strategies employed by his contemporaries, especially the Stoics, and concludes that Paul emerges as the harbinger of change in the ancient practice of emotional therapy through how he valorizes λύπη and attributes to it a constructive rather than merely utilitarian value in the pursuit of moral progress. For Welborn, Paul – who expresses 'pain given and pain received' in his letter – had 'reflected deeply upon the nature and function of the emotions "in Christ"', and found his answer in how Christ's suffering disclosed a λύπη that was in accordance with God's will and led through repentance to salvation.[51] Noteworthy in Welborn's study is its implied endorsement of a reasoned, ethical basis for λύπη, and its contextual rootedness, evidenced in the widespread use of Greco-Roman literary sources for comparison.

1.2.2.c. Paul's Notion of Joy

In the past few years, several essays by New Testament scholars have appeared in which Paul's view of joy is central to the discussion.[52]

N. T. Wright's observations about joy in the New Testament[53] highlight its theological dimensions as well as its ethical nature. For Wright, the character of early Christian joy is definitively shaped by the events surrounding Jesus, while remaining within ancient Israelite parameters: joy has to do with discovering that Israel's God is now fulfilling his promises to bring restoration.[54] These ideas are crystallized in Paul's missive to the Philippians. At one level, joy has to do with the bonds of mutual affection between him and his converts. But at a deeper level, joy has to

---

[47] Barclay, 'Death', 227–8 (quote from 228), 234; see also 217–18.
[48] I discuss in detail the question of whether or not 1 Thess. 4.13 enshrines a prohibition against grief in Section 4.3.4.
[49] So also Barton, 'Eschatology', 587 n.51.
[50] Larry L. Welborn, 'Paul and Pain: Paul's Emotional Therapy in 2 Corinthians 1.1–2.13; 7.5–16 in the Context of Ancient Psychagogic Literature', *NTS* 57 (2011): 547–70.
[51] Welborn, 'Paul and Pain', 570.
[52] See also Barton, 'Spirituality', which was discussed in Section 1.2.1.b.
[53] N. T. Wright, 'Joy: Some New Testament Perspectives and Questions', in *Joy and Human Flourishing: Essays on Theology, Culture, and the Good Life*, ed. Miroslav Volf and Justin E. Crisp (Minneapolis, MN: Fortress, 2015), 39–61. This collection of essays, the result of a series of consultations hosted by the Yale Center of Faith and Culture, represents an effort to help to remedy the paucity of contemporary theological reflection on joy.
[54] Wright, 'Joy', 46–9.

do with the resurrection and enthronement of Jesus, and the new world that his lordship has inaugurated. Those who follow Jesus are part of this new world; and so Paul rejoices – even in suffering, for it is 'an indication that the new world and the old are chafing together' – and summons the Philippians to rejoice with him.[55] For Wright, this joy certainly involves 'internal mental or emotional states'; but he also suggests, while acknowledging that it is impossible to prove, that on the basis of Phil. 1.27-30 and 4.4-5 Paul might even have in mind an outward, public, activity of celebration, perhaps as a kind of protest against the celebrations of *Kyrios Caesar* or pagan religion.[56]

Helpful in Wright's discussion is his reminder that the joy of which the New Testament speaks is capable of overlapping with quite different emotions, such as sorrow, which alerts one to the fact that something rather different from 'ordinary' joy is envisaged; indeed, joy has to do with 'the Lord'.[57] The basis for joy is thus theological: as Wright notes, 'The sovereign lordship of Christ frames and renders joyful his [Paul's] reflections on his likely fate (Phil. 1.18-26).'[58] Wright also alerts us to the sociality of joy – that there is a sense in which it is socially generated and also to be socially performed. However, his suggestion that Paul is promoting a regular, highly visible, and countercultural celebration of joy seems rather unlikely, given the belligerent environment in which the believers lived.

In a relatively short yet perceptive essay, Colleen Shantz brings Paul's notion of happiness into interdisciplinary dialogue with recent research on emotion in positive psychology and other fields.[59] Applying Martin P. Seligman's typology of the three kinds of lives that bring people happiness to her reading of Paul, Shantz finds that it is the meaningful life (where one looks beyond oneself to a transcendent purpose) rather than the pleasurable life or the good life that encapsulates how Paul is able to achieve happiness despite his frequent experiences of affliction.[60] Paul's participation in the Christological pattern of dying and rising allows him to articulate a hermeneutic for all of life in which conventional standards of honour are turned on their heads: suffering thus becomes 'an actual participation in the way of Christ that has defeated the powers of death and sin'.[61] This revised understanding of meaning and happiness in life enables Paul to establish and nurture his new faith communities, which in turn generates

---

[55] Wright, 'Joy', 49–55 (quote from 55).
[56] Wright, 'Joy', 56–8.
[57] Wright, 'Joy', 40–1.
[58] Wright, 'Joy', 53.
[59] Colleen Shantz, '"I Have Learned to Be Content?": Happiness According to St. Paul', in *The Bible and the Pursuit of Happiness: What the Old and New Testaments Teach Us about the Good Life*, ed. Brent Strawn (New York: Oxford University Press, 2012), 187–201. The essays in this collection originated in a 2009 conference in Atlanta which was part of a five-year project focused on the Pursuit of Happiness, hosted by the Centre for the Study of Law and Religion at Emory University.
  We should note that while the emotion term that Shantz uses throughout her essay is 'happiness' (which is in keeping with the theme of the collection and also of the larger project of which it is a part), when it comes to her discussion of Paul's letters she is referring, in actual fact, to 'joy'. We may therefore take her references to happiness as a terminological proxy for joy.
[60] Shantz, 'Happiness', 189–97.
[61] Shantz, 'Happiness', 199.

the happiness that comes from group cohesion and shared values.[62] Shantz's study is instructive in how she engages in heuristic fashion with the work of neuroscientists, psychologists, and social scientists on emotion. Theories regarding happiness, the link between cognition and emotion, and the social character of emotion are carefully mapped onto Paul's experience to produce an account that remains grounded in the realities of the text while being alert to viable ways of understanding it in more comprehensive terms.

1.2.3. Summary

What we are seeing in New Testament studies is a budding interest in drawing on resources in modern emotions studies to investigate the role of emotion in early Christianity. The growing attention to emotion in biblical studies has its parallel in the field of classics, with scholars from both disciplines making important contributions as to how the emotions were viewed in antiquity.[63] This interest arguably provides further evidence for what many academics term as an 'emotional turn' or 'affective turn' – a theoretical engagement with emotion since the mid-1990s in the humanities and social sciences[64] – which is itself part of a veritable explosion of interest in the academic study of emotion in recent decades, an interest that is unusually widespread and remarkably interdisciplinary. The eminent development psychologist Jerome Kagan has observed that 'the corpus of scholarly writing on emotion is so extensive that it would seem presumptuous for anyone to assume they could add to the existing record of wisdom'.[65] Indeed, the literature continues to expand at such a breathtaking pace that to offer any kind of critical overview of recent research on emotion is a dauntingly ambitious undertaking. In the section that follows, I can do little more than outline the main contours of the arguments surrounding the nature of emotion, especially as they pertain to my study.

---

[62] Shantz, 'Happiness', 197–8.
[63] See John T. Fitzgerald, 'The Passions and Moral Progress: An Introduction', in *Passions and Moral Progress in Greco-Roman Thought*, ed. John T. Fitzgerald (Abingdon: Routledge, 2008), 1–2.

In classics, important book-length examples include Nussbaum, *Therapy*; Richard Sorabji, *Emotion and Peace of Mind: From Stoic Agitation to Christian Temptation* (Oxford: Oxford University Press, 2000); Margaret R. Graver, *Cicero on the Emotions: Tusculan Disputations 3-4* (Chicago: University of Chicago Press, 2002); Margaret R. Graver, *Stoicism and Emotion* (Chicago: University of Chicago Press, 2007); Teun Tieleman, *Chrysippus' On Affections: Reconstructions and Reinterpretations* (Leiden: Brill, 2003); Robert A. Kaster, *Emotion, Restraint, and Community in Ancient Rome* (New York: Oxford University Press, 2005); David Konstan, *The Emotions of the Ancient Greeks: Studies in Aristotle and Classical Literature* (Toronto: University of Toronto Press, 2006).

Significant collections of essays include Susanna Morton Braund and Christopher Gill, eds, *The Passions in Roman Thought and Literature* (Cambridge: Cambridge University Press, 1997); Juha Sihvola and Troels Engberg-Pedersen, eds, *The Emotions in Hellenistic Philosophy* (Dordrecht: Kluwer Academic, 1998); John T. Fitzgerald, ed., *Passions and Moral Progress in Greco-Roman Thought* (Abingdon: Routledge, 2008).

[64] See e.g. Patricia Ticineto Clough and Jean O'Malley Halley, eds, *The Affective Turn: Theorizing the Social* (Durham, NC: Duke University Press, 2007); for more references see Jan Plamper, *The History of Emotions: An Introduction*, trans. Keith Tribe (Oxford: Oxford University Press, 2015), 63 n.120.
[65] Jerome Kagan, *What Is Emotion? History, Measures, and Meanings* (New Haven, CT: Yale University Press, 2007), 4.

1.3. Contemporary Emotions Research: Selected Aspects

1.3.1. Overview

The study of emotion is complex and continues to be steeped in debates related to the definition, constitution, and function of emotion. In a recent survey, Carroll Izard canvasses thirty-five prominent academics – representing scientific disciplines concerned with emotions research (behavioural and cognitive neuroscience, computational cognitive science, and clinical, developmental, and social psychological science) – on their working definitions of emotion.[66] Based on their responses, Izard delineates a composite picture of the main features of emotion:

> Emotion consists of neural circuits (that are at least partially dedicated), response systems, and a feeling state/process that motivates and organizes cognition and action. Emotion also provides information to the person experiencing it, and may include antecedent cognitive appraisals and ongoing cognition including an interpretation of its feeling state, expressions or social-communicative signals, and may motivate approach or avoidant behavior, exercise control/regulation of responses, and be social or relational in nature.[67]

Izard's findings show that scholars in the psychological and behavioural sciences have yet to converge on a consensus definition of emotion. In addition, his multivalent description highlights the difficulties that theorists face in articulating the relationships between the various processes that are thought to be integral to emotion. It is interesting that some of the scientists who were surveyed opined that emotion may have also a social facet; this takes us to the heart of the debate concerning the nature of emotions – whether they are universal or socially constructed.

As Jan Plamper observes, since the mid-nineteenth century at the very latest, academic discussion of emotion has revolved around these two polarities: the universal, essentialist, transhistorical nature of emotion on the one hand, and its being socially conditioned, culturally contingent, and historical on the other.[68] One of the most difficult challenges facing emotions researchers today is how to establish a middle ground, by bridging scientific discourse in neuroscience and psychology with the work of social scientists and scholars in the humanities. While certain universalist conceptions of emotion allow for a degree of cultural contingency,[69] in the same way

---

[66] Carroll E. Izard, 'The Many Meanings/Aspects of Emotion: Definitions, Functions, Activation, and Regulation', *Emotion Review* 2 (2010): 363–70.
[67] Izard, 'Many Meanings', 367.
[68] Plamper, *History*, 5–6, 74. On the historical development of both views up to the present day, see Plamper, *History*, 75–250; a succinct analysis of their theoretical underpinnings is in John Corrigan, 'Introduction: Emotions Research and the Academic Study of Religion', in *Religion and Emotion: Approaches and Interpretations*, ed. John Corrigan (Oxford: Oxford University Press, 2004), 7–13.
[69] E.g. in studies on empathy in social neuroscience; for discussion see Plamper, *History*, 248–9.

that some cognitive theories leave room for physiological influences,[70] a conclusive theoretical synthesis of both paradigms remains elusive.[71]

1.3.2. Emotions Research in the Social Sciences and Humanities

It is beyond the scope of my study to attempt to adjudicate between the two paradigms. However, since my approach to emotion revolves around, broadly speaking, historical investigation, the constructivism that continues to influence emotions research in the humanities and social sciences is of far more direct applicability than the universalist paradigm. Social constructionist approaches to emotion have their origin in the field of anthropology. Until the publication in the 1980s of influential emotional ethnographies, especially those by Michelle Rosaldo, Lila Abu-Lughod, and Catherine Lutz,[72] it was widely assumed that emotions were prelinguistic and invariant across cultures.[73] These new findings, which were part of a broader social constructionist trend in anthropology,[74] undermined any notions of pancultural emotions and ushered constructionist arguments for emotion onto centre stage. Thus Lutz, for example, insists that 'emotional experience is not precultural but pre*eminently* cultural';[75] and Rosaldo, reiterating her views in a subsequent, seminal essay, argues that emotion is shaped by thought, and is indeed embodied thought – and as such, emotions should be interpreted as processes structured by the forms of cognition and reason that arise from a person's embeddedness within a particular sociocultural milieu.[76]

Since the mid-1990s or so, however, some anthropologists have moved beyond these views of emotion to promote, among other things, the supersession of dichotomous emotional constructs, and even certain universalist tendencies.[77] Nonetheless, as Plamper rightly concludes, 'No other discipline has done so much to shatter the idea that feelings are timeless and everywhere the same as has anthropology.'[78]

In the related field of sociology, the contemporary interest in emotion began to be discernible in the 1970s, with the diminishing influence of grand theory and a

---

[70] E.g. Batja Mesquita and Michael Boiger, 'Emotions in Context: A Sociodynamic Model of Emotions', *Emotion Review* 6 (2014): 298–302.

[71] Perhaps the most well-known attempt is that of William M. Reddy, *The Navigation of Feeling: A Framework for the History of Emotions* (Cambridge: Cambridge University Press, 2001). Reddy's aim is to bring together the universalism of cognitive psychology and the social constructivism of the anthropology of emotions, but his proposals are not uncontroversial; see Plamper, *History*, 251–65.

[72] Michelle Z. Rosaldo, *Knowledge and Passion: Ilongot Notions of Self and Social Life* (Cambridge: Cambridge University Press, 1980); Lila Abu-Lughod, *Veiled Sentiments: Honor and Poetry in a Bedouin Society* (Berkeley: University of California Press, 1986); Catherine A. Lutz, *Unnatural Emotions: Everyday Sentiments on a Micronesian Atoll & Their Challenge to Western Theory* (Chicago: University of Chicago Press, 1988).

[73] On the earlier anthropology of emotions, see Plamper, *History*, 80–98.

[74] On this see Plamper, *History*, 109–14. This trend is a devolution of what is often known as the linguistic or cultural turn, or the advent of postmodernism, within the social sciences and humanities.

[75] Lutz, *Unnatural Emotions*, 5 (emphasis original).

[76] Michelle Z. Rosaldo, 'Towards an Anthropology of Self and Feeling', in *Culture Theory: Essays on Mind, Self, and Emotion*, ed. Richard A. Schweder and Robert A. LeVine (Cambridge: Cambridge University Press, 1984), 137–57, especially 137–43.

[77] For discussion see Plamper, *History*, 129–30, 136–46.

[78] Plamper, *History*, 146.

turn to microsociology. It was arguably the work of Arlie Hochschild[79] that marked the emergence of the sociology of emotions as a distinct subfield of study.[80] For Hochschild, social interactions are construed as a scripted drama in which actors abide by 'feeling rules' that form the basis for the 'emotional work' that they have to perform in order to make their feelings conform appropriately to society's emotional norms. Emotional life is regulated through the assessment and modification of personal feeling in relation to the operative feeling rules, which set standards of what is owed and owing in emotional exchanges.[81] Though one might wish for a more nuanced account of emotion that grants individual agents more leeway in their responses to emotional pressure,[82] Hochschild's basic notion of feeling rules remains influential in the sociology of emotions. In his survey of the field, Jonathan Turner notes that since the late 1970s the study of emotion has made remarkable progress, and it now stands at the forefront of microsociology and, increasingly, macrosociology, with theoretical research traditions already in evidence.[83]

A recent contribution to the broader field comes from Ole Riis and Linda Woodhead, who in 2010 published *A Sociology of Religious Emotion*, drawing inspiration from across a wide range of disciplines that deal with emotion (philosophy, psychology, behavioural studies, neuroscience, cultural studies, linguistics, anthropology, and sociology) to produce a multidimensional conceptual framework for emotion that is attentive to its variegated character.[84] They propose a model in which emotion is generated in the interactions between individual agents, societal structures, and cultural symbols;[85] and to consolidate these interactions they posit the concept of an 'emotional regime'.[86] Eschewing the need to choose between scientific and cultural approaches to emotion, they argue that recent work in cognitive and neurological science and in philosophical phenomenology is further destabilizing the overly simplistic dichotomy between these poles.[87] For Riis and Woodhead, emotion is '"both-and" rather than

---

[79] Arlie Russell Hochschild, *The Managed Heart: Commercialization of Human Feeling* (Berkeley: University of California Press, 1983); see also Arlie Russell Hochschild, 'Emotion Work, Feeling Rules, and Social Structure', *American Journal of Sociology* 85 (1979): 551–75.

[80] So Plamper, *History*, 123; see n.198 for major subsequent publications in the field. For an overview of the trajectory of research, see Jonathan H. Turner, 'The Sociology of Emotions: Basic Theoretical Arguments', *Emotion Review* 1 (2009): 340–54.

[81] Hochschild, *Managed Heart*, ix–x, 18, 56–75, 85; see also Hochschild, 'Emotion Work', especially 571–3.

[82] So e.g. Deborah Lupton, *The Emotional Self: A Sociocultural Exploration* (London: Sage, 1998), 169–70.

[83] Turner, 'Sociology', 340; on these research trajectories see Jan E. Stets and Jonathan H. Turner, eds, *Handbook of the Sociology of Emotions* (New York: Springer, 2006).

[84] Ole Riis and Linda Woodhead, *A Sociology of Religious Emotion* (Oxford: Oxford University Press, 2010), 20–53.

[85] Riis and Woodhead, *Sociology*, 5–9.

[86] Riis and Woodhead, *Sociology*, 10–12. To be sure, the term 'emotional regime' is not new. William Reddy seems to have introduced it: he defines the term formally as 'the set of normative emotions and the official rituals, practices, and emotives that express and inculcate them; a necessary underpinning of any stable political regime' (*Navigation*, 129). Certainly, as Plamper observes (*History*, 265), the term is now often heard in various settings, detached from its context and used for the general idea of emotional norms or standards. Riis and Woodhead assign to it a very specific meaning in their scheme (see further my discussion in Section 5.3.1).

[87] Riis and Woodhead, *Sociology*, 24–30.

"either/or": both personal and relational; private and social; biological and cultural; active and passive';[88] it is 'a label for a range of coordinated psychophysical elements, in and through which we relate to other beings and symbols, and in terms of which they relate to us'.[89] Furthermore, Riis and Woodhead specifically contextualize *religious* emotion within their conceptual framework, and demonstrate comprehensively how religious emotion is integral to, and configured by, its social and symbolic relations.[90]

1.3.3. Emotion: Nature and Terminology

To conclude this brief, and necessarily only representative, overview of current emotions research, we attend now to the closely related questions of definition and terminology. What is meant by 'emotion'? And is there a fundamental linguistic unity of meaning in the various terms that have represented 'emotion' across history, cultural space, and disciplinary specialization?

1.3.3.a. The Nature of Emotion and Its Conceptual History

Plamper observes that the sheer difficulty of defining emotion is often treated as its leading characteristic.[91] As James Russell writes at the beginning of his introduction to a specially designated section of a recent volume of *Emotion Review* treating the matter, 'Emotion researchers face a scandal: We have no agreed upon definition for the term – *emotion* – that defines our field.'[92] Indeed, even within each of the disciplines that study emotion, there is incomplete agreement about what constitutes emotion; this state of affairs hampers the progress of research and stymies interdisciplinary work. An academic consensus as to what emotion is might be next to impossible to achieve, not least because each field of study privileges different aspects of emotion. Nonetheless, scholars of different disciplinary commitments continue to try to move the discussion forward constructively: examples include, from neuroscience, Joseph LeDoux; from psychology, Jerome Kagan; from philosophy, Martha Nussbaum; and the collaborative proposals of a philosopher, Kevin Mulligan, and a psychologist, Klaus Scherer.[93] My own theoretical position follows the eclectic but broadly sociological approach of Riis and Woodhead, who present emotion as cognitive, psychophysical stances and interventions embedded in complex socio-symbolic structures of meaning.[94]

---

[88] Riis and Woodhead, *Sociology*, 5.
[89] Riis and Woodhead, *Sociology*, 47.
[90] Riis and Woodhead, *Sociology*, 54–5, 69–73, 93–4.
[91] Plamper, *History*, 11. Among the studies Plamper cites is Beverly Fehr and James A. Russell, 'Concept of Emotion Viewed from a Prototype Perspective', *Journal of Experimental Psychology: General* 113 (1984): 464–86: 'everyone knows what an emotion is, until asked to give a definition' (here 464).
[92] James A. Russell, 'Introduction to Special Section: On Defining Emotion', *Emotion Review* 4 (2012): 337 (emphasis original).
[93] Joseph LeDoux, 'A Neuroscientist's Perspective on Debates about the Nature of Emotion', *Emotion Review* 4 (2012): 375–9; Kagan, *Emotion*; for a summary of its main themes see Jerome Kagan, 'Once More into the Breach', *Emotion Review* 2 (2010): 91–9; Martha C. Nussbaum, *Upheavals of Thought: The Intelligence of Emotions* (Cambridge: Cambridge University Press, 2001), especially 1–16; Kevin Mulligan and Klaus R. Scherer, 'Toward a Working Definition of Emotion', *Emotion Review* 4 (2012): 345–57.
[94] Riis and Woodhead, *Sociology*, 29, 47–53. See in my study Sections 1.3.2 and 5.3.

In regard to terminology, the English term 'emotion' shares a capacious semantic domain with several other commonly used terms. Riis and Woodhead speak for many in suggesting that these alternative terms highlight different dimensions of emotion:

> 'Passions' conveys the power of emotion, 'feeling' their embodied aspect, 'sentiments' the way they relate to character and education, while 'affect' suggests their passive and reactive dimension. 'Emotion' is good at conveying its dynamic, motivating force of 'e-motion', but tends to support an individualistic conception of emotions as inner states.[95]

These kinds of observations find broad support in Thomas Dixon's account of the conceptual history of the term 'emotion',[96] in which he argues that 'emotion' displaced other more specific terms when, as an everyday word used in common parlance to refer to any kind of mental feeling, it was commandeered as a theoretical term in the science of the mind in the early nineteenth century.[97] Until then, theorists like philosophers, physicians, and theologians had tended to use more than one term to refer to those states that would later be designated as 'emotion'. Influenced by Augustine and Aquinas (who were in turn influenced by ancient debates between Stoicism and Christianity), these theorists had especially distinguished between 'passions', which were involuntary, troubling lusts and desires to be avoided, and 'affections', which were the virtues such as love and compassion to which one should voluntarily aspire.[98] The linguistic ascendancy of 'emotion' as a theoretical term in the nineteenth century reflected the shifts in institutional and intellectual authority that were occurring:

> The term 'emotion' suited the purposes of a self-consciously secularizing and scientific cadre of psychological theorists of the late 19th century, detached as it was from the centuries of moral and theological connotations that had accrued to the terms 'passion' and 'affection'.[99]

The final stage in the semantic history of 'emotion' has been the popularization of scientific ideas associated with it, such as 'emotional intelligence' and 'emotional well-being', in ways that have traded on the psychological and medical authority of the term.[100]

---

[95] Riis and Woodhead, *Sociology*, 20. They note also that no one term captures the full complexity of what it seeks to articulate.
[96] Thomas Dixon, *From Passions to Emotions: The Creation of a Secular Psychological Category* (Cambridge: Cambridge University Press, 2003); I refer below primarily to his own precis, published as Thomas Dixon, '"Emotion": The History of a Keyword in Crisis', *Emotion Review* 4 (2012): 338–44.
[97] Dixon, 'History', 339–40; Dixon, *From Passions*, 109–27.
[98] Dixon, 'History', 339; Dixon, *From Passions*, 26–61. However, Barbara Rosenwein finds a greater overlap between 'passions' and 'affections', seeing the presence of a continuum between the terms; Barbara H. Rosenwein, *Emotional Communities in the Early Middle Ages* (Ithaca, NY: Cornell University Press, 2006), 4.
[99] Dixon, 'History', 342; see also Dixon, *From Passions*, 233–42.
[100] Dixon, 'History', 343.

The intellectual history of 'emotion' also helps to explain the conceptual confusion and debate that has marked so much of emotions research. Here we must outline Dixon's account a little more fully.[101] In the early nineteenth century, when the new theoretical term 'emotion' was first put into use by the philosopher Thomas Brown, he championed the notion that 'emotions' were vivid feelings that could not be embodied in any verbal definition. Brown's was also an explicitly non-cognitive concept of 'emotion' in which intellectual thought was separated from feeling. The physician Charles Bell, who regarded 'emotions' as certain changes in the mind that were manifested in bodily ways, was also influential. Brown's and Bell's ideas were endorsed by many psychologists and scientists and exercised a formative influence on the emotions theories of William James and Charles Darwin. Dixon concludes,

> The founders of the discipline of psychology in the late 19th century bequeathed to their successors a usage of 'emotion' in which the relationship between mind and body and between thought and feeling were confused and unresolved, and which named a category of feelings and behaviours so broad as to cover almost all of human mental life including as Bain (1859) had put it, all that was previously understood by the terms 'feelings, states of feeling, pleasures, pains, passions, sentiments, affections'.[102]

Modern psychology has had to deal with this muddled legacy in which emotional feeling and intellectual thought were bifurcated, and 'emotion' left bereft of a clear definition.

The above discussion is germane to our discussion because it helps us to be alert to certain unconscious biases that may be inadvertently carried into the study of emotion in the New Testament. First, there is a popular and academic tendency to dichotomize thought and feeling based on the premise that emotion is non-cognitive and irrational compared to properly evaluated thinking and volition.[103] Second, if emotions are regarded as irrational, then they are seen to hamper sensible and intelligent action – which can cause a negative assessment of people or situations in which emotion is evident: 'People tend to see emotions as a disruption of, or barrier to, the rational understanding of events. To label someone "emotional" is often to question the validity, and more, the very sense of what they are saying.'[104] Third, with the corporeality of emotions comes the assumption that they are natural, and culturally universal. For Hockey, it is not surprising, given all these commonly held assumptions, that emotion in the New Testament has been overlooked in modern scholarship. The privileging of rationality has led to a trivializing of emotion, and, furthermore, the assumption that emotions are universal can mean that one makes the further assumption that emotions

---

[101] Here I summarize Dixon, 'History', 340–2.
[102] Dixon, 'History', 342–3, citing Alexander Bain, *The Emotions and the Will* (London: Parker, 1859), 3.
[103] Here I am indebted to Hockey, *Role*, 23–5, where she uses the work of Catherine Lutz (*Unnatural Emotions*, 53–80) to highlight Western historical biases that we need to be aware of when exploring the writings of an ancient author.
[104] Hockey, *Role*, 24 (quote from Lutz, *Unnatural Emotions*, 60).

in a text do not need to be thoroughly investigated because they can be automatically understood from personal experience.[105]

1.3.3.b. Emotion and Cognition

Although definitional and other issues are still debated, present-day emotions scholarship in psychology has largely moved beyond the thought/feeling dualism that marks non-cognitive approaches.[106] The authors of a review to mark *Cognition and Emotion*'s twenty-fifth year of publication in 2011 note that 'although occasional grumbling was once heard about "cognitive imperialism" the idea of a cognitive approach to emotions is now firmly at the centre of any articulated understanding of emotion'.[107] In cognitive models of emotion, a typical emotion 'combines appraisal, physiological change, experience, expression, and action';[108] however, theorists do not agree as to the precise number and nature of these components, nor their sequence, in emotional arousal.[109] But at the heart of all cognitive approaches is the premise that an emotion is a judgement of value – an evaluation or appraisal in relation to a person's needs or goals – that gives rise to one or several modes of action readiness.[110] As such, cognitive theories ascribe great importance to the role of emotions in human life, since they relate outer events and other people to inner concerns.[111]

1.3.3.c. 'Emotion' as a Portmanteau Term

We end our survey of research by considering if the present-day term 'emotion' is conceptually equivalent to the terms that were in use in the Greco-Roman world. Certainly, 'emotion' is a contested word in terms of its precise definition and nature. Yet, as we have also seen, the intellectual history of the term shows that there is significant overlap with the other terms with which it is associated. Before 'emotion' was endowed with its modern meaning by the scientific community in the nineteenth century, people spoke more often and more precisely of things like 'passions', 'affections', and 'sentiments'; all such terms therefore referred to subsets of the ideas that today come under the umbrella of 'emotion'.[112] Terms like 'passion' and 'affection' especially were influenced by Augustine's and Aquinas's understanding of them; and they were in turn

---

[105] Hockey, *Role*, 25.
[106] Non-cognitive theories are still held by a few psychologists; on this see the discussion in Elliott, *Faithful Feelings*, 24–7.
[107] Keith Oatley et al., '*Cognition and Emotion* over Twenty-Five Years', *Cognition and Emotion* 25 (2011): 1345. See also the survey by Izard discussed earlier (Section 1.3.1).
[108] Keith Oatley and P. N. Johnson-Laird, 'Cognitive Approaches to Emotions', *Trends in Cognitive Science* 18 (2014): 134; see also Agnes Moors, 'Theories of Emotion Causation: A Review', *Cognition and Emotion* 23 (2009): 626, who aggregates these elements slightly differently and expresses them in terms of cognitive, feeling, motivational, somatic, and motor components.
[109] Moors, 'Theories', 627–30; Oatley and Johnson-Laird, 'Cognitive Approaches', 134–7.
[110] Oatley et al., 'Twenty-Five Years', 1345. On appraisal theory generally, see Agnes Moors et al., 'Appraisal Theories of Emotion: State of the Art and Future Development', *Emotion Review* 5 (2013): 119–24; see also the useful overview in Hockey, *Role*, 27–31.
[111] Oatley and Johnson-Laird, 'Cognitive Approaches', 134.
[112] See Rosenwein, *Emotional Communities*, 3.

influenced by Stoic philosophical conceptions of those states that we would today call emotions – in particular, the passions, and the category of 'good emotions' called the *eupatheiai*.[113] Thus our conclusion is that all the above terms track the same lexical field in overlapping if not strictly synonymous fashion, and as such can be represented in my study by 'emotion' – a broad, inclusive portmanteau word that aggregates the various meanings that are embedded in these alternative terms, and can therefore be used in a generic sense to designate all of them. In order to vary my prose, and in common with much of academic writing today, I will occasionally use words such as 'feeling' and 'affect' as equivalents for 'emotion'. However, I will not use 'passion' and 'affection', with their moralizing connotations, unless I am referring to specific historical contexts where these terms refer to ethical mores.

1.4. Aims of the Study

We are now in a position to set out the aims of this study and to delineate the methodological approach that it will take.

Our survey of current research in emotion in early Christianity in general, and in Paul in particular, reveals that it is still at a very early stage. It was only in 2019 that the first full-scale examination of emotion in a New Testament letter (1 Peter) was produced.[114] Certainly, scholarly work on specific emotions in the Pauline letters, carried out in dialogue with modern emotions research, is beginning to suggest several things about Paul's view of these emotions – that for him, they have a rational basis, that they are linked in some way to his theological agenda, and that they are connected also to processes of social engagement. However, further work is needed to develop these findings and elucidate their implications. In addition, and importantly, more can be done to investigate the broader role of emotion in Paul's writings, beyond its use in persuasive discourse.

These questions drive my study: For Paul, what is the main role of emotion, and why is this important for him? Since we will operate on the assumption that emotion is cognitive, how precisely are thought, faith, and feeling correlated to each other? What is the rationale behind Paul's promotion of certain emotions, such as joy, and banishment (or at least moderation) of other emotions, like grief? How are 'right' emotions fostered and 'wrong' ones curbed, and long-term emotional dispositions established and reinforced? How does Paul's handling of emotion compare to that of the most significant ancient parallel, the Stoics? My study, which is the first monograph-length study of emotion in Paul's letters, aims to fill a gap in New Testament research by addressing precisely these questions, and by taking the discussion forward through the articulation of a robust account of the function of emotion in Paul's writings. I will show that Paul regards emotion as being integral to, and an embodiment of, belief, and that he also understands emotion to be both socially formed and socially formative. The thrust of my argument is that for Paul, emotion plays a critical role alongside

---

[113] These will be investigated in the following chapter of this study.
[114] As noted earlier; see Section 1.2.1.c.

belief in the shaping of identity and community, and is therefore integral to the proper acculturation and social formation of the early Christians – a role that is only beginning to be recognized and explored in New Testament scholarship.

In broader terms, my hope is that this study will make a modest contribution towards the much larger enterprise of deepening our understanding of Pauline Christianity and the social world of the New Testament. Furthermore, I hope that it will be a useful example of how appropriate social-scientific resources can be put to use alongside exegetical analysis to mount a thoroughgoing historical investigation of emotion in the Pauline letters. In a 2014 journal article surveying the state of play of cognitive approaches to emotion, Oatley and Johnson-Laird concluded that for any account of emotion, 'a central task for future emotion research is to focus on the functions of emotions in social relationships'.[115] I hope that such a focus will be fruitful even in an interdisciplinary investigation like this present one.

1.5. Methodological Approach

It remains for me to outline how this study is laid out; but first, some general comments concerning the theoretical underpinnings of my approach are in order.

In line with the mainstream understanding of emotion in current scholarship, this study adopts a cognitive approach to emotion, which involves, at its core, an appraisal of an object's value that gives rise to some form of action tendency. At the same time, as mine is a historical study of emotion, I take also the view – prevalent in emotions theories in the social sciences and humanities – that emotion is socially constructed and culturally conditioned. As I see it, an approach to emotion that deliberately incorporates the interplay of these two ideas – that emotion is a cognitive as well as a social phenomenon – holds much promise for my inquiry because it recognizes the personal dimensions of affective response while also being attentive to the impact on emotion of social dynamics and cultural influences since, after all, Paul's letters are written to, and for, communities.

If, as we say, emotion is socially constructed, then it is vital that we are familiar with thinking concerning emotion in the first-century Greco-Roman world so that our reflection on Paul's treatment of emotion is firmly tethered to its historical and sociocultural context. Accordingly, in the chapter to follow (Chapter 2), I will provide a comprehensive discussion of the Stoic understanding of emotion and its therapy. We will allow the Stoics to speak for themselves, to ensure that we are not anachronistically importing modern conceptions of emotion into ancient texts. And in the course of our work on Paul in the subsequent chapters of this study, we will return to this material on Stoicism and interact with it by highlighting points of similarity and difference and drawing out their implications. I have chosen to focus my attention on the Stoics – and *only* the Stoics – for several reasons. First, it is commonly held that Stoicism was the most important philosophical influence in that era;[116] Anthony Long notes that

---

[115] Oatley and Johnson-Laird, 'Cognitive Approaches', 138.
[116] So e.g. Anthony A. Long, *Hellenistic Philosophy*, 2nd ed. (Berkeley: University of California Press, 1986), 107; F. H. Sandbach, *The Stoics*, 2nd ed. (Indianapolis, IN: Hackett, 1989), 16.

'in the Roman world of the first two Christian centuries Stoicism was the dominant philosophy among educated pagans'.[117] Second, the Stoics were known for their explicit emphasis on philosophy as a way of life;[118] by any reading, Pauline Christianity, too, was at least also a way of life.[119] Third, and related to the foregoing, there is an astonishingly long-established scholarly tradition of using Stoicism as a conversation partner for Christianity, which suggests that juxtaposing the two traditions is, as Kavin Rowe elegantly puts it, 'a particularly promising way of eliciting creative thought about complex cases in which rival traditions negotiate each other's claims to truth through time'.[120] Fourth, the Stoics had by far the most fully developed account of emotion of the day, which is helpful in terms of constructing comparisons with Paul's views.

In Chapters 3 and 4 of my study I investigate joy in Philippians and grief in 1 Thessalonians, respectively: though both emotions occur across a number of Paul's letters, joy is an especially significant theme in Philippians, and grief in 1 Thessalonians. Due to the constraints of space, I have had to be very selective as to which emotions to focus on. Joy and grief have been chosen because they are powerful, contrasting emotions that Paul categorically deals with, and at some length; in Philippians he expressly commands joy, while in 1 Thessalonians he forbids a certain type of grief. The prominence of joy and grief in these letters suggests that they have something to do with the thrust of Paul's theological thinking; and it would therefore seem that a careful study of these emotions can help to take us to the heart of Paul's pastoral agenda.

In terms of specifics, both Chapters 3 (Joy in Philippians) and 4 (Grief in 1 Thessalonians) will be prefaced by a discussion of the background of the letter in question, its genre, and its distinctives – all of which help us to have a sense of Paul's purposes for writing. Moreover, since our study proceeds on the assumption of the unity of each letter, this fact will have to be established. In regard to my approach to the texts themselves, here in Chapters 3 and 4 I will not deploy modern emotions theories in my reading of Paul, beyond their general role in alerting us to the cognitive and social dimensions of emotion. Instead, we will endeavour to hear him on his own terms and in his own historical context through a rigorous exegetical analysis of what he has to say. At the same time, we will keep an eye also on what he might be trying to do to shape Christian community. Where appropriate, I will introduce Stoic thinking as a foil for Paul's views, so as to make his understanding of joy and grief come into even sharper focus.

Finally, in Chapter 5, I bring modern emotions theory to bear on my study. The understanding that emotion is related to cognition and that it is not only personal, but has also a social cast, suggests that the use of Riis and Woodhead's sociological model of the emotional regime (see Section 1.3.2) might be a particularly fruitful means of heuristic engagement with how Paul deals with joy and grief. Accordingly, Riis and

---

[117] Long, *Hellenistic Philosophy*, 232.
[118] See John Sellars, *The Art of Living: The Stoics on the Nature and Function of Philosophy*, 2nd ed. (London: Bloomsbury, 2009), 55–85.
[119] A recent and intelligently provocative reading of the relationship between emergent Christianity and Stoicism as rival traditions of life is C. Kavin Rowe's *One True Life: The Stoics and Early Christians as Rival Traditions* (New Haven, CT: Yale University Press, 2016).
[120] See Rowe, *One True Life*, 3–4.

Woodhead's framework will be discussed and then used to elucidate how desired emotional patterns are produced and reinforced, and how their strength and longevity are sustained. I will then correlate these findings to my proposals concerning how Paul is using emotion in his letters. To end, I will contrast the Pauline emotional regime with Stoic thinking on emotion by bringing together the key findings from this and earlier chapters of my study, and in so doing, also highlight the distinctiveness of Paul's account of emotion.

2

Emotion in Stoicism

2.1. Introduction

In this chapter, I delineate the Stoic understanding of emotion through an examination of extant primary sources. The trajectory of the discussion is straightforward. We begin by considering the broader philosophical context, after which I set out the Stoic account of emotion: we look first at the Stoic construal of the causation of affective events, then their classification of emotion, and finally the therapy of emotion. The chapter ends with an investigation of how Seneca and Epictetus view grief and joy.

2.1.1. Translating πάθος

First, however, some important clarifications are needed in regard to terminology. The Stoic doctrine of affective events uses a specific term, πάθος, which in earlier Greek philosophical thought had encapsulated a wide-ranging set of phenomena that we would today designate by the use of the English term 'emotion'.[1] However, the Stoics applied the term πάθος in a more narrow, technical sense: they regarded the πάθη as being inherently wrong and thus a non-normative component of the rational human condition. The English word 'emotion' – which, as we have discussed earlier (see Section 1.3.3.c), is used today both in everyday language and academic discourse to denote the generic body of experiences that are commonly regarded as such – is therefore a potentially misleading translation of πάθος, with its ethical connotations.[2]

Following the lead of scholars such as Anthony Long and D. N. Sedley,[3] Brad Inwood,[4] Troels Engberg-Pedersen,[5] Susanna Morton Braund and Christopher Gill,[6] and others, I have chosen to render πάθος as 'passion' instead of 'emotion', which is

---

[1] According to Diogenes Laertius 5.23 and 5.45, Aristotle and Theophrastus each produced a work concerning the πάθη.
[2] LS 1.420: 'Passion is ... an unhealthy state of mind, not synonymous with emotion in ordinary language.'
[3] LS 1.410–23.
[4] Brad Inwood, *Ethics and Human Action in Early Stoicism* (Oxford: Clarendon, 1985), 127–8.
[5] Troels Engberg-Pedersen, *The Stoic Theory of Oikeiosis: Moral Development and Social Interaction in Early Stoic Philosophy* (Aarhus: Aarhus University Press, 1990), 170–206.
[6] Susanna Morton Braund and Christopher Gill, eds, *The Passions in Roman Thought and Literature* (Cambridge: Cambridge University Press) (in the title of their volume).

perhaps the more popular translation.⁷ This allows us to distinguish πάθος as a subset of that broad category of human experience that is understood as 'emotion' in common parlance, which is very useful for our purposes, because we are then able to retain in our discussion that same basic understanding of 'emotion' as is found in language today, and simultaneously assign to 'passion' the distinctive meanings associated with Stoic theory – which includes the fundamental notion that every πάθος is out of place in the life of the wise man.⁸

2.2. The Broader Philosophical Background

There is some consensus that in recent decades the salient features of Stoic thinking on the emotions have emerged with increasing clarity.⁹ The founders of the Stoic school did not set out to eradicate all trace of emotion in humans; on the contrary, identifying false belief as the cause of the experiences of feelings with which they were dissatisfied, they sought to determine what the natural feelings of a person should be, in the absence of all false belief. Through careful observation the Stoics developed psychological explanations for affective responses that harmonized with their ideas concerning the causation of mental experiences. These explanations were integrated into a comprehensive theory of emotion.

However, the Stoic theory of emotion cannot be understood in isolation from its philosophical context. The Stoics prided themselves on the coherence of their philosophy,¹⁰ and Stoic thinking on emotions can only be understood by reference to their broader theories of psychology, ethics, epistemology, and physics.¹¹ It was an organic part of a much larger conceptual framework that the Stoics constructed to make sense of human nature and behaviour. A fundamentally important and pervasive element of that framework is reason; and it is with the Stoic understanding of reason that we begin our exploration.

2.2.1. Rationality, Virtue, and *Eudaimonia*

In Stoic thinking, rationality permeated the entire cosmos: divine reason or λόγος, which the Stoics equated with universal nature, and with their conception of deity, pervaded all things and shaped every event.¹² The universe was regarded as an organized system

---

⁷ Used by, e.g. Julia Annas, *Hellenistic Philosophy of Mind* (Berkeley: University of California Press, 1992), 103–20; Tad Brennan, 'The Old Stoic Theory of Emotions', in *The Emotions in Hellenistic Philosophy*, ed. Juha Sihvola and Troels Engberg-Pedersen (Dordrecht: Kluwer Academic, 1998), 21–70; Richard Sorabji, *Emotion and Peace of Mind: From Stoic Agitation to Christian Temptation* (Oxford: Oxford University Press, 2000); Simo Knuuttila, *Emotions in Ancient and Medieval Philosophy* (Oxford: Clarendon, 2004), 47–80.
⁸ On the Stoic ideal of the sage, see John Sellars, *The Art of Living: The Stoics on the Nature and Function of Philosophy*, 2nd ed. (London: Bloomsbury, 2009), 59–64.
⁹ Margaret R. Graver, *Stoicism and Emotion* (Chicago: University of Chicago Press, 2007), 2; Brennan, 'Stoic Theory', 21.
¹⁰ Anthony A. Long, *Hellenistic Philosophy*, 2nd ed. (Berkeley: University of California Press, 1986), 108, citing Cicero, *Fin.* 3.74.
¹¹ Brennan, 'Stoic Theory', 21.
¹² See Cicero, *Nat. d.* 1.39 (= LS 54B); Diogenes Laertius 7.134 (= LS 44B); Seneca, *Ep.* 124.13–14.

that was amenable to rational explanation. Since λόγος was present in human beings, the individual person at the essence of his nature shared the property of rationality with the cosmos. As such, to live in agreement with nature was to act in accordance with the best of human reason.[13] The Stoics believed that rational contemplation and action would facilitate the living of life according to nature's purposes,[14] for nature's activity was one of perfect rationality.[15] Therefore, that which was of greatest good for a person was the perfection of his own reason – which led to virtue:

> And what quality is best in man? It is reason; by virtue of reason he surpasses the animals, and is surpassed only by the gods. Perfect reason is therefore the good peculiar to man ... When this is right and has reached perfection, man's felicity is complete. Hence, if everything is praiseworthy and has arrived at the end intended by its nature, when it has brought its peculiar good to perfection, and if man's peculiar good is reason; then if a man has brought his reason to perfection, he is praiseworthy and has reached the end suited to his nature. This perfect reason is called virtue, and is likewise that which is honourable. (Seneca, *Ep.* 76.9–10)

Summed up as 'the natural perfection of a rational being qua rational',[16] virtue was a rational consistency (ὁμολογία, literally, 'harmony with reason') that ensued in happiness or *eudaimonia* (εὐδαιμονία) – which was wholly constituted by virtue.[17] If virtue was rational consistency, then its opposite, vice, was irrationality that stemmed from aberrant thinking and erroneous judgement.[18] The Stoic position on the nature of the soul did not allow for degrees of virtue and vice. The soul was a unitary whole, and as such its powers were not divisible into the rational and the irrational; thus a person's reasoning faculty was either consistent or inconsistent.[19]

Eudaimonia was by no means unique to Stoicism: most of the major systems of moral philosophy in antiquity are broadly eudaimonist in their structure.[20] The Stoics

---

[13] Stobaeus 2.75.11–76.8 (= LS 63B).
[14] Diogenes Laertius 7.130. See also the similar statement in Cicero, *Nat. d.* 2.37–9 (= LS 54H); here Cicero refers to man's purpose, which is to contemplate and imitate the world, in order to be perfected in virtue.
[15] Seneca, *Ep.* 124.13–14: 'that alone is perfect which is perfect according to nature as a whole, and nature as a whole is possessed of reason.'
[16] Diogenes Laertius 7.94.
[17] Diogenes Laertius 7.89; Plutarch, *Virt. mor.* 441B–C (= LS 61B). Cicero, in *Tusc.* 4.34, opines that virtue may, in its most concise formulation, be termed 'right reason'. On the translation of *eudaimonia* as 'happiness', see Anthony A. Long, 'Stoic Eudaimonism', in *Stoic Studies* (Cambridge: Cambridge University Press, 1996), 181; here Long argues that 'happiness' is the normal and indeed correct translation of *eudaimonia* because it includes both the objective features of happiness (the attainment of good) and its subjective connotations (a profoundly content state of mind). See also his *Epictetus: A Stoic and Socratic Guide to Life* (Oxford: Clarendon, 2002), 190.
[18] Stobaeus 2.66.14–67.4 (= LS 61G); Cicero, *Tusc.* 4.29, 34–5 (= LS 61O); Plutarch, *Virt. mor.* 441C–D (= LS 61B); Plutarch, *St. rep.* 1046E–F (= LS 61F).
[19] LS 1.383, citing Diogenes Laertius 7.127 (= LS 61I).
[20] For a comparative study of ancient Greek eudaimonistic theories see Julia Annas, *The Morality of Happiness* (New York: Oxford University Press, 1993). On eudaimonism in Stoicism see Long, 'Eudaimonism', 179–201; John M. Cooper, 'Eudaimonism, the Appeal to Nature, and "Moral Duty" in Stoicism', in *Reason and Emotion: Essays on Ancient Moral Psychology and Ethical Theory* (Princeton, NJ: Princeton University Press, 1999), 427–48; LS 1.398–401.

share with Socrates, Plato, Aristotle, and Epicurus the general claim that *eudaimonia* is a condition that depends on a person's beliefs, values, desires, and moral character; where they stand alone is in their tenet that *eudaimonia* consists entirely in ethical virtue and is thus not dependent on the possession of goods that partly depend on chance.[21] In Stoicism, then, the cultivation of rationality was the key to *eudaimonia*. A happy life was a life of perfected reason in accordance with nature; moreover, such a condition was within one's power to achieve

> since they [the Stoics] have perceived the final good to be agreement with nature and living consistently with nature, which is not only the wise man's proper function, but also in his power. It necessarily follows that the happy life is in the power of the man who has the final good in his power. So the wise man's life is always happy. (Cicero, *Tusc.* 5.82 (= LS 63M))

As Long expresses it, the Stoic specification of happiness 'involves the fulfilment of all desires that it is *reasonable* for human beings to have'; such a condition is certainly attainable provided that one completely limits these desires (and aversions) to the domain in which one is capable of being autonomous, that is, in such things as rationality, judgement, and volition.[22] Hence we see that *eudaimonia* is inextricably linked both to reason and virtuous agency;[23] indeed, its benefits are constituted by virtue.[24]

2.2.2. Stoic Physics and the *Pneuma*

Along with the Stoic emphasis on the norms that could be established as a result of rational evaluation was an insistence also on the physical nature of all events in the mind. For them, mental events were always constituted by some kind of psychophysical change. Earlier, Aristotle had proposed that in investigating the nature of emotions, biological and non-biological understandings were both valid:

> But the natural philosopher and the logician will in every case offer different definitions, e.g., in answer to the question what is anger. The latter will call it a craving for retaliation, or something of the sort; the former will describe it as a surging of the blood and heat around the heart. The one is describing the matter, the other the form or formula of the essence. (Aristotle, *De an.* 1.1.403a29–403b3)

Stoicism adopted Aristotle's methodological stance and propounded a hypothesis in which mental events could be construed either in intentional terms (by articulating their propositional content) or in physical terms (by specifying some material shift within a somatic locale). Though greater emphasis was placed on the intentional

---

[21] Long, 'Eudaimonism', 182.
[22] See Long, *Epictetus*, 191 (emphasis original).
[23] Cooper, 'Eudaimonism', 427–8.
[24] LS 1.399; citing Seneca, *Ep.* 92.3 (= LS 63F).

dimensions of their theory, the Stoics made significant effort also to explain the processes of the mind in physical terms, in a manner that was consistent with their understanding of natural science.

The Stoic belief that the mind was necessarily a material substance and that all mental events were also manifested physically came from their claim that anything that interacted with a body had to be itself corporeal in some way. Indeed, for the Stoics, the tangible bodily reactions that accompanied emotional upheavals were proof that thoughts and emotions were also alterations in some kind of psychic material.[25] This animating mind-material consisted of *pneuma* (πνεῦμα) – a highly energized compound of fire and air. In early Stoicism, Zeno had identified the heat that was in all things as the 'designing fire' (πῦρ τεχνικόν) which supplied the 'seminal principle' (λόγος σπερματικός) that explained their structure and function; indeed the universe as a whole was a macrocosm of this structural and functional complexity, because of the presence of the designing fire in it.[26] However, from Chrysippus onwards, it was the *pneuma* that was assigned this cosmological function and associated with rationality; all things owed their identity and properties to the *pneuma*.[27] It was therefore the *pneuma* that endowed humans with all the capacities necessary for life, perception, and response.[28] This helps to account for the readiness of the Stoics to assume a connection between human rationality and cosmological ordering: individual living things are parts of the cosmos and derive their psychic capacities from the psychic material of the whole.[29]

The term *psychē* (ψυχή), often rendered in English as 'soul', referred to the entire innate expanse of *pneuma* present in a human,[30] but in its common and more restrictive usage it designated the centralized portion of the *pneuma* – the *hēgemonikon* (ἡγεμονικόν) or 'directive faculty' – that was responsible for what we would call the person's psychological operations.[31] Here, cognition was also coordinated with locomotion and other motor functions.[32] The *hēgemonikon* was therefore regarded as a command centre, located at the heart, which received sensory inputs from, and initiated behaviours to, other portions of the psychic material extending into the sense

---

[25] Nemesius, *De natura hominis* 78.7–79.2 (= LS 45C). On corporealism see also Cicero, *Acad.* 1.39 (= LS 45A); Sextus Empiricus, *Math.* 8.263 (= LS 45B); and the useful discussion in David E. Hahm, *The Origins of Stoic Cosmology* (Columbus: Ohio State University Press, 1977), 3–28.
[26] Stobaeus 1.213.15–21 (= LS 46D); Diogenes Laertius 7.135–6 (= LS 46B); Eusebius, *Praep. evang.* 15.14.2 (= LS 46G).
[27] Plutarch, *St. rep.* 1053F–1054B (= LS 47M); Galen, *Intr.* 14.726.7–11 (= LS 47N); see further Long, *Hellenistic Philosophy*, 152–8.
[28] More specifically, it was the variations in the 'tension' (τόνος) between the fire and air in the *pneuma* as they worked together upon the two passive elements of water and earth that explained differences in the qualities imparted by *pneuma* to things; see Graver, *Stoicism*, 19–21. For a fuller discussion see Hahm, *Stoic Cosmology*, 165–74.
[29] See Hahm, *Stoic Cosmology*, 163.
[30] *SVF* 2.885 (= Galen, *PHP* 7.1.112).
[31] The two meanings of ψυχή are distinguished in Sextus Empiricus, *Math.* 7.234 (= LS 53F).
[32] The Stoics divided the soul into eight parts: the five senses, the speech and reproductive faculties, and the *hēgemonikon*. See Aetius, *Doxographi Graeci* 4.21.1–4 (= LS 53H), 4.4.4 (= *SVF* 2.827); also Diogenes Laertius 7.110, where the mind is called δοανοία.

organs and limbs.³³ In Stoic nomenclature, *hēgemonikon* is the closest equivalent to our term 'mind'.

2.2.3. Stoic Psychology of Knowledge and Action

The Stoics also provided psychophysical explanations for how information in the mind was conceptualized and acted upon. In this psychology of knowledge and action, the main elements are impression, assent, and impulse; these generate the action that is to be explained.³⁴ The sequence is provided by the Stoicizing Academic Antiochus of Ascalon and cited by Cicero,³⁵ who attributes these same ideas to Chrysippus.³⁶ Further support for these elements as being integral to the Stoic theory comes from the fact that they correspond to three of the four powers of the rational soul in Iamblichus's report as found in Stobaeus: here the *hēgemonikon* is the seat of impression (φαντασία), assent (συγκατάθεσις), impulse (ὁρμή), and reason (λόγος).³⁷

2.2.3.a. Knowledge

An impression is an alteration that occurs in the *psychē* through which something seems to be present or to be the case.³⁸ The Chrysippan account runs as follows:

> An impression is an affection occurring in the soul (φαντασία μὲν οὖν ἐστι πάθος ἐν τῇ ψυχῇ γιγνόμενον), which reveals itself and its cause. Thus, when through sight we observe something white, the affection is what is engendered in the soul through vision; and it is this affection which enables us to say that there is a white object which activates us. (Aetius, *Doxographi Graeci* 4.12.1 (= LS 39B))

An impression is thus essentially sentient in nature. Further, in having an impression, the mind produces thought that is linguistically formulable and therefore propositional ('which enables us to say there is').³⁹ Elsewhere, the relationship of impressions to articulate thought is expressed very clearly: 'For impression comes first; then thought, which is capable of expressing itself, puts into the form of a proposition that which the subject receives from an impression.'⁴⁰ However, this does not imply that the mind receives raw data that it then subsequently interprets. All impressions of rational persons are rational 'processes of thought',⁴¹ and all rational impressions may be

---

[33] Chrysippus is described as likening it to a spring that flows through the whole body, a tree with its branches, and a monarch with his network of spies, in Calcidius, *On the Timaeus of Plato* 220 (= LS 53G), and an octopus and its tentacles in Aetius, *Doxographi Graeci* 4.21.1–4 (= LS 53H).
[34] For a comprehensive discussion, see Inwood, *Ethics*, 42–101.
[35] Cicero, *Acad.* 2.24–5.
[36] Cicero, *Fat.* 41–2. See also Stobaeus 1.368.12–20 (= LS 53K).
[37] Stobaeus 1.368.12–20 (= LS 53K).
[38] Graver, *Stoicism*, 24.
[39] Engberg-Pedersen, *Oikeiosis*, 147–52, especially 150.
[40] Diogenes Laertius 7.49; I translate φαντασία as 'impression' instead of 'presentation'. See also Sextus Empiricus, *Math.* 8.70 (= LS 33C). For a succinct discussion of the Stoic argument for a linguistic dimension to rationality, see Long, *Hellenistic Philosophy*, 124–5.
[41] Diogenes Laertius 7.51.

classified as being either true or false on the basis of the assertions that can be made about them.[42] These claims combine to produce a scenario in which the mind's stock of conceptions is instantly activated upon receiving an impression, such that it presents its object in a conceptualized form.[43]

In addition, the Stoics had a specific term for the true impression which was unmistakably trustworthy because it represented its real object with complete accuracy: this was the 'cognitive' or 'kataleptic' impression (φαντασία καταληπτική) – literally, 'impression capable of grasping (its object)'.[44] Sextus Empiricus reports,

> Of true impressions, some are cognitive, others not (τῶν δὲ ἀληθῶν αἱ μέν εἰσι καταληπτικαὶ αἱ δὲ οὔ). Non-cognitive are ones people experience when they are in abnormal states. For very large numbers of people who are deranged or melancholic take in an impression which is true but non-cognitive, and arises purely externally and fortuitously, so that they often do not respond to it positively and do not assent to it. A cognitive impression is one which arises from what is (καταληπτικὴ δέ ἐστιν ἡ ἀπὸ ὑπάρχοντος) and is stamped and impressed exactly in accordance with what is, of such a kind as could not arise from what is not ... For the Stoics say that one who has the cognitive impression fastens on the objective difference of things in a craftsmanlike way, since this kind of impression has a peculiarity which differentiates it from other impressions. (*Math.* 7.247–52 (= LS 40E))[45]

As Engberg-Pedersen observes, whether an impression is kataleptic or merely true is a difference of degree with respect to the mind's contribution. The nature of this contribution may be elucidated from Sextus's description of the person having a kataleptic impression as one noticing 'in a craftsmanlike way' (τεχνικῶς) the uniqueness of its properties. The person does this not by having an impression in the sense of an image with some special property that marks it outs as veridical, but by recalling previous knowledge to help him determine what the thing or event is that impinges on his mind. Thus in a kataleptic impression such knowledge is articulated more and more precisely until the description of the thing or event that forms the impression matches exactly that thing or event.[46]

However, to have an impression – whatever its type – is still simply to entertain a thought, without any implication of commitment to it. Impression is not belief;[47] that which transmutes thought into belief is a subsequent mental event called an

---

[42] Sextus Empiricus, *Math.* 7.242–6 (= LS 39G).
[43] LS 1.240.
[44] See LS 1.250–3, in which there is also a useful summary of the debate between the Stoics and the Academics concerning the self-certifiability of such impressions. For the sake of consistency, in my study I shall refer to these impressions as 'kataleptic' impressions.
[45] See also Diogenes Laertius 7.54, who notes that the Stoics regarded the kataleptic impression as 'the criterion of truth, i.e. the impression arising from what is'.
[46] Engberg-Pedersen, *Oikeiosis*, 157–60.
[47] See LS 1.239–40, where Long and Sedley helpfully explain that 'a Stoic impression in not an impression *that* something is the case – which in modern English, does imply some degree of belief – but just the impression *of* something's being the case' (emphases theirs).

assent. Specifically, one assents to the unique proposition that is intrinsic to, and the proper object of, any impression.[48] This implies making a commitment to the veracity or desirability of the state of affairs that form the content of an impression, and also having the capacity to refrain from doing so.[49] Assents can be strong or weak: the wise man's strong assent is one that is not only firm and certain but is also irreversible, while the weak, less reliable assent of an ordinary person is characterized by precipitancy and changeability.[50] In regard to kataleptic impressions, the Stoics assumed that the rational human being was endowed with the mental ability to make accurate discriminations that were congruent with living according to nature. As such, he was naturally predisposed to give his assent to such impressions,[51] the outcome of which was 'cognition' or *katalēpsis* (κατάληψις), that is, assent to a kataleptic impression.[52]

In summary, the Stoic framework for understanding the formation of belief has two components: impression and assent. Any occurrent thought, desire, or belief that a person may have is a combination of these two components. In Stoic epistemology, the highest cognitive state of 'knowledge' (ἐπιστήμη) occurs only when an impression is kataleptic and the corresponding assent is strong. Though *katalēpsis* is a necessary condition of knowledge, it is not sufficient to constitute it because the cognition has to be impregnable to any thinking that might engender a change of mind. All other combinations of impression and assent produce 'opinion' (δόξα), for our sources also tell us that *doxa* involves weak assent, or assent to what is not kataleptic.[53] We may depict all this in tabular form, showing how two kinds of assent to three kinds of impression result in either opinion or knowledge (see Table 1).

Table 1 Impression and Assent in the Formation of Belief

			Assent	
			Weak	Strong
Impression	False		Opinion	Opinion
	True	Merely true	Opinion	Opinion
		Kataleptic	Opinion	Knowledge

---

[48] Stobaeus 2.88.2–3.
[49] LS 1.322; Long and Sedley observe also that Epictetus calls assent 'the power to use impressions' (*Diatr.* 1.1.12).
[50] Stobaeus 2.111.18–112.8 (= LS 41G); Plutarch, *St. rep.* 1057B (= LS 41F). As Graver, *Stoicism*, 26, expresses it, 'The ordinary mind is, as it were, a pushover, yielding easily to impressions which the wise person would resist.'
[51] Cicero, *Acad.* 2.30–1, 2.37–8 (= LS 40N).
[52] Cicero, *Acad.* 1.40–1 (= LS 40B).
[53] See e.g. Sextus Empiricus, *Math.* 7.151–7 (= LS 41C); Cicero, *Acad.* 1.41–2 (= LS 41B). Brennan, 'Stoic Theory', 27, notes that as the definition of knowledge is conjunctive, with knowledge and opinion between them exhausting the options, DeMorgan's laws confirm that opinion's definition should be disjunctive in this fashion.

We should note that knowledge requires a strong assent, and can only be found in the wise person, whose perfected reason contains no inconsistencies. All beliefs found in the non-wise person, even if kataleptically true, are only opinions.

2.2.3.b. Action

Having elucidated how the Stoics understood belief to be constructed, we turn now to their analysis of action, which centred on the concept of impulse (ὁρμή). An impulse was not some vague instinctual urge or underlying drive. It was that psychophysical event that caused an action.[54] According to Stobaeus,

> What activates impulse, they [the Stoics] say, is precisely an impression capable of directly impelling a proper function (φαντασίαν ὁρμητικὴν τοῦ καθήκοντος αὐτόθεν). In genus impulse is a movement of the soul towards something. (Stobaeus 2.86.17–19 (= LS 53Q))

Furthermore,

> They [the Stoics] say that all impulses are acts of assent, and the practical impulses also contain motive power. But acts of assent and impulses actually differ in their objects: propositions are the objects of acts of assent, but impulses are directed towards predicates, which are contained in a sense in the propositions. (Stobaeus 2.88.2–6 (= LS 33I))

From this we may learn several things. First, an impulse is stimulated by a 'hormetic impression' (φαντασία ὁρμητική): one that indicates to the person something that is 'proper' (καθῆκον) – that is, relevant or appropriate – because it will contribute to the fulfilment of his nature. Second, an impulse is a motion of the *psychē* towards the predicate in the endorsed proposition.[55] Third, an impulse is a type of assent involving impressions that have a special evaluative and practical character: thus, on the Stoic theory all occurrent practical attitudes – all desires, intentions, flights, and so on – are impulses, and therefore assents to these hormetic impressions.[56] Elsewhere, our sources tell us that an impulse is the necessary[57] and sufficient[58] condition of an action,

---

[54] LS 1.420: 'Impulses are that activity of the soul's commanding-faculty which converts its judgements of what it should pursue or avoid into purposive bodily movements.'
[55] See also Inwood, *Ethics*, 51, 272 n.53.
[56] See Brennan, 'Stoic Theory', 28. See also 29, where, using a helpful example, Brennan explains the apparent conundrum of how an assent to an impression can be simultaneously a belief (an assent to a full proposition, e.g. 'the cake is to be eaten by me') and an impulse (an assent to a predicate contained by that proposition, e.g. 'to eat the cake'). Impulses and beliefs are both assents, and impulses are correlated with beliefs in such a way that the impulse for an action (to eat the cake) and the belief that the action is to be carried out by the person (the cake is to be eaten by me) always entail one another. However, as Brennan admits, the state of our sources denies us further insight into the details.
[57] Alexander of Aphrodisias, *Fat.* 183.5–10; Seneca, *Ep.* 113.2.
[58] Cicero, *Acad.* 2.108.

and that unless an external obstacle hinders the physical execution of the act, an impulse invariably produces an action.[59]

That all impulses are acts of assent logically entails a view in which individuals are held responsible for their thoughts and desires.[60] Indeed, by performing much of the work of intention as part of its essential role in human action, impulse 'isolates the ethically significant aspect of an action'.[61] Long and Sedley are correct to argue that assent, for the Stoics, seems to be a distinguishing mark of rationality.[62] This brings us to λόγος, the fourth of the four powers of the *hēgemonikon* (see Section 2.2.3). This uniquely human endowment – decisively lacking in animals – fundamentally qualifies the *hēgemonikon* as a unitary rational agent, by making its impressions, impulses, and assents rational. While the four powers of the human soul work seamlessly as a single entity, reason is the key function: it works with impressions through an act of assent, thereby shaping impulses.[63]

2.3. The Stoic Understanding of Emotion

2.3.1. The Passions as 'Excessive' Impulses

We are now in a position to detail how the Stoics incorporated affective events into their account of mental functioning. The Stoics defined passions as 'excessive' impulses, or, in other words, particularly compelling motivations towards actions of certain kinds. The standard definition as found in Stobaeus's report runs as follows:

> Πάθος δ᾽ εἶναί φασιν ὁρμὴν πλεονάζουσαν καὶ ἀπειθῆ τῷ αἱροῦντι λόγῳ ἢ κίνησιν ψυχῆς <ἄλογον> παρὰ φύσιν (εἶναι δὲ πάθη πάντα τοῦ ἡγεμονικοῦ τῆς ψυχῆς).

> They [the Stoics] say that passion is impulse which is excessive and disobedient to the dictates of reason, or a movement of soul which is irrational and contrary to nature; and that all passions belong to the soul's commanding-faculty. (Stobaeus 2.88.8–10 (= LS 65A))[64]

Since passions are impulses and therefore involve assenting to some hormetic impression, it follows that passions depend on the formulation and ratification of specific propositions about oneself and one's surroundings. In effect, the person has assented to a false value judgement, and in so doing issued himself with the excessive impulse to either pursue or avoid something.

---

[59] On this see Inwood, *Ethics*, 52; Brennan, 'Stoic Theory', 28.
[60] Stobaeus 2.88.2–6 (= LS 33I); Plutarch, *St. rep.* 1057A (= LS 53S).
[61] Inwood, *Ethics*, 53.
[62] LS 1.322.
[63] Inwood, *Ethics*, 52–3. See also Anthony A. Long, 'Soul and Body in Stoicism', *Phronesis* 27 (1992): 50–1.
[64] See also Diogenes Laertius 7.110; Cicero, *Tusc.* 4.11.

The meaning of 'excessive' is explained by Chrysippus in relation to people who 'overstep the proper and natural proportion of their impulses', and he illustrates this using the imagery of a person walking and running. When the person walks in accordance with his impulse, he remains in control of his movements and is able to stop or change direction; the movement of his legs is commensurate with the impulse and not excessive. However, in running, the person loses the sense of this control: the movement in his legs 'exceeds' the impulse such that they are carried away by their motion. By analogy, Chrysippus argues, an impulse is excessive if it goes beyond the natural control of reason.[65]

The important and original insight expressed by the analogy is the continuity, and also the difference, between normal, healthy impulses and passions.[66] We have already seen that in Stoic psychology, any impulse is an effective cause of action. Since reason characterizes the *hēgemonikon*, there is nothing intrinsically irrational about impulses as such. However, as Chrysippus insists, the passions are 'irrational' because they run contrary to the natural limits and dictates of reason; their unnaturalness consists in the immoderation of their movement.[67] Passions do not stem from ordinary errors of fact,[68] but are 'vicious and uncontrolled reason which acquires vehemence and strength from bad and erroneous judgement'.[69]

Passions, then, are characterized by their 'excess' in terms of the nature of the judgements that give rise to them. At the same time, as we have seen, the standard Stoic definition of passions also relates this 'excess' to the concomitant psychophysical movements ('movement of soul') that form their coordinate definitions. These movements are elsewhere described in greater detail, in terms of the four generic types of passion with which they are correlated.

> They [the Stoics] say that desire (ἐπιθυμία) is a stretching (ὄρεξις) which is disobedient to reason, and its cause is forming an opinion (δοξάζειν) that a good

---

[65] Galen, *PHP* 4.2.10–18 (= LS 65J). The person with an excessive impulse is 'not obedient' (μὴ εὐπειθῶς ἔχειν) to reason. Another example cited, by Cicero and Seneca, is that people falling from a high place do not have control over their movements; they can neither hold back nor delay their physical reactions; see Cicero, *Tusc.* 4.42; Seneca, *Ira* 1.7.4.

[66] LS 1.420.

[67] Galen, *PHP* 4.2.10–18 (= LS 65J). See the Stobaean account at 2.89.4–12, where we learn that passions, being irrational and disobedient to reason, overpower people with their intensity. This is not to say that the process has not been evaluated, as Stobaeus's quoting of a commonly heard phrase shows ('Although I have [better] judgement, nature forces me to do this' (Pomeroy)), but rather that the act does not conform to normal rational choices. Commenting on this, Arthur Pomeroy notes that the effect 'is to reinforce the moral responsibility of individuals for their acts, rather than excuse them as outside their control' (*Arius Didymus: Epitome of Stoic Ethics* (Atlanta, GA: Society of Biblical Literature, 1999), 118 n.128.

[68] Stobaeus 2.89.16–18 tells us: 'All those in the grips of passion turn their backs on reason, not in the same way as those who have been thoroughly deceived in any matter, but in a special way (ἀλλ' ἰδιαζόντως)' (Pomeroy). Long and Sedley, 1.420, argue that this implies that the pro or contra judgement underlying a passion is perfectly natural in itself: the wise man will naturally try to seek or avoid the things that form the objects of passions – but he will do so at a walking pace, as it were, i.e. on the basis of a properly rational judgement of such things' moral indifference. In this way, he experiences nothing in contrary to his desire or impulse; since he 'acts with reserve', his impulses are rationally regulated so as to accord with his environment (see Stobaeus 2.155.5–17 (= LS 65W)).

[69] Plutarch, *Virt. mor.* 441D (= LS 61B).

is approaching and that when it is present we shall do well by it; this opinion that it is really worth stretching for has a fresh power to stimulate irregular motion. Fear (φόβος) is a shrinking (ἔκκλισις) which is disobedient to reason, and its cause is forming an opinion that something bad is approaching; this opinion that it is really worth shrinking away from has a fresh power to stimulate motion. Grief (λύπη) is a contraction (συστολή) of the soul disobedient to reason, and its cause is forming a fresh opinion that a bad thing is present, for which it is appropriate to be contracted. Delight (ἡδονή) is a swelling (ἔπαρσις) of the soul disobedient to reason, and its cause is forming a fresh opinion that a good thing is present, for which it is appropriate to be swollen. (Stobaeus 2.90.7–18 (= SVF 3.394); my translation)[70]

As expected, the phrase 'it is appropriate' (καθήκει) in relation to contraction in grief and swelling in delight corresponds precisely to the description of appropriateness in our earlier discussion of the Stobaean account of Stoic impulse (Section 2.2.3.b). Just as in impulse generally the *psychē* views some predicate as appropriate and moves to fulfil it, so in the passions it sees certain conditions as being appropriate and therefore experiences the physical movement associated with the passion. Thus in the passage above we note that in grief the person sees 'being contracted' as appropriate and therefore suffers the type of movement termed a contraction (συστολή); in delight he regards 'being swollen' as appropriate and so experiences a swelling (ἔπαρσις). Though καθήκει is absent in relation to the movements associated with desire and fear, the use of language of similar force denotes clearly the presence of appropriateness.[71] All these alterations in the *psychē* can be sensed because of its continual proprioceptive awareness.[72] The precise form of each type of alteration is not important; for our purposes it is sufficient to highlight that in the Stoic account some kind of *felt* psychosomatic change accompanies each type of passion.[73]

But what precisely is the relationship between these felt movements and the judgements that are also involved in affective events? According to Galen, while Zeno identified the passions with the contractions, shrinkings, and other psychophysical motions that followed or supervened upon (ἐπιγίγνεσθαι) the judgements, Chrysippus subsequently revised the Zenoian view to equate the passions with the judgements

---

[70] See also the similar accounts in Andronicus, *De passionibus* 1, Cicero, *Tusc.* 4.14–15, and Diogenes Laertius 7:111–14. Also, in referring to a 'fresh' (πρόσφατον) power or opinion, the Stoics are stressing its immanent force rather than specifying some notion of temporal recentness (which Posidonius tries to do; see *PHP* 4.7.1–5 (= *SVF* 3.481), with Inwood, *Ethics*, 146). The term, used frequently of food and also of new corpses, implies that no decomposition has yet set in and that the item in question has retained its pristine character; see Martha C. Nussbaum, *The Therapy of Desire: Theory and Practice in Hellenistic Ethics* (Princeton, NJ: Princeton University Press, 1994), 381–2.

[71] The idea of appropriateness is wide and not confined to judgements made on moral grounds, though, as Sorabji observes, it includes in Cicero, *Tusc.* 3.83, and Seneca, *Marc.* 1, the case in which mourners come to think that they have a moral duty to react (*Emotion*, 30).

[72] As discussed at Section 2.2.2.

[73] See Knuuttila, *Emotions*, 60–2, for the scholarly interpretations of the precise nature of these psychophysical movements. An expanded list of these movements is provided by Galen in *PHP* 4.2.4–6 and 4.3.2 (of note is the term 'bitings', which was long established as a way of speaking of the pain of grief). See also Cicero, *Tusc.* 4:15, where Cicero's Latin terminology for these movements corresponds closely to what Galen reports. For a fuller discussion see Graver, *Stoicism*, 28–34.

themselves.⁷⁴ However, as Graver argues, even though there is certainly a difference in wording, there is much similarity in the two accounts: both hold that a passion involves a psychophysical change and a judgement. In addition, they describe the relation between the two in very much the same way; for Zeno the change supervenes on the judgement and would not be a passion if it did not supervene on such a judgement, while for Chrysippus the change is induced by the judgement, which would not be a passion if such a movement was not produced. The chief difference between the two philosophers is in the exact application of the term 'passion' within the sequence. In reformulating the definition, Chrysippus clarifies what was already implied in Zeno's version: that it is the nature of the judgement that defines what sort of impulse has occurred.⁷⁵ Graver concludes that a distinction can therefore be made between the passions as judgements (i.e. strictly for their intentional content, which may be either true or false) and the feeling one gets from a certain passion. In itself, the feeling merely registers the physical event that necessarily occurs with the passion. Moreover, because the felt psychophysical event merely supervenes on the judgement, rather than being itself the passion, it is possible to experience something which *feels* like delight or fear but which is not actually one of these passions because it lacks the pertinent intentional criteria.⁷⁶ We shall pick this up again in our exploration of the *propatheiai*, or 'pre-passions' (Section 2.3.3.c).

2.3.2. The Passions as Value Judgements

However, more than being mere psychic motions, passions – being certain kinds of impulses – necessarily contain propositional content: evaluative construals of external objects as being either advantageous or injurious to oneself.⁷⁷ These evaluations comprise both an occurrent element (e.g. 'this is desire') and a dispositional one ('desire is good, and it is appropriate to react in an emotional way to it'), and these two elements are brought together syllogistically to produce the judgements that are intrinsic to affective response. Thus a fundamental feature of the Stoic theory of the passions is its position concerning the propriety or impropriety of these judgements, which is based on normative claims as to the types of objects that one could legitimately value as a result of properly rational thinking. The classification of affective responses proceeds accordingly: imperfectly reasoned evaluations give rise to the passions, while

---

⁷⁴ Galen, *PHP* 5.1.4; 4.3.2–3.
⁷⁵ Graver, *Stoicism*, 33. See also Christopher Gill, 'Competing Readings of Stoic Emotions', in *Metaphysics, Soul, and Ethics in Ancient Thought: Themes from the Work of Richard Sorabji*, ed. Ricardo Salles (Oxford: Clarendon, 2005), 453–4. I concur with Graver and Gill, who do not agree with the arguments for a substantive difference between Zeno and Chrysippus in Sorabji, *Emotion*, 55–65.
⁷⁶ Graver, *Stoicism*, 33–4.
⁷⁷ I use the term 'external object' to designate those things that are external to one's sphere of control; the Stoic term is ἀδιάφορα ('indifferents'). Although some indifferents may be 'preferable' (προηγμένα) because they have some sort of positive value, they are still intrinsically indifferents; the fact is that nothing is really good except the perfection of one's reason, which is virtue. See Cicero, *Fin.* 3.50–4; Diogenes Laertius 7.104–7. For an overview of the Stoic ethical stance regarding the objects of evaluation, see Graver, *Stoicism*, 46–51.

there is another ideal or 'eupathic' class of emotions which are generated through proper reasoning.

The source that illuminates most clearly the interplay between the occurrent and dispositional dimensions of the evaluative process is the Stobaean account of the causation of affective events at the level of genus that was quoted earlier (Stobaeus 2.90.7–18). In all four genera (desire, fear, grief, and delight) the person experiencing these passions is credited with a belief that something either good or bad is present or in prospect. It is important to highlight that here, in the case of grief for instance, the judgement is not that 'a present thing is bad' but that 'a bad thing is present'. As such, the evaluative component comes in not because the person makes the decision there and then that something is bad, but because the occurrent judgement engages dispositional attitudes that are already in place concerning the badness of certain object types.

However, this ascription of value still does not produce a passion on the Stoic account. The Stobaean summary also informs us that in the genesis of the passions, the evaluation of a contingent object is followed by a further judgement that some sort of predicative response is appropriate under the circumstances. This same sequence is found in Cicero's analysis of the causes of grief. He describes grief as 'a belief (*opinio*) that some serious evil is present', and then adds,

> Specifically it is a fresh belief (*recens opinio*), and the evil is of such a nature that it seems right to be pained by it – seems so, at least, to the person who is suffering and who believes that it is appropriate for him to suffer. (*Tusc.* 3.25 (Graver))[78]

More specifically, it is a combination of two judgements that brings about grief:

> But when our belief in the seriousness of our misfortune is combined with the further belief that it is right, and an appropriate and proper thing, to be upset by what has happened, then, and not before, there comes about that deep emotion which is distress. (*Tusc.* 3.61–2 (Graver))

Hence Cicero's claim is that when an external trigger occurs, the conjunction of two related judgements – an evaluation of an external object, and a belief in the appropriateness of a predicative response to it – generates distress in the person.[79]

The Stoic theory is based on the assumption that the object of a passion is either good or bad. As we have seen earlier, only behaviour that is rational and therefore in accordance with virtue is intrinsically good; behaviour that is irrational is a deviation from the norms of nature and therefore intrinsically bad. People who are driven by irrational thinking wrongly believe that external objects are of significance in their lives, and as a result both their judgements about the value of these objects and the appropriateness of their reactions to them are systemically misguided.[80]

---

[78] For the meaning of a 'fresh' belief, see Cicero's own explanation in *Tusc.* 3.75, where he explains that 'freshness' relates not only to matters of time but also to the vigour of the imagined evil.
[79] This two-component analysis is reiterated, for grief at *Tusc.* 3.74, 76, 79, and for grief and the other generic passions at 4.14.
[80] Knuuttila, *Emotions*, 59.

Therefore, on the Stoic account, the passions are the consequence of reason gone astray. The Stoics rejected the Platonic model of a divided soul in which emotional conflict was explained by how passion was often at odds with reason.[81] Instead, such conflict arose from extremely rapid fluctuations in the unitary *hēgemonikon*;[82] Zeno uses the ornithological metaphor of 'fluttering' to convey this notion of volatility.[83] Thus the dominant Stoic conception of those subject to passion is their instability and lack of consistent direction.[84] Since human beings are responsible for the state of their rationality, they are also held responsible for their passions and any ensuing actions. According to Epictetus,

> It is not the things themselves that disturb men, but their judgements about these things. For example, death is nothing dreadful, or else Socrates too would have thought so, but the judgement that death is dreadful, *this* is the dreadful thing. When, therefore, we are hindered, or disturbed, or grieved, let us never blame anyone but ourselves, that means, our own judgements. (*Ench*. 5; emphasis translator's)[85]

For the Stoics, the passions followed directly upon faulty judgements based on a mistaken interpretation of one's mental impressions or an erroneous description of one's experiences.[86]

2.3.3. The Taxonomy of the Emotions

2.3.3.a. The Passions

As we already know, the Stoic account of the causation of the passions informs us that there are four generic ones: desire (ἐπιθυμία), the opinion that something in prospect is a good of such a sort that one should reach out for it; fear (φόβος), the opinion that something in prospect is an evil of such a sort that we should avoid it; grief (λύπη), the opinion that some present thing is an evil of such a sort that we should be downcast about it; and delight (ἡδονή), the opinion that some present thing is a good of such a sort that we should be elated about it.[87] Clearly, these four passions are the product of two dichotomies, between present and future, and good and evil, and are often depicted graphically by scholars as shown in Table 2.

---

[81] Plutarch, *Virt. mor*. 446F–447A (= LS 65G).
[82] Plutarch, *Virt. mor*. 441B–D (= LS 61B).
[83] Stobaeus 2.88.11–12 (= LS 65A): 'Therefore every fluttering is also a passion, and likewise, every passion is a fluttering.'
[84] LS 1.422; here attention is drawn to references to the soul's 'weakness' and 'lack of tension' in Galen, *PHP* 4.6.2–3 (= LS 65T) and Stobaeus 2.88.22–89.3 (= LS 65C). For Galen's and Posidonius's objections to the Chrysippan doctrine of passion, see LS 1.422–3; Engberg-Pedersen, *Oikeiosis*, 182–93; Graver, *Stoicism*, 75–81.
[85] See also Epictetus, *Diatr*. 1.12.20–1, and Seneca, *Ira* 2.3.1–2.4 (= LS 65X).
[86] LS 1.421.
[87] Our main sources are Stobaeus 2.90.7–18; Andronicus, *De passionibus* 1; Cicero, *Tusc*. 4.14–15; Diogenes Laertius 7.111–14. The fourfold classification was very widely attested; for examples see Graver, *Stoicism*, 231 n.38.

Table 2 The Passions

	Present	In Prospect
Good	Delight	Desire
Evil	Grief	Fear

The above generic passions are each further broken down into a number of species. The surviving lists of these species are all different, both in terms of the number of them included and their names.[88] The unsystematic structure of these lists is exacerbated by the presence of overlapping definitions as well as gaps; no reasonable amount of emendation would produce anything like the neat taxonomy at the level of genus that is seen in all the Stoic sources. Margaret Graver's solution to this mystery is compelling: she argues that the point of offering such lists can only have been to demonstrate that the broad-brush classification by genus could be made fine-grained enough to capture the nuances of ordinary emotional experience. This approach probably reflected a deliberate choice, made early in the history of the school, that its philosophical needs would be better served by a list that included a wide variety of everyday terms and definitions than by some neat and exhaustive classification which employed unfamiliar language.[89]

2.3.3.b. The *Eupatheiai*

The Stoics also had a class of emotions that belonged to the person of wise understanding: these affective responses are to the passions what the Stoic sage is to the ordinary person. The collective term ἐυπάθειαι (the term designated to mean 'good emotions' or 'proper feelings')[90] is attested from an early date and may have been the term used in the early treatises.[91] For Inwood, the proper understanding of the Stoic ideal of freedom from the passions may be summed up in the slogan '*apatheia* is *eupatheia*', from which it follows that a *eupatheia* is simply the impulse of a fully rational person.[92] In the psychology of the wise person, then, the *eupatheiai* were analogous to, and indeed replaced, the passions of the non-wise.

There are three genera of eupathic responses: joy (χαρά), the knowledge that some present thing is a good of such a sort that one should be elated about it; wish (βούλησις), the knowledge that something in prospect is a good of such a sort that one should reach out for it; and caution (ἐυλάβεια), the knowledge that something in prospect

---

[88] For the canonical definitions see Stobaeus 2.90.19–92.20; Diogenes Laertius 7.111–14; Cicero, *Tusc.* 4.16–21; Andronicus, *De passionibus* 2–5; Nemesius, *De natura hominis* 19.229–21.235.
[89] Graver, *Stoicism*, 57–8.
[90] As is common, I will retain the Greek term and speak of *eupatheiai* or eupathic responses rather than use vague language like 'good feelings'.
[91] Graver, *Stoicism*, 51, citing Plutarch, *Virt. mor.* 449A–B; *St. rep.* 1037F–1038A. Inwood, *Ethics*, 172, notes that it is not clear when the term came to be first used in the Stoa. The main (and almost sole) evidence for them is in Cicero, *Tusc.* 4.11–14, Diogenes Laertius 7.116, and Andronicus, *De passionibus* 1–6.
[92] Inwood, *Ethics*, 172.

is an evil of such a sort that one should avoid it.[93] The absence of a fourth *eupatheia* follows organically from the Stoic definitions. The corollary of grief would have to be the knowledge that some present thing is an evil. The wise, however, can never have the knowledge that some evil was present to them. Putting it another way: 'the wise never are affected emotionally by anything they regard as, and that in truth *is*, bad.'[94] On this basis, there can be no fourth genus of eupathic response.[95] We should note also that like the passions, within each genus the *eupatheiai* may be broken down into species.[96]

Since the *eupatheiai* gave rise to normative responses, their evaluations are necessarily completely accurate, veridical attributions of goodness and badness. In the *eupatheiai*, then, opinion has been replaced by knowledge, and external objects or indifferents have been rejected in place of genuine goods and evils (which is to say, virtue and vice), for the impulses that are correlated with the *eupatheiai* are wholly rational.[97] Phenomenologically, as Graver argues, since the *eupatheiai* are instances of the same felt psychic movements, they should resemble the passions at the psychosomatic level of description; where they differ at the level of feeling, it should be that the *eupatheiai* are without any sense of conflict or contradiction. However, far from being flat and diminished versions of emotions, the *eupatheiai* are corrected versions of them, and as such may be likened to 'the easy movements of a powerful athlete, forceful but without strain'.[98] We may depict the *eupatheiai* as shown in Table 3.

Table 3 The *Eupatheiai*

	Present	In Prospect
Good	Joy	Wish
Evil	NA	Caution

2.3.3.c. The *Propatheiai*

Even before the Stoics came on the scene, there was discussion about the relationship between spontaneous physiological reactions and thought. Aristotle, for example, observed that involuntary movements such as changes in heart rate and sexual arousal

---

[93] Adapted from Tad Brennan's reconstruction of the full forms of the *eupatheiai*. As he notes, we have well-attested definitions for the *eupatheiai* that mirror the impulse formations for the passions, but their full forms must be reconstructed; see Brennan, 'Stoic Theory', 34. See also Diogenes Laertius 7.116 and Cicero, *Tusc.* 4.12–14.
[94] John M. Cooper, 'The Emotional Life of the Wise', in *Ancient Ethics and Political Philosophy: Proceedings of the Spindel Conference 2004*, Southern Journal of Philosophy Supplement 43 (Memphis, TN: University of Memphis, 2005), 180, interpreting Cicero at *Tusc.* 4.14 (emphasis original).
[95] See Cicero, *Tusc.* 4.14; and Brennan, 'Stoic Theory', 35.
[96] These species are named in Diogenes Laertius 7.116, with full definitions appearing only in Andronicus, *De passionibus* 6.
[97] Brennan, 'Stoic Theory', 34–5.
[98] Graver, *Stoicism*, 52. Similarly, Cooper, 'Emotional Life', 179, describes the emotions of the non-wise as 'agitated and effusive' when compared to the good feelings of the wise, which are 'calm, steady, smooth, and so on'.

responded merely to impressions.[99] This connection was later also made in a fragment of Chrysippus, preserved by Galen, in which he records his observations concerning involuntary weeping and cessations of weeping.[100] The Stoic founders seem also to have devised specific terms like 'biting' (δῆγμα) and 'troubling' (συνθρόησις) to designate certain types of affective responses which did not have the status of genuine emotions because they did not meet the assent criterion.[101]

The fullest account of feelings that occur in the absence of assent is provided by Seneca in Book 2 of *On Anger*. He gives a succinct presentation of what he takes to be the Stoic view of the causation of anger: for him, it is a response that requires both impression of injury and assent to that impression. Most interestingly, Seneca also refers explicitly to the presence of an involuntary psychological event, a 'single mental process' (*simplex*) that 'follows immediately upon the impression and springs up without assistance from the mind'.[102] This prior event – which occurs without the mind's volition – is not the same as anger, which Seneca understands to be a complex process that requires the forming of an impression of injury and the thought that one ought not to have been wronged and therefore should be avenged.[103]

What then is this *simplex* event? Quite clearly, it is not an impulse, since there is no assent. However, this is not to say that one's cognitive faculties are not involved. The event requires some conceptualization of the experience of injury – which draws on a sophisticated array of concepts such as personhood, intention, and fairness.[104] That Seneca conceives of this prior event in rational terms is further confirmed by the extensive listing of examples of such events that he furnishes, to demonstrate how fully articulate thoughts can come about without meeting the condition of voluntariness.[105] However, such prior events are not passions:

> None of these things which move the mind through the agency of chance should be called passions (*adfectus*); the mind suffers them, rather than causes them. Passion, consequently, does not consist in being moved by the impressions that are presented to the mind, but in surrendering to these and following up such chance prompting. (*Ira* 2.3.1–2)

For Seneca, anger has not occurred unless the person judges that a certain response is appropriate for oneself, and chooses to act upon this response:

---

[99] Aristotle, *De an.* 3.9.432b26–433a1 and *Mot. an.* 11.703b–704a.
[100] Galen, *PHP* 4.7.16–17.
[101] See Plutarch, *Virt. mor.* 449a: here Zeno and Chrysippus are very likely those who claim that 'tremblings and changes of colour' need not be indications of fear but of a 'troubling', and that tears are not evidence of grief but only of a 'biting'. In *Tusc.* 3.82–3, Cicero, following Chrysippus, explains that the wise person is not susceptible to grief, but allows that a lesser response which he terms 'the sting and certain minor symptoms of shrinking' (*morsus tamen et contractiunculae quaedam*) is natural to the wise, and can occur with regularity.
[102] Seneca, *Ira* 2.1.3–5.
[103] Seneca, *Ira* 2.1.4–5.
[104] Graver, *Stoicism*, 94–5.
[105] Seneca, *Ira* 2.2.1–2.3.3. Here he gives twenty-six highly varied scenarios which range from crude reflex actions (e.g. recoiling from certain types of touch) to responses that require complex mental processing (e.g. having certain feelings when reading of past events, such as Sulla's proscriptions or Hannibal's siege after the Battle of Cannae).

Anger must not only be aroused but must rush forth, for it is an active impulse; but an active impulse never comes without the consent of the will, for it is impossible for a man to aim at revenge and punishment without the cognizance of the mind. A man thinks himself injured, wishes to take vengeance, but dissuaded by some consideration immediately calms down. This I do not call anger, this prompting of the mind which is submissive to reason; anger is that which overleaps reason and sweeps it away. Therefore that primary disturbance of the mind which is excited by the impression of injury is no more anger than the impression of injury is itself anger; the active impulse consequent upon it, which has not only admitted the impression of injury but also approved it, is really anger – the tumult of a mind proceeding to revenge by choice and determination. (*Ira* 2.3.4–5)

Clearly, Seneca does not regard the unassented feelings of which he speaks as passions.[106] As such, these feelings are not only non-culpable experiences but also perfectly normal – and indeed, expected – feelings in even the wise person.[107]

Seneca's discussion coheres substantially with what Stoic-influenced authors in Alexandria wrote about *propatheiai* or 'pre-passions': involuntary feelings that were not to be seen as passions because assent did not accompany the relevant impression. The Alexandrian *propatheiai* tradition appears quite early, in the commentaries of Philo, and finds fuller expression later in the exegetical writings of Origen and others.[108] The correspondences in the views of the authors in Rome and in Alexandria concerning unassented feelings suggest clearly the influence of a common source: authoritative material from the early Stoics, whose precise formulations had been lost. The points of similarity include the involuntary nature of such feelings, their dependence on rational impression, and their continued occurrence in the wise.[109]

Though their theological commitments were markedly different, the writers at Alexandria shared with the Stoics a strong interest in providing a description of the perfection of human nature. For Philo and the Christian writers, Abraham and the incarnate Christ, respectively, were the prime exemplars of virtue; however, as the passions were thought to arise from an irrational valuation of external objects, passages of Scripture that seemed to attribute such emotions to these exemplar figures were of particular concern. The concept of the *propatheiai* was sometimes pressed into service to help resolve this difficulty.[110] One clear instance occurs in Philo's comments on his quotation of Gen. 23.2 ('Abraham came to bewail Sarah and to mourn'); here

---

[106] Seneca's term for them is *principia proludentia adfectibus* ('beginnings preliminary to passion').
[107] Seneca, *Ira* 2.2.1–3. Elsewhere, Seneca discusses various types of involuntary affects that arise in the wise; for him these unassented feelings are 'natural' and reflect nature's intentions for human psychology (see *Ep.* 11.1–2; 57.4–5; 71.29). In *Marc.* 7 Seneca pursues this idea of 'natural' affect and argues that it is natural to miss a family member not only in bereavement but also in separation; for him it is 'inevitable' that such partings bring about 'a biting and a contraction of even the stoutest minds'.
[108] The term is used by Origen, Jerome, and other Christian writers; see M. Pohlenz, *Die Stoa: Geschichte einer geistigen Bewegung*, 2 vols (Göttingen: Vandenhoeck & Ruprecht, 1947), 1.307–8; 2.154.
[109] See Graver, *Stoicism*, 102.
[110] Graver, *Stoicism*, 102–8.

Philo opines that Scripture, which informs the reader that Abraham came to mourn Sarah, does not represent him as finally doing so.

> But excellently and carefully does [Scripture] show that the virtuous man did not resort to wailing or mourning but only came there for some such thing. For things that unexpectedly and against his will strike the pusillanimous man weaken, crush and overthrow him, whereas everywhere they merely bow down the man of constancy when they direct their blows against him, and not in such a way as to bring [their work] to completion, since they are strongly repelled by the guiding reason, and retreat. (Philo, QG 4.73)

To be sure, Abraham is 'struck' by 'things', namely, impressions that represent his circumstances as evil; however, the equanimity that ensues from his 'constancy' and state of rationality means that he does not give in to grief, but is only 'bowed down' for the moment. For Philo, though Abraham experiences involuntary feelings akin to grief, his virtuous state is not compromised by the appearance of any passion.[111]

To summarize: the concept of the *propatheiai* allowed the Stoics and those influenced by them to accommodate within their theoretical framework for human psychology those affective reactions that were beyond the voluntary control of the agent, and therefore not to be construed as passions.[112] According to Seneca, these 'first movements' (*primi motus*) cannot be overcome by reason, 'although perchance practice and constant watchfulness will weaken them'.[113] The Roman anthologist Aulus Gellius tells the story of an impending shipwreck that some people were facing. In such a terrifying situation, it was entirely natural for even the wise person to be beset by uncontrollable feelings and physical sensations – 'certain swift and unconsidered motions which forestall the action of the intellect and reason'. However, by withholding assent from any occurrent impressions, he 'rejects and repudiates them, and sees in them nothing to cause him fear'. Though 'his colour and expression have changed for a brief moment', he 'keeps the even tenor and strength of the opinion which he has always had about mental impressions of this kind'.[114]

2.3.3.d. 'Moral Emotions'

There is a fourth category of emotions that our Stoic sources seem to reveal. In an often-recounted story, the young man Alcibiades comes to a realization of his errors when they are revealed to him by his teacher, Socrates. Alcibiades is deeply remorseful, and implores him for help in amending his life.[115] Alcibiades's emotional turmoil is precipitated by his acknowledgement of the presence of a genuine evil, namely his

---

[111] See also Margaret R. Graver, 'Philo of Alexandria and the Origins of the Stoic Προπάθειαι', *Phronesis* 44 (1999): 306–7.
[112] Inwood, *Ethics*, 174–80; Sorabji, *Emotion*, 66–75.
[113] Seneca, *Ira* 2.4.1–2.
[114] Aulus Gellius, *Noct. att.* 19.1.17–20 (= Epictetus fr. 9, part).
[115] Cicero, *Tusc.* 3.77–8; the portrait of Alcibiades appears also in several other sources, e.g. Plato, *Symp.* 215e–216c and *Alc.* 118b–c, 127d; Plutarch, *Alc.* 4.

own vices, not some external object. His response problematizes the supposition that every passion is constituted by a false judgement that an external object is good or evil. Indeed, the anecdote undermines simultaneously the assumptions for three of the four passions: for in addition to the grief that Alcibiades experiences for his present vice, he feels also a desire for his future virtue and a fear for his future vice.[116]

We have already seen that the four generic passions are concerned with external goods, while the *eupatheiai* have their basis in genuine goods, that is, virtue and vice. However, the experience of Alcibiades resists this classification: while it resembles the *eupatheia* because of the type of object with which it is correlated, it is not the response of the wise person, who could not experience any feelings of moral inadequacy.[117] Yet even those who are non-wise, like Alcibiades, can respond emotionally to integral objects that are features of one's own character. That such responses – remorse over one's vices, the desire for moral improvement, and the fear of future errors – were considered by the Stoics to be bona fide psychological events is shown by Chrysippus's and Cicero's inclusion of them among the phenomena to be considered by a theory of consolation, and Seneca's and Epictetus's use of them in ethical therapy.[118]

In modern psychology, the term 'moral emotions' is often used to designate this category of affective response.[119] However, the Stoic authors did not use such a catch-all term. Instead, they referred to specific responses, for example, μεταμέλεια or remorse, which Stobaeus defines as 'distress over things that have been done, that they were done in error by oneself'.[120] The ordinary, non-wise person, who constantly did things badly, would be expected to experience remorse with much frequency.[121] A genus grid of such a person's set of affective responses – not towards external objects as with the standard passions, but towards genuine goods or evils as with the *eupatheiai* – would, like the *eupatheiai*, result in three genera, with remorse instead of joy being the pre-eminent one[122] (see Table 4).

Table 4 The 'Moral Emotions'

	Present	In Prospect
Good	NA	Desire for improvement
Evil	Remorse	Fear of future error

---

[116] Cicero, *Tusc.* 3.77. The remaining passion, delight, cannot be veridically orientated, as the other three can be, for the same sort of reason that there is no fourth *eupatheia*: if someone is delighted by the true belief that something good is present to them, then it must indeed be so – but this means that they must be a sage, who cannot have any sort of passion; see Brennan, 'Stoic Theory', 51.
[117] Graver, *Stoicism*, 192.
[118] Graver, *Stoicism*, 192. See e.g. Cicero, *Tusc.* 3.76; 4.60–2; Epictetus, *Diatr.* 3.23.27–38; Seneca, *Tranq.* 1.1–17.
[119] See Gabriele Taylor, *Pride, Shame, and Guilt: Emotions of Self-Assessment* (Oxford: Clarendon, 1985); Julia Price Tangney, Jeff Stuewig, and Debra J. Mashek, 'Moral Emotions and Moral Behavior', *Annual Review of Psychology* 58 (2007): 345–72.
[120] Stobaeus 2.102.25–6 (my translation).
[121] Stobaeus 2.102.23–5.
[122] Graver, *Stoicism*, 195.

The Stoics clearly believed that the responses described for Alcibiades are true to life, since even those who are unwise may respond emotionally to integral objects. It certainly seems possible that such a person's responses are at least sometimes generated on the basis of true beliefs; if so they have the status of καθήκοντα, or the ordinary person's appropriate actions – the same status as other actions that are premised on true beliefs about appropriateness.[123] Thus we have good cause to think that the 'moral emotions' fall within Stoic parameters for acceptable affective responses to integral goods and evils.[124] As long as one's subjective states of feeling are not associated with any falsehood, there is no reason why the experience of them should be deleterious to the goal of rational perfection.

With this, we complete our survey of the Stoic theory of emotion, situating it within its wider philosophical context. We now turn to the question of how the Stoics treated the problem of emotions that had run out of control.

2.4. The Stoic Therapy of Emotion

2.4.1. Reason, Nature, and *Oikeiōsis*

We have already seen how the Stoics saw the perfection of reason in accordance with nature, which was virtue, as the greatest good for a person. Not surprisingly, the bedrock of Stoic thinking about emotional therapy was an unyielding belief in the dignity of human reason. This belief stemmed from how nature was regarded as the ultimate source of everything that had value, such that the value of anything else in the world, like reason, depended upon its relationship to universal nature. Agreement with nature denoted positive value, and contrariness to nature the opposite.[125]

For the Stoics, reason was not just the foundational element of what made one human but also, crucially, something that was fully within one's own power to cultivate. The attainment of rational understanding did not require any help from without, divine or otherwise. Indeed, as Seneca tells Lucilius,

> It is foolish to pray for this when you can acquire it for yourself ... God is near you, he is with you, he is within you. This is what I mean, Lucilius: a holy spirit indwells within us, one who marks our good and bad deeds, and is our guardian. As we treat this spirit, so are we treated by it. (*Ep.* 41.1–2)[126]

---

[123] The starting point of appropriate acts is reason; appropriate actions are defined as 'all those which reason prevails with us to do', with inappropriate actions defined the opposite way (Diogenes Laertius 7.108–9); see also Stobaeus 2.85.12–86.4.

[124] Graver, *Stoicism*, 210–11.

[125] Diogenes Laertius 7.88. For further discussion see Troels Engberg-Pedersen, 'Discovering the Good: Oikeiōsis and Kathēkonta in Stoic Ethics', in *The Norms of Nature: Studies in Hellenistic Ethics*, ed. Malcolm Schofield and Gisela Striker (Cambridge: Cambridge University Press, 1986), 145–83; Long, *Hellenistic Philosophy*, 179–84; Anthony A. Long, 'The Logical Basis of Stoic Ethics', in *Stoic Studies* (Cambridge: Cambridge University Press, 1996), 134–55.

[126] The 'holy spirit' which Seneca speaks of is equated with God; Seneca, like his Stoic predecessors, identifies God with the material universe (see *Ep.* 92.30).

Martha Nussbaum observes that this is not at all an atheist view: reasoning is not only divine internally in the human being, but his piece of the divinity that inhabits the whole framework of the universe. Yet it is certainly a rationalist view that repudiates the subservience to external anthropomorphic and capricious divinities that were a central feature of conventional Roman religion.[127] At a fundamental level, reason went hand in hand with the practical decisions that one made; for the Stoics, the power of choice wholly resided within the human person. Epictetus thus asserts,

> Consider who you are. To begin with, a man; that is, one who has no quality more sovereign than moral choice (προαίρεσις), but keeps everything subordinate to it, and this moral choice itself free from slavery and subjection. (*Diatr.* 2.10.1–2)[128]

Underlying all this was the belief that human beings were predisposed to living rationally in the first place, although it was a process of natural development – a process that the Stoics termed *oikeiōsis*. The basic idea was that humans, and indeed all animals, possessed a fundamental orientation towards what was best for themselves, towards what was truly good. It was the human person's natural inclination to preserve and take care of the things that it saw as belonging to it.[129] There were two dimensions of *oikeiōsis*: the personal[130] and the social.[131] A young infant had an initial natural bent towards self-preservation,[132] but between infancy and adulthood were distinct stages of rational development in which nature sanctioned modes of thinking and behaviour that changed a creature whose responses were purely animal-like and reflexive into an adult fully endowed with reason.[133] In parallel with increasing maturity came also a natural extending of that *oikeiōsis* to the people around oneself, beginning with one's children, and moving in ever-widening circles to encompass all of one's social sphere and beyond.[134] *Oikeiōsis* can therefore be understood as a sort of continuum: at one end was the instinctive self-preservation of a young infant, at the other, the outward-looking disposition and sociability of a rational adult (the so-called 'social *oikeiōsis*'[135]), who was 'designed by nature to safeguard and protect his fellows'.[136] As we might expect, this normative

---

[127] Nussbaum, *Therapy*, 326.
[128] See also Epictetus, *Diatr.* 1.1.12–13. On προαίρεσις see Section 2.5.1.c.
[129] In Diogenes Laertius 7.85–6 (= LS 57A), Chrysippus uses the notion of 'appropriation' (οἰκείωσις) to frame the connections between nature's constitution of animals, their inherent impulses, and their innate ability to respond discriminatingly to their external environment. For Sandbach, '*Oikeiōsis* is then the process of making a thing belong, and this is achieved by the recognition that the thing is *oikeion*, that it belongs to you, that it is yours'; *Stoics*, 32.
[130] Cicero, *Fin.* 3.17–21.
[131] Cicero, *Fin.* 3.62–8.
[132] Cicero describes this as preserving 'oneself in one's constitution' (*Fin.* 3.20).
[133] Long, *Hellenistic Philosophy*, 187–8, referring to Cicero, *Fin.* 3.20–1; see also Seneca, *Ep.*121.
[134] Cicero, *Fin.* 3.62–8.
[135] E.g. Brad Inwood, 'Comments on Professor Görgemanns' Paper: The Two Forms of Oikeiōsis in Arius and the Stoa', in *On Stoic and Peripatetic Ethics: The Work of Arius Didymus*, ed. W. W. Fortenbaugh (New Brunswick, NJ: Transaction Books, 1983), 193.
[136] Cicero, *Fin.* 3.68. For detailed discussion on *oikeiōsis* see Gisela Striker, 'The Role of Oikeiosis in Stoic Ethics', *OSAP* 1 (1983): 145–67; Engberg-Pedersen, *Oikeiosis*, 64–100; Annas, *Happiness*,

account of the development of human nature was grounded completely in a singular commitment to a fully reasoned way of life.

It is on the basis of *oikeiōsis* that Epictetus poses this rhetorical question:

> Who has come into being without an innate concept of what is good and evil, honourable and base, appropriate and inappropriate, and happiness, and of what is proper and falls to our lot, and what we ought to do and what we ought not to do? (*Diatr.* 2.11.3-4)

Epictetus goes on to insist that the task is to cultivate that which nature has already endowed one with, and also to apply what one knows to one's circumstances.[137] For him, one's innermost moral intuitions could serve as a worthy guide to those things in the universe that were truly good.

2.4.2. Philosophy as Therapy

The ideals outlined above – that life in accordance with nature and reason is man's chief end, and that the power of reason can be nurtured through the proper exercise of choice – were key aspects of Stoic teaching that underscored how philosophy had inherent practical value in everyday life. Seneca commends Lucilius for his diligence in his studies and implores him to keep at it, for the point of philosophical study is that 'you make it each day your endeavour to become a better man'.[138] There were at least two results that would accrue to those who diligently pursued philosophical study. At the societal level, 'the first thing which philosophy undertakes to give is fellow-feeling with all men; in other words, sympathy and sociability'.[139] At a personal level, philosophy

> moulds and constructs the soul; it orders our life; guides our conduct, shows us what we should do and what we should leave undone; it sits at the helm and directs our course as we waver amid uncertainties. (Seneca, *Ep.* 16.3)

The point is that philosophical study was thought to bring tremendous practical benefit to humanity; this produced an obligation to extend to all the advantages of such an education.[140] The Stoics therefore paid careful attention to such matters as rhetoric and the literary aspects of their teachings, aiming not at philosophical jargon that would appeal only to a small elite, but for maximum reach across a general audience.[141]

For philosophical study to be effective, there had to be regular self-scrutiny. Living actively in conformity with one's reason, instead of being passively dominated

---

262–76; Gretchen Reydams-Schils, 'Human Bonding and Oikeiōsis in Roman Stoicism', *OSAP* 22 (2002): 221–51.
[137] *Diatr.* 2.11.4–18.
[138] Seneca, *Ep.* 5.1.
[139] Seneca, *Ep.* 5.4.
[140] Seneca, *Ep.* 16.1.
[141] See Nussbaum, *Therapy*, 330–2.

by wrong thinking and habitual dispositions, required constant watchfulness and perseverance.[142] Indeed, the most general strategy of Stoic therapy was that one had to be aware of how one saw one's circumstances – a priority that Epictetus frequently expressed in his cardinal rule of life: 'making use of impressions'.[143] Hence the task of philosophy was to prompt rigorous and sustained reflection that would enable one to take charge of one's own thinking.[144] It was the goal of the teacher of philosophy to facilitate this process, which involved exacting work with his pupil.[145]

Some brief comments should be made regarding the media through which philosophical therapy was to be applied. According to Seneca, personal conversation provided the greatest benefit, because 'it creeps by degrees into the soul'.[146] Public fora were not as effective: 'Lectures prepared beforehand and spouted in the presence of a throng have in them more noise but less intimacy. Philosophy is good advice; and no one can give advice at the top of his lungs.'[147] Written communication was generally inferior to personal communication; Epictetus certainly carried out his teaching in oral form – we have his pupil Flavius Arrian to thank for his stenographic record of his teacher's *ipsissima verba*. Yet, in what is often regarded as the greatest showpiece of Stoic philosophical therapy in action, Seneca's *Epistulae Morales*, Seneca ingeniously creates within the written text an intimate dialogue between teacher and pupil that demonstrates to his readers how epistolary paraenesis could be carried out in a way that was effective and fruitful.[148]

2.4.3. The Case for Stoic Therapy

The most comprehensive description of the Stoic view of the passions is found in the third and fourth books of Cicero's *Tusculan Disputations*, which have their basis in Chrysippus's understanding of the extirpation of the passions and the therapy of the soul. In Cicero's view, 'souls which have been ready to be cured and have obeyed the instructions of wise men, are undoubtedly cured';[149] this was the central thrust of Chrysippan therapeutic thinking. In book four, after a survey of the Stoic definitions of the passions, Cicero draws an analogy between physical and psychological ailments:

> Just as when the blood is in a bad state or there is an overflow of phlegm or bile, bodily sickness and disease begin, so the disturbing effect of corrupt beliefs warring against one another robs the soul of health and introduces the disorder of disease. (Cicero, *Tusc.* 4.23)

---

[142] Seneca, *Ep.* 16.1–3.
[143] Long, *Epictetus*, 85, referring to Epictetus, *Diatr.* 1.1.7; 1.3.4; 1.6.13; 1.7.33; 1.12.34; 1.20.15. Epictetus in *Diatr.* 3.22.19–22 also connects the priority of making one's *hēgemonikon* pure with the right use of one's impressions.
[144] Nussbaum, *Therapy*, 328.
[145] Galen, *PHP* 5.2.23–4= *SVF* 3.471.
[146] Seneca, *Ep.* 38.1.
[147] Seneca, *Ep.* 38.1.
[148] For an overview of letter writing as a means of philosophical paraenesis, see Stanley K. Stowers, *Letter Writing in Greco-Roman Antiquity*, LEC 5 (Philadelphia, PA: Westminster Press, 1986), 36–40.
[149] Cicero, *Tusc.* 3.5.

In both cases, treatment was possible. In the case of mental distress, as Cicero enunciates,

> there is an art of healing the soul – I mean philosophy, whose aid must be sought out, not, as in bodily diseases, outside ourselves, and we must use our utmost endeavour, with all our resources and strength, to have the power to be ourselves our own physicians. (Cicero, *Tusc.* 3.6)

Indeed, without philosophical intervention, there was no cure.[150] As such 'diseases of the soul' were 'both more dangerous and more numerous than those of the body',[151] the goal was not only to cut away the external manifestations of the passion but also to 'tear out all the fibres of its roots'.[152] Cicero's vivid language emphasizes the Stoic ideal of the wise man as being completely free from passions of any sort.[153] Enshrined in the modus operandi of Stoic philosophical therapy was thus a profound respect for the integrity of the reasoning abilities of every person.[154] As such, the function of philosophical therapy was understood as that of strengthening the soul, or, as Nussbaum puts it, 'developing its muscles, assisting it to use its own capabilities more effectively'.[155]

As we have seen, in the Stoic account of emotion, the judgements which give rise to the passions are based on one's appraisals concerning whether something is good or bad, beneficial or baneful. These evaluations are all marked by the ascription of a high value to external objects, or things that do not fall under one's control.[156] Of paramount importance in Stoic therapy was therefore its insistence that the judgements with which the passions are identified are false, because externals are devoid of any intrinsic ethical value. Cicero is in agreement with the Stoics that as sick and irrational motions of the soul, the passions are injurious to the individual; in several places he provides rhetorical illustrations of the morbidity of irrational affective action,[157] and contrasts such behaviour with the restraint, consistency, and serenity of the wise man.[158]

The Stoics advanced several other arguments for their position. One that Cicero seems to have found compelling was that passions are never reliable motivations for virtuous action.[159] In fact, it is the person who is unable to resort to reason who resorts

---

[150] Cicero, *Tusc.* 3.13.
[151] Cicero, *Tusc.* 3.5.
[152] Cicero, *Tusc.* 3.13, 83.
[153] Diogenes Laertius 7.117.
[154] Epictetus, *Diatr.* 2.10.1–2.
[155] Nussbaum, *Therapy*, 317–18, referring to Seneca, *Ep.* 15. See also Cicero, *Tusc.* 4.31.
[156] Nussbaum observes that the evaluative beliefs on which the major passions rest 'all embody a conception of the agent's good according to which the good is not simply "at home" inside of him, but consists, instead, in a complex web of connections between the agent and unstable worldly items such as loved ones, city, possessions, the conditions of action'; see *Therapy*, 370.
[157] Speaking of anger, Cicero asks, 'Is there anything more like unsoundness of mind than anger? ... What share have change of colour, voice, eyes, breathing, ungovernableness of speech and act in soundness of mind?' (*Tusc.* 4.52; see also e.g. 4.35, 48).
[158] See e.g. Cicero, *Tusc.* 4.37.
[159] Cicero uses the example of bravery in battle, which 'does not need the backing of irascibility' and 'stands in no need of loss of temper' (*Tusc.* 4.53). See also Seneca, *Ira* 1.12.1–13.5, which concludes with Seneca's argument that 'no man is ever made braver through anger, except the one who would never have been brave without anger. It comes, then, not as a help to virtue, but as a substitute for it' (1.13.5).

to impassioned modes of conduct; such a person is manifestly unwise.[160] This notion of the non-necessity as well as counter-effectiveness of the passions is supported by a slippery slope argument: tiny motions of affect may seem innocuous, but they are actually irrational movements that quickly become ungovernable.[161] In Cicero's view, when an emotional judgement of any kind is repeated, the soul's power of reasoning is progressively weakened, such that 'it is impossible for a disordered and excited soul to control itself or stop where it wishes'.[162] Furthermore, due to the interconnections between the passions, when one experienced an emotional upheaval of some sort, there was a ripple effect that brought about alterations in other emotional dispositions.[163]

It should be noted that Cicero's analysis of the passions reflected his personal experience of them. He was grief-stricken by the death of his only daughter and first child, Tullia, and in book three of the *Tusculan Disputations* he summarizes the rival approaches to consolation that he applied and wrote about in his lost *Consolatio*.

> Some hold that the comforter has only one responsibility: to teach the sufferer that what happened is not an evil at all. This is the view of Cleanthes. Others, including the Peripatetics, would teach that it is not a great evil. Still others, for instance Epicurus, would draw attention away from evils and toward good things, and there are yet others who think it sufficient to show that nothing has happened contrary to expectation. And the list goes on. Chrysippus, for his part, holds that the key to consolation is to get rid of the person's belief that mourning is something that he ought to do, something just and appropriate. Finally there are those who bring together all these types of consolation, since different methods work for different people. In my *Consolation*, for instance, I combined virtually all these methods into a single speech of consolation. For my mind was swollen, and I was trying out every remedy I could. (*Tusc.* 3.76 (Graver))

He continues,

> The most dependable method as regards the validity of its reasoning is that of Chrysippus, but it is a hard method to apply in time of distress. It's a big task to persuade a person that he is grieving by his own judgment and because he thinks he ought to. (*Tusc.* 3.79 (Graver))

Though Cicero prefers his own eclectic consolatory strategy, he endorses the Chrysippan approach as the one which best combines a sound theoretical basis with the possibility of success;[164] Cicero sees it as superior because attention is placed not on the evaluation of an external object but on the assessment of the appropriateness

---

[160] Cicero, *Tusc.* 4.55.
[161] Knuuttila, *Emotions*, 77.
[162] Cicero, *Tusc.* 4.38–42, quote from 41. There are similar arguments in Seneca, *Ep.* 85.6–16 and Epictetus, *Diatr.* 2.18.1–14.
[163] Cicero, *Tusc.* 3.19–20.
[164] See Cicero, *Tusc.* 3.79 and Graver, *Cicero*, 122. On Cicero's views of the competing approaches, see Knuuttila, *Emotions*, 74.

of the emotional response itself; he confirms later that dealing with the emotions themselves as the starting point is didactically and therapeutically the most efficacious strategy.[165] The Chrysippan approach helped the individual to recognize that an affective response incorporated a voluntary assent to the prescription that one should have such a response. It was then possible to demonstrate that such a response was neither fitting nor useful, and that it ensued in behaviour that sabotaged the quest for true happiness.[166]

2.4.4. Stoic Therapy in Practice

Having reviewed the arguments in favour of the Stoic position, we can now outline the practicalities of their cognitive therapy. The arguments that were mounted against the passions and for an ideal of *apatheia* had a therapeutic function as a general orientation, but a focus on the concrete, and the use of instructive examples, together with an emphasis on understanding the background and circumstances of the individual, were also indispensable components of their approach.[167]

A primary task of the teacher was to help his student to reach the goal of rational self-determination. This involved the creation of a space, internal to the pupil, for critical self-examination:

> Make it, therefore, your study at the very outset to say to every harsh impression, 'You are an external impression and not at all what you appear to be.' After that examine it and test it by these rules which you have, the first and foremost of which is this: Whether the impression has to do with the things which are under our control, or with those which are not under our control; and if it has to do with some one of the things not under our control, have ready to hand the answer, 'It is nothing to me.' (Epictetus, *Ench.* 1.5)

Epictetus here shows his students how to deconstruct an external impression without recourse to an emotion-filled reading of it. Elsewhere, he also advises his pupils to reject bad impressions and replace them with good ones.[168] Alongside these strategies, he prescribes other practical exercises, such as putting key Stoic doctrines into action, participating in a range of life situations without affective reactions, and preparing for eventualities through careful premeditation.[169] In addition, as we have observed, vituperation of the passions was part of the Stoic approach.

In Stoic teaching, the use of example figures is prominent. One reason had to do with motivation: portraits of exemplars helped the individual to see that conceptual notions of right thinking could have concrete expression.[170] But as Nussbaum points out, the Stoics were concerned not only with getting the general content of an act right but also

---

[165] Cicero, *Tusc.* 4.60-2.
[166] Cicero, *Tusc.* 3.61-6.
[167] See Knuuttila, *Emotions*, 78; and especially Nussbaum, *Therapy*, 335-41.
[168] Epictetus, *Diatr.* 2.18.23-6.
[169] See e.g. *Ench.* 4-5, 9-10; *Diatr.* 2.2.1-7; 2.13; 2.16; 3.3; 3.8.1-6.
[170] Cicero, *Tusc.* 3.79; 4.60.

with promoting fully virtuous acts. Since this was a highly contextual matter, general rules could not guarantee a correct result. Ultimately, what was needed was a strategy for rational assessment that would, in a specific scenario, show one 'when he should do certain things, and to what extent, and in whose company, and how, and why' (Seneca, *Ep.* 95.5). Certainly, *exempla* had to be supplemented by philosophical explication, but they demonstrated as nothing else could what it was to think and act wisely.[171]

However, the success of the Stoic method depended also on the pupil's practical response to the sorts of cognitive therapy outlined above. He had to take an active role in the introspective supervision of his own motivations, thoughts, and actions.[172] Writing about anger, Seneca highlights the benefits of a regular self-appraisal of the quality of one's actions and moral development:

> Anger will cease and become more controllable if it finds that it must appear before a judge every day. Can anything be more excellent than this practice of thoroughly sifting the whole day? And how delightful the sleep that follows this self-examination – how tranquil it is, how deep and untroubled, when the soul has either praised or admonished itself, and when this secret examiner and critic of self has given report of its own character! (Seneca, *Ira* 3.36.2–3)[173]

Clearly, what is implied here is that regular self-examination leads to the betterment of one's state, by reducing one's proneness to unregulated emotional behaviour.[174] At its heart, Stoic philosophy was not about the promulgation of abstract theory, but was a way of life that transformed the individual's modes of seeing and being. Rigorous self-examination was integral to this process, because such a transformation required the reawakening of the mind's powers of rational self-consciousness and active vigilance, and the discarding of old habits.[175]

2.5. The Early Roman Empire Stoics on Grief and Joy

We shall conclude our discussion with a focused examination of how the Stoics of the early Roman Empire, who were Paul's contemporaries, dealt with emotion. Our

---

[171] See Nussbaum, *Therapy*, 339–40.
[172] Epictetus, *Diatr.* 4.12; *Ench.* 33.
[173] See also Epictetus, *Diatr.* 2.18.12–18.
[174] See also Epictetus, *Diatr.* 4.12.6.
[175] See further Nussbaum, *Therapy*, 340–1, and especially Pierre Hadot, *Philosophy as a Way of Life: Spiritual Exercises from Socrates to Foucault*, ed. Arnold I. Davidson, trans. Michael Chase (Oxford: Blackwell, 1995), 83–6. Hadot notes that no systematic treatise codifying the instructions and techniques for what he terms 'spiritual exercises' has come down to us; yet the presence of frequent allusions to them in Stoic writings suggests that they were very much part of the philosophical curriculum. However, we have Philo's two lists of spiritual exercises (in *Alleg. Interp.* 3.18 and *Heir* 253), which provide us with a fairly complete panorama of Stoic-Platonic-inspired therapeutics. Hadot aggregates the elements of the two lists into four groups of exercises: first, attention; then meditation and the remembrance of good things; then the more intellectual exercises of reading, listening, research, and investigation; and finally the more active exercises of self-mastery, accomplishment of duties, and indifference to externals.

best sources are Seneca and Epictetus; and as Stoicism had by that time become an established doctrinal system, moral exhortation rather than matters of theory was their concern. Even if for the most part they confirm rather than add to our knowledge of Stoic theory, what they have to say furnishes us with invaluable information about what it meant to live as a committed Stoic. In order both to give our exploration precision and to facilitate the comparisons that we shall later make with Paul's views, our study will be limited to two key emotions: grief and joy. Given the theoretical consistency which frames and indeed finesses Stoicism, we can be assured that such a delimitation will not disadvantage our study; on the contrary, the use of specific foci will help us to appreciate how Stoic therapeutic concepts took on flesh and translated into real-life practice.

2.5.1. Grief

2.5.1.a. Consolation in Antiquity

By the time of the late Republic and the early Roman Empire, the *consolatio* – a piece of writing which employed rational argument to combat grief and other misfortunes – had become a distinct genre with its own tropes.[176] A number of consolations have come down to us from this period, with the most common type being the consolatory letter, examples of which are found within the letter collections of Cicero, Seneca, and Pliny, and also among the letters of Apollonius of Tyana.[177] In addition, six longer works are extant: three by Seneca, two by Plutarch, and one attributed to Plutarch.[178] Quite clearly, the practice of consolation was by that time already widespread in the Greco-Roman world. Its origin dates to at least the eighth century BCE, because consolatory topoi are found as early as Homer;[179] this means that consolation predates the rise of philosophy as a specialized branch of thought. However, it was not until the late fifth and early fourth centuries that the problem of grief began to be treated in a more systematic fashion – in writings that dealt with death and loss either explicitly or indirectly,[180] and in several treatises and other types of literature on topics that included consolatory aspects.[181]

---

[176] Useful general surveys of consolation in antiquity are Robert C. Gregg, *Consolation Philosophy: Greek and Christian Paideia in Basil and the Two Gregories*, Patristic Monograph Series 3 (Cambridge: Philadelphia Patristic Foundation, 1975), 1–50; J. H. D. Scourfield, *Consoling Heliodorus: A Commentary on Jerome, Letter 60* (Oxford: Clarendon, 1993), 15–33; Paul A. Holloway, *Consolation in Philippians: Philosophical Sources and Rhetorical Strategy*, SNTSMS 112 (Cambridge: Cambridge University Press, 2001), 55–83. The literary sources are collected by Carl Buresch, 'Consolationum a Graecis Romanisque scriptarum historia critica', *Leipziger Studien zur classichen Philologie* 9 (1886): 1–170. On the conceptual notion of a consolatory genre in antiquity, see J. H. D. Scourfield, 'Towards a Genre of Consolation', in *Greek and Roman Consolations: Eight Studies of a Tradition and Its Afterlife*, ed. Hans Baltussen (Swansea: Classical Press of Wales, 2013), 1–36.

[177] Cicero, *Fam.* 4.5; 5.16; 5.18, 6.3; *Att.* 12.10; 15.1; *Ep. Brut.* 1.9; Seneca, *Ep.* 63; 99 (some scholars include also *Ep.* 93); Pliny, *Ep.* 1.12; 3.21; 9.9; Apollonius of Tyana, *Ep.* 55; 58.

[178] Seneca, *Helv., Marc., Polyb.*; Plutarch, *Exil., Cons. ux.*; Ps.-Plutarch, *Cons. Apoll.*

[179] E.g. in *Il.* 6.486–9, where Hector attempts to comfort Andromache by appealing to the inevitability of fate, or in *Il.* 24.522–51, where Achilles stresses to Priam that grief is pointless.

[180] From doxographical tradition we learn that death and bereavement were the focus of most of these early writings (see e.g. Diogenes Laertius 4.11; 6.15; 6.80; 9.46) but topics such as poverty and exile were also given attention (e.g. Diogenes Laertius 2.84; 5.42; 9.20).

[181] These include the Περὶ εὐθυμίας of Democritus (Diogenes Laertius 9.46) and Hipparchus (Stobaeus 4.44.81), and the Περὶ παθῶν of Theophrastus (Diogenes Laertius 5.42), Xenocrates (Diogenes

In subsequent centuries, two particularly influential works emerged. The most significant early treatise was the Περὶ πένθους of Crantor of Soli, the fourth-century Academician, which was accorded a paradigmatic status by the many philosophers who took it as a model.[182] Of at least equal importance for later tradition was Cicero's aforementioned *Consolatio*, which was also influenced by Crantor's work.[183] C. E. Manning notes that the *consolatio* was a natural literary development of the Hellenistic Age, when the prime concern of philosophy was to equip the individual to meet the challenges of life, and that it became part of the armoury of all the major schools of philosophy.[184] Though the range of circumstances that consolers addressed was very broad,[185] bereavement was the most prevalent subject matter.[186] Greco-Roman letters of consolation contained traditional materials such as quotations from the poets, examples, precepts, and arguments against excessive grieving.[187] The content of these arguments tended towards the philosophical commonplace, with platitudes of general application such as would find ready acceptance with the bereaved.[188] To be sure, each major school of philosophy developed its own distinctive position in regard to comforting the grieving person;[189] but consolations of the period often displayed a studied eclecticism in which school lines were regularly crossed.

2.5.1.b. Seneca on Grief

In their approach to the treatment of grief, Seneca's consolatory writings share many similarities with Greco-Roman letters of consolation in general.[190] Seneca freely utilizes several ideologically neutral stock arguments: for example, that death is inevitable,[191] that the intensity of grief diminishes over time,[192] and that death delivers from present

---

Laertius 4.11), Zeno (Diogenes Laertius 7.4), Herillus (Diogenes Laertius 7.166), Sphaerus (Diogenes Laertius 7.178), Chrysippus (Diogenes Laertius 7.111), and Hecastus (Diogenes Laertius 7.110).

[182] See Cicero, *Acad.* 2.135; Diogenes Laertius 4.27; and also Fitzgerald, 'Introduction', 9–10. Only fragments remain; for details see Holloway, *Consolation*, 58 n.20.

[183] This too has been lost, but much of its substance is preserved in *Tusc.* books 1 and 3. Cicero refers to his *Consolatio* at *Tusc.* 1.65, 76, 83; 3.70, 76; 4.63.

[184] C. E. Manning, *On Seneca's 'Ad Marciam'*, Mnemosyne Supplement 69 (Leiden: E. J. Brill, 1981), 12.

[185] Cicero in *Tusc.* 3.81 names specific situations such as *de paupertate ... de vita inhonorata et ingloria ... de exsilio, de interitu patriae, de servitute, de debilitate, de caecitate, de omni casu, in quo nomen poni solet calamitatis*.

[186] It forms the subject matter of the following extant prose *consolationes* from the period of the early Roman Empire: Cicero, *Fam.* 4.5; 5.16; 6.3; *Att.* 12.10; 15.1; *Ep. Brut.* 1.9; Seneca, *Marc.*; *Polyb.*; *Ep.* 63; 99; Plutarch, *Cons. Ux.*; Ps.-Plutarch, *Cons. Apoll.*

[187] Stowers, *Letter Writing*, 142.

[188] Margaret R. Graver, 'The Weeping Wise: Stoic and Epicurean Consolations in Seneca's 99th Epistle', in *Tears in the Graeco-Roman World*, ed. Thorsten Fögen (Berlin: Walter de Gruyter, 2009), 235.

[189] Cicero in his *Consolatio* identifies five major theories of consolation: those of Cleanthes, the Peripatetics, the Epicureans, the Cyreniacs, and Chrysippus (*Tusc.* 3.76); for a concise summary see Holloway, *Consolation*, 64–74.

[190] Five of Seneca's texts are conventionally referred to as coming within the ambit of consolatory literature: *Marc.*; *Polyb.*; *Helv.*; *Ep.* 63; and *Ep.* 99. On the construction of a Senecan consolatory corpus see Marcus Wilson, 'Seneca the Consoler? A New Reading of His Consolatory Writings', in *Greek and Roman Consolations: Eight Studies of a Tradition and Its Afterlife*, ed. Hans Baltussen (Swansea: Classical Press of Wales, 2013), 94–5.

[191] *Marc.* 11; 17.1; *Polyb.* 1.4; *Ep.* 99.7–9.

[192] *Marc.* 8.1–2; *Ep.* 63.12.

and future misfortunes.[193] To these we may add standard exhortations to responsible behaviour: two common ones were not to neglect one's familial or public duties and not to complain against God or fate.[194] As with philosophical paraenesis generally, the use of exemplars featured prominently in ancient consolation.[195] In addition, Seneca valorizes rigorous philosophical study: 'encircle yourself with them as bulwarks for your mind in order that sorrow may find no point that will give entrance to you.'[196]

These platitudes are accompanied by other arguments that come from a range of philosophical traditions, giving ancient consolation its characteristically eclectic quality while at the same time reinforcing its intensely practical goal.[197] At several places in his consolations, Seneca promotes Epicurean therapy by steering the grieving person's mind away from his or her present misfortunes towards more pleasurable experiences, such as good recollections of the past[198] and thoughts of family, books and reading, and Caesar[199] – all of which should help to compensate for any present misfortune. He also modifies this Epicurean approach by connecting the making of pleasant memories to discourse on the virtues of the diseased person.[200] Elsewhere, Seneca endorses the Cyreniac strategy of contemplating possible future evils in order to lessen the shock of any sudden calamity.[201] Initially associated with the Cyreniacs, in a slightly less bald form, it was adopted by the Stoics who from the time of Chrysippus maintained that foreseen evils strike more lightly.[202] More explicitly Chrysippan influences are found in Seneca's arguments against the appropriateness of grief. Scattered across his letters is the charge that grieving is useless, and accomplishes nothing whether for oneself

---

[193] *Marc.* 19.4–5; 20.6; 22.1–2; *Polyb.* 9.4–5.
[194] See Holloway, *Consolation*, 64–5, citing *Polyb.* 5.4–6.5; *Helv.* 18.7–8 (on fulfilling familial and public duties); and *Marc.* 10.2; *Polyb.* 2.2; 4.1 (on not complaining).
[195] *Marc.* 2.1–4.4; *Polyb.* 14.1–16.3; 17.1–6.
[196] *Polyb.* 18.1–2. See also *Helv.* 17.2–5.
[197] As Scott LaBarge observes concerning ancient consolation, 'Schools that are so divergent in other ways seem largely to have converged in their treatment of grief. The consensus view is that grief should be indulged as little as possible, and many thought that ideally we should not grieve at all'; Scott LaBarge, 'How (and Maybe Why) to Grieve Like an Ancient Philosopher', in *Virtue and Happiness: Essays in Honour of Julia Annas*, ed. Rachana Kamtekar, OSAP Supplementary Vol. 2012 (Oxford: Oxford University Press, 2012), 323.

LaBarge however does not discuss *why* there was a convergence of views. C. E. Manning suggests, quite plausibly, that the historical context in which Seneca was writing was one in which intellectuals were openly disputing which form of advanced education was most beneficial. It was therefore natural for Seneca and others to avoid dogmatic writing that might result in philosophy being dismissed as useless. Instead of giving an exposition of his own views, 'such a teacher must aim to create the right disposition to receive the doctrine; he must lead gently from common ground to his own position'; see his 'The Consolatory Tradition and Seneca's Attitude to the Emotions', *Greece and Rome* 21 (1974): 73–4.
[198] One could be thankful that the person lived at all, 'for it is better to have blessings that will flee than none at all' (*Marc.* 12.1–3, quote from 3); see also *Polyb.* 10; *Ep.* 99.4–5.
[199] *Helv.* 18–19; *Polyb.* 8; 12–13.
[200] *Marc.* 24.1–4; *Polyb.* 18.7–8. On Epicurean consolatory theory, see Cicero, *Tusc.* 3.33, 76; Manning, 'Consolatory Tradition', 79–81; Manning, *Marciam*, 47–8; more generally, see Nussbaum, *Therapy*, 102–39; Malte Hossenfelder, 'Epicurus – Hedonist Malgré Lui', in *The Norms of Nature: Studies in Hellenistic Ethics*, ed. Malcolm Schofield and Gisela Striker (Cambridge: Cambridge University Press, 1986), 245–63.
[201] *Marc.* 9–10; *Helv.* 5.3. On Cyreniac thinking see Cicero, *Tusc.* 3.28, 52, 76; Manning, *Marciam*, 60.
[202] Manning, *Marciam*, 60, citing Cicero, *Tusc.* 3.52.

or the person for whom one mourns.[203] Moreover, since grief is inherently irrational, it is always beneath human dignity.[204] These arguments appear together with another distinctively Stoic notion: that false opinion has a key role in fuelling one's irrational grief. Seneca writes, 'What tortures us, therefore, is an opinion (*opinio*), and every evil is only as great as we have reckoned it to be.'[205]

Does Seneca advocate the complete rooting out of one's emotions of grief (*apatheia*), or their moderation (*metriopatheia*)?[206] In several places, Seneca evidently admits that to grieve is both natural and reflexive. However, he also insists that due confines must be placed on one's grieving. Addressing Marcia, who after three years was still mourning her son, Seneca writes,

> 'But', you say, 'Nature bids us grieve for our dear ones'. Who denies it, so long as grief is tempered? For not only the loss of those who are dearest to us, but a mere parting, brings an inevitable pang and wrings even the stoutest heart. (*Marc.* 7.1–2)

The same views are found in Seneca's consolation to Polybius upon the death of his brother. Referring to the sorrow and weeping which constantly intrude upon human life, he tells Polybius,

> Thus we spend our lives, and therefore we ought to do in moderation this thing that we must do so often; and as we look back upon the great mass of sorrows that threatens us behind we ought, if not to end our tears, yet at any rate to keep watch over them. (*Polyb.* 4.3)

Seneca's approval of moderate grief is confirmed when he discloses to Polybius that 'nature requires from us some sorrow ... But never will I demand of you that you should not grieve at all'.[207] Moreover, it is the proper application of reason to one's grief that is effective in curtailing its excessiveness.[208]

---

[203] *Marc.* 6.1–2; *Polyb.* 2.1; 5.1–3; 9.1–3; *Ep.* 99.4; see also Cicero, *Tusc.* 3.66–7.

[204] Cicero, *Tusc.* 4.59. The argument that grief is inappropriate and unworthy often takes the form of short asides that misfortune should be borne with manly courage: see *Marc.* 1.1; 7.3; *Polyb.* 6.2; *Ep.* 99.1–2.

[205] *Marc.* 19.1; see also 7.1.

[206] 'Moderate emotion' (μετριοπάθεια), a view often taken to be Peripatetic or Old Academic, is discussed by Cicero in *Tusc.* 3.22; 3.74; *Acad. pr.* 2.135 (where it is attributed to Crantor, whose views were taken to be the same as Aristotle's). For its approval see Ps.-Plutarch, *Cons. Apoll.* 102d (quoting Crantor); for Stoic objections see *Tusc.* 4.38–47 with Graver, *Cicero*, 163–5.

[207] *Polyb.* 18.4–5. See also *Marc.* 3.3.

[208] *Polyb.* 18.6–7:

> Reason will have accomplished enough if only she removes from grief whatever is excessive and superfluous; it is not for anyone to hope or to desire that she should suffer us to feel no sorrow at all. Rather let us maintain a mean which will copy neither indifference nor madness, and will keep us in the state that is the mark of an affectionate, and not an unbalanced, mind. Let your tears flow, but also let them cease, let deepest sighs be drawn from your breast, but let them also find an end; so rule your mind that you may win approval both from wise men and from brothers.

In the *consolationes*, Seneca comes across as a defender of *metriopatheia*. Yet in his letters to Lucilius, which were written later,[209] his views become more nuanced. At the beginning of *Ep.* 63, Seneca tells his pupil,

> I am grieved to hear that your friend Flaccus is dead, but would not have you sorrow more than is fitting. That you should not mourn at all I shall hardly dare to insist; yet I know that it is the better way. (*Ep.* 63.1)

That for Seneca the expunction of grief is 'the better way' is substantiated by the revelation later of his regret at weeping excessively, to the point of being 'overcome with grief', when his friend Serenus died.[210] Seneca thus acknowledges that his own sorrow had been beyond his ability to quell; subsequently, he – using, twice, in the final section the jussive subjunctive verb form (*cogitemus*, 'let us think')[211] – casts himself in the role of the patient, as he often does in the *Epistulae*.[212] However, Seneca's uncompromising stance is then immediately tempered by his concession that tears are forgivable if they remain within one's power to control them (*si ipsi illas repressimus*). He therefore adjures Lucilius to exercise self-control in the midst of grief: 'Let not the eyes be dry when we have lost a friend, nor let them overflow. We may weep, but we must not wail.'[213] Seneca is in *Ep.* 63 still giving some leeway to grief exercised under restraint, but he also seems to want to highlight the danger of allowing that grief to descend into unappeasable sorrow – a state to which he had succumbed against his better wishes.

Appearing as a long enclosure within *Ep.* 99 is Seneca's letter to Marullus, which is the last and also least conventional of his consolations.[214] Here, Seneca's doctrinal commitments are foregrounded by his argument that a life of virtue, one that is circumscribed by natural rationality, is wholly incompatible with the expressions of emotion that are properly called grief. Consolatory arguments from tradition continue to be pressed into service, but in more restricted fashion. In accordance with Stoic principles, Seneca now explicitly contends that Marullus, despite the death of his son, has not suffered any real evil that justifies his grief. In contrast with the hypothetical case of the wise man who despite losing an intimate friend (which for the Romans was 'the greatest blow of all') still finds joy because of the privilege of having had that friendship, the death of a child is an illusory evil – one of those 'shadowy troubles over which men make moan through force of habit'.[215] He chides Marullus for his

---

[209] Miriam Griffin dates the three *consolationes* to 39–49 CE, the *Epistulae Morales* to 64–65 CE; see her *Seneca: A Philosopher in Politics* (Oxford: Clarendon, 1976), 349–50, 395–400, 518.
[210] *Ep.* 63.14.
[211] *Ep.* 63.15–16.
[212] See Marcus Wilson, 'The Subjugation of Grief in Seneca's "Epistles"', in *The Passions in Roman Thought and Literature*, ed. Susanna Morton Braund and Christopher Gill (Cambridge: Cambridge University Press, 1997), 49. On Seneca's self-identification as a fellow patient, see e.g. *Ep.* 27.1; 68.9.
[213] *Ep.* 63.1. We should note that Seneca continues to use therapeutic arguments from a range of schools, e.g. Chrysippus (63.3), the Epicureans (63.4–7), and the Cyreniacs (63.15); for details see Manning, 'Consolatory Tradition', 78.
[214] A fact which Seneca himself admits: 'I have not observed the usual form of condolence'; *Ep.* 99.1. For a detailed literary analysis of *Ep.* 99 see Wilson, 'Subjugation of Grief', 48–67.
[215] *Ep.* 99.3.

false belief that death is inherently evil,[216] and for conforming to societal norms of mourning behaviour that required an exaggeration of natural responses.[217] Seneca does not deny that there are indeed natural responses – tears, changes in facial expression, and felt inner pain – that accompany bereavement; in fact, he pre-empts the charge of *inhumanitas* by saying that it is unnatural to suppress these responses.[218] For him, then, certain natural expressions of bereavement are associated with a life of virtue; but grief and some of its accompanying practices are clearly excluded.

Seneca continues by stating that there are two forms of weeping which occur in the wise person's experiences.[219] One type are the tears that emerge 'by their own force', being 'wrung from us by the necessity of Nature' at those times when the immediacy and intensity of one's loss is most keenly experienced.[220] Earlier, in our examination of the *propatheiai* (see Section 2.3.3.c), we saw how the Stoic founders apparently distinguished from genuine emotions another level of affective response, for which a special terminology was used. These 'bitings' and 'troublings' were involuntary sensations that lacked the necessary belief structures to make them passions as defined by the Stoics. We also discussed how Seneca applied this 'pre-emotion' concept in his *De ira*. Here, in *Ep*. 99, he is merely restating his position and lending further support to the older Stoic stand.

It is the second category of tears which now concerns us. Noting that such tears 'fall by consent', and that they come about 'when we muse in memory of those whom we have lost', Seneca contends that they express positive rather than negative feelings, and as such may be likened to tears of joy: *tunc oculi velut in gaudio relaxantur*.[221] I am persuaded by the view of several scholars who suppose that Seneca, in referring to tears as a voluntary reaction of the wise person, is drawing on his understanding of the Stoic doctrine of eupathic response.[222] The *eupatheiai*, as we have already seen, are impulses which result from fully accurate assessments of goodness and badness. In Margaret Graver's hypothesis, the mention of joy (*gaudium*) at *Ep*. 99.1 is confirmation of this supposition, because joy figures prominently in Seneca's writings as that feature of the wise person's inner experience that corresponds to pathological delight in the non-wise person.[223] Graver argues that the best indication that Seneca means to refer to an existing doctrine lies less in his exact choice of words than in the inclusion of a keyword within the relevant conceptual frame. He has already stated that the wise response to the

---

[216] *Ep*. 99.7–13. See also *Ep*. 74, which concerns virtuous living: in 74.24–6 and 74.30–1, Seneca argues that the integrity of the wise man's virtue means that even if his friends or children die, no distress is experienced, for 'the sage will retain the firm belief that none of these things is evil, or important enough to make a healthy mind break down' (74.31).
[217] *Ep*. 99.16–17.
[218] *Ep*. 99.15.
[219] *Ep*. 99.18–19.
[220] Seneca gives as examples the initial news of an untimely death and the final embrace before a body's cremation.
[221] *Ep*. 99.18–19.
[222] See Graver, 'Weeping', 244–8; Graver, *Stoicism*, 101; Gretchen Reydams-Schils, *The Roman Stoics: Self, Responsibility, and Affection* (Chicago: University of Chicago Press, 2005), 140–1.
[223] Graver, 'Weeping', 244–5, notes that the concept appears as early as *Vit. beat*. 4.2–5 and is explained in relation to integral goods at some length in *Ep*. 23.1–6 and 27.2–3; furthermore, in *Ep*. 59.2 it is clearly marked as Stoic (*ad nostram albam*), with the Stoic definition also quoted.

death of a friend is joy, occasioned by memories of the friendship (*Ep.* 99.3–4); as such, this same joy is to characterize the response of the person at *Ep.* 99.18–19.[224]

If a type of grief that could be considered a *eupatheia* is indeed in view here, the question is whether this is one of those points where Seneca is marshalling ideas from Stoic tradition and putting them to use, or an innovation in which he takes his Stoic inheritance in a new direction. Graver is open to the developmental view, but does not want to dismiss the former possibility. She cites a passage in Philo's *On the Migration of Abraham* (*Migration*, 156–7) in which Philo gives a physicalist explanation of joyful tears which strongly resembles *Ep.* 99.18–19, and suggests that it is entirely reasonable to suppose that Philo's explanation is one he remembered from reading Chrysippus – who had, according to Galen, provided phenomenological explanations for affective sensations including those of fear, distress, confidence, and joy. If Philo's language reflects old Stoic material referring to tears of joy, then Seneca's presumably does as well.[225] For Reydams-Schils, Seneca is walking a fine line between the well-established categories of his Stoic predecessors and breaking new ground. In *Ep.* 99.20–1, Seneca speaks of proper behaviour even in grief which results in tears that do not impair the dignity and authority of the wise man. Reydams-Schils sees in this an attempt by Seneca to move beyond traditional Stoic categories to posit an acceptable counterpart to grief that is analogous to joy: a fourth eupathic response, concomitant with the correct use of reason – which in effect fills the empty box in the symmetric schema of the Stoic doctrine of the *eupatheiai*.[226]

To summarize: Seneca's consolatory writings demonstrate that he made use of the majority of theories of that era, Stoic or otherwise, provided that they suited his purpose in writing to a particular addressee. However, our evidence also clearly indicates that Seneca was not afraid to push back the boundaries of Stoic thinking. By advocating a position of moderate emotion, he was not merely parroting Peripatetic theory. Much more than that, as Reydams-Schils elegantly words it,

> Seneca is struggling to find a way compatible with Stoic doctrine to tell Cicero (and indirectly Plato) that even in public and at a burial not only a mother but also any philosophically inclined human being has neither to be stone-faced nor stone-hearted in order to preserve dignity and virtue.[227]

Despite being bound by the rhetorical and contextual limitations of the consolatory genre in which he was working, Seneca was trying to find a place in Stoicism for the wise person's weeping – the non-culpable, eupathic antithesis of pathological grief.

---

[224] Graver, 'Weeping', 245.
[225] Graver, 'Weeping', 246–8, referring to Galen, *PHP* 4.7.3–4. Concerning the extent of Philo's knowledge of Stoic views on emotion, see David Winston, 'Philo of Alexandria on the Emotions', in *Passions and Moral Progress in Greco-Roman Thought*, ed. John T. Fitzgerald (Abingdon: Routledge, 2008), 201–20. On eupathic joy specifically, see Philo, *QG* 4.15–16, 4.19, 4.101.
[226] Reydams-Schils, *Roman Stoics*, 140–1, and also 136.
[227] Reydams-Schils, *Roman Stoics*, 141.

2.5.1.c. Epictetus on Grief

We now turn to Epictetus, who did not pen a consolation per se. In his understanding and treatment of the emotions, Epictetus endorses fully the teachings of his Stoic forebears. Since his protreptic addresses are works of informal moralizing rather than explanations of Stoic moral theory, he avoids technicalities in his writing and also does not proffer an explicit theory of the emotions. Nevertheless, his position clearly reflects orthodox Stoicism: the passions are, in his view, the consequence of erroneous judgements and the misuse of reason.[228] In Epictetus's scheme, a key term is *prohairesis* (προαίρεσις), which Long translates as 'volition' – 'the purposive and self-conscious centre of a person'; for Epictetus, nothing except this God-given rational faculty of evaluation, choice, and action truly belongs to the human person and lies within the ambit of his or her control.[229] All other things in life, including external circumstances whether *prima facie* good or bad, are not in one's control and are therefore ultimately not of any real concern. This fundamental distinction allows Epictetus to correlate human autonomy with his cardinal rule of 'making the right use of impressions'; indeed, as Long expresses it, Epictetus insists that 'impressions have only the effects that we permit them to have'.[230] The upshot of all this is that the person who chooses to live within the sphere of his *prohairesis* (and who therefore necessarily also upholds the notion that any occurrent external event is to be set in the context of a divinely benevolent ordering of the universe) is able to experience uncurbed tranquillity.[231]

Epictetus's position as outlined above is seen very clearly in his *Diatr.* 3.3, in which he discusses how the good and virtuous man, working upon his own *hēgemonikon*, can succeed in the task of dealing with his impressions in accordance with nature (3.3.1). Right action consists in acting within one's sphere of volition (*prohairesis*) and disregarding all external situations that fall outside one's ability to control them (3.3.14–16). Epictetus acknowledges the fact that it is all too easy to be 'caught gaping straightway at every external impression that comes along' (3.3.17). Yet it is possible, through the vigilant appraisal of one's judgements, to maintain in every situation a state of equanimity:

> If we see a man in grief, we say, 'It is all over with him'; if we see a Consul, we say, 'Happy man'; if we see an exile, 'Poor fellow'; or a poverty-stricken man, 'Wretched man, he has nothing with which to get a bite to eat'. These, then, are the vicious judgements which we ought to eradicate; this is the subject upon which we ought

---

[228] On Epictetus and emotion, see Long, *Epictetus*, 244–54; Anthony A. Long, 'Epictetus on Understanding and Managing Emotions', in *From Epicurus to Epictetus: Studies in Hellenistic and Roman Philosophy* (Oxford: Clarendon, 2006), 377–94; and Edgar M. Krentz, 'ΠΑΘΗ and ΑΠΑΘΕΙΑ in Early Roman Empire Stoics', in *Passions and Moral Progress in Greco-Roman Thought*, ed. John T. Fitzgerald (Abingdon: Routledge, 2008), 126–31.

[229] Quote from Long, *Epictetus*, 207; on the concept of *prohairesis* (including its relationship with the *hēgemonikon*), and its translation, see 207–20, 232–3. A succinct discussion of the various aspects of *prohairesis* is found also in Troels Engberg-Pedersen, 'Self-Sufficiency and Power: Divine and Human Agency in Epictetus and Paul', in *Divine and Human Agency in Paul and His Cultural Environment*, ed. John M. G. Barclay and Simon J. Gathercole (London: T&T Clark, 2006), 120–1.

[230] Long, *Epictetus*, 216.

[231] See John M. G. Barclay, 'Security and Self-Sufficiency: A Comparison of Paul and Epictetus', *Ex Auditu* 24 (2008): 61–2.

to concentrate our efforts. Why, what is weeping and sighing? A judgement. What is misfortune? A judgement. What are strife, disagreement, fault-finding, accusing impiety, foolishness? They are all judgements, and that, too, judgements that lie outside the province of moral purpose (*prohairesis*), assumed to be good or evil. Let a man but transfer his judgements that lie within the province of the moral purpose (*prohairesis*), and I guarantee that he will be steadfast, whatever the state of things about him. (3.3.17–19)[232]

However, such a state of unflappable self-composure is not tantamount to a callous detachment from other people and the misfortunes that may befall them. Epictetus insists that in one's relationships and dealings with others, one 'ought not to be unfeeling (ἀπαθής) like a statue', and couples this stance with the characteristically Stoic notion of appropriate action (τὸ καθῆκον) (*Diatr.* 3.2.4). Elsewhere he makes it clear that one should not hesitate to show sympathy to a grieving person, and, if the occasion warrants it, even 'groan with' (συνεπιστενάζω) the person. However, to this he immediately appends a caveat: 'be careful not to groan also in the centre of your being' (*Ench.* 16). Hence one can – and in fact, should – grieve with the bereaved person, but not to the extent that one's imperturbability is imperilled. For Epictetus, the correct performance of one's social roles has both an outward and inward orientation;[233] in other words, the human person's attitudes and actions towards others are to be structured by a judicious sociability that both reflects one's appropriate duty to others and maintains the integrity of one's volition and freedom. We should therefore be affectionate (φιλόστοργος) towards others, but without becoming abject, broken-spirited, dependent on another, slavish, or miserable (*Diatr.* 3.24.58–9). As John Barclay observes, 'The Stoic, while bound in a network of duties *to* others, is never bound by anything he needs *from* them.'[234]

It comes as no surprise that Epictetus does not have very much to say about the practical therapy of grief. The wise man has no place in his life for grief, and the Stoic teacher's task is to help his students rid themselves of this and other passions – all of which are evidence of the presence of mistaken judgements of value.[235] Specifically, in Epictetus's view, grief is the result of a false judgement that death is something terrible.[236] Furthermore, the control of grief is a problem for the individual: 'Now another's grief is no concern of mine, but my own grief is' (*Diatr.* 3.24.23). Even though one may strive to help others in their grief, it is one's own freedom from disturbance that is paramount (3.24.24). Beyond this, Epictetus shows no further interest in how one might comfort the bereaved. Contrasting him with Seneca, Marcus Wilson notes that for Epictetus there is no place for rhetorical persuasion or for the adaptation of multiple arguments to the particular character and situation of the bereaved. Seneca is more alert to the overwhelming power of grief and far more ready to address the grief of others than to focus exclusively, as Epictetus urged, on the control of the

---

[232] On training oneself to deal with impressions, see also *Diatr.* 3.8.1–6.
[233] Long, *Epictetus*, 237.
[234] Barclay, 'Security', 65 (emphases original); see further 60–5.
[235] See e.g. Epictetus, *Diatr.* 4.1.111–12, where he speaks of the need to 'purify' one's judgements concerning one's possessions, body, and familial relationships.
[236] E.g. *Diatr.* 3.8.5; *Ench.* 3, 5, 26.

individual's own mind.[237] It is interesting that in Seneca and Epictetus a common set of conceptual apparatuses led to the construction of partially divergent practical philosophies of grief. We can already see here that Stoicism made room for a more rich and complex emotional life than is often assumed.

2.5.2. Joy

2.5.2.a. Joy as a Eupathic Response

We have already seen how on the Stoic account the *eupatheiai* were that set of perfected emotions, free from the grounds of criticism on which the passions were rejected, which were regularly the experience of the wise person. John Cooper argues convincingly that the doctrine of eupathic responses arose early in the development of Stoicism as a reaction against the accusation that the Stoics were insensitive to situations in which attachments to or aversions from certain people or things were justified.[238] Given the defensive context in which this aspect of Stoic theory was worked out, it is not surprising that we have only limited details about how precisely the *eupatheiai* would function in a perfected human life. It seems that the Stoics did not develop the theory very far as a positive account in its own right of what they certainly regarded as important aspects of the moral life.[239] This means that we have considerably less information about Stoic thinking on joy, for example, compared to the material on grief that we have already discussed. Yet I think that our sources do still allow us to adumbrate what the Roman Stoics – or more precisely, Seneca, since Epictetus does not seem to say very much here – thought about joy as a eupathic response.

But first, it is helpful at this point to summarize very briefly what earlier Stoicism has to tell us about joy. Unlike its eupathic relations, wish and caution, joy does not motivate actions of pursuit or avoidance; it is instead a reactive response. Putting together the accounts in Cicero, Diogenes Laertius, and Andronicus, we learn that joy is a feeling of 'rational uplift' or 'elation' (εὔλογος ἔπαρσις) at being in the presence of true goods – that is, virtue itself, virtuous deeds, and their essential accompaniments.[240] Since wise people are, on Stoic principles, continually aware of their own virtuous condition, and since this awareness never fails to generate actions that are wholly virtuous, the wise will experience a steady joy both at their condition and its practical expression.[241]

2.5.2.b. Seneca on Joy

Seneca's fullest exposition about joy is found in *Ep.* 23, where he describes what true joy is and how it can be achieved through the application of philosophy. He begins his letter to Lucilius with the assertion that joy (*gaudium*) is both the 'foundation'

---

[237] See Wilson, 'Seneca the Consoler?', 112.
[238] Cooper, 'Emotional Life', 176.
[239] Cooper, 'Emotional Life', 177–8.
[240] Cicero, *Tusc.*4.13; Diogenes Laertius 7.116; Andronicus, *De passionibus* 6.
[241] Cooper, 'Emotional Life', 186–7.

and 'pinnacle' of a sound mind and that joy may be found 'if we have not placed our happiness in the control of externals' (*qui felicitatem suam in aliena potestate non posuit*).[242] Seneca is in effect restating standard theory about the *eupatheiai*, for in the person of wise understanding, joy and its fellow eupathic responses emanate from fully veridical judgements of the goodness or badness of genuine goods or evils. Such a wise person, whose actions are always fully coordinated with the proper exercise of virtue, is able to experience eupathic joy consistently. Seneca writes,

> Real joy (*gaudium*), believe me, is a stern matter. Can one, do you think, despise death with a care-free countenance, …? Or can one thus open the door to poverty, or hold the curb on his pleasures, or contemplate the endurance of pain? He who ponders these things in his heart is indeed full of joy; but it is not a cheerful joy. It is just this joy, however, of which I would have you become the owner; for it will never fail you … do the one thing that can render you really happy (*felicem*): cast aside and trample under foot all those things that glitter outwardly and are held out to you by another or as obtainable from another; look toward the true good (*verum bonum*), and rejoice only in that which comes from your own store. And what do I mean by 'from your own store'? I mean from your very self, that which is the best part of you. (*Ep.* 23.4–6)

Seneca clearly sees joy as the affective state that especially marks the normative human agent. Yet this state is only accessible to Lucilius when he is transformed by moral progress, whose aim is virtue; thus the 'true good' in which he is called to rejoice is his potential for virtue – the 'best part' of him. Elsewhere, Seneca reaffirms his thinking: writing to console his mother during his exile, he reminds her that as the human person is already imbued with such a potential, she is able to actualize it and achieve joy through the judicious evaluation of external goods:

> Nature intended that we should need no great equipment for living happily; each one of us is able to make his own happiness (*beatum*). External things are of slight importance, and can have no great influence in either direction. Prosperity does not exalt the wise man, nor does adversity cast him down; for he has always endeavoured to rely entirely upon himself, to derive all of his joy (*gaudium*) from himself. (Seneca, *Helv.* 5.1–2)

The parallels with *Ep.* 23 may be readily discerned. There, the joy that Seneca has in view is a joy that is to be 'born' in one's being – as he tells Lucilius: *Volo illam tibi domi nasci* (*Ep.* 23.3). This joy has no commerce with 'objects of cheer' (*hilaritates*) that are superficial and transient; while these things may possibly elicit laughter, they do not reflect the presence of real joy. As Seneca emphasizes, joy causes the wise person's soul to be 'happy and confident, lifted above every circumstance' (*Ep.* 23.3).[243]

---

[242] *Ep.* 23.1–2.
[243] See also *Ep.* 59.2, 16, where Seneca tells Lucilius that for the wise man, joy stems from the awareness and enjoyment of one's own virtue; as such, joy is independent of one's circumstances and is 'unbroken and continuous'.

We find analogous ideas in Seneca's *De Vita Beata*, which was written for his elder brother Gallio.[244] Here Seneca considers the question of how true happiness (i.e. in a eudaimonist sense) is to be obtained. He argues that the answer is to be found in living according to nature (*Vit. beat.* 3.1-3; 8.1-2). The result is a life of inner harmony, ruled by reason, where there is constancy in one's perceptions and convictions. The 'highest good' – a life of virtue – is attained, and in consequence 'no crookedness, no slipperiness is left to it, nothing that will cause it to stumble or fall' (8.5). Untouched by external goods, the person experiences 'unbroken tranquillity and enduring freedom' (3.3-4)[245] and 'a boundless joy (*gaudium*) that is firm and unalterable' (3.4), a joy that 'is deep and issues from deep within, since he finds delight in his own resources, and desires no joys greater than his inner joys' (4.4). In this and the examples cited earlier, Seneca's conception of joy is in keeping with standard Stoic thought about eupathic joy.

However, as Margaret Graver has recently argued, there is a passage (*Ep.* 66) in which Seneca's construal of joy does not fully square with the usual Stoic account.[246] Here Seneca speaks of 'deriving joy from the dutiful behaviour of one's children and from the well-being of one's country' (*gaudere liberorum pietate, patriae incolumitate*, 66.37). That this joy is an affective responsive is shown by the use of terms that reflect Stoic theory concerning sensed alterations in the *psychē*: thus, for example, this joy is 'effusive and expansive' (*remissa et laxa*, 66.12) and involves a 'natural effusion and expansion of the mind' (*naturalis animi remissio et laxitas*, 66.14).[247] Graver theorizes that *gaudium* here in relation to the safety of one's homeland and the piety of one's children is an occurrent response of the virtuous mind to what the Stoics would term as preferred indifferents. It is not another name for the delight that an ordinary person experiences, even though similar affective sensations may be experienced, because the ordinary person's response is predicated on the assumption that these objects are good. The wise person knows that they are preferred indifferents, yet responds to them with real joy, as a 'natural effusion of the mind'. Thus there appears here to be a divergent Stoic account of how normative affect works.[248]

Our evidence earlier tells us that Seneca is certainly committed to the idea of joy as that emotional state which especially characterizes the wise person. Yet, if Graver is correct, what we have here in *Ep.* 66 is an effort by Seneca to account for the possibility of occurrent, wise joy that is based on the presence of non-integral goods. As in the curious case of the wise person's weeping (Section 2.5.1.b), Seneca reveals himself as a Stoic philosopher who is unafraid to show his ingenuity while broadly remaining within school boundaries.

---

[244] The same Gallio as is mentioned in Acts 18.12-17.
[245] See also 8.3-4.
[246] Margaret R. Graver, 'Anatomies of Joy: Seneca and the Gaudium Tradition', in *Hope, Joy, and Affection in the Classical World*, ed. Ruth R. Caston and Robert A. Kaster (Oxford: Oxford University Press, 2016), 123-42, especially 133-6.
[247] Graver, 'Anatomies', 134-5.
[248] Graver, 'Anatomies', 135-6 (quote from 136).

2.6. Conclusion

The Stoic understanding of personhood was wholly integrated within a philosophical framework in which the entire universe – all of nature – was understood to be shaped and ordered by divine rationality. The goal of life therefore consisted in a life in agreement with nature, the result of which was *eudaimonia*. This meant the rational selection of those things which accorded with nature, or, in other words, the perfection of virtuous agency. Since rationality characterized the human soul, one's emotional states, far from being irrational drives, were primarily specified by their cognitive content. Emotions embodied certain ways of interpreting the world. However, in the non-wise, imperfections of rationality gave rise to the passions – which were false judgements about the value of external goods. As the Stoics were committed to rational self-determination, the passions, which violated the integrity of human agency, had to be extirpated.

Yet not everything that we would today consider an 'emotion' was considered by the Stoics to be a passion that required elimination; there were other classes of affective response – the 'good emotions' or *eupatheiai*, the 'pre-emotions' or *propatheiai*, and also what one might term the 'moral emotions' – which were deemed to be appropriate and indeed even normative. Alongside these we might place also the curious instance of the wise person's weeping, which seems to have been the eupathic antithesis of pathological grief. The Stoics have long been caricatured as being almost inhumanly disengaged from the emotions that make life and its relationships meaningful. In fact, our sources suggest that they allowed – and perhaps even deliberately made room for – a considerable variety of affective states and thus for a rich and complex emotional life.

The passions, however, were problematic and had to be eradicated. Since they arose from false beliefs, it was thought that the treatment of the mind was the best way to achieve this. Stoic cognitive therapy was in part a philosophical analysis of what the passions were, and in part a battery of cognitive devices (which were often not philosophical, and often shared with other schools) for attacking the objectionable aspects of emotion. The work was performed by the coaction of both parts of the therapeutic package.[249] However, it is important to note that the chief demand of Stoic ethics was not that one should suppress or deny one's feelings, but that one should perfect one's rational core. A proper understanding of Stoic axiology makes it clear that the Stoics did not seek to attain *apatheia* only because of the disruptive effects of emotional disquiet, but because no rational person would want to continue to believe that which was false.

---

[249] See Sorabji, *Emotion*, 160.

3

Joy in Philippians

3.1. The Background to Philippians

3.1.1. Overview

Philippians is one of Paul's[1] most personal letters, one in which we may readily observe the heartfelt emotions that arise from the close relationship that he enjoys with this community of believers. The Philippians, who have been so supportive of Paul, are 'his beloved and longed-for brothers and sisters'[2] and his 'joy and crown' (Phil. 4.1). These strong feelings of affection have their basis in the Philippians' stalwart participation in the gospel mission – a mutual partnership (κοινωνία) that is both spiritual and practical. In the course of this partnership, the Philippians have repeatedly sent to Paul moneys to support his work of ministry (4.15-16), thereby demonstrating their commitment to their common cause. Most recently one of their members, Epaphroditus, had been tasked to bring to Paul a financial gift and also to be of general service to him (4.10, 18; 2.25-30). Epaphroditus had fallen dangerously ill, either along the way to Paul or in his company,[3] but now that he is recovered, Paul is sending him back. This provides Paul with the opportunity to send a letter to the Philippians.

Internal evidence suggests that Paul has several interrelated purposes for writing.[4] He expresses joy over the Philippians' support and acknowledges their gift, commends

---

[1] The Pauline authorship of Philippians has only very rarely been questioned; for details see Gerald F. Hawthorne and Ralph P. Martin, *Philippians*, revised ed., WBC 43 (Nashville, TN: Thomas Nelson, 2004), xxviii–xxx.

[2] As Gordon Fee notes, that the vocative ἀδελφοί means 'brothers and sisters' in the Pauline letters is made clear from Phil. 4.1-2, where Paul uses this vocative and then specifically addresses two women; *Paul's Letter to the Philippians*, NICNT (Grand Rapids, MI: Eerdmans, 1995), 109 n.9.

[3] Paul Holloway (*Consolation in Philippians: Philosophical Sources and Rhetorical Strategy*, Society for New Testament Studies Monograph Series 112 (Cambridge: Cambridge University Press, 2001), 25) argues that the most reasonable way to read Paul's statement in 2.30 that διὰ τὸ ἔργον Χριστοῦ μέχρι θανάτου ἤγγισεν παραβολευσάμενος τῇ ψυχῇ is that in bringing the gift from Philippi Epaphroditus became sick and, rather than stopping to recover, pressed ahead so that Paul would not suffer from need in prison. However, nothing conclusive can actually be said about when or where Epaphroditus fell ill or recovered.

[4] There is considerable scholarly opinion concerning the occasion of the letter; see e.g. Fee, *Philippians*, 29–39; Markus Bockmuehl, *A Commentary on the Epistle to the Philippians*, BNTC (London: A & C Black, 1997), 33; Paul A. Holloway, *Philippians: A Commentary*, Hermeneia (Minneapolis, MN: Fortress, 2017), 24–31. However, it seems to me rather difficult – and perhaps altogether

Epaphroditus (and Timothy), provides the Philippians with an update of his own situation, and addresses aspects of theirs that he is concerned about. Reporting his own situation, Paul repeatedly mentions being 'in chains' (1.7, 13, 14, 17). However, instead of curtailing the progress of the gospel, as the Philippians might have expected, his incarceration, most likely in Rome,[5] and the circumstances surrounding it are turning out for its very advancement (1.12-14). In relation to the situation affecting the Philippian believers, Fee argues convincingly that at least two matters – suffering because of opposition, and some sort of internal unrest – coalesce in some way as the driving force behind the letter's two blocks of hortatory material (1.27–2.18 and 3.1–4.3).[6] In his letter to the Philippians, then, Paul produces a multifaceted message that brings together pastoral sensitivity and the practical outworking of doctrine: a message of solidarity, encouragement, hope, and the possibility of joy even in turmoil and suffering.

3.1.2. Literary Integrity

A generation ago, many critical scholars were of the view that Philippians is a composite of two or three separate letters. This view has now largely been rejected, though there are still a number of scholars who hold to some kind of partition theory.[7] Their case rests primarily on the construal of two seemingly abrupt transitions within the letter. The first is the sudden change in tone at 3.1-2, where Paul seems to be preparing to end the letter but instead launches into polemical invective. This has led some commentators to conclude that a fragment from another letter has been spliced in here; on this reading, at 3.1 τὸ λοιπόν means 'finally', while χαίρετε ἐν κυρίῳ is a farewell formula akin to 2 Cor. 13.11. The second uneven seam concerns the location

---

unnecessary – to make a case for a single factor, from among several interrelated ones, to form the occasion for writing.

[5] The question of the place of writing remains controversial, but is ancillary to my study. I follow many scholars in favouring the traditional view of a Roman provenance over an Ephesian or Caesarean origin: see the discussion in Holloway, *Philippians*, 19–24.

[6] Fee, *Philippians*, 29. He notes that both of these matters appear in the initial imperative of 1.27-8: 'that you *stand firm* in the *one Spirit, striving together as one person* for the faith of the gospel, without being frightened in any way by *those who oppose you*' (emphases his), followed by a clause explaining their suffering (1.29-30) and by an appeal to have the same mindset (2.1-2). These same verbs ('stand firm'; 'have the same mindset') are used in the appeals that conclude the second hortatory section (4.1-3). For Fee, these two concerns, viz. suffering and disunity, bookend Paul's hortatory material.

Much scholarly attention has been devoted to the identities of the opponents to whom Paul alludes in 1.14-17; 1.27-8; 3.2, 18-19. I follow those interpreters who take the view that Paul is referring to Judaizers, especially in chapter 3; see the succinct analysis in Jerry L. Sumney, 'Studying Paul's Opponents: Advances and Challenges', in *Paul and His Opponents*, ed. Stanley E. Porter (Leiden: Brill, 2005), 25–9. However, the question is hardly settled: see the recent discussion in Mark A. Jennings, *The Price of Partnership in the Letter of Paul to the Philippians: 'Make My Joy Complete'*, LNTS 578 (London: T&T Clark, 2018), 5 n.16.

[7] E.g. Hans Dieter Betz, *Studies in Paul's Letter to the Philippians*, WUNT 343 (Tübingen: Mohr Siebeck, 2015), 9–10; John Reumann, *Philippians: A New Translation with Introduction and Commentary*, AB 33B (New Haven, CT: Yale University Press, 2008), 8–13; Jean-Baptiste Edart, *L'Épître aux Philippiens, Rhétorique et Composition Stylistique*, EBib 45 (Paris: Gabalda, 2002), 15–41; Lukas Bormann, *Philippi: Stadt und Christengemeinde zur Zeit des Paulus*, NovTSup 78 (Leiden: Brill, 1995), 108–18.

of Paul's thanksgiving for their gift (4.10-20). Its placing within an ancient letter is unusually late; and again, the τὸ λοιπόν of 4.8 should lead to concluding remarks rather than to an expression of thanks.

Though the various partition theories are not all agreed, the most common proposal is that Philippians comprises three letter fragments, which are (in chronological order): Letter A (4.10-20), a short note of thanks sent immediately after the arrival of Epaphroditus; Letter B (1.1–3.1), a letter of reassurance dispatched with Epaphroditus upon his return to Philippi; and Letter C (3.2–4.3), a polemical letter sent later, perhaps after Paul's release, when he had become more fully apprised of the theological debate at Philippi.[8] The remaining material (4.4-9 and 4.21-3) is variously assigned, with 4.4-7 and 4.21-3 often shoehorned into Letter B.[9]

However, the presence of redactional seams has been challenged. It is unnecessary to conclude in 3.1a that Paul is bringing the letter to a close: τὸ λοιπόν is best understood here as a transitional instead of concluding particle ('furthermore', instead of 'finally'),[10] and χαίρετε ἐν κυρίῳ means 'rejoice [not goodbye] in the Lord'.[11] Furthermore, βλέπετε in 3:2 can simply mean 'consider' and not 'beware' – in which case the tonal shift is minimal.[12] As to the supposedly delayed 'thank you' (4.10-20): it has been demonstrated that this section forms an *inclusio* with the introductory thanksgiving at the beginning (1.3-11), thus precluding its excision as a separate letter. The presence of numerous clear parallels between these two sections proves that 4.10-20 is not the only place where Paul thanks the Philippians for their gift.[13] In the first place, in a Hellenistic letter, an expression of thanks for a gift need not occur near its beginning; in fact, formal expressions of thanks might be absent.[14]

Several important studies, undertaken from different perspectives, also uphold the unity of Philippians. David Garland's literary approach reveals the extensive use of *inclusio* which mark out several shorter sections as well as the overall paraenesis of 1.27–4.3.[15] Duane Watson's seminal rhetorical-critical inquiry demonstrates that Philippians systematically develops the proposition found in 1.27-30 and is thus a cohesive whole.[16] For Gordon Wiles, the introductory thanksgiving of 1.3-11 is an

---

[8] Holloway, *Consolation*, 7–8.
[9] See the table in Bormann, *Philippi*, 110.
[10] Margaret E. Thrall, *Greek Particles in the New Testament: Linguistic and Exegetical Studies* (Leiden: Brill, 1962), 25–30, especially 28; Loveday Alexander, 'Hellenistic Letter-Forms and the Structure of Philippians', *JSNT* 37 (1989): 96–7.
[11] Alexander, 'Hellenistic Letter-Forms', 97.
[12] George D. Kilpatrick, 'ΒΛΕΠΕΤΕ, Philippians 3:2', in *In Memoriam Paul Kahle*, ed. Matthew Black and G. Fohrer (Berlin: Töpelmann, 1968).
[13] Gerald W. Peterman, *Paul's Gift from Philippi: Conventions of Gift-Exchange and Christian Giving*, SNTSMS 92 (Cambridge: Cambridge University Press, 1997), 90–3. Peterman notes that 'the large-scale inclusio forces us to view the thought of the letter as more concerned with providing a response to the Philippians' support than has commonly been recognized' (92–3).
[14] Alexander, 'Hellenistic Letter-Forms', 97–8.
[15] David E. Garland, 'The Composition and Unity of Philippians: Some Neglected Literary Factors', *NovT* 27 (1985): 141–73, especially 159–61. He also highlights (157–9) the numerous thematic and verbal parallels between chapters 2 and 3, not least between the hymn of 2.5-11 and 3.20-1.
[16] Duane F. Watson, 'A Rhetorical Analysis of Philippians and Its Implications for the Unity Question', *NovT* 30 (1988): 57–88, especially 66–7, 84. See also Peter Wick, *Der Philipperbrief: Der formale Aufbau des Briefs als Schlüssel zum Verständnis seines Inhalts*, BWANT 135 (Stuttgart: Kohlhammer, 1994), 11, 187–91.

epistolary anticipation, controlled by liturgical idiom, of the major themes that run through the letter.[17] Loveday Alexander observes that the arguments typically adduced for partition are not reflected in Hellenistic epistolary conventions.[18]

However, rhetorical and epistolographic arguments for unity are not without their problems, as Bockmuehl points out.[19] As a way out of the impasse, he furnishes two considerations about the text and the composition of Philippians that suggest that one may reasonably continue to interpret the letter in its received form. First, the manuscript transmission of Philippians *as a whole* is consistent without exception – a fact which is significant especially given the well-documented tenacity of textual variants.[20] Second, it is difficult to imagine how an editor clever enough to carry out such a sophisticated splicing operation would be so inept as to leave such obvious breaks in the redacted document.[21]

It seems clear that partition hypotheses do not hold water, and I shall therefore proceed on the assumption of the literary integrity and unity of Philippians, and interpret the letter as an integral whole. We turn next to the question of Philippians as a letter: precisely what kind of letter is it?

3.1.3. Genre

3.1.3.a. A Hortatory Letter of Friendship

On the basis of evidence from Greco-Roman epistolography, some scholars posit that Philippians reflects many characteristics of both a 'letter of friendship' and a 'letter of moral exhortation',[22] and is therefore best described as 'a hortatory letter of

---

[17] Gordon P. Wiles, *Paul's Intercessory Prayers: The Significance of the Intercessory Prayer Passages in the Letters of St Paul*, SNTSMS 24 (Cambridge: Cambridge University Press, 1974), 194–215.
[18] Alexander, 'Hellenistic Letter-Forms', 87–101.
[19] See Bockmuehl, *Philippians*, 23–4, 38–40.
[20] Bockmuehl, *Philippians*, 24–5.
[21] Bockmuehl, *Philippians*, 24–5.
[22] L. Michael White, 'Morality between Two Worlds: A Paradigm of Friendship in Philippians', in *Greeks, Romans, and Christians: Essays in Honor of Abraham J. Malherbe*, ed. David J. Balch, Everett Ferguson, and Wayne A. Meeks (Minneapolis, MN: Fortress, 1990), 201–15; Stanley K. Stowers, 'Friends and Enemies in the Politics of Heaven: Reading Theology in Philippians', in *Pauline Theology 1: Thessalonians, Philippians, Galatians*, ed. Jouette M. Bassler (Minneapolis, MN: Fortress, 1991), 107–14; Fee, *Philippians*, 2–14. For a survey of the scholarship see John Reumann, 'Philippians, Especially Chapter 4, as a "Letter of Friendship": Observations on a Checkered History of Friendship', in *Friendship, Flattery, and Frankness of Speech: Studies in Friendship in the New Testament World*, ed. John T. Fitzgerald, NovTSup 82 (Leiden: Brill, 1996), 83–106.
  See also Alexander, 'Hellenistic Letter-Forms', 87–101, on the closely related category of the so-called 'family letter': since the content of family letters was similar to that of letters of friendship, family letters were grouped together with them by the ancient theorists, and not regarded as a distinct type (on this, see Fee, *Philippians*, 2 n.8). Ben Witherington, *Paul's Letter to the Philippians: A Socio-Rhetorical Commentary* (Grand Rapids, MI: Eerdmans, 2011), 17–21, has recently made a case for Philippians to be regarded as a family letter because key aspects of the grammar of friendship such as direct reciprocity and explicit references to friendship itself are absent. Witherington draws support from the work of Alexander and from Reidar Aasgaard's study of the Pauline sibling metaphor, in which he argues that the familial metaphor is used to strengthen the ties between Paul and his readers and to support his drive for unity and mutual responsibility; see Reidar Aasgaard, *'My Beloved Brothers and Sisters!': Christian Siblingship in Paul*, JSNTSup 265

friendship'.²³ Certainly, the letter seems to abound with allusions to the *topoi* of friendship.²⁴ Examples are the presence-absence motif (1.19-26; 2.12), expressions of affection and desire to be with the readers (1.7-8; 4.1), the reciprocity between writer and readers (1.7, 30; 2.17-18; 4.14), the pattern of giving and receiving (4.10-20), the importance of mutual participation (1.5; 2.1; 3.10; 4.15), the push for agreement and equality (1.27-2.4; 4.2), the need for a single mind (2.2, 5; 4.2) and the sharing of common enemies (1.27-30; 3.2, 17-19).²⁵ Philippians also contains significant elements of moral instruction: two large hortatory sections (1.27-2.18 and 3.1-4.3) take up a large part of the letter. Consistent with the goal of Greco-Roman letters of exhortation (which often took place in the context of friendship),²⁶ the aim of this hortatory material is to advocate a certain kind of behaviour and deprecate another, and this is evident in Paul's explicit appeal throughout the letter to exemplary paradigms (Christ, 2.6-11; Timothy, 2.20-2; Epaphroditus, 2.29-30; and Paul himself, 3.4-14).²⁷

However, critics argue that while some of the phraseology that is characteristic of Greco-Roman friendship is found in Philippians, Paul does not actually make explicit reference, or unambiguous allusion, to friendship; moreover, he does not use here (or in any other letter) the terms φίλος/φιλία.²⁸ In addition, the social equality that was thought to be ideal in friendship – between two males of equal standing – is lacking; Paul's seniority in the relationship is implicit throughout the letter.²⁹ Also, there is no parallel example of one person entering into a friendship with a group of people, as is the case here.³⁰ Furthermore, while one might argue that a Greco-Roman

(London: T&T Clark, 2004), 309, 311. However, our evidence indicates that the family letter was not regarded as a distinct type.

On letter writing in the Greco-Roman world, see Abraham J. Malherbe, *Ancient Epistolary Theorists*, SBLSBS 19 (Atlanta, GA: Scholars, 1988), 1-14; Stanley K. Stowers, *Letter Writing in Greco-Roman Antiquity*, Library of Early Christianity 5 (Philadelphia, PA: Westminster Press, 1986), 27-40. As Malherbe (6-7) and Stowers (32-5) explain, formal schooling would have included instruction in letter writing. Two manuals for such instruction are extant: 'Epistolary Types', by Pseudo-Demetrius, and 'Epistolary Styles', by Pseudo-Libanius, both of which are reproduced by Malherbe in *Theorists*, 30-41 and 66-81, respectively. Pseudo-Demetrius illustrates twenty-one different types of letters, with the 'friendly' type heading his list and the 'advisory' letter listed as the eleventh type. Pseudo-Libanius expands the list from twenty-one to forty-one styles, with the 'paraenetic' and 'friendly' letters listed as the fifth and eleventh styles.

²³ Fee, *Philippians*, 12. Cf. White, 'Morality', 206 ('Philippians … is primarily a friendly hortatory letter'); Stowers, 'Friends', 107 ('a hortatory letter of friendship').
²⁴ On friendship in classical antiquity see Aristotle, *Eth. nic.* Book 8; Cicero, *Amic.*; Seneca, *Ep.* 1, 9, 35; Plutarch, *Amic. mult.*; for discussion of the vast secondary literature, see especially David Konstan, *Friendship in the Classical World* (New York: Cambridge University Press, 1997); Peter Marshall, *Enmity in Corinth: Social Conventions in Paul's Relations with the Corinthians*, WUNT 2.23 (Tübingen: Mohr, 1987), 1-34; John T. Fitzgerald, 'Paul and Friendship', in *Paul in the Greco-Roman World: A Handbook*, ed. J. Paul Sampley (Harrisburg: Trinity Press International, 2003), 319-43.
²⁵ Charles B. Cousar, *Philippians and Philemon: A Commentary*, NTL (Louisville, KY: Westminster John Knox, 2009), 12.
²⁶ On this see Stowers, *Letter Writing*, 91-112; Abraham J. Malherbe, *Moral Exhortation: A Greco-Roman Sourcebook* (Philadelphia, PA: Westminster, 1986), 79-80 and *passim*.
²⁷ Fee, *Philippians*, 11-12.
²⁸ Bockmuehl, *Philippians*, 34. However the absence of explicit friendship terms in Paul has been variously explained; for a summary see Reumann, *Philippians*, 684.
²⁹ Bockmuehl, *Philippians*, 34-5. However, one may argue that friendship was found also among social unequals: see David E. Briones, *Paul's Financial Policy: A Socio-Theological Approach*, LNTS 494 (London: T&T Clark, 2013), 75-7.
³⁰ Carolyn Osiek, *Philippians, Philemon*, ANTC (Nashville, TN: Abingdon, 2000), 24.

paradigm of friendship can shed light on some aspects of the two-way relational dynamics between Paul and his readers, it does not account for one factor that some interpreters see as being central to the understanding of Paul's relationship with the Philippians – God's presence in it.[31] On balance, Bockmuehl is probably correct in his assessment: 'Philippians certainly manifests many informal aspects of a warm human friendship ... That recognition alone, however, does not suffice to confirm the requisite social and epistolary conventions of Greco-Roman *philia*.'[32]

3.1.3.b. A Letter of Consolation

An interesting proposal comes from Paul Holloway, who situates Philippians within the literature of consolation in antiquity. He argues that Philippians should be seen in the light of ancient consolers, who 'understood their primary task to be not one of sharing in the grief of others, but one of removing that grief by rational argument and frank exhortation'.[33] For Holloway, Paul diagnoses the chief problem at Philippi to be discouragement; his primary purpose in writing is thus to console the Philippians that things were going much better than they imagined.[34] To correct their distress and restore them to responsible behaviour, Paul exploits two key consolatory motifs: the distinction between things that matter and things that do not (he introduces the 'adiaphora' topos at 1.10: εἰς τὸ δοκιμάζειν ὑμᾶς τὰ διαφέροντα), and the disposition of 'joy' (χαρά), which characterized the wise person in both good times and bad.[35]

3.1.3.c. Other Proposals and Conclusion

Though the above proposals are inconclusive, in my view they remain among the most promising. To be sure, other approaches have been championed. These include efforts to locate Paul's implied relationship with the Philippians within the milieu of societal conventions and structures, such as mutual benefaction,[36] the Roman *societas*,[37] or patron-client relationships.[38] Other scholars have interpreted Philippians against the

---

[31] However, Fee seems fully cognizant of this possible objection. On his reading, Philippians is an especially Pauline and therefore intensely Christian expression of a 'hortatory letter of friendship', one in which first-century epistolary conventions are mere scaffolding for Paul, in whose hands friendship is thus radically transformed from a two-way bond to a three-way bond – between him, the Philippians, and Christ; see *Philippians*, 12–14.

[32] Bockmuehl, *Philippians*, 35. See also the discussion and similar conclusion in Reumann, *Philippians*, 678–85.

[33] Holloway, *Consolation*, 1. He offers a useful survey of the genre of ancient consolation in 55–74.

[34] Holloway, *Consolation*, 45–8.

[35] Holloway, *Consolation*, 74–83, 87–145.

[36] Marshall, *Enmity*, 157–64; White, 'Morality'.

[37] J. Paul Sampley, *Pauline Partnership in Christ: Christian Community and Commitment in Light of Roman Law* (Philadelphia, PA: Fortress, 1980). See recently also Julien M. Ogereau, *Paul's Koinonia with the Philippians: A Socio-Historical Investigation of a Pauline Economic Partnership*, WUNT 2.377 (Tübingen: Mohr Siebeck, 2014), who affirms Sampley's views and finds that Paul and the Philippians had formed a financial partnership 'where they cooperated in his missionary activities by providing material and financial resources, while he performed the work of ministry' (15).

[38] E.g. Bormann, *Philippi*, 187–217.

background of ancient rhetoric,[39] or even as a *praemeditatio mortis*.[40] However, just as efforts to classify Philippians on the basis of literary genre have proven ambiguous, attempts to read it in the light of ancient social conventions or rhetoric have been equally inconclusive. Arguing that many of these highly precise models are proving less than helpful as tools for the analysis of Philippians, not least because few of them tend to agree, Bockmuehl wisely pleads for a cautious and light-handed application of all these approaches[41] – an approach that this study will adopt.

3.1.4. Distinctives

3.1.4.a. Lexical Distinctives

The profiling of a document's character using statistics based on vocabulary can generate more than merely superficial results and provide useful clues about the author's priorities, if one proceeds with discrimination and due regard for the overarching themes of the piece of writing. There are in Philippians some terms that occur with disproportionate frequency. Most noticeable is the remarkable frequency of χαρά and its verbal cognates, which are found a total of sixteen times in Philippians[42] (more than anywhere else in Paul), out of a total of some fifty occurrences in the undisputed Pauline letters;[43] this is a clear indication of the importance of joy in Paul's thinking.[44] Two verbs that relate to the activity and disposition of the mind occur also with unusual frequency: φρονέω (ten times;[45] otherwise used only twelve times in the undisputed Pauline letters, nine of which are in Romans) and ἡγέομαι (six times;[46] elsewhere only three times in the undisputed Paulines).

3.1.4.b. Thematic Distinctives

It has become something of a hackneyed commonplace to speak of Philippians as a 'letter of joy', as if it was written to an exemplary church that did not have to deal with any serious problems. The obvious affection that unites Paul and his readers only reinforces this jejune notion in the popular Christian imagination. This may have led

---

[39] E.g. Watson, 'Rhetorical Analysis'. See the discussion in Walter Hansen, *The Letter to the Philippians*, PilNTC (Grand Rapids, MI: Eerdmans, 2009), 12–15.
[40] Betz, *Studies*, 133–54, especially 153.
[41] Bockmuehl, *Philippians*, 39; see also 34–40 for a shrewd assessment of these approaches.
[42] In noun form: χαρᾶς (1.4); χαράν (1.25); χαράν (2.2); χαρᾶς (2.29); χαρά (4.1). In verbal form: χαίρω, χαρήσομαι (1.18); χαίρω, συγχαίρω (2.17); χαίρετε, συγχαίρετε (2.18); χαρῆτε (2.28); χαίρετε (3.1); χαίρετε (twice) (4.4); ἐχάρην (4.10).
[43] Hans Conzelmann, '*χαίρω, χαρά, συγχαίρω*', TDNT 9:359–72; William G. Morrice, 'Joy', DPL 511–12.
[44] N. T. Wright rightly notes that though it is sometimes claimed that there is theological significance in the etymological proximity between χαρά and χάρις, the New Testament writers themselves do not make this link explicit; thus we must be wary of going beyond the usual rule of locating the meaning of a word in its context and not in its history or family resemblances; 'Joy', 47.
[45] φρονεῖν (1.7); φρονῆτε, φρονοῦντες (2.2); φρονεῖτε (2.5); φρονῶμεν, φρονεῖτε (3.15); φρονοῦντες (3.19); φρονεῖν (4.2); φρονεῖν, ἐφρονεῖτε (4.10).
[46] ἡγούμενοι (2.3); ἡγήσατο (2.6); ἡγησάμην (2.25); ἥγημαι (3.7); ἡγοῦμαι (twice) (3.8).

to a downplaying of both the nature of the problems at Philippi and the theological content of the letter. A second factor pulls in a different direction, but has also led to potential misunderstanding about Paul's central concerns: so much attention has been given to the Christ poem of Phil. 2.6-11 in contemporary New Testament scholarship – which tends to focus on the pre-Pauline origins of the passage and thus isolate it from its literary context – that questions of Christology may have obscured other important features of the letter.[47]

It becomes apparent, when the Christ poem is seen in its context, that its point is to showcase the pattern of selflessness and humility to which the Philippians must be conformed if they are to live in a manner worthy of the gospel (1.27). For this to happen the Philippians need to have the correct mindset; that this is a major concern for Paul is shown in his repeated use of φρονέω.[48] He first models for his readers what it means to think rightly about others (1.7), and then uses the same verb at several key points: to encourage them towards unity in Christ (2.2), to mandate the same self-abasing attitude that Christ displayed (2.5), and to emphasize the contrast between mature thought and its opposite (3.15, 19). Paul adjures Euodia and Syntyche to think the same things in the Lord (4.2). His final use of the verb is in connection with the commendable attitude of the Philippians towards him (4.10). To further impress on the reader the significance of all this, Paul uses comparable terms throughout: ἡγέομαι (see n.46 in this chapter), σκοπέω (2.4; 3.17), and λογίζομαι (3.13, 4.8). There is also an abundance of 'knowledge' terminology throughout the letter: most notably in 1.9-10, where Paul prays that the Philippians' love may increasingly abound ἐν ἐπιγνώσει καὶ πάσῃ αἰσθήσει εἰς τὸ δοκιμάζειν ὑμᾶς τὰ διαφέροντα, and in 3.8-10, where Paul speaks of the surpassing value of the knowledge of Christ (τὸ ὑπερέχον τῆς γνώσεως Χριστοῦ Ἰησοῦ) and expresses his desire to know Christ more fully (γνῶναι αὐτὸν καὶ τὴν δύναμιν τῆς ἀναστάσεως αὐτοῦ καὶ [τὴν] κοινωνίαν [τῶν] παθημάτων αὐτοῦ). Paul also employs military and athletic imagery to express the notion of mental determination (1.27, 30; 3.12-14; 4.1-3). It is clear that in Philippians there is a strong focus on right thinking.[49]

The reason for this emphasis is that the faith of the believers and its practical expression are being stymied by much adversity and disunity. Accordingly, Paul emphasizes the need to stand firm (1.27-8; 4.1) and persevere (3.13-15); right thinking about Christian truth will lead to a repristination of the ways in which suffering and opposition are faced. Specifically, Paul reminds the Philippians of their assured future with its eschatological victory (2.9-11; 3.12-14, 20-1). The end result is joy: indeed, the motif of joy in Philippians is pervasive, more so than in any other Pauline letter. The importance of this theme is not accidental: 2 Cor. 8.1-2 reveals that joy in the midst of great affliction is a hallmark of the Macedonian churches (cf. 1 Thess. 1.6, in which

---

[47] Moisés Silva, *Philippians*, 2nd ed., BECNT (Grand Rapids, MI: Baker, 2005), 20–1.

[48] Wayne Meeks has drawn attention to Paul's frequent use of φρονέω in Philippians – a frequency comparable only with the latter part of his letter to the Romans; 'The Man from Heaven in Paul's Letter to the Philippians', in *In Search of the Early Christians: Selected Essays*, ed. Allen R. Hilton and H. Gregory Snyder (New Haven, CT: Yale University Press, 2002), 109–10.

[49] I am indebted to the insights of Silva, *Philippians*, 21.

Paul recalls how the gospel was received in Thessalonica ἐν θλίψει πολλῇ μετὰ χαρᾶς πνεύματος ἁγίου).

Our broad analysis thus far already yields some tantalizing clues about what joy is, for Paul: it seems that has something to do with correct thinking, and the relativization of present suffering in the light of eschatological hope. Since suffering is, in this sense, a foil for joy, it is helpful for our purposes to specify in some detail the suffering that Paul refers to. The way in which various descriptions of suffering (Paul's, his co-workers', the Philippians', and Christ's) are woven into the letter – and also tied together – indicates that it is for Paul an important motif. Hence we now turn our attention to suffering in Philippians, before we investigate what Paul says about joy.

3.2. Suffering in Philippians

3.2.1. Paul's Suffering

3.2.1.a. Paul in Prison (Phil. 1.7, 13-14, 17)

The notion of suffering makes its first appearance early in the letter, in the middle of Paul's thanksgiving for the Philippians' partnership in the gospel (1.3-8).[50] Paul's speaking of 'chains' (δεσμοί, 1.7) indicates that he is under some form of custody.[51] He mentions these chains again in 1.13-14, 17; and probably refers again to his detention in 4.4 when he commends the Philippians for sharing in his 'affliction' (πλὴν καλῶς ἐποιήσατε συγκοινωνήσαντές μου τῇ θλίψει; in this regard, it is instructive that earlier in 1.17 the notion of θλῖψις is linked with δεσμοί). Fee argues that although 'chains' could possibly be a metonymy for imprisonment as such,[52] it is most likely that Paul was literally chained to his guards, since imprisonment without the use of chains was a concession to high status.[53] Some scholars have suggested, on the basis of the account in Acts 28.30-1 (which indicates that for a length of time Paul, in Rome, was undergoing a less severe form of remand), that at the time of writing to the Philippians, Paul was certainly chained to a guard – but under house arrest.[54]

---

[50] For the historical interpretation of the motif of suffering in Philippians, see L. Gregory Bloomquist, *The Function of Suffering in Philippians*, JSNTSup 78 (Sheffield: Sheffield Academic Press, 1993), 18–70.

[51] Ernst Lohmeyer, *Die Briefe an die Philipper, an die Kolosser und an Philemon*, 14th ed., KEK 9 (Göttingen: Vandenhoeck & Ruprecht, 1974), 5, sees here one of many indications of persecution and impending martyrdom in Philippians. Though Lohmeyer's perspective of Philippians as a disquisition on the experience of martyrdom is widely criticized for going beyond the realities depicted in the letter, his approach highlights the pervasiveness of the language of suffering in the letter. See Bloomquist, *Function*, 50–2, for an analysis of Lohmeyer's approach.

[52] So BDAG 219.

[53] Fee, *Philippians*, 92, drawing on the work of Brian Rapske, *The Book of Acts and Paul in Roman Custody*, The Book of Acts in Its First Century Setting 3 (Grand Rapids, MI: Eerdmans, 1994), 25–8.

[54] So recently Witherington, *Philippians*, 9–10. But such a reading may owe too much to Acts 28.30-1; see Angela Standhartinger, 'Letter from Prison as Hidden Transcript: What It Tells Us about the People at Philippi', in *The People beside Paul: The Philippian Assembly and History from Below*, ed. Joseph A. Marchal (Atlanta, GA: SBL Press, 2015), 111–12.

However, though we cannot be certain about the precise mode of Paul's confinement at this time, on balance the language and structure of communication of the letter seem to indicate that he was incarcerated in prison.[55] In general, the Roman penal system did not seek to rehabilitate people: prisons were basically holding tanks where people were detained awaiting trial or execution, and conditions of life in prison were often gruesome.[56] The support and material help of friends was crucial,[57] but the stigma associated with imprisonment made it socially costly, if not downright dangerous, to identify publicly with a prisoner.[58] In short, incarceration in any form was grim and degrading; Fee is probably correct to say that the repetition of the phrase 'my chains' (1.7, 13-14, 17) indicates that Paul is smarting under the imprisonment.[59]

3.2.1.b. The Actions of Paul's Rivals (Phil. 1.15-17)

Furthermore, while Paul's confinement has catalyzed an increasingly strong sense of evangelistic fervour among the believers who have been inspired by his example of courage (1.14; see also 1.16, where Paul seems to draw a connection between his present sufferings and 'the defence of the gospel'), it has also created an opportunity for his rivals to achieve their own goals by capitalizing on his misfortunes. They proclaim Christ, but their motives stem from envy and rivalry (διὰ φθόνον καὶ ἔριν, 1.15), unlike others who do so out of goodwill towards Paul (δι' εὐδοκίαν, 1.15).[60] Driven by their own selfish ambitions and insincere in their aims, they are more than willing to allow further distress to fall upon Paul (οἱ δὲ ἐξ ἐριθείας τὸν Χριστὸν καταγγέλλουσιν, οὐχ ἁγνῶς, οἰόμενοι θλῖψιν ἐγείρειν τοῖς δεσμοῖς μου, 1.17).[61] It seems accurate to think, therefore, that the already considerable physical suffering and mental distress resulting from Paul's imprisonment are being compounded by the emotional pain wreaked upon him through the actions of his rivals.

3.2.1.c. Paul's Common Suffering with the Philippians (Phil. 2.17-18)

Paul returns to a discussion of his suffering at 2.17-18. In ancient Mediterranean religious practice, sacrifices were often completed with a libation or drink

---

[55] So e.g. Standhartinger, 'Letter', 124–30, noting the presence of coded references to people and situations, e.g. the unnamed 'loyal companion' (Phil. 4.3), in order to lessen the dangers of writing in prison.
[56] On the varieties of imprisonment in the Roman world, see Rapske, *Custody*, 10–35; Craig S. Wansink, *Chained in Christ: The Experience and Rhetoric of Paul's Imprisonments*, JSNTSup 130 (Sheffield: Sheffield Academic Press, 1996), 28–32. On conditions in prison, see Rapske, *Custody*, 196–225; Wansink, *Chained*, 33–40, 44–95.
[57] Rapske, *Custody*, 370–88.
[58] Rapske, *Custody*, 293–4, 388–92.
[59] Fee, *Philippians*, 92.
[60] Bockmuehl, *Philippians*, 78–9, detects in the phrase δι' εὐδοκίαν the possibility that Paul here refers to the desire of the second group of evangelists to pursue the divine will, rather than their wish to show him some sort of goodwill. His argument, based on the contemporary usage of εὐδοκία elsewhere, does not lack cogency; however, it perhaps downplays too much the juxtaposition of the phrases διὰ φθόνον καὶ ἔριν and δι' εὐδοκίαν, which surely has a contrastive function in terms of emphasizing two antithetical attitudes towards Paul and his ministry.
[61] On the identity of this group of evangelists who are opposed to Paul, see the proposals in Reumann, *Philippians*, 202–7.

offering.⁶² Paul is thus using a familiar metaphor in describing his suffering as a libation that is 'poured out' onto the 'sacrificial service' of the Philippians' faith (Ἀλλὰ εἰ καὶ σπένδομαι ἐπὶ τῇ θυσίᾳ καὶ λειτουργίᾳ τῆς πίστεως ὑμῶν, 2.17).⁶³ Commentators are divided as to whether Paul is drawing on a pagan or a Jewish cultic background,⁶⁴ but the question need not detain us. In either case, it is evident that for Paul, the Philippians' faith constitutes a sacrifice to God, with his own ministry being the complementary drink offering.⁶⁵

There is some debate concerning Paul's self-description as a libation: is he referring generally to his ongoing missionary work (which includes his present suffering) or specifically to the eventuality of martyrdom?⁶⁶ Some interpreters find it likely that Paul's imagery here incorporates the supposition of a possibility of martyrdom. Hansen, for example, argues that the present tense σπένδομαι (2.17) is used in a concessive clause (εἰ καὶ, 'even if, although') to portray a real possibility, that is, 'even if I am martyred'.⁶⁷ Further, other uses of σπένδω (2 Tim. 3.6 and *Ign. Rom.* 2.2) demonstrate that the verb's cultic associations made it suitable for use with reference to imminent martyrdom.⁶⁸ Paul has of course already alluded to the possibility of martyrdom at 1.20-1, and does so again at 3.10.

However, others do not see here any allusion to Paul's death. Hawthorne and Martin note that while libation accompanied most sacrifices in both the Greek world and Jewish cultus, 'never in the Greek bible nor in the Hellenistic world is this term ever used to denote libations of blood'.⁶⁹ Moreover, the present tense, σπένδομαι, indicates that Paul sees his ministry as ongoing and not one that will terminate prematurely in death. The libation metaphor is to be understood in conjunction with the earlier two metaphors of running and labouring (2.16) as describing the rigours of his current apostolic activities. Hence when Paul uses the libation metaphor, he does not have death in mind; indeed, within a few sentences, in 2.24, he confidently assures the Philippians

---

⁶² See e.g. Num. 28.7; Plutarch, *Arist.* 21.2-5.
⁶³ The verb σπένδω means 'offer as a libation/drink offering' (BDAG 937) and in the New Testament appears only here and in 2 Tim. 4.6, both in the passive and employed figuratively. On the use of σπένδω as a cultic term in the Hellenistic world, see Otto Michel, 'σπένδομαι', *TDNT* 7.528-36; A. M. Denis, 'La fonction apostolique et la liturgie en Esprit. Étude thématique des métaphores paulinieres du culte nouveau', *RSPT* 42 (1958): 631-4. On its use in the LXX together with the cognate noun σπονδή, see Reumann, *Philippians*, 398.
⁶⁴ See Reumann, *Philippians*, 397-8.
⁶⁵ Bockmuehl, *Philippians*, 160. For a discussion of the possible meanings of the Philippians' 'sacrifice and service', see especially Reumann, *Philippians*, 398-401. Reumann concludes by noting that both terms within the hendiadys had cultic applications, Greco-Roman and Jewish, and also wider non-cultic applications; there is no consensus on which term dominates. Even so, along with several other interpreters (e.g. Hawthorne and Martin, *Philippians*, 148), he takes λειτουργίᾳ as basic and θυσίᾳ as adjectival; hence, 'sacrificial service'.
⁶⁶ See the useful overview in Joseph H. Hellerman, *Philippians*, EGGNT (Nashville, TN: Broadman and Holman, 2015), 140-1.
⁶⁷ Hansen, *Philippians*, 188.
⁶⁸ Hansen, *Philippians*, 188. See also J. B. Lightfoot, *Saint Paul's Epistle to the Philippians*, 6th ed. (London: Macmillan, 1881), 118-19, who in connection with this cites the examples of Seneca and Thrasea who used similar metaphors when at the point of death (Tacitus, *Ann.* 15.64; 16.35).
⁶⁹ Hawthorne and Martin, *Philippians*, 149, citing Jean-François Collange, *The Epistle of Saint Paul to the Philippians*, trans. A. W. Heathcote (London: Epworth, 1979), 113 (following Denis, 'La fonction', 630-45).

of a future visit to them.[70] Rather, 'he is picturesquely referring to his sufferings as an apostle'; these sufferings 'act as a seal on whatever sacrifice the Philippians may make, just as a libation completes any offering made to God'.[71]

Clearly, there is no consensus on the matter. However, Bockmuehl offers a helpfully conciliatory perspective: in his opinion, Paul most likely takes a comprehensive view of things: his work and ministry – whether in life or in death – is offered to God as a complement to the sacrifice of the Philippians.[72] As we shall see below in Section 3.3.2.c, for Paul and for the Philippians, such a view is cause indeed for mutual joy. For now, however, we should note that Paul is clearly tying his own experience of suffering – even unto death, if need be – to that of the Philippians in a very specific way: as partners in the work of the gospel.

3.2.2. The Philippians' Suffering (Phil. 1.27-30)

From 1.27-30 it is clear that the Philippian believers are also experiencing some form of adversity. Here, Paul exhorts them to live worthily of the gospel of Christ and to stand firm together in their faith (1.27), and not to be intimidated in any way by those who oppose them (μὴ πτυρόμενοι ἐν μηδενὶ ὑπὸ τῶν ἀντικειμένων, 1.28). Some commentators discern here the presence of pagan opposition: the Philippians' adversaries come from outside the Christian community, since they are destined for 'destruction' (ἀπώλεια, 1.28); and they are possibly linked with the Roman civic authorities, since they are of the same kind as those who confronted Paul when he first came to Philippi (1.30; see also Acts 16.19-39).[73] Others identify the ἀντικείμενοι with the Judaizers, since this is the group that Paul appears to be greatly concerned about elsewhere (3.2).[74] This latter proposal is much the weaker of the two: the context (1.27-30) indicates actual suffering, and it is difficult to imagine the Philippians putting tensions caused by the presence of false teachers into this category. Furthermore, πτύρω[75] is much too forceful a choice of term to use to describe a response to false teaching; that danger is surely one of being persuaded rather than being panicked.[76] However, whatever view one takes, the fact is that the Philippians are facing opposition; and according to Paul, the presence of this opposition is evidence (ἔνδειξις) of the Philippians' salvation (1.28). Paul provides a

---

[70] Hawthorne and Martin, *Philippians*, 149. Fee, *Philippians*, 253, argues that Paul nowhere in the larger context of the letter suggests (or even hints) that he expects his imprisonment to end in death: he might yearn that it did (1.23), but actually expects to be vindicated (1.19-20), and that out of divine necessity he will live, and revisit them (1.24-6; 2.24).

[71] Hawthorne and Martin, *Philippians*, 149. See also the similar conclusion reached by Fee, *Philippians*, 254.

[72] Bockmuehl, *Philippians*, 161–2; see also Reumann, *Philippians*, 415.

[73] E.g. Bockmuehl, *Philippians*, 100–1.

[74] E.g. Silva, *Philippians*, 82–3.

[75] Hapax legomenon in the New Testament. It occurs almost always in the passive, and means 'let oneself be intimidated, be frightened, terrified' (BDAG 895). Thus it can denote the panicked stampede of startled horses; Lightfoot, *Philippians*, 106.

[76] See Peter Oakes, *Philippians: From People to Letter*, SNTSMS 110 (Cambridge: Cambridge University Press, 2001), 81–2; also Fee, *Philippians*, 167 n.50.

theological précis of why this is so,[77] contextualizing their suffering in terms of their relationship with Christ (1.29) and with him (1.30).

In 1.29, Paul explains that to suffer for the sake of Christ is as much a gift of divine grace as it is to believe in Christ (ὅτι ὑμῖν ἐχαρίσθη τὸ ὑπὲρ Χριστοῦ, οὐ μόνον τὸ εἰς αὐτὸν πιστεύειν ἀλλὰ καὶ τὸ ὑπὲρ αὐτοῦ πάσχειν, 1.29). Paul's markedly Christological emphasis in describing their suffering[78] indicates that he is not offering encouragement about suffering in general. Rather, he is reminding believers that it is not just their lot but their privilege 'to suffer for the sake of Christ' (τὸ ὑπὲρ αὐτοῦ πάσχειν)[79] in a world that is hostile to God; indeed, it is precisely because their believing in Christ and their suffering for his sake have both been 'graciously given' (ἐχαρίσθη)[80] by God that they can be assured that whatever they are undergoing is a sure sign of their future salvation.[81]

Paul augments these comments on suffering by calling attention to the parallels between the Philippians' experiences and his own (1.30). Already in 1.7 he had referred to them as his co-participants in the grace of God – the grace manifested in his imprisonment and in the defence and propagation of the gospel (ἔν τε τοῖς δεσμοῖς μου καὶ ἐν τῇ ἀπολογίᾳ καὶ βεβαιώσει τοῦ εὐαγγελίου συγκοινωνούς μου τῆς χάριτος πάντας ὑμᾶς ὄντας); that he could address them in this way demonstrates their resolute solidarity with him in his gospel mission and hence also in his suffering. Now he explicitly correlates their suffering to his: they and he are engaged in the very same struggle (τὸν αὐτὸν ἀγῶνα ἔχοντες, 1.30). Since Paul is suffering at the hands of the Roman authorities, the implication may be that the Philippians are being troubled likewise by them.[82] Some commentators assert that the point of the comparison is not the similarity of the circumstances, but their shared theological rubric: they were all part of the one same apostolic ἀγών.[83] However, even if the parallel is limited to this level of abstraction (a view which I am not fully persuaded by), Paul's incorporation of the Philippian believers into his sphere of suffering demonstrates clearly that he sees them going through harsh treatment on behalf of the gospel, as he does. As such, a paradigmatic understanding of the narrative of 1.12-26 is surely in view (cf. 1.30: οἷον εἴδετε ἐν ἐμοὶ καὶ νῦν ἀκούετε ἐν ἐμοί). Also, their common experience for the sake of Christ represents something of the 'participation in his sufferings' of which Paul goes on to speak in 3.10.

---

[77] As Fee, *Philippians*, 170 n.59, observes, this is similar to what Paul does elsewhere, e.g. 1 Thess. 3.2-3; 2 Cor. 4.17-18; Rom. 5.3-4; 8.17-18.
[78] On this see further Fee, *Philippians*, 171, especially n.63.
[79] Hellerman, *Philippians*, 86, notes that ὑπέρ, when used with verbs of suffering, gives the reason for it; see also BDAG 1031.
[80] BDAG 1078: χαρίζομαι, 'to give freely as a favour, give graciously'.
[81] 'God has granted you the high privilege of suffering for Christ; this is the surest sign, that He looks upon you with favour'; Lightfoot, *Philippians*, 106.
[82] Fee, *Philippians*, 172.
[83] Joachim Gnilka, *Der Philipperbrief*, HTKNT 10.3 (Freiburg: Herder, 1976), 102; Hawthorne and Martin, *Philippians*, 77.

3.2.3. Christ's Suffering (Phil. 2.5-11)

We turn our attention, next, to the suffering of Christ. An extraordinary amount of scholarship has centred on the famous encomium to Christ of 2.5-11. Our interest, however, lies solely in how Paul uses this passage in its epistolary context to draw out the motif of suffering. As such, I am assuming that the text is a unity; moreover, concerns about its religious origin and authorship are of only secondary importance to my inquiry.[84] Even if Paul merely quotes the passage, Morna Hooker argues most reasonably that 'even if the material is non-Pauline, we may expect Paul himself to have interpreted and used it in a Pauline manner'.[85]

Paul launches into the hymn with an opening imperative that serves a double purpose: it both sums up the habits of reasoning and behaviour which he has just outlined to the Philippians at 2.2-4 and emphasizes the paradigmatic nature of the φρόνησις of Christ, the contours which he is about to describe: Τοῦτο φρονεῖτε ἐν ὑμῖν ὃ καὶ ἐν Χριστῷ Ἰησοῦ (2.5).[86] In no uncertain terms Paul exhorts his readers to adopt the very mindset of Christ[87] – the possession and practical expression of which will result in faithful living that is 'worthy of the gospel' (1.27) and the assurance of salvation in the face of opposition (1.28), as the Philippians apply their knowledge of the gospel to the specific circumstances that they find themselves in. As Fowl rightly observes, 'Within this scheme the story of Christ narrated in 2.6-11 functions as an exemplar, a concrete expression of a shared norm from which Paul and the Philippians can make analogical judgments about how they should live.'[88]

One primary way in which Christ functions as an exemplar in his φρόνησις lies in his willingness to embrace abasement, suffering, and even an ignominious death for the benefit of others (2.6-8). As a slave (δοῦλος, 2.7), Christ enters human history without rights or privileges; instead, he is the servant of all.[89] Clearly, 2.3-4 is in

---

[84] Many scholars, following the seminal work of Ernst Lohmeyer, *Kyrios Jesus: Eine Untersuchung zu Phil 2.5-11*, SHAW, Philosophisch-historische Klasse, Jahrgang 1927-8, 4. Abhandlung, 18 (Heidelberg: Carl Winter, 1928), take the passage to be a pre-Pauline hymn; see especially Ralph P. Martin, *Carmen Christi: Philippians 2.5-11 in Recent Interpretation and in the Setting of Early Christian Worship*, 2nd ed. (Grand Rapids, MI: Eerdmans, 1983). The various views concerning the interrelated issues of background and authorship are helpfully summarized in Fee, *Philippians*, 43-6.

[85] Morna D. Hooker, 'Philippians 2:6-11', in *Jesus und Paulus: Festschrift für Werner Georg Kümmel zum 70. Geburtstag*, ed. E. E. Ellis and E. Grässer (Göttingen: Vandenhoeck & Ruprecht, 1975), 152.

[86] Meeks argues that 'this letter's most comprehensive purpose is the shaping of a Christian *phronēsis*, a practical moral reasoning that is "conformed to [Christ's] death" in hope of his resurrection'; see 'Man from Heaven', 110.

[87] That the φρόνησις of Christ is also to be that of the Philippians is made even clearer by some further structural parallels that Paul composes: ἡγούμενοι (2.3) / ἡγήσατο (2.6b); μηδὲν ... μηδὲ ... ἀλλὰ (2.3), μὴ ... ἀλλὰ (2.4) / οὐχ ... ἀλλὰ (2.6b, 7a). As Dorothea Bertschmann notes, the presence of these parallels 'makes it even clearer that the point of correspondence between the Philippians and Christ which Paul wants to point out is one of *attitude*. The unselfish behaviour of Christ is contrasted with the potentially selfish behaviour of the Philippians and vice versa' (*Bowing before Christ – Nodding to the State?: Reading Paul Politically with Oliver O'Donovan and John Howard Yoder*, LNTS 502 (London: T&T Clark, 2014), 96, emphasis original).

[88] Stephen E. Fowl, 'Christology and Ethics in Philippians 2:5-11', in *Where Christology Began: Essays on Philippians 2*, ed. Ralph P. Martin and Brian J. Dodd (Louisville, KY: Westminster John Knox, 1998), 145-6.

[89] Only here in all his letters does Paul use δοῦλος to specify Christ. On the basis of certain conceptual and linguistic affinities, scholars often posit a connection between the δοῦλος here and the Suffering Servant of Isaiah; see e.g. N. T. Wright, *Paul and the Faithfulness of God* (London: SPCK, 2013),

view: Christ exhibits and indeed exemplifies, in superlative fashion, the spirit of self-abnegation and selflessness of mind and behaviour that the Philippian believers are urged to have. Among other things, then, the Christ poem highlights that the one who truly follows Christ will also willingly take on the role of a slave for the sake of others. As Fee concisely expresses it, 'The Philippians are to pursue the mindset of the one who as God emptied himself and as man humbled himself, even to death on the cross.'[90] The basic paradigmatic concern of the Christ poem, found in 2.6-8, thus has to do with 'the pattern of service provided by Jesus in his dying'.[91]

However, as Paul goes on also to emphasize, the death of Christ is not the end of the story. The poem concludes on a stunning note of exaltation, as Christ is bestowed with the title of κύριος and accorded universal worship (2.9-11). Paul thus affirms the rightness of the paradigm to which he has called the Philippians, while at the same time highlighting the eschatological vindication that also awaits them as followers of Christ – a thought that runs throughout the letter.[92]

3.2.4. The Examples of Paul's Co-workers (Phil. 2.19-30)

Next, in 2.19-30, Paul turns his attention to Timothy and Epaphroditus, casting them as examples for the Philippians.[93] Timothy is commended as one who is like-minded (οὐδένα γὰρ ἔχω ἰσόψυχον[94] (2.20a); lit. 'I have no one of equal soul') and who therefore, like Paul, manifests in his thinking a genuine concern for the welfare of the Philippians (2.20b-21); the context suggests that this concern has to do with how they are faring in the gospel mission in the face of growing opposition (1.27-30). Epaphroditus, too, is commended: though severely ill, he chose to put his life on the line in order to complete the task that was entrusted to him by the Philippian church, and thereby honour his commitment to them and to Paul (2.25-30).[95] As such, Paul instructs the Philippians to receive him 'in the Lord' with due honour and great joy

---

680-4, though some would demur, e.g. Reumann, *Philippians*, 360-1. However, whether or not such a link can be established, the key point remains the same: Christ voluntarily gives up his divine privileges in order to serve as a slave, descending from the highest status to the lowest (Bockmuehl, *Philippians*, 136).

[90] Fee, *Philippians*, 218 n.3.

[91] I. Howard Marshall, 'The Theology of Philippians', in *The Theology of the Shorter Pauline Letters*, by Karl P. Donfried and I. Howard Marshall (Cambridge: Cambridge University Press, 1993), 137.

[92] See Fee, *Philippians*, 219.

[93] Peter-Ben Smit rightly argues that although Timothy and Epaphroditus are introduced in the letter because Paul needs to tell the Philippians about his plans concerning the two men, it is reasonable to read his characterizations of them as *exempla*, since the surrounding context in which information is given about them is dominated by *exempla*: Paul has presented Christ's example as a model for emulation, and his own *periautological exemplum* is about to come in chapter 3 (*Paradigms of Being in Christ: A Study of the Epistle to the Philippians*, LNTS 476 (London: T&T Clark, 2013), 107-9). We would add that Paul has already described his attitude and actions in 1.12-26 in paradigmatic terms as well, via 1.30, as we saw earlier (see Section 3.2.2).

[94] Hapax legomenon in the New Testament. As Fee notes, attempts to give it a more precise nuance have not met with success (*Philippians*, 265 n.27).

[95] The grammar at 2.30 indicates that Paul is saying that Epaphroditus came close to death in his willingness to put his life at risk in order to fulfil his mission. The main clause (ὅτι διὰ τὸ ἔργον Χριστοῦ μέχρι θανάτου ἤγγισεν) is modified by a participial clause (παραβολευσάμενος τῇ ψυχῇ) that is connected to a purpose clause (ἵνα ἀναπληρώσῃ τὸ ὑμῶν ὑστέρημα τῆς πρός με λειτουργίας).

(2.29), as one who has risked his life 'for the work of Christ' and been willing to give up his life on behalf of another.

In the latter part of chapter 2, then, the Philippian church is presented with three examples of the self-renouncing φρόνησις that Christ has and which is enjoined (2.5). There is Paul, who regards his life and ministry as an offering that accompanies the Philippians' sacrifice. Timothy has served faithfully in the work of the gospel and shown a selfless concern for them. Finally, Epaphroditus's devotion to the service of Christ has put his life in jeopardy. In two of these examples (Paul's and Epaphroditus's) suffering for the sake of the gospel is described in explicit terms; in Timothy's ministry, it is implicit – but is not unreasonable, on the basis of the evidence, to read into his example a willingness to suffer likewise for the same cause.

3.2.5. Conclusion

The motif of suffering is threaded right through the letter. However, this suffering – that which Paul is himself undergoing and gives voice to, and which he also describes in the lives of others – is not some generalized notion of mental or physical distress. It refers specifically to suffering that is borne for the sake of Christ and his gospel. Paul sets up this suffering as a correlative of faith in Christ: both are 'graciously given' (1.29) by God and are therefore integral to his divine purposes in the life of the believer. Such suffering is evidence of the Philippians' salvation, because the God who has granted to them the gift of salvation has also graced them to be Christ's people in the world, which entails suffering for his sake. As Paul goes on to demonstrate in 2.5-11, Christ's own death and resurrection prefigures and provides the warrant for the experiences of those who follow him. Thus believers are to live (and suffer) for the sake of Christ who himself lived (and suffered) for the sake of this world; in this way, they – as with their Lord – move from present suffering to future glorification.

Paul thus looks to Christ as the ultimate paradigm: in possessing a totally selfless mindset and by being willing to suffer and even die for the sake of another, Christ advances the gospel and receives eschatological vindication. By setting up himself, Timothy, and Epaphroditus as exemplars, Paul teaches the Philippians that those who pattern their thinking and behaviour after that of Christ will likewise advance his gospel and receive that same prize at the Parousia. Suffering for the sake of Christ is thus the harbinger of resurrection glory. However, the picture of suffering as Paul paints it is not yet complete. For while it is the lot of the believer in this age to bear suffering for the sake of Christ, along with that suffering there can also be the experience of joy in Christ – which in a very profound way signals the believer's entry into the eschatological practice of life in the age to come.[96] Hence, it is not surprising that in the course of the letter suffering is often articulated with joy. We will now investigate in detail Paul's account of joy in Philippians.

---

[96] Wright, 'Joy', 54–5.

3.3. Joy: Exegetical Considerations

3.3.1. Joy in Partnership in the Gospel (Phil. 1.3-5; 2.28-30; 4.10-19)

Paul's first mention of joy occurs within the introductory thanksgiving, where he tells the Philippians that he thanks God each time he remembers them (1.3), and that his prayers for them are always made 'with joy' (μετὰ χαρᾶς, 1.4). These thankful remembrances and the prayers of joy that accompany them have their foundation ἐπὶ τῇ κοινωνίᾳ ὑμῶν εἰς[97] τὸ εὐαγγέλιον ἀπὸ τῆς πρώτης ἡμέρας ἄχρι τοῦ νῦν (1.5); Paul's joy thus reflects a profound partnership in the spread of the gospel that he has shared with the Philippian church since the beginning of his missionary endeavours in Macedonia.[98] In the New Testament the phrase κοινωνία … εἰς τὸ εὐαγγέλιον is unique to Philippians; Paul's use of it here defines his relationship with them early on and removes all doubt as to the character of their partnership: it is a partnership in the gospel's advancement.[99] This partnership is certainly 'spiritual' in nature (in that it has its basis in their shared theological understanding of God and his work),[100] but it also finds expression in concrete terms, both in the task of evangelism and in the matter of finances.[101] More than once, the Philippians have sent pecuniary aid to Paul; by so doing they have demonstrated their backing of Paul's ministry and their solidarity with him in his troubles (4.14-16). Most recently, their ongoing support has been shown again in their sending of Epaphroditus to Paul with a monetary gift and, presumably, also to be of general help to him (4.18; cf. 2.25-30).

Apparently very touched by the Philippians' gift – which he regards as a renewed and concrete expression of their concern for his welfare – Paul expresses great joy (Ἐχάρην[102] δὲ ἐν κυρίῳ μεγάλως ὅτι ἤδη ποτὲ ἀνεθάλετε[103] τὸ ὑπὲρ ἐμοῦ φρονεῖν, 4.10).[104] Interestingly, this is the only place where Paul quantifies his own experience

---

[97] The Greek εἰς has here the sense of 'unto', i.e. 'with the furtherance of the gospel in view'; Fee, *Philippians*, 81 n.46.
[98] Jennings, *Price*, 4, and *passim*, has recently argued that Paul wrote Philippians with the sole intent of persuading the church to maintain its partnership with him in the gospel mission. For Jennings, 'Paul presents χαίρω/χαρά as the character or response to the advance of the gospel' (157).
[99] Peterman, *Gift*, 100–1.
[100] See 1.7, 'my partners in God's grace'; 2.1, 'fellowship in the Spirit'; 3.10, 'fellowship of his [Christ's] sufferings'.
[101] See Stephen C. Barton, 'Spirituality and the Emotions in Early Christianity: The Case of Joy', in *The Bible and Spirituality: Exploratory Essays in Reading Scripture Spiritually*, ed. Andrew T. Lincoln, J. Gordon McConville, and Lloyd K. Pietersen (Eugene, OR: Cascade Books, 2013), 185.
[102] On whether ἐχάρην is a genuine or epistolary aorist, see especially the discussion in Fee, *Philippians*, 428 n.17. I am persuaded by Fee's arguments for the former interpretation.
[103] Grammatically the unusual verb ἀναθάλλω (lit. 'to bloom again'; hapax legomenon in the New Testament) can be either intransitive, taking τὸ ὑπὲρ ἐμοῦ φρονεῖν as an accusative of reference (hence, 'you flourished again in your concern for me'), or transitive, taking τὸ ὑπὲρ ἐμοῦ φρονεῖν as its direct object ('you caused your concern for me to flourish again'); both meanings are possible here and the difference is insignificant. See BDAG 63; Fee, *Philippians*, 429.
[104] Many have found it strange that Paul acknowledges in 4.10-20 gifts from Philippi without actually expressing thanks by using a verb like εὐχαριστέω; the various explanations offered for Paul's *danklose Danke* are documented in Reumann, *Philippians*, 685–8. Among them is the view of Wolfgang Schenk, *Die Philipperbriefe des Paulus* (Stuttgart: Kohlhammer, 1984), 43, that joy and thanks occupy the same semantic field; against this Peterman, *Gift*, 128–9, argues that Schenk relies too heavily on the etymological connection between εὐχαριστέω and χαίρω and on the fact

of joy: the adverb μεγάλως appears only here in the New Testament, and its very uniqueness intensifies what he is saying about the depth of his feelings.[105] It is clear that the concern (φρονεῖν) of the Philippians and the way it continues to find tangible expression draw from him immense joy. Peterman notes that the same expression 'to rejoice greatly' is found in various papyri (e.g. P.Oxy. 1676 and 3356), where it serves to confirm the bond between the parties, and is typically used in connection with the receipt of a letter. In his view, Paul's expression of joy here fits well with such expressions because it is based on contact with, and good news from, the Philippians, even though, in more specific terms, his joy is linked not so much to the receipt of a letter but to their remembrance of him.[106] However, even so – and consistent with the exhortations of 3.1 and 4.4 (which we shall examine below, at Section 3.3.3) – Paul's joy is first and foremost ἐν κυρίῳ. Although the immediate occasion for Paul's joy has to do with the Philippian church's concern for him, its ultimate basis is 'in the Lord', since, among other things, it is he who has begun the good work in the Philippians (1.6) that has led to their work of partnership with him.[107] Also, we should not read any hint of reproach in Paul's words here in 4.10: the adverbial expression ἤδη ποτέ points to the conclusion of the hiatus in the Philippians' giving rather than to any insinuation that it was long overdue[108] – a point of view that is surely confirmed by the clause that follows, ἐφ' ᾧ καὶ ἐφρονεῖτε, ἠκαιρεῖσθε δέ.[109]

This joy, then, has nothing to do with the satisfaction of his physical or financial needs, as 4.11a (οὐχ ὅτι καθ' ὑστέρησιν λέγω) makes clear.[110] The reason (γάρ) that he gives for not speaking to the Philippians of these needs is that he has learned to be content in whatever circumstance he might find himself in (ἐγὼ γὰρ ἔμαθον[111] ἐν οἷς

---

that thanks to God in the Old Testament often takes the form of an expression of joy. Peterman's own view (*Gift*, 74–83) – that first-century social conventions between friends did not call for a statement of thanks – has won some scholarly endorsement (see e.g. Reumann, *Philippians*, 686–8), but is not without its detractors; see recently Briones, *Financial Policy*, 124–8, who argues that Paul's so-called thankless thanks actually reflects a theological conviction that only God occupies the position of benefactor.

[105] Hawthorne and Martin, *Philippians*, 261.
[106] Peterman, *Gift*, 129.
[107] I. Howard Marshall, *The Epistle to the Philippians*, Epworth Commentaries (London: Epworth, 1991), 12, rightly draws attention to the recurrent theme in Philippians of Christian growth being simultaneously ascribed to God's activity and to enrolling the believer's own efforts. As such, as Bockmuehl, *Philippians*, 64, expresses it (in reference to 1.6): 'God's good work in these Christians, then, is to make them active participants in the gospel and its benefits. This participation includes, but goes far beyond, their material contribution to Paul's ministry.'
[108] Contra F. F. Bruce, 'St. Paul in Macedonia. 3. The Philippian Correspondence', *BJRL* 63 (1980–1): 274, who claims that the modern reader 'finds it difficult not to discern a nuance of "And high time too!"' in these words.
[109] The imperfect tenses of ἐφρονεῖτε and ἠκαιρεῖσθε, together with the intensive καί (which emphasizes the φρονέω repeated from the previous clause; on this see Thrall, *Greek Particles*, 90), imply strongly that the Philippians had all along been concerned for Paul's welfare but faced an ongoing lack of opportunity to do something about it; see Fee, *Philippians*, 430. For hypotheses concerning the circumstances surrounding this lack of opportunity, see Hellerman, *Philippians*, 256.
[110] ὑστέρησιν stems from ὑστέρησις, 'the condition of lacking that which is essential' (BDAG 1044). Hence Hellerman, *Philippians*, 258, rightly argues that Paul's joy is not that of a poor man whose need has been met, but of 'a man whose Christian family has found renewed opportunity to tangibly express its Christlike mind-set of concern for him'.
[111] Most likely a constative aorist, used of completed experiences; see Bockmuehl, *Philippians*, 260.

εἰμι αὐτάρκης εἶναι, 4.11b). Long exegetical tradition has interpreted this clause in the light of Stoicism.[112] On this reading, the adjective αὐτάρκης[113] is freighted with Stoic introspection: the truly contented person, being sufficient unto himself in all things, is one whose state of inner tranquillity is never disturbed by the vicissitudes of life and the actions of others.[114] Other scholars, however, argue that since αὐτάρκεια was also used widely to denote contentment in a general, non-technical sense, we cannot be sure that Paul was consciously drawing on Stoic sources.[115] Malherbe locates Paul's language outside the technical Stoic idea of αὐτάρκεια altogether, placing it instead in the context of ancient discussions of friendship.[116]

However, it seems to me that a careful consideration of the context of Paul's language can help to settle the matter. When Paul later in 4.12 reveals that he has 'learned the secret'[117] of having plenty and being in need and so forth, he is actually making the claim that he is indifferent to matters which are outside the sphere of one's control. This is because his contentment now wholly derives from his relationship with Christ, who empowers him to face any challenge (πάντα ἰσχύω ἐν τῷ ἐνδυναμοῦντί με, 4.13). As we have earlier seen, the concept of the 'indifferents' (ἀδιάφορα), or external goods, is important in Stoic thought. Virtue alone is the only good and thus the one thing which fits the bill of making up the Stoic *telos*; as such, virtue alone is self-sufficient and all else is indifferent. It seems likely that Paul adopts the same ideas here; the parallels with Stoicism are too clear to be put aside.[118] Paul is αὐτάρκης: his personal situation with regard to material goods is a matter of complete indifference to him. However, his is not the cultivated imperturbability of the Stoic sage, who, by relying on his own inner resources, has trained himself to face any situation with equanimity. Instead, Paul's self-sufficiency has its basis in a special kind of strength and empowering that originates from a profound, ongoing sense of connection with Christ. As Fee deftly

---

[112] See e.g. Lightfoot, *Philippians*, 163–4; Rudolf Bultmann, *Primitive Christianity in Its Contemporary Setting* (Cleveland, OH: Collins, 1956), 138, 185–6; and more recently Fee, *Philippians*, 431–2.
[113] αὐτάρκης appears only here in the New Testament; its cognate noun (αὐτάρκεια) twice, in 2 Cor. 9.8 and 1 Tim. 6.6.
[114] Many commentators note the similarity of Paul's language at 4.11 with that of Seneca's, e.g. in *Vit. beat.* 6.2: 'the happy man is content with his present lot, no matter what it is, and is reconciled to his circumstances'; see e.g. Fee, *Philippians*, 432 n.37; J. N. Sevenster, *Paul and Seneca*, NovTSup 4 (Leiden: Brill, 1961), 113–14. Cf. Epictetus, *Diatr.* 4.7.14: 'Wherever I go it will be well with me, for here where I am it was well with me, not because of my location, but because of my judgments, and these I shall carry away with me; … and with the possession of them I am content, wherever I be and whatever I do' (quoted by Fee, *Philippians*, 432 n.37).
[115] E.g. Silva, *Philippians*, 204.
[116] Abraham J. Malherbe, 'Paul's Self-Sufficiency (Philippians 4:11)', in *Friendship, Flattery, and Frankness of Speech: Studies in Friendship in the New Testament World*, NovTSup 82 (Leiden: Brill, 1996), 125–39.
[117] The verb μεμύημαι (lit. 'I have been initiated'; hapax in the New Testament) came from the vocabulary of the mystery religions and was used in relation to initiatory rites, but like other mystery terminology also acquired more general meanings (BDAG 660). However, as Bockmuehl observes, 'Initiation in a metaphorical sense may well still be intended, in which case Paul's point is that Christian contentment remains unintelligible to those outside and can only be "learned" from the God of peace' (*Philippians*, 261).
[118] So Troels Engberg-Pedersen, 'Stoicism in Philippians', in *Paul in His Hellenistic Context*, ed. Troels Engberg-Pedersen (Edinburgh: T&T Clark, 1994), 270, referring to Cicero, *Fin.* 3.23–6, 32. See also his *Paul and the Stoics* (Edinburgh: T&T Clark, 2000), 101; and Bockmuehl, *Philippians*, 260–1.

puts it, 'He [Paul] turns "self-sufficiency" into "contentment" because of his "Christ-sufficiency."'[119] Paul's self-sufficiency is wholly constituted by his relationship to Christ.

Only after qualifying his opening statement of joy against possible misunderstanding, and after elaborating why the Philippians' ministering to his material lack was *not* the cause of his joy, does Paul proceed to explain further the question of what it *is* about in 4.14-18 – thereby returning to his earlier train of thought. At 4.10, as we have seen, Paul had joyfully received the Philippians' gift, seeing it as tangible proof of the revival of their care for him. He now hastens to reassure them that he is by no means ungrateful for their generosity (πλήν[120] καλῶς ἐποιήσατε[121], 4.14), and that his remarks in 4.11-13 should not be taken to imply that he regards their gift as unnecessary (4.15-18). However, Paul does more than just these things. He continues to contextualize what he says within a candid but carefully calibrated affirmation of the special partnership that he shares with the Philippian Christians, an affirmation in which he combines his appreciation for their gift with assertions about his financial independence.

Since their gift was aimed at meeting his material needs while in prison – though he has no actual need of the gift – it stands as evidence of their being partners with him in his affliction (συγκοινωνήσαντές μου τῇ θλίψει, 4.14).[122] At the same time, the Philippians are partners with him in the gospel mission through their financial contributions to his work (ἐν ἀρχῇ τοῦ εὐαγγελίου, ὅτε ἐξῆλθον ἀπὸ Μακεδονίας, οὐδεμία μοι ἐκκλησία ἐκοινώνησεν εἰς λόγον δόσεως καὶ λήμψεως εἰ μὴ ὑμεῖς μόνοι ... καὶ ἅπαξ καὶ δὶς εἰς τὴν χρείαν μοι ἐπέμψατε, 4.15-16). Paul's description of the κοινωνία in which he and the Philippians jointly participate recalls and adds to what he has earlier said (1.5, 7; 2.1). His language is now couched in terms of 'giving and receiving' (δόσις καὶ λήμψις) – commercial parlance that in the first century was also regularly co-opted to refer to the mutual obligations inherent to contexts of friendship and social reciprocity.[123] It is almost certain that Paul is drawing on familiar notions and conventions of friendship to acknowledge the recent gift from the Philippians and to express his gratitude to them.[124]

---

[119] Fee, *Philippians*, 434.

[120] With πλήν ('nevertheless'), Paul does two things: he underscores for the Philippians that he could just as well have done without their contributions, and returns to the task of affirming them for their care and concern; see Hawthorne and Martin, *Philippians*, 267. Thrall, *Greek Particles*, 21, claims that in 4.14 (in relation to 4.11) we have the clearest example in Paul of πλήν functioning as a balancing adversative (used to contrast two truths of divergent tendency).

[121] Some commentators suggest that the expression καλῶς ἐποιήσατε (lit. 'you did well') is the closest that Paul comes to saying 'thank you'; see e.g. Bockmuehl, *Philippians*, 262 (citing F. F. Bruce, *Philippians*, NIBCNT (Peabody, MA: Hendrickson, 1989), 154). Fee, *Philippians*, 438 n.7, offers the American slang 'you did good' as a translation which captures better the sense of the Greek.

[122] Fee, *Philippians*, 438 n.8, notes that the redundant συν prefix of the modal participle συγκοινωνήσαντες 'emphasizes their participation together with him *in his affliction*' (emphasis original); cf. Lightfoot, *Philippians*, 164 (cited by Fee): 'It was not the actual pecuniary relief, so much as the sympathy and companionship in his sorrow, that the apostle valued.' That they were suffering as he was has already been intimated at 1.29-30.

[123] On δόσις καὶ λήμψις in the Greco-Roman world, see Peterman, *Gift*, 51–65; Marshall, *Enmity*, 157–64. The term also appears in Jewish-Hellenistic writings, both in its financial sense (e.g. Sir. 42.7) and metaphorically of a socially reciprocal relationship (e.g. Sir. 41.21).

[124] So e.g. Fee, *Philippians*, 442–5. See also 446–7, where Fee offers two perspicacious reasons why Paul even sees the need to tell the Philippians what (by his own admission) they well know, and why he emphasizes their being the only church to have entered into this kind of partnership with him.

With another οὐχ ὅτι (4.17; cf. 4.11),[125] Paul immediately qualifies what he has just said. Aware that the Philippians might misinterpret his words as a request for more aid, he tells them in no uncertain terms, still using accounting terminology, that what he 'strives for'[126] is not any gift of theirs (οὐχ ὅτι ἐπιζητῶ τὸ δόμα, 4.17a), but rather, 'the interest that accrues to your account' (ἐπιζητῶ τὸν καρπὸν[127] τὸν πλεονάζοντα εἰς λόγον ὑμῶν, 4.17b). Its meaning, as 4.18 goes on to show, is theological: the 'fruit' is not their enhanced standing vis-à-vis Paul, but their practical praise offering to God.[128] Using metaphorical language (ὀσμὴν εὐωδίας, θυσίαν δεκτήν) drawn from the LXX, Paul likens the Philippians' gift to an aromatic sacrifice that is pleasing to God.[129] Paul then closes his thoughts in this section with an assurance that would have been very striking to his readers, because of the way it radicalized the social conventions that structured relationships. Here in 4.19, a third party, God, is explicitly introduced as an integral member of the partnership that Paul shares with them; it is God, not Paul, who will supply (πληρώσει[130]) *all* the Philippians' needs (πᾶσαν χρείαν ὑμῶν), that is, whether these needs are associated with material lack (cf. 2 Cor. 8.1-2) or spiritual concerns (which are mentioned throughout the letter).[131] This divine provision is not according to the balanced reciprocity of a Greco-Roman friendship, but κατὰ τὸ πλοῦτος αὐτοῦ ἐν δόξῃ ἐν Χριστῷ Ἰησοῦ. Paul's partnership with the Philippians is not predicated on the social expressions of mutuality that one would expect, but instead upon their common participation in a heavenly citizenship (3.20) in which all notions and norms of giving and receiving are relativized. For Paul, this partnership – specifically, what it consists in and how it is lived out – forms the basis for his joy here.

That Paul expects the Philippians also to find joy in this gospel partnership is seen in his instructions concerning Epaphroditus's return. To be sure, this occasion is, naturally, already cause for rejoicing (2.28). However, Paul makes it clear that joy is to come also because Epaphroditus has exemplified selfless service both to him and them in relation to the work of the gospel (2.29-30).

> First, as often happens between friends, one partner in the friendship takes delight in reminding the other how that one has expressed friendship in the past; Paul's point, then, is that their gift represents yet another in their long and laudatory history in this regard. Second, in keeping with social convention, Paul is most likely expressing his thanks indirectly, but even more tellingly, by rehearsing in this manner the history of his benefitting from their generosity.

[125] In both 4.11 and 4.17, οὐχ ὅτι is used to introduce a correction. See further Schenk, *Philipperbriefe*, 44–6, for the linguistic and syntactical parallels in two verses.

[126] ἐπιζητῶ: in Paul, only here (twice) and at Rom. 11.7; an intensified form of ζητέω, meaning here 'to be seriously interested in or have a strong desire for' (BDAG 371).

[127] Lit. 'fruit' (appearing also at 1.11, 22); used here metaphorically in a commercial sense (Hellerman, *Philippians*, 266).

[128] Bockmuehl, *Philippians*, 265–6. Bockmuehl also highlights the plausibility of 'fruit' being read in eschatological terms too; i.e. relating to the future reckoning on the 'day of Jesus Christ' (1.6; 2.16) when the Philippian gift will accrue not only to their own account, but they themselves will be Paul's 'joy and crown' (4.1; cf. 2.16), i.e. his eschatological reward.

[129] On this see especially Reumann, *Philippians*, 667–70.

[130] I follow the majority of recent commentators in preferring the better attested future indicative πληρώσει rather than the aorist optative πληρώσαι. However, even if the optative is original, Paul's note of assurance is not significantly diminished. For discussion see Reumann, *Philippians*, 670–1.

[131] See e.g. Fee, *Philippians*, 452–3; contra those who understand πᾶσαν χρείαν in eschatological terms (e.g. Ralph P. Martin, *Philippians*, NCB (London: Oliphants, 1976), 169), or in present material terms (e.g. Hawthorne and Martin, *Philippians*, 273).

Summarizing our findings thus far: for Paul, joy arises because of his partnership with the Philippians in the advance of the gospel – a partnership that is at once both spiritual and material. Most recently, he has had cause to find particular joy on the occasion of the receipt of a financial gift from the Philippians. However, since Paul derives his sense of contentment solely from his relationship with Christ, the actual ground for his joy does not consist in any pecuniary benefit that this gift might bring; instead, it consists in what the gift represents – a renewal of the Philippians' concern for his welfare, and an offering to God that is pleasing to him. In a sense, then, along with Peterman we may infer that Paul's joy has to do with 'delight in the spiritual maturity of the Philippians', since their display of concern (φρονεῖν) in 4.10 is in keeping with the Christian mindset (φρόνησις) that he has delineated throughout the letter (especially at 2.2, 5; cf. 4.14 in which Paul pays tribute to their willingness to share in his afflictions).[132] Furthermore, given that such Christian maturity – and the right thinking and action that mark it – have their basis in God's work, Paul sees his joy over the Philippians' concern as being 'in the Lord' (4.10).

3.3.2. Joy in the Gospel's Advancement

3.3.2.a. Joy and the Progress of the Gospel in Rome (Phil. 1.15-18)

Paul's joy, however, also has a dimension that is predicated on the spread of the gospel itself. In 1.18, the apostle rejoices because Christ is being preached through the evangelistic efforts of the believers in Rome; this is the 'progress' (προκοπή) of the gospel that he has earlier referred to at 1.12. The motives of these believers, as we have noted, are mixed; among these fellow Christians are those who are quite willing to let further distress fall upon Paul (1.17; see also Section 3.2.1.b). However, this is clearly a secondary concern for him. Even if there is duplicity rather than sincerity in the ministry of some of the other evangelists, what matters is that Christ is being preached; as long as this happens, Paul will rejoice (Τί γάρ; πλὴν ὅτι παντὶ τρόπῳ, εἴτε προφάσει εἴτε ἀληθείᾳ, Χριστὸς καταγγέλλεται, καὶ ἐν τούτῳ χαίρω, 1.18).[133] Moreover, in expressing this singular joy in the advancement of the gospel rather than in self-advancement, Paul demonstrates to the Philippians the kind of mindset and practical behaviour that he wants them to imitate (see 3.17 and 4.9). In Christ, Paul's ambition and desire have now found a true and satisfying goal – one in which all pain and gain are reconfigured in the light of God's call upon his life (3.7-14).[134] The gospel of Christ is being increasingly heard in Rome; for Paul, this fact alone is cause for joy.

---

[132] Peterman, *Gift*, 128; see especially n.42.
[133] Fee, *Philippians*, 124, notes, 'Without doubt the newly emboldened, fearless preaching of the gospel by his friends was cause for joy under any circumstances. What he wants the Philippians to hear is that the preaching which intended as one of its side effects to afflict him is also a cause for joy.'
[134] See Bockmuehl, *Philippians*, 81.

3.3.2.b. Joy and the Progress of the Gospel in the Philippians' Lives (Phil. 1.18-26; 2.1-4; 4.1)

Paul's reflection on the matter of the progress of the gospel, which began with evangelism, ends on a related note: the progress of the gospel in the lives of the Philippians themselves. Despite what he is presently undergoing, Paul is confident that he will remain alive and continue his ministry (1.19-26), the immediate focus of which concerns the Philippians' 'progress and joy in the faith' (εἰς τὴν ὑμῶν προκοπὴν καὶ χαρὰν τῆς πίστεως, 1.25)[135] – which is almost certainly the progress of the gospel (1.12) now applied specifically to the Philippians.[136] The deliberate co-location of the themes of progress and joy in relation to faith is instructive: we may say that progress denotes the objective aspect of faith, while joy (and, we as shall later discuss, mutual joy) is its appropriation in the experience of the believer, because it emerges from a renewed outlook on the world that is made possible only through genuine progress in the faith. These twin themes of progress and joy, which have characterized Paul's description of his own situation since 1.12, will also guide his concern for the believers throughout the rest of the letter. Progress in the faith and joy in the faith are to go hand in hand.[137]

However, Paul's joy over the Philippians has yet to reach full flower. Despite the enthusiastic affirmations with which he begins the letter at 1.3-11, it is clear from 2.1-4 that his joy over them is curtailed by what he perceives to be a lack of love and harmony among them. Even so, there is insufficient evidence to conclude that disunity was at this point in time already a dire problem in the church.[138] Only at 4.2-3 is there an explicit mention of a division within the church. Hence Paul's language in chapter 2 may merely reflect his identification of disunity as a potentially serious risk[139] – something that he hopes to nip in the bud through an impassioned yet tactful appeal that presupposes the secure bonds of friendship and mutuality that exist between him and the Philippians. This strongly personal appeal – πληρώσατε[140] μου τὴν χαρὰν (2.2) – is far from being egotistical and self-serving;[141] instead, it reveals much about the nature of the relationship between Paul and his church. His heart and apostleship are deeply bound up with the well-being of his converts. The Philippians' progress in

---

[135] With regard to εἰς τὴν ὑμῶν προκοπὴν καὶ χαρὰν τῆς πίστεως (1.25): most commentators see the single preposition and article (εἰς τὴν) as holding the two nouns together as one thought unit, while ὑμῶν and the genitive τῆς πίστεως qualify both nouns. On this reading, the phrase is understood as 'for your progress and joy in the faith', with τῆς πίστεως taken as a genitive of reference and ἡ πίστις used to denote the content of belief, i.e. the faith of the gospel (cf. 1.27); see Fee, *Philippians*, 153. For alternative interpretations see Reumann, *Philippians*, 227–9.

[136] προκοπή at 1.12 and at 1.25 form an *inclusio*.

[137] Bockmuehl, *Philippians*, 94.

[138] *Pace* Davorin Peterlin, *Paul's Letter to the Philippians in the Light of Disunity in the Church*, NovTSup 79 (Leiden: Brill, 1995), 59–65 and *passim*.

[139] Bockmuehl, *Philippians*, 108 (following G. B. Caird, *Paul's Letters from Prison*, New Clarendon Bible (Oxford: Oxford University Press, 1976), 129), argues that such a risk is heightened in Paul's mind because tensions in the church in Rome have become evident (1.15, 17; 2.20-1).

[140] This is best understood in the sense of 'to bring to completion that which was already begun' (Reumann, *Philippians*, 304).

[141] *Pace* Robert T. Fortna, 'Philippians: Paul's Most Egocentric Letter', in *The Conversation Continues: Studies in Paul and John in Honor of J. Louis Martyn*, ed. Robert T. Fortna and Beverly R. Gaventa (Nashville, TN: Abingdon, 1990), 220–34, who produces a caricatured reading of Paul that is based more on modern psychologizing than on the realities of the text.

the faith, expressed in unity for the sake of the gospel (see 1.25, 27) and in like-minded, harmonious relationships in which the interests of others have priority (2.1-4), will fill up his own measure of joy (2.2) – and given their bonds of friendship, that in itself should be incentive enough for them to pursue it.[142]

To be sure, as we have noted earlier, Paul *already* experiences joy because of the Philippians (1.4; 4.10); indeed, he expresses delight in, and further desire for, their progress in the faith (1.3-11; 25). Now, through the like-mindedness and unity of soul of the Philippians (2.2-4), Paul's joy will be enlarged – even though his joy will reach its final goal only on the 'day of Christ', as he has first intimated at 1.6. At the Parousia, it will be evident that Paul has not laboured in vain (2.16), and the Philippians will be his cause for joy; hence, by metonymy, they are already now his 'joy and crown' (χαρὰ καὶ στέφανός μου, 4.1).[143]

3.3.2.c. Mutual Joy in the Face of Suffering (Phil. 2.17-18)

The subject of joy appears again at 2.17-18. Here, while at the same time referring to his suffering, Paul enjoins the Philippians to rejoice with him – a thought that has been anticipated at 1.18. As we have earlier seen, Paul regards his present circumstances as a form of libation – the giving of himself and his apostolic experiences as a sacrifice to God to complement the sacrificial service of the Philippians: Ἀλλὰ εἰ καὶ σπένδομαι ἐπὶ τῇ θυσίᾳ καὶ λειτουργίᾳ[144] τῆς πίστεως ὑμῶν,[145] χαίρω καὶ συγχαίρω πᾶσιν ὑμῖν· (2.17). The imagery makes it clear that Paul's focus of attention is not on himself, however, but on the Philippians: theirs is the main offering that is offered to God, and Paul is more than willing to expend his ministry – and indeed, his very life – on their behalf if one thing remains to make that sacrificial service acceptable.

Paul's joy therefore consists in the fact that he continues to make a contribution to the sacrificial service that his Philippian converts offer, just as he has previously identified their faith (1.4-5) and progress in the gospel (1.25) as a cause for joy.[146] Specifically, he takes joy in the fact that his own sacrifice will complete their act of offering and make it perfectly acceptable to God.[147] Interestingly, Paul also rejoices *with* the Philippians: συγχαίρω πᾶσιν ὑμῖν (2.17); this strongly suggests that they were themselves already rejoicing in their own participation and sacrificial service

---

[142] Bockmuehl, *Philippians*, 108.

[143] Since στέφανος in the New Testament often has eschatological connotations, and since the parallel passage (1 Thess. 2.19) is used of the Parousia, many commentators take both χαρά and στέφανος to refer to the future; see Hellerman, *Philippians*, 226-7.

[144] On τῇ θυσίᾳ καὶ λειτουργίᾳ ('sacrificial service') see also Section 3.2.1.c. It seems likely that Paul sees this sacrificial service in comprehensive terms, i.e. to refer to all that the Philippians have done as an expression of their faith; contra e.g. Hansen, *Philippians*, 188–90, who limits the notion to just 'sacrificial financial support'.

[145] τῆς πίστεως ὑμῶν qualifies the Philippians' sacrificial service. I follow most commentators in taking the genitive τῆς πίστεως as subjective (i.e. 'your sacrificial service, prompted by your faith'); for discussion see Reumann, *Philippians*, 148.

[146] Bockmuehl, *Philippians*, 162.

[147] Fee captures Paul's thought well: 'But if indeed my present struggle represents a kind of drink offering to go along with your own suffering on behalf of the gospel, then I rejoice over that'; *Philippians*, 255.

in the gospel mission. Indeed, evidence of their joy comes from several ingredients in that sacrificial service: their prayers, their pecuniary support, and the sending of Epaphroditus to him. Paul rejoices in the Philippians' joyful sacrificial service for the sake of the gospel. The social dimension of joy is clearly apparent.

The emphasis on mutual joy continues in 2.18 where Paul instructs them: τὸ δὲ αὐτὸ καὶ ὑμεῖς χαίρετε καὶ συγχαίρετέ μοι. The resultant fourfold (συγ)χαίρειν produces an awkward redundancy for some, but I suggest that the most natural way to understand Paul's thrust, factoring in the τὸ δὲ αὐτό, is to see it as some kind of pleonastic parallelism: 'Just as I take joy in my service, and I rejoice with you in yours, so you must take joy in your service, and rejoice with me in mine.' Fee is correct to say that Paul's emphasis is that 'first, he and they rejoice on their own accounts for the privilege of serving the gospel, even in the midst of great adversity, and second that they do so mutually, as they have done so much else mutually'.[148]

It is on this highly striking note of shared joy – with the emphatic repetition of verbs to do with joy (χαίρω, χαίρετε) and mutuality in joy (συγχαίρω, συγχαίρετε) – that Paul brings his thoughts here to a close. The Philippians are beginning to make 'progress and joy in the faith' (1.25), and there is no doubt at all that these interrelated ideals are crucial things which Paul wishes to nurture in their lives. In particular, here at least, the aspect of joy is accentuated: it is the 'experienced' concomitant of genuine progress in the Christian life, and thus capable of flourishing even in times of deprivation and suffering. Moreover, joy for Paul is not just an emotion belonging to the individual; it is equally a 'social' emotion – the Philippians are to express their joy corporately, and they are also to share in Paul's joy, just as he shares in theirs. These emphases are reflected in Paul's handling of the theme of joy. As Fee notes, up to 2.17-18 every mention of joy, except in 1.25, has had to do with Paul himself; but a subtle but noticeable shift towards the Philippians now takes place (Paul's own 'rejoicing' occurs only once more in the letter, at 4.10). What began in 1.25 as concern for the Philippians' 'progress and *joy* in the faith' is now expressed with imperatival force in 2.18 (an emphasis that will appear again later at 3.1 and 4.4). Significantly, the first appearance of joy as an imperative is intertwined with Paul's joy, and also found in the context of affliction and opposition.[149] Our conclusion must be that joy – and *mutual* joy – even in the face of suffering is surely the goal of Paul's preceding instructions and exhortations. As Paul goes on to highlight, that such joy is possible in the first place is because it is predicated on the work of Christ, both past and future.

3.3.3. Joy 'in the Lord': The Eschatological Horizon (Phil. 3.1; 4.4-9)

In the final analysis, for Paul, joy is to be found 'in the Lord'. At 3.1, Paul picks up the earlier χαίρετε from 2.18 and adds ἐν κυρίῳ to it. The imperative therefore explicitly recalls his earlier mentions of joy but is now couched in explicitly theological terms. As with the Psalmists whose language Paul is borrowing (there are numerous references, e.g. Ps. 32.11; 33.21; 35.9), the Lord is both the ground and object of joy.[150] This

---

[148] Fee, *Philippians*, 256.
[149] Fee, *Philippians*, 256.
[150] Fee, *Philippians*, 291 n.27, observes that the LXX translators consistently avoided χαίρω for this idiom in the Psalms, using instead either ἀγαλλιάω or εὐφραίνω. Paul, on the other hand, uses

perspective on joy is to form the framework, both theological and experiential, in which the Philippians are to understand Paul's injunctions in this section,[151] and indeed in the entire epistle. This joy is neither a psyched-up satisfaction in feeling miserable nor a superficial triumphalism that blithely disregards the realities of one's circumstances. What Paul is describing is a joy that emerges *in spite of* the presence of suffering, not because of it; he is inculcating in the Philippians a perspective on joy in which suffering can be seen in the light of the bigger picture of God's working in and through adversity to achieve his purposes in Christ. Indeed, it is Christ who in his service, suffering, and exaltation provides the example and assurance of future victory and glory for the believer (2.5-11; 3.20-1). Christ, then, is the source and occasion of the Philippians' joy – a joy that begins here on earth and reaches its final fulfilment in the eschaton.

These theologically charged ideas are reinforced at 4.4 where Paul begins a set of final imperatives (4.4-9); here, he repeats the interim conclusion at 3.1 not once, but twice, and adds the important qualifier 'always': Χαίρετε ἐν κυρίῳ πάντοτε· πάλιν ἐρῶ, χαίρετε (4.4). Just as Paul has in 3.1 reinforced his prior exhortations to joy in the letter, so here at 4.4 he underlines – doubly – that previous encouragement as standing at the very heart of his message to the Philippians.[152] Once again, some sort of cosmetic happiness that appears when things go well is not in view here. The joy that Paul speaks of can be had πάντοτε, 'because it depends not on changing circumstances but on the one who does not change'.[153] The imperative to rejoice is followed by two further exhortations which are related to this joy.[154]

The first of the two is to have an attitude of forbearance towards others: τὸ ἐπιεικὲς[155] ὑμῶν γνωσθήτω πᾶσιν ἀνθρώποις (4.5a). In the midst of their present adversity, the

---

the latter terms only once (2 Cor. 2.2), not counting the LXX citiations, preferring χαίρω and its cognates. Fee concludes that given the flexible way this idiom is handled in the LXX and given Paul's linguistic preferences, χαίρετε ἐν κυρίῳ is best understood as Paul's own rendering of this Old Testament idiom.

I follow Fee in taking ἐν κυρίῳ to denote that the Lord is *both* the object and ground of joy (*Philippians*, 291); similarly, Bockmuehl, *Philippians*, 60, thinks that the fact that joy is 'in the Lord' indicates that it arises 'from belonging to him who is both its source and its object'. Some scholars, however, here distinguish – unnecessarily, in my opinion – between the two senses: e.g. Bruce, *Philippians*, 76, who takes it (and the Psalms) to indicate that the Lord is the object of the believer's rejoicing, and Fritz Neugebauer, *In Christus: Eine Untersuchung Zum Paulinischen Glaubensverständnis* (Göttingen: Vandenhoeck & Ruprecht, 1961), 144 n.17 (against any Old Testament derivation) who emphasizes the incorporative sense of being 'in the Lord', i.e. that it is union with the Lord that provides the ground for rejoicing.

[151] Fee, *Philippians*, 291, is correct in saying that this framework serves as Paul's first antidote to the Philippians' being taken in by the possible attractiveness of the Judaizing option (on which see Fee, *Philippians*, 293–303).
[152] Bockmuehl, *Philippians*, 243–4.
[153] Silva, *Philippians*, 194.
[154] The asyndetic injunctions in 4.4-6 (χαίρετε … γνωσθήτω … μεριμνᾶτε) have led some scholars to look beyond syntax to semantics to connect the imperatives, with differing conclusions (see discussion in Reumann, *Philippians*, 634; Reumann himself takes them as 'aphoristic dicta but linked at points'). I follow Fee, who reads them as sharing ground with the 'threefold expression of Jewish piety – rejoicing in the Lord, prayer, and thanksgiving – which are basic to the Psalter' (*Philippians*, 402–3). It is noteworthy that these three things form also that familiar Pauline triad of practices that mark the mature believer (see 1.3-4; 1 Thess. 3.9-10; 5.16-18; also Col. 1.9-12).
[155] ἐπιεικές is from the adjective ἐπιεικής ('not insisting on every right of letter of law or custom, yielding, gentle, kind, courteous, tolerant', BDAG 371); this range of meanings is reflected in the

Philippians' unbridled joy in the Lord is to be accompanied by a noticeable quality of gentle forbearance towards one another and towards all; this seems to include the patient bearing of abuse from those who are making life difficult for them.[156] More precisely, the context suggests that ἐπιείκεια here denotes 'a humble, patient steadfastness, which is able to submit to injustice, disgrace and maltreatment without hatred or malice, trusting God in spite of it all'.[157] The second exhortation relates to the believer's prayer life: μηδὲν μεριμνᾶτε, ἀλλ' ἐν παντὶ τῇ προσευχῇ καὶ τῇ δεήσει μετὰ εὐχαριστίας τὰ αἰτήματα ὑμῶν γνωριζέσθω πρὸς τὸν θεόν (4.6). Only in prayer about 'everything' can they be anxious about 'nothing': the comprehensive positive πᾶς sets up a contrast with the comprehensive negative μηδείς.[158] The result of heeding this exhortation is the promise[159] of God's peace,[160] bestowed on his people and standing guard over their hearts and minds (4.7).[161]

Lying in the middle of the exhortations of 4.4-6 is a terse, important formulation about the 'nearness' of Christ: ὁ κύριος ἐγγύς (5b). Its meaning is slightly ambiguous, as ἐγγύς can be understood either temporally or spatially;[162] furthermore, its function in relation to the surrounding instructions is in dispute because there is no grammatical connection to them.[163] I follow many modern exegetes in taking the nearness of the Lord in a temporal sense, and therefore understand ὁ κύριος ἐγγύς to mean the

---

varied English translations of the word. It appears elsewhere in the Paulines only in 1 Tim. 3.3 and Tit. 3.2; Paul uses the noun ἐπιείκεια alongside πραΰτης at 2 Cor. 10.1 to denote Christ's attitude of humility and gentleness.

[156] As Hellerman, *Philippians*, 237, observes, the word group is often used to describe the superior party, e.g. Felix (Acts 24.4), Christ (2 Cor. 10.1), and slave owners (1 Pet. 2.1); so some see Paul here enjoining the Philippians to exhibit ἐπιείκεια in the sense of 'magnanimity', since the Lord is at hand (so e.g. Hawthorne and Martin, *Philippians*, 244). However, other uses of the word group describe the weaker party (e.g. Wis. 2.19; Tit. 3.2). Hellerman is correct to argue that the context indicates that the latter situation is the better description of the Philippians' circumstances, as those who face serious opposition.

Silva makes the interesting suggestion that Paul is here in 4.5a most likely recalling 2.3-4 (where he had instructed the Philippians to place the interests of others above their own). Christian joy is not inward-looking, and the believer is to find godly satisfaction in focusing on others and their needs; in this way joy can be learnt, and the call to show forbearance towards others can be seen as a way of reinforcing Christian joy (*Philippians*, 194). However, a proactive consideration of the interests of others does not seem to be a basic semantic component of ἐπιείκεια.

[157] R. Lievestad, "'The Meekness and Gentleness of Christ" II Cor. X.1', *NTS* 13 (1965–6): 158.
[158] See Ulrich B. Müller, *Der Brief des Paulus an die Philipper*, THKNT 11.1 (Leipzig: Evangelische Verlagsanstalt, 1993), 198.
[159] As Müller, *Brief*, rightly emphasizes, this is a promise, not a wish.
[160] ἡ εἰρήνη τοῦ θεοῦ appears only here in the New Testament, though a similar expression, ἡ εἰρήνη τοῦ Χριστοῦ, is found in Col. 3.15. The genitive is subjective, and the phrase is therefore best understood as 'the peace that God himself has and guarantees' (Karl Barth, *The Epistle to the Philippians*, trans. James W. Leitch (Louisville, KY: Westminster John Knox, 2002), 123), rather than signifying an inward peace of the soul that comes from God (as many older commentators think, e.g. M. R. Vincent, *A Critical and Exegetical Commentary on the Epistles to the Philippians and to Philemon*, ICC (Edinburgh: T&T Clark, 1897), 135).
[161] Recent commentators rightly draw attention to the fact that 4.4-7 'reflects the conjunction between individual and corporate piety' (Fee, *Philippians*, 403).
[162] See further Hellerman, *Philippians*, 237–8.
[163] I take ὁ κύριος ἐγγύς to ground both v. 5a and v. 6; so e.g. Fee, *Philippians*, 407–8; Silva, *Philippians*, 194–5.

imminent Parousia of Christ.[164] On this interpretation, the return of the Lord provides eschatological motivation to respond confidently to all the apostolic injunctions of 4.4-6.[165] It is this sure hope that provides the essential underpinning of Paul's exhortations here and hence also of Paul's approach to joy. Earlier in the letter, Paul had spoken of his joyful confidence in the fact of his own final vindication before God: Ἀλλὰ καὶ χαρήσομαι, οἶδα γὰρ ὅτι τοῦτό μοι ἀποβήσεται εἰς σωτηρίαν[166] (1.18-19). He now enjoins the Philippians, who are suffering as he is, to keep their sight on that same eschatological horizon, and thereby find their joy 'in the Lord' (3.1; 4.4).

3.4. The Basis and Function of Joy

Our exegetical spadework has revealed that the theme of joy runs right through Philippians. Far from being merely incidental, joy often occupies a central place in Paul's thinking and certainly integral to much of the hortatory material in the letter. Noteworthy is the fact that Paul's call to joyful living emerges from the privations of imprisonment; this in itself is significant because it emphasizes to the believers his ability to rise above the thoroughly adverse circumstances in which he finds himself and to experience joy in spite of the hardships and opprobrium that he has had to bear. However, in the letter, joy is inflected in other important ways as well – so much so that it may be said that what Paul offers to the Philippians is careful, deliberate instruction on how to live the Christian life victoriously while in the very midst of suffering and affliction: it is a 'pedagogy in joy'.[167] Indeed, Paul's indefatigable efforts both to exemplify this joy himself and to inculcate and guide – and even regulate – its expression within the Philippian church seem to suggest that he views joy as being crucial to the establishment of early Christian culture. The question is: why is so much weight put on joy as the goal of Paul's instructions?

3.4.1. The Theological Basis of Joy

That Paul's promoting of joy in the Philippian Christians is practicable and, indeed, makes good sense in the first place is because God's work of redemption – the death and resurrection of God's Christ, the coming of the Spirit, and the certainty of the Parousia – has meant that new terms of engagement with the world are now available.

---

[164] See Reumann, *Philippians*, 613. Fee however thinks both meanings are probably in view (*Philippians*, 407–8). Bockmuehl opines that it is theologically pointless to choose between the two interpretations, because the evidence in the New Testament is that each one in any case implies the other (*Philippians*, 246).

[165] So correctly J. Ernst, who argues that for Paul, awaiting the Parousia is a key paraenetic motif; *Die Briefe an die Philipper, an Philemon, an die Kolossser, an die Epheser*, RNT (Regensburg: Pustet, 1974), 115. See 1.6, 10; 2.16; 3.20-1.

[166] τοῦτό μοι ἀποβήσεται εἰς σωτηρίαν is Job 13.16a (LXX) verbatim. The majority of scholars argue that σωτηρία in Paul always refers, directly or indirectly, to eschatological salvation and vindication, and never to physical deliverance; that eschatological salvation and vindication are in view here seems highly likely in light of the Job citation, so e.g. Bockmuehl, *Philippians*, 82–3. Hawthorne and Martin's advocacy of the latter view is a minority position (*Philippians*, 49–50).

[167] Being the expression used by Barton, 'Spirituality', 185.

For the believer, it is no longer only visible, corporeal manifestations of reality that feed his consciousness and govern his sense of existence; instead, his metaphysical horizon is to be definitively reshaped by eschatological reality. This has, as its corollary, a profound effect on his mental and emotional engagement with the world around him. A radical reconfiguration of his sense and conception of identity, value, meaning, and purpose has taken place.

As such, to rejoice in the face of suffering is to reject any notion that one's sense of well-being depends on one's circumstances, for the present age no longer has the last word. Paul regards joy as being for the believer's taking, because it is grounded in the confident assurance that in the end all will be made right through God's work in Christ (Phil. 3.20-1; cf. 1 Cor. 15.24-8). Putting it a different way: this revised hermeneutic for all of life that reads in it the possibility of joy at all times is rooted in the transfiguration of meaning that emerges from the believer's participation in the Christological pattern of dying and rising (Phil. 3.10-11).[168] The basis of Christian joy is therefore intrinsically theological; this joy simultaneously signals and celebrates the profound connection between the believer and God and his work in the world, past, present, and future. For the believer, then, the experience of suffering for the sake of the gospel throws into sharp relief the painful tensions that result from a life lived both in this world and the one to come. However, joy is attainable in spite of these tensions, because the presence of such suffering is proof of – and a precursor to – eschatological salvation (Phil. 1.27-30).

In the letter to the Philippians, the theological basis of the believer's joy is made most explicit in 3.1 and 4.4, where the summons to rejoice is articulated to the fact that this joy is 'in the Lord', and similarly in 4.10, where Paul expresses much joy 'in the Lord' over the Philippians' renewed concern for him (though ἐν κυρίῳ is absent at 1.18 and 2.17-18, the verbs for 'rejoicing' in these verses surely stand in this same theological correlation). It is precisely because Christian joy has a firm theological basis that it can be called forth with imperatival force.

Closely related to the theological underpinning of joy is the emphasis on thinking and on the mind that runs through Paul's letter. We have noted earlier the significance of the numerous appearances of verbs that relate to the disposition or activity of the mind (φρονέω, ἡγέομαι, σκοπέω, and λογίζομαι), the abundance of 'knowledge' vocabulary, and the use of military and athletic imagery to flesh out the notion of mental tenacity. It is right thinking about Christian truth, and the possession of a mindset that reflects the character and disposition of Christ, that will help the Philippians to overcome the suffering and trials that they are going through – and to do so with joy. Quite clearly, for Paul, there is a significant cognitive dimension to living the Christian life well.

Interestingly, the cognitive aspect of the Pauline reality framework that makes joy possible is in some respects parallel to that of the Stoic account of affective response, but, as we shall see, at a fundamental level the two schemes are completely different. A recapitulation of the Stoic theory is helpful at this juncture. For the Stoics, joy

---

[168] See Colleen Shantz, '"I Have Learned to Be Content?": Happiness According to St. Paul', in *The Bible and the Pursuit of Happiness: What the Old and New Testaments Teach Us about the Good Life*, ed. Brent Strawn (New York: Oxford University Press, 2012), 198–9.

belongs to a select group of emotions called the *eupatheiai*, which are acceptable, non-culpable ways of experiencing affect. The wise person – whose perfected rationality mirrors the universal reason that governs the cosmos, and who therefore always acts in conformity with nature and its ends – would regularly be subject to the *eupatheiai*. Such a person would not be overwhelmed emotionally by any circumstance, whether (in the eyes of the ordinary person) beneficial or baneful. This is because the wise person has redirected his capacity to perceive and ascribe value correctly through his judgements and affective responses, so that they are appropriate for a rational human being. At the heart of Stoic ethics is the doctrine that virtue alone is good, vice alone bad; everything else is an indifferent. The wise person is incapable of being emotionally impacted by anything that others would regard as a present evil. To be sure, like any other person, in life he encounters suffering (and other circumstances that an ordinary person would consider as bad) – but he would not count them as bad. Suffering is not for him a present evil, because vice is the only evil there is; the Stoic sage is, by definition, free of vice and its effects. He would not mistake an indifferent for genuine goods and evils, which is to say, virtue and vice.

Instead, the wise person would experience the *eupatheiai* on a regular basis. He would be able to experience joy often, because the perfection of reason produces virtue and the actions that are the immediate practical expression of such a state of mind – virtue and virtuous acts being the genuine goods towards which the wise person's rational impulses are directed and in relation to which he consistently forms fully accurate, veridical judgements. So Seneca, as we have seen, speaks of a 'boundless joy' that emanates from deep within the wise man because he delights in his own inner resources (*Vit. beat.* 3.4, 4.4), a joy that causes one's soul to be 'happy and confident, lifted above every circumstance' (*Ep.* 23.3). The wise maintain a steady joy both at their virtuous condition and its practical expression, and remain unaffected by externals – the things that lie beyond their sphere of control. Stoic joy is therefore premised on a belief about the rational ordering of the world and its inhabitants.

Like the Stoics, Paul has a cognitive interest in what makes joy reasonable. In his scheme, right thinking can also produce a profound sense of joy that is able to transcend all adversity. However, Paul's ideological framework has a totally different basis; for him, joy is grounded in a proper understanding of – and, one might add, a participation in – God's continuing action in the world. Paul's inaugurated eschatology speaks of a world in which God's perfect order is yet to be fully established: the πολίτευμα of believers is in heaven, from which they expect the arrival of Christ, who will transfigure and glorify their bodies through the same power that will subject all things to his rule (Phil. 3.20-1; cf. 2.11). Therefore, though there is an already present reality that governs the lives of Christians, their orientation is one of forward anticipation, as 3.12-14 has already made very clear,[169] because the 'day' is not yet here (1.6, 10; 2.16).

However, this forward-looking thrust makes present joy possible, but also precarious: there is a danger that a severe or prolonged ordeal of some sort might severely weaken, or even totally extinguish, the believer's joy. Paul's solution seems to be threefold. First, throughout the letter, and in different ways, he stresses the importance

---

[169] See Bockmuehl, *Philippians*, 235.

of developing and maintaining a Christian mindset – one that demonstrates right thinking, maturity, and perseverance and, above all, is patterned after Christ's. This mindset is thus to be a common mindset: one that consists in the Philippians having the same outlook on the world, on the work of God in the world, and on one's responsibilities in light of these truths.[170] Second, he himself models such a mindset for the Philippians, and shows them what Christian joy looks like, even in the presence of great adversity. Third, he calls for the corporate reinforcement of this joy, knowing that the Philippians' faith would be buttressed by the mutual encouragement that shared joy can bring. For Paul, joy very clearly also has a social dimension – and as we shall see, this distinctive Christian sociality not only protects and promotes joy but also helps to complete it.

3.4.2. The Social Character and Function of Joy

While the ground of joy in Philippians is theological, its expression is manifestly social. Joy here is not simply a matter of the emotions construed as private experiences and expressions that occur within the individual's thought-world and remain embedded within its confines, important though this aspect is. The way in which Paul describes his own joy and how it comes about shows beyond any doubt that it is dependent – and to no small degree – on the attitudes and actions of the Philippians. Furthermore, this joy is not to be contained within the individual, but is to be enacted and shared. In other words, for Paul, joy is very much a matter of sociality and public performance; it is both socially generated and socially expressed.

The sociality of joy in Philippians is made evident several times during the course of the letter. We note, first, that the ongoing, flourishing mission partnership between Paul and the Philippian church is a key ingredient in the production of joy. In chapter 1, Paul speaks of the joy that accompanies his prayers of thanksgiving for his Philippian brethren – a joy that arises from their faithful partnership with him in the work of evangelism. In chapter 4, we learn that this partnership includes also an important financial dimension: the Philippian believers have, on a number of separate occasions, sent money to Paul to help him to meet his needs. They have recently despatched Epaphroditus to Paul with another monetary gift, which he receives with much joy, though (as we have discussed earlier) he hastens to inform them that his joy comes not so much from the economic value of the gift but from the fact that it is a concrete expression of their ongoing concern for his welfare and interest in his ministry.

Second, and related to the above, Paul speaks of a joy that he and the Philippian believers are to have because of their common commitment to the gospel mission. Paul's and the Philippians' evangelistic efforts take place against a backdrop of suffering. Yet, even in the midst of great adversity, it is apparent that both Paul and the Philippians have been able to take joy in the privilege of serving the gospel. What is even more striking is that this joy is also a *shared* joy: Paul rejoices in his own service to God and also in that of the Philippians, and he expects them likewise to rejoice in his service even as they rejoice together in their own (2.17-18). Quite clearly, the joy

---

[170] Lynn H. Cohick, *Philippians*, SGBC (Grand Rapids, MI: Zondervan, 2013), 89.

that Paul refers to here does not belong only to the realm of personal experience. It is also very much a mutual, social joy that stems from the fact that in the very face of suffering both Paul and the Philippians believers are giving themselves wholeheartedly to God in sacrificial service, and gladdened by the salutary example of the other. It is, I think, not unreasonable to suggest that such a joy would have a strongly mutually reinforcing quality.

Another depiction of a social basis for joy in the letter occurs at 2.1-4. Here, Paul attempts to galvanize his readers towards a vision of solidarity and like-minded relationships within the church. The achieving of this ideal state of affairs would induce an even fuller flowering of the joy that he already experiences from his evangelistic partnership with them and investment in their lives. To be sure, the Philippians are already his 'joy and crown' (4.1) – but growth in unity of mind and spirit among the believers would intensify Paul's sense of joy and indeed 'complete' it (2.2). Once again, the sociality of joy comes to the fore: joy is now directly correlated to the quality of the relationships within the church, or, to be more specific, to the extent to which the Philippians display to each other Christ's attitudes of humility and self-abnegation (2.2-5), and thereby '"think" in a manner appropriate to where they *are*, which is "in Christ Jesus"'.[171] For Paul, a unified church brings deep joy, because unity is a clear indicator of the presence in the believers of a Christ-like φρόνησις, and thus also a marker of their maturity in the faith.

Finally, we note that joy is a matter also of public performance: it is to be *socially expressed*. This is already evident in Paul's exhortation to mutual joy in the face of suffering at 2.17-18 (discussed earlier); and certainly, Paul himself models it through the ways in which he describes and communicates his own joy throughout the letter. Paul also expects the Philippians to welcome with joy the returning Epaphroditus, who has faithfully served both him and them (2.28-9). We meet this notion again at 3.1 and 4.4, where he summons again the believers at Philippi to joy 'in the Lord' in spite of the trials and pressures through which they are called to pass. Their joy is to be visible – and not only that, but visibly celebrated.[172] This is, again, a shared joy – certainly premised on a particular view of salvation history, but also at once a joy that is indispensably social in its orientation and manifestation.

Indeed, to a degree that would have made his Stoic contemporaries rather nervous, the way Paul describes his joy shows that it is intentionally bound up with the outlook and behaviour of others. Specifically, Paul's joy is generated in relationship with the Philippian believers, for the expression of warm concern and friendship that their gift to him represents brings him immense delight and comfort; indeed, it is obvious that he desires their φρονεῖν more than the material expression of it.[173] Also, the Philippians' unity and like-mindedness, and their continuing progress in the faith, are for Paul rich sources of joy, as is their committed and faithful partnership with him in the work of

---

[171] Francis B. Watson, 'Barth's *Philippians* as Theological Exegesis', in Barth, *Philippians*, xlix.

[172] As Barth (commenting on Phil. 4.4-5) puts it, 'And perhaps we are to think at the same time of the fact that the Lord is near: the time of rejoicing is at the door – see that all men notice it!' (*Philippians*, 121).

[173] Cf. 2 Cor. 12.14, where Paul tells the Corinthians: οὐ γὰρ ζητῶ τὰ ὑμῶν ἀλλὰ ὑμᾶς.

the gospel. This joy, however, is not to be his alone; Paul expects the Philippians to exhibit in their demeanour a lively, mutual joy.

All this indicates that Paul's thinking – and that which he also wants to see among his Christian brethren – is far removed from the relational self-sufficiency that marks the Stoic sage. Paul's attitude, as a Stoic would understand and interpret it, involves the evaluative construal of an external object (the actions of fellow Christians) as being beneficial in some way for oneself, such that one should reach out for it. However, the Stoic wise person, whose rationality has been perfected, would not allow an external object to affect in any way his state of complete inner equanimity. Furthermore, Paul's joy is not eupathic joy, which derives from one's virtuous condition and its practical expression, and is untouched by the presence of externals. The implication is that in the Stoic schema, Paul's joy would most likely be classified instead as one of the four generic passions – ἡδονή (delight), the opinion that some present thing is a good of such a sort that one should be elated about it – and, as such, to be extirpated, since the passions followed directly upon faulty judgements of one's impressions.

The comparison of Pauline joy with Stoic thinking about emotion throws the sociality of Christian joy into sharp relief, and leads to some rather intriguing questions. First, Paul is obviously *not* self-sufficient at a relational level (in the sense of not needing any encouragement and care); he certainly values – and indeed, deeply so – the ongoing, thoughtful concern of his friends at Philippi. Would he still rejoice if they had forgotten about him and his needs, if they had not responded at this time and in such a manner? Second, all these human relationships are, in a sense, embedded in the common relationship with Christ that believers share. For Paul, to what extent could this relationship with Christ substitute for his relationship with the Philippians when it came to the engendering of joy? Third, the presence of Christ serves to embolden and empower Paul's ministry, even without material supply. Could Paul's work still be carried out effectively and his mission be accomplished, without interaction and fellowship with other believers? And finally, what about the Philippian church – would it continue to grow without the vivifying presence of joy, expressed at both the individual and corporate level?

Our answers to these questions can be at best only speculative. However, from what we have elucidated, Paul's attitude towards joy seems to show that in certain very important ways its promotion and social flourishing are seen to be integral to the health of the fledgling Christian community at Philippi and to the success of the gospel mission, and also to his personal well-being.

3.5. Conclusion

The evidence before us indicates that joy, for Paul, is a crucially important emotional corollary of certain key theological values in the Christian life. More specifically, we may say that Paul sees joy as the believer's deep-seated, embodied, and enacted pleasure that emerges through his or her discernment of, and active participation in, God's eschatological renewal of creation and creature in the light of the work of Christ and the coming of the Spirit.[174] The good news is that Christ has come, and that he is coming again; Christian joy is grounded in these realities and therefore profoundly connected to the advancement of this good news and to the growth in faith of those who accept it. To be joyful is thus to believe rightly in the truths that the gospel of Christ proclaims; and the implication is that the quality of a person's joy is in some sense an indication of the extent to which these truths have actually taken hold of the person's thinking[175] – and thereby shaped his or her Christian identity, outlook in life, and sense of mission.

Moreover, since the basis of joy consists in God's eschatological act of renewing the world, the presence of suffering in the here and now does not need to cripple the believer's joy. Paul does not shy away from telling the Philippians that suffering for the sake of the gospel is part of what it means to follow Christ. For just as it was for Christ, lying behind such suffering is the promise of ultimate vindication. Therefore suffering becomes, in a way, a theological crucible in which the melding together of pain and a renewed, Christ-focused perspective on such pain produces the possibility of a deeper and richer understanding of the Christian life, as the believer learns to fix his gaze on the eschatological horizon, thereby becoming increasingly cognizant of the hope – and accompanying joy – that are also present realities.[176] Joy is thus an experience of revitalization – one that is 'so profound, so touched by transcendence, that it makes possible the transcendence of suffering, grief, shame, and all that is death-dealing, even and especially death itself'.[177] Putting these things together, it seems entirely reasonable to conclude that for Paul joy is to be regarded as a primary, and perpetual, orientation within the life of the believer (cf. Rom. 14.17).[178]

In addition, Paul clearly regards joy as being also a social phenomenon: socially generated in relationship with fellow believers, and socially displayed through expressions of mutual joy that reflect and reinforce the fact that each believer's story is part of a larger narrative, one in which God has the final word. We may therefore say that joy is the collective manifestation of salvation and spiritual transformation in the lives of individual believers. Throughout the letter, Paul places joy within the context of his special relationship with the Philippians: he repeatedly makes clear his desire that they know and share his joy, and so attain a greater fullness of joy in their own lives. The mutuality and sociality of joy are thus foregrounded; it would certainly seem that Paul sees joy as being a critical ingredient in the establishment of a distinctively Christian culture, in view of its powerful potential to structure both personal sensibility and public behaviour. One might even say that here in Philippians Paul regards joy as a responsibility of the believer, because of the far-reaching ways

---

[174] See also Barton, 'Spirituality', 183.
[175] As Wright, 'Joy', 61, observes, 'Not to celebrate, not to express joy in the lordship of the crucified and risen Jesus, would be tacitly to acknowledge that one did not really believe.'
[176] To use Nicholas Lash's apt expression: joy is 'the felt form of Christian hope' (*Seeing in the Dark* (London: Darton, Longman & Todd, 2005), 201; quoted in Barton, 'Spirituality', 190 n.40).
[177] Barton, 'Spirituality', 191.
[178] Paul writes elsewhere that joy is a fruit of the Spirit and thus serves as evidence of the Spirit's presence and ministry in the life of the believer (Gal. 5.22).

in which joy expresses key aspects of Christian belief and is thus constitutive of the emotional ethos of a community that is truly Christian.

All this helps to explain why Paul takes such great pains to call forth joy from the Philippians by making it the subject of repeated pedagogy, as well as to exemplify it in his own life and ministry. It is interesting to note that like the Stoics, Paul develops a process to inculcate Christian joy: Paul knows that it can be taught (and conversely, also learned), modelled, requested, and also reinforced through the solidarity of shared feelings. And like the Stoics, in his understanding of joy Paul assumes that some kind of grand ordering of the cosmos is at work. But here any superficial similarities end, not least because Pauline joy and Stoic joy are premised on entirely different ideological realities. For in the final analysis Paul derives his joy from his relationship with his Lord, and from his relationship with others who also call Christ Lord. True Christian joy will emerge when these relationships are what they should be.

4

Grief in 1 Thessalonians

4.1. The Background to 1 Thessalonians

4.1.1. Overview

Paul's first letter to the church at Thessalonica was most likely written from Corinth,[1] several months after his abrupt flight from Thessalonica, where his evangelistic mission had fomented much hostility (Acts 17.1-10; 1 Thess. 1.6). Following Paul's departure, the opposition against the fledgling church that he had planted intensified. Deeply concerned about the well-being of his new converts (1 Thess. 3.5) – not only because they were suffering (2.14-16; 3.3-4) but also because he had been forced to leave them before he had finished instructing them in their newfound faith (2.17; 3.10) – and repeatedly frustrated in his efforts to return to Thessalonica to see them again (2.18), Paul sent Timothy to them to strengthen them (3.1-5). Timothy has since returned with a favourable report – of the believers' faith and love, their good memories of Paul, and desire to see him again (3.6).

In response, Paul writes this warm pastoral letter to the Thessalonians to encourage them to continue to stand firm in the Lord (3.8) in the midst of the severe adversity they are experiencing. The missive gives the impression that Paul is generally pleased with the progress of his converts; there are no major issues identified for censure, nor doctrinal aberrations for correction. Paul does provide teaching on certain aspects of their corporate ethics (in various parts of chapters 4–5), but the main problem that he concerns himself with has to do with the Thessalonians' eschatological outlook (4.13–5.11): the recent deaths of some of their number have brought on immense grief – which, for Paul, indicates that their understanding of the resurrection of believers at the return of Christ is incomplete. Hence Paul takes time to help the Thessalonians deal with their grief; and as we shall see, the consolation he offers is firmly rooted in his theology, and has profound personal and social implications for his addressees.

---

[1] I follow the traditional view of the provenance of the letter; see e.g. Abraham J. Malherbe, *The Letters to the Thessalonians*, AB 32B (New Haven, CT: Yale University Press, 2000), 72–3. For an evaluation of alternative views see Malherbe, *Thessalonians*, 71–4; Robert Jewett, *The Thessalonian Correspondence: Pauline Rhetoric and Millenarian Piety* (Philadelphia, PA: Fortress, 1986), 49–60.

4.1.2. Literary Integrity

There is an overwhelming scholarly consensus concerning Paul's authorship of 1 Thessalonians as a whole. However, the literary integrity of the letter has on occasion been challenged by arguments that it is interpolated, or a compilation of a number of Pauline letters. The various compilation theories do not have a following and may be set aside.[2] In relation to the matter of interpolation, only 1 Thess. 2.13-16 has garnered some limited support that it did not emerge from Paul's hand.[3] The contemporary debate was given its impetus during the second half of the twentieth century, primarily through the work of Birger Pearson.[4]

In sum, Pearson marshals three types of arguments – historical, theological, and form-critical – to make the case that 1 Thess. 2.13-16 is a post-Pauline interpolation. In regard to matters of history, Pearson contends that 2.16c is about the destruction of Jerusalem in 70 CE, as the aorist ἔφθασεν refers to a past event of wrath, with εἰς τέλος underscoring its catastrophic finality.[5] He also finds it problematic that in 2.14 the Thessalonians' sufferings are compared with those of the churches in Judea at the hands of the Jews, because there is no evidence of any significant persecution of the Judean Christians before the first Jewish-Roman War.[6] Pearson reinforces these arguments with the claim that there are theological incompatibilities between 2.15-16 and Paul's thoughts elsewhere – principally the fact that it is impossible to ascribe to Paul the anti-Semitic invective of 2.15-16 when in Rom. 9-11 he speaks far more positively of the Jews.[7] Finally, Pearson argues that a form-critical investigation substantiates the fact that 2.13-16 is a later interpolation. Structurally, 2.11-12 introduces the apostolic parousia, but this actually begins only at 2.17. The appearance at 2.13 of a second thanksgiving (indicated by εὐχαριστοῦμεν) is not only an anomaly in Paul's letters but also interrupts his flow of thought.[8]

However, Pearson's arguments have been refuted. It has been shown that the past event that the ἔφθασεν of 2.16c refers to could be any of several calamitous situations preceding Paul's writing of the letter;[9] while, in relation to 2.14, scholars have demonstrated that the Judean Christians did suffer at the hands of their fellow Jews before the outbreak of the Jewish-Roman War.[10] Pearson's more theologically grounded assertions have also been called into question. For example, Jeffrey Weima argues that Paul's positive statements about the Jews in Rom. 9-11 must not overshadow the

---

[2] See the discussion in Charles A. Wanamaker, *The Epistles to the Thessalonians*, NIGTC (Grand Rapids, MI: Eerdmans, 1990), 34–5. Among contemporary commentators, only Earl J. Richard, *First and Second Thessalonians*, SP 11 (Collegeville, PA: Liturgical, 1995), 11–19, espouses a compilation theory.
[3] See Todd D. Still, *Conflict at Thessalonica: A Pauline Church and Its Neighbours*, JSNTSup 183 (Sheffield: Sheffield Academic Press, 1999), 24 n.2; Jeffrey A. D. Weima, *1-2 Thessalonians*, BECNT (Grand Rapids, MI: Baker, 2014), 41–2.
[4] Birger A. Pearson, '1 Thessalonians 2:13–16: A Deutero-Pauline Interpolation', *HTR* 64 (1971): 79–94.
[5] Pearson, 'Interpolation', 82–3.
[6] Pearson, 'Interpolation', 86–7.
[7] Pearson, 'Interpolation', 85–6.
[8] Pearson, 'Interpolation', 88–91.
[9] See Weima, *Thessalonians*, 43.
[10] Weima, *Thessalonians*, 43–4.

many negative statements that he also makes about them in the same passage.[11] The form-critical basis for regarding 1 Thess. 2.13-16 as an interpolation has also been undermined; several scholars have shown that the passage is integral to the letter.[12] Furthermore, even if 2.13 can be properly classified as a thanksgiving, Paul consistently demonstrates in his letters that he is never straitjacketed by epistolary conventions; he is certainly capable of adding a second thanksgiving if it suits his purposes for writing.[13]

In conclusion, the arguments put forward for the inauthenticity of 2.13-16 are not persuasive. There are compelling reasons to regard the text as being part of the letter – a conclusion that is only strengthened by the fact that it is found within every extant manuscript of 1 Thessalonians. My study will therefore proceed on the assumption of the literary integrity of the letter.

4.1.3. Genre

4.1.3.a. A Paraenetic Letter

Abraham Malherbe has built a forceful case for understanding 1 Thessalonians as a paraenetic letter,[14] which was one of the recognized forms of epistolography in the Greco-Roman world.[15] For Malherbe, the paraenetic intention of 1 Thessalonians is highly pronounced: chapters 4 and 5 are clearly paraenetic, while chapters 1-3, which are autobiographical, function paraenetically by laying the foundation for the specific advice that would follow in the second half of the letter.[16] He opines that the heavy use of paraenesis may lie in the fact that Paul is writing to recent converts to Christianity sooner than he writes to his other converts; these new believers need to be nurtured in their faith and given more basic instruction in Christian behaviour. Hence, 'its paraenetic features perform what we would call pastoral care'.[17]

Malherbe identifies in Paul's letter many key features of paraenesis. These include (1) the frequent use of material that is already known to one's readers;[18]

---

[11] Weima, *Thessalonians*, 42. For a discussion of other theologically grounded objections to the interpolation approach, see Nijay K. Gupta, *1 & 2 Thessalonians*, ZCINT (Grand Rapids, MI: Zondervan, 2019), 114-21.

[12] See e.g. Jewett, *Thessalonian Correspondence*, 38.

[13] See Still, *Conflict*, 29-30.

[14] See especially Abraham J. Malherbe, 'Exhortation in 1 Thessalonians,' in *Paul and the Popular Philosophers* (Minneapolis, MN: Fortress, 1989); Abraham J. Malherbe, *Paul and the Thessalonians: The Philosophic Tradition of Pastoral Care* (Philadelphia, PA: Fortress, 1987), 68-78; Malherbe, *Thessalonians*, 81-6 (85: '1 Thessalonians is clearly a paraenetic letter; indeed, it is one of the best examples of such a letter'). Malherbe acknowledges that his identification of 1 Thessalonians as paraenesis is not new; Patristic commentators, especially John Chrysostom and Theodoret, have frequently commented on Paul's pastoral sensibilities by using the language of paraenesis and psychagogy (*Thessalonians*, 86).

[15] Pseudo-Libanius lists the 'paraenetic' style as the fifth style in his instruction manual for letter writing; this broadly corresponds to Pseudo-Demetrius's 'advisory' type, which is the eleventh type of letter in his manual (see further n.22 of Chapter 3 of my book).

[16] Malherbe, 'Exhortation', 49-51.

[17] Malherbe, *Thessalonians*, 85. We should note, however, that it is difficult to use the adjective 'pastoral' unambiguously because of possible connotations that may be anachronistic.

[18] See Malherbe, 'Exhortation', 51, for further details. As Malherbe notes in *Pastoral Care*, 76, the frequent use of language such as the paraenetic 'as you know' subtly makes the point to the

(2) complimenting them for living as they should, along with the encouragement to do so more and more (4.1, 10; 5.11);[19] (3) the offering of models for imitation (1.6; 2.14);[20] and related to this, (4) the delineation of such models in antithetical terms, for the sake of emphasis ('not ... but', 2.1-8);[21] (5) employing a wide range of hortatory terms;[22] and (6) the use of philophronetic, even familial, language and imagery that are redolent with positive feeling designed to strengthen one's readers.[23] Attention is drawn also to the unique character of 4.13-18, where Paul consoles those who are grieving: for Malherbe, the pericope exhibits similarities to the genre of the letter of consolation, which was discussed in the epistolographic handbooks of the era in terms that reflected its paraenetic character.[24] Paul's use of such hortatory motifs thus demonstrates his continuity with the hortatory tradition and reflects his pastoral method; however, he often radically reshapes the material so that it squares with his understanding of theology.[25] At the same time, Paul freely modifies conventional epistolary form so that his letter can take on certain functions.[26]

4.1.3.b. A Letter of Consolation

Based on his investigation of the Greco-Roman consolatory tradition, where consolatory visits and letters played central roles, Abraham Smith proposes that the letter of consolation, which was a notable form of psychagogy in antiquity, 'can account for virtually every aspect of 1 Thessalonians'.[27] In his argument that the consolatory letter is a generic model for 1 Thessalonians, Smith looks beyond epistolary structural parallels and focuses on how Paul co-opts the *topoi* of the consolatory tradition in the Hellenistic world as literary expressions of the typical pattern of social interaction associated with consolation.[28] Smith's conclusion is that Paul's consolatory goal is not limited to 4.13-18; instead, the entire letter reflects its shared origin with contemporaneous consolatory writing, through how its readers are furnished throughout with consolatory examples and commonplaces to help them overcome their experiences of grief.[29]

Thessalonians that despite their novice status in their new faith, they already share a history in the faith that is documented by their own experience.

[19] Malherbe, 'Exhortation', 51; Malherbe, *Pastoral Care*, 76.
[20] Malherbe, 'Exhortation', 51.
[21] Malherbe, *Pastoral Care*, 71.
[22] See Malherbe, 'Exhortation', 51-2, for details.
[23] Malherbe, 'Exhortation', 52-5; Malherbe, *Pastoral Care*, 72-5.
[24] Malherbe, 'Exhortation', 64-5, citing the fifth type in Pseudo-Demetrius's 'Epistolary Types' (see further n.22 of Chapter 3 of my book).
[25] Malherbe, 'Exhortation', 56-66.
[26] Malherbe, *Thessalonians*, 90-1.
[27] Abraham Smith, *Comfort One Another: Reconstructing the Rhetoric and Audience of 1 Thessalonians* (Louisville, KY: Westminster John Knox, 1995), 47-60 (quote from 48).
[28] Smith, *Comfort*, 45-6, 52-7; Smith builds on the work of Stowers (*Letter Writing in Greco-Roman Antiquity*, Library of Early Christianity 5 (Philadelphia, PA: Westminster Press, 1986), 144) who notes three fundamental elements of typical social interaction reflected in ancient consolatory letters: (1) The writer may have a wide range of positive relationships with the recipient. (2) The recipient has experienced some major misfortune that is apt to produce grief. (3) The writer expresses his grief and provides reasons why the recipient should bear up under this grief.
[29] Smith, *Comfort*, 59.

Reaching a similar conclusion, Donfried argues that Paul writes to the Thessalonians primarily to console them and encourage them in the face of persecution; in order to do this effectively he must also emphasize the divine origin of the message he had proclaimed while he was in their company, and defend himself against charges made against his motivation and behaviour.[30] At the heart of Paul's purpose, however, lies the desire to bring consolation and encouragement to the discouraged; thus, as Donfried explains, 'we understand 1 Thessalonians not primarily as a "paraenetic" letter but as a "paracletic" letter, as a *consolatio*'.[31]

4.1.3.c. Other Proposals and Conclusion

With the rise of rhetorical criticism in the latter decades of the twentieth century, a number of studies of 1 Thessalonians have been carried out on the assumption that its interpretation as a letter is better served by prioritizing a concern for its rhetorical genre over its epistolary features. The earliest explicit attempt at the rhetorical analysis of 1 Thessalonians as a letter seems to have been the short discussion by Kennedy, who regards it as deliberative rhetoric.[32] Subsequent studies have led several scholars to conclude instead that it is an example of epideictic rhetoric.[33] Even so, we cannot speak of a consensus view: there are a number of scholars who see 1 Thessalonians as deliberative rhetoric,[34] or find it unhelpful to have to choose between epideictic and deliberative rhetoric,[35] or even delineate a new rhetorical genre for it because it does not square with the traditional ones.[36]

---

[30] Karl P. Donfried, 'The Theology of 1 Thessalonians as a Reflection of Its Purpose', in *Paul, Thessalonica, and Early Christianity* (London: T&T Clark, 2002), 119–38, especially 119–20.

[31] Donfried, 'Purpose', 119–20. Donfried does not deny Malherbe's claim that there are paraenetic elements in 1 Thessalonians, but he rejects the idea that it is the overriding genre: 'Much closer to Paul's intention is the genre *consolatio*, a genre which, like many other subcategories, includes paraenesis. 1 Thessalonians is a λόγος παραμυθητικός to a Christian church suffering the effects of persecution' ('Purpose', 137–8).
  However, Juan Chapa, 'Is First Thessalonians a Letter of Consolation?', *NTS* 40 (1994): 150–60, while identifying features that 1 Thessalonians shares with Greco-Roman consolatory letters, stops short of classifying it as such because it does not adhere to the structural guidelines of the consolatory letter type as outlined in the standard handbooks. Against this, David Luckensmeyer and Bronwen Neil, 'Reading First Thessalonians as a Consolatory Letter in Light of Seneca and Ancient Handbooks on Letter-Writing', *NTS* 62 (2016): 31–48, have recently argued that since the Senecan consolatory epistles do not rigidly follow such guidelines, there is some justification in locating 1 Thessalonians within a reinterpreted understanding of the consolation genre.

[32] George A. Kennedy, *New Testament Interpretation through Rhetorical Criticism* (Chapel Hill: University of North Carolina Press, 1984), 142.

[33] See e.g. George Lyons, *Pauline Autobiography: Towards a New Understanding*, SBLDS 73 (Atlanta, GA: Scholars, 1985), 219–21; Jewett, *Thessalonian Correspondence*, 71–6; Steve Walton, 'What Has Aristotle to Do with Paul? Rhetorical Criticism and 1 Thessalonians', *TynBul* 46 (1995): 249–50.

[34] E.g. Bruce C. Johanson, *To All the Brethren: A Text-Linguistic and Rhetorical Approach to 1 Thessalonians*, ConBNT 16 (Stockholm: Almqvist & Wiksell, 1987), 189.

[35] E.g. Jan Lambrecht, 'A Structural Analysis of 1 Thessalonians 4–5', in *The Thessalonians Debate: Methodological Discord or Methodological Synthesis?*, ed. Karl P. Donfried and Johannes Beutler (Grand Rapids, MI: Eerdmans, 2000), 177.

[36] So Thomas H. Olbricht, 'An Aristotelian Rhetorical Analysis of 1 Thessalonians', in *Greeks, Romans, and Christians: Essays in Honor of Abraham J. Malherbe*, ed. David J. Balch, Everett Ferguson, and Wayne A. Meeks (Minneapolis, MN: Fortress, 1990), 216–36, especially 225–6. However, Olbricht's

The nature of the relationship between rhetorical criticism and epistolary approaches continues to be debated. To be sure, the advocates of rhetorical analysis recognize that its effectiveness is heightened when it is carried out alongside a corresponding epistolary analysis – but its most fervent proponents argue that it is rhetorical analysis that brings the interpreter closer to the author's literary intention.[37] However, on the other side of the hermeneutical fence are those who question the value of applying the rules of Greco-Roman rhetoric to 1 Thessalonians, not least because the various studies of the letter have elicited much disparity in its rhetorical disposition,[38] but, more fundamentally, because of concerns about the very legitimacy of using the categories of rhetorical theory to analyse the Pauline letters.[39]

4.1.4. Distinctives

Whatever one's views might be as to the genre of Paul's letter, it seems clear that he aims to nurture the Thessalonians in their new-found faith since he is unable to be physically present with them (3.10-11). Evidently, these recent converts lack a basic grounding in the proprieties of Christian living, because running through the letter is a distinct interest in matters of behaviour (e.g. 2.1-12; 4.1-18; 5.1-22). It is thus not surprising to find in the letter a preponderance of paraenetic discourse.[40]

Paul's loving concern for the Thessalonian believers is woven into the fabric of the letter. He constantly refers to them as ἀδελφοί[41] and speaks passionately of his affection for them (e.g. 2.8, 17-20; 3.6-11). Forced to leave them against his will, he describes himself as a bereft orphan (ἀπορφανίζω,[42] 2.17). He recounts how he and

---

proposal of 1 Thessalonians as 'church rhetoric' does not have much of a following, perhaps because of his failure to offer any other examples of it.

[37] See e.g. Charles A. Wanamaker, 'Epistolary vs. Rhetorical Analysis: Is a Synthesis Possible?', in *The Thessalonians Debate: Methodological Discord or Methodological Synthesis?*, ed. Karl P. Donfried and Johannes Beutler (Grand Rapids, MI: Eerdmans, 2000), 283–6.

[38] On this see in particular Krentz, '1 Thessalonians: Rhetorical Flourishes and Formal Constraints', in *The Thessalonians Debate: Methodological Discord or Methodological Synthesis?*, ed. Karl P. Donfried and Johannes Beutler (Grand Rapids, MI: Eerdmans, 2000), 295–304.

[39] See Weima, *Thessalonians*, 55–6.

[40] See Section 4.1.3.a above.

[41] The fictive-kinship term ἀδελφός occurs proportionately more often in 1 Thessalonians than in any of Paul's other letters (1.4; 2.1, 9, 14, 17; 3.2, 7; 4.1, 6, 10 (x2), 13; 5.1, 4, 12, 14, 25, 26, 27): a total of nineteen times, compared to thirteen times in Romans, thirty-three times in 1 Corinthians, and nine times in 2 Corinthians – all three of which are considerably longer letters. For further details and for the function of the term in 1 Thessalonians see especially Trevor J. Burke, *Family Matters: A Socio-Historical Study of Kinship Metaphors in 1 Thessalonians*, JSNTSup 247 (London: T&T Clark, 2003), 165–75. See also Reidar Aasgaard, *'My Beloved Brothers and Sisters!': Christian Siblingship in Paul*, Journal for the Study of the New Testament Supplement Series 265 (London: T&T Clark, 2004), 151–66.

[42] The verb is hapax in the New Testament, and occurs only infrequently in the extant Greek literature where it consistently refers to children who are orphaned from their parents, and not the reverse; see further John B. Faulkenberry Miller, 'Infants and Orphans in 1 Thessalonians: A Discussion of Ἀπορφανίζω and the Text-Critical Problem in 1 Thess. 2:7' (Paper presented at the Annual Meeting of the Society of Biblical Literature, Boston, 20 March 1999). Paul's placement of the orphan metaphor within a passive participle, coupled with his earlier mention of being driven out (2.15), strongly indicates that he was forcibly separated from his new converts (which squares with the account in Acts 17.10).

his co-workers had treated the Thessalonians as a nursing mother (τροφός, 2.7) would care for her own infants; such was their love for them that they had shared with them not only the gospel but also their 'own selves' (ἡ ἑαυτῶν ψυχή, 2.8). As a father with his own children (2.11), he and his colleagues had exhorted (παρακαλέω, 2.12; cf. 3.2, 7; 4.1, 10, 18; 5.11, 14), encouraged (παραμυθέομαι, 2.12; cf. 5.14), and urged (μαρτύρομαι,[43] 2.12) the Thessalonian believers to live a life that was worthy of God (2.12), which would please (ἀρέσκω, 4.1; cf. 2.4, 15) him.

We may conjecture with some justification that Paul's heartfelt concern for the Thessalonians is precipitated by two related exigencies: first, the fact that he and his co-workers had had to leave Thessalonica abruptly, without having completed the task of instructing them in the basics of Christian belief and praxis (as 3.10 seems to indicate); and second, because they are presently undergoing much suffering for their faith.

Indeed, the motif of suffering and conflict is highly significant. The Thessalonians had received the gospel 'in much affliction' (ἐν θλίψει πολλῇ, 1.6), and they were suffering the same things as did the churches in Judea (2.14). Suffering for the sake of the faith would continue to mark their lives (3.3), as it did Paul's own life (3.7). Several times in the letter, Paul speaks of his own sufferings. He had previously suffered (προπάσχω, 2.2) at Philippi and been shamefully mistreated (ὑβρίζω, 2.2) there; however, taking courage in God, he had brought the good news to Thessalonica in spite of much opposition (ἐν πολλῷ ἀγῶνι, 2.2).[44] Paul describes some of this opposition: there are those who have been persecuting him and his co-workers, thus hindering their task of evangelism (καὶ ἡμᾶς ἐκδιωξάντων ... κωλυόντων ἡμᾶς τοῖς ἔθνεσιν λαλῆσαι ἵνα σωθῶσιν, 2.15-16). Also lined up against them is Satan, whose actions have 'prevented' (ἐγκόπτω, 2.18) Paul from returning to Thessalonica.

Yet in spite of suffering, the Thessalonians had accepted the gospel with joy that was inspired by the Holy Spirit, thus becoming imitators of both Paul and the Lord (1.6). Paul links joy with a 'crown of boasting' (2.19) in which he will glory at the coming of Christ; and indeed, as he tells them: ὑμεῖς γάρ ἐστε ἡ δόξα ἡμῶν καὶ ἡ χαρά (2.20). Joy cannot be said to be a major motif in 1 Thessalonians, but it serves to bridge two themes that are key to the letter: suffering and eschatology – which we shall now very briefly outline, before we return to a discussion of the theme of suffering and conflict.

Paul makes explicit mention of the Parousia several times in the letter. At the end of chapter 1, he reminds the Thessalonians that they are waiting for the return of Christ, who would deliver believers from the coming wrath (1.10; cf. 1.3). At 2.19-20, as we have already seen, the Parousia forms the context in which the Thessalonians are to be celebrated as Paul's crown of boasting; at that eschatological event they are pictured as being blameless in holiness before God (3.13). The Parousia takes centre stage in the pericopes of 4.13-18 and 5.1-11, where Paul explains how the return of Christ relates to the status of believers, whether deceased (4.13-18) or living (5.1-11). Indeed, since the 'day of the Lord' is imminent (5.2), the believers are to wait for Christ's

---

[43] BDAG 619: 'to urge something as a matter of great importance'.
[44] If credence is given to the parallel account in Acts 17.1-10, there is here a depiction of aggressive, possibly also physical, opposition.

coming from heaven (1.10), in full assurance that they are called into God's kingdom and glory (2.12). Then, as he brings the letter to a close, Paul makes a final reference to the Parousia (5.23). The letter is shot through with the language and imagery of apocalyptic.

4.2. Conflict and Suffering in 1 Thessalonians

4.2.1. Introduction

We now take a closer look at the theme of conflict and suffering in 1 Thessalonians. Such a notion is readily apparent in the letter at a number of levels: thus we find a reference to violent conflict culminating in the death of Jesus and his prophets (2.15); conflict arising from the Gentile mission (2.2, 15-16); conflict between spiritual powers (1.9; 2.18; 3.5); Paul's anxiety associated with the possibility that his work would be in vain (3.1-5); ideological conflict between the Christian message and that of ancient Rome (5.3); and conflict among members of the community (5.12-15).[45] However, for the purposes of this study what I wish to discuss is the social aspect of such conflict from the perspective of the Thessalonians themselves. What precisely is the nature of the conflict that the Thessalonian Christians are facing? How might this conflict have affected them as a community of believers? The answers to these questions may help us to understand further the background to Paul's paraenesis in the letter, especially as it pertains to the quelling of the Thessalonians' grief (4.13-18).

4.2.2. The Nature of the Thessalonians' Suffering (1 Thess. 1.6)

As we have already noted, it is evident that the Thessalonian believers had encountered a considerable degree of hostility when they first heard and accepted the gospel that Paul had proclaimed to them (1.6). That this θλῖψις had continued may be inferred from Paul's reference to the fact that the Thessalonians had suffered (πάσχω, 2.14) at the hands of their compatriots (συμφυλέται, 2.14), and is confirmed when he reveals that Timothy was sent to strengthen them (3.2) because of his concern that they would be shaken by these afflictions[46] (τὸ μηδένα σαίνεσθαι ἐν ταῖς θλίψεσιν ταύταις,[47] 3.3a). Yet

---

[45] As David Luckensmeyer, *The Eschatology of First Thessalonians*, NTOA/SUNT 71 (Göttingen: Vandenhoeck & Ruprecht, 2009), 22, helpfully summarizes.

[46] Contra a minority of interpreters (e.g. Richard, *Thessalonians*, 141–2) who take the verb σαίνομαι (hapax legomenon in the New Testament) to mean 'to flatter' and argue that Paul is therefore saying that Timothy was sent to the Thessalonians to prevent them from being talked out of their new faith. For further discussion see Weima, *Thessalonians*, 211–12.

[47] The antecedent of ταύταις is not entirely certain, and this has led a few commentators (e.g. more recently Traugott Holtz, *Der erste Brief an die Thessalonicher*, EKKNT 13 (Zürich: Benziger, 1986), 127; Malherbe, *Thessalonians*, 193) to suggest that Paul is referring to his own suffering. On this reading, Paul is worried that the faith of his converts will be shaken once they discover that he is undergoing persecution. However, this seems rather unlikely: first, the Thessalonians surely already knew this fact (2.2), and second, the second-person pronouns that Paul employs in the preceding verse (εἰς τὸ στηρίξαι ὑμᾶς καὶ παρακαλέσαι ὑπὲρ τῆς πίστεως ὑμῶν, 3.2c; cf. 3.5) surely indicate that the Thessalonians are in view (so rightly Weima, *Thessalonians*, 212–13).

Paul takes the view that such suffering is part and parcel of the Christian life (αὐτοὶ γὰρ οἴδατε ὅτι εἰς τοῦτο κείμεθα, 3.3b); he had already warned the Thessalonians that they would have to endure these afflictions – which was apparently what did happen (3.4).

What was the precise nature of the conflict that the Thessalonian believers found themselves embroiled in? The mimetic parallel that Paul draws at 1.6 between the experiences of the Thessalonians and those of himself and Jesus clearly suggests that Paul, in referring to the Thessalonians' θλῖψις, has in view at least some form of social oppression connected with the proclamation or reception of the gospel;[48] it is not entirely improbable that this may have also been manifested in terms of physical opposition, especially if credence is given to the account in Acts 17.1-10. Malherbe holds a decidedly minority position in arguing that θλῖψις refers instead to the 'distress and anguish of heart experienced by persons who broke with their past as they received the gospel'.[49] We may certainly grant that the Thessalonian believers have experienced significant social dislocation, but it seems most unlikely that Paul has only some kind of inner psychological turmoil in view.[50]

On the other hand, is it possible that this conflict had led to the death, or even martyrdom, of a number of the Thessalonian believers? As we shall see later in greater detail in Section 4.3.3.a, such a conclusion is generally arrived at by correlating what Paul says about the Thessalonians' θλῖψις with his discussion in 4.13-18 of the death of certain believers. However, the presence of martyrdom seems unlikely, given the fact that Paul nowhere in his letter mentions or celebrates the fact that any of the believers had died for their faith.[51] Barclay therefore rightly concludes that the Thessalonians' θλῖψις is best understood as social harassment of the kind that became common for Christians in the Greco-Roman world.[52]

4.2.3. The Cause of the Thessalonians' Suffering (1 Thess. 2.14)

Next, what can be said concerning the source of the Thessalonian Christians' suffering? Our evidence comes from 2.14, where one may logically deduce that Paul in referring to the συμφυλέται[53] of the Thessalonians must be using the term in its ethnic sense to indicate a Gentile source for their afflictions, since the Thessalonians are themselves

---

[48] So the majority of commentators, e.g. Ernest Best, *A Commentary on the First and Second Epistles to the Thessalonians*, BNTC (London: A & C Black, 1972), 79, who thinks Paul is referring to persecution; and Holtz, *Thessalonicher*, 49 (followed by Wanamaker, *Thessalonians*, 80–2), referring to the presence of social oppression at the time of the Thessalonians' conversion.

[49] Malherbe, *Pastoral Care*, 48 (see also the wider discussion in 46–52); also Malherbe, *Thessalonians*, 127–9.

[50] See the discussion in Still, *Conflict*, 208–17.

[51] John M. G. Barclay, 'Conflict in Thessalonica', *CBQ* 55 (1993): 514, argues that Paul would surely have celebrated them as martyrs if so. In support Barclay cites (n.6) Phil. 2.25-30 and Rom. 16.4, where Paul lauds those who have risked their lives for the gospel; no such eulogy is present here in 1 Thessalonians.

[52] Barclay, 'Conflict', 513–16.

[53] BDAG 960: 'one's people'; hapax legomenon in Paul and in the rest of the New Testament. However, its cognate φυλή occurs twice in Paul (Rom. 11.1; Phil. 3.5); on both these occasions it is in relation to Paul's belonging to the tribe of Benjamin.

Gentile converts to Christianity (1.9). This conclusion is supported by the fact that Paul is always mindful of the matter of race and careful to distinguish between Jews and Gentiles in his writings (e.g. in Gal. 2) – it would therefore be completely inconsistent of him to employ the term in its geographic sense to designate *all* the denizens of Thessalonica irrespective of their ethnicity.[54] Hence (and notwithstanding the mention of Jewish troublemakers in Acts 17.5-6) Paul is saying that the source of the church's afflictions was unconverted Gentiles.[55]

It seems most likely then that the chief cause of the harassment was the fact that the Thessalonian believers had turned their backs on common Greco-Roman religion as a result of their conversion (1.9). De Vos outlines a situation of social conflict that 'centered on the rejection of traditional religious practices and a withdrawal from social/religious activities'.[56] Still makes a similar observation: 'the conflict occurred because unbelievers wanted to control and to censure a novel religious movement which they viewed as ideologically and socially deviant.'[57] The discrimination and pressure that was effected against the Thessalonian Christians was therefore presumably aimed at reversing their beliefs and practices.[58]

From the viewpoint of the wider community, the behaviour of the converts was utterly reprehensible. First, their religious mores and social exclusiveness disrupted normal familial and cultic activity and thereby both offended and injured public sensibility.[59] Second, given the way that politics and religion were so closely integrated in Greco-Roman society, it was highly probable that the religious ideals of the Christians – with their claim to be subjects of another king – became overlaid with political overtones that were thought to be subversive; all this would have loudly sounded alarm bells in a city like Thessalonica, which was acutely aware of its continuing dependence on imperial benefaction.[60] Third, it was very likely that the Christians' rejection of traditional religion not only branded them as ἄθεοι but was also seen to compromise the city's overall well-being as far as its dealings with the gods was concerned; if even one segment of the community raised the ire of the gods, the entire city was put at risk because their wrath could lead to the meting out of severe punishments such as famine, flooding, or other natural calamities.[61] As Still summarizes succinctly, the conflict between the Christians and non-Christians

---

[54] As Barclay, 'Conflict', 514, stresses, 'With his acute consciousness of the racial distinction between Jews and non-Jews, Paul could hardly refer to Jews as *symphyletai* (2.14) of his non-Jewish converts (1.9).'

[55] See Still, *Conflict*, 218–27, for a persuasive articulation of this view.

[56] Craig Steven de Vos, *Church and Community Conflicts: The Relationship of the Thessalonian, Corinthian, and Philippian Churches with Their Wider Civic Communities*, SBLDS 168 (Atlanta, GA: Scholars, 1999), 176; see also the wider discussion at 155–60.

[57] Still, *Conflict*, 267.

[58] de Vos, *Conflicts*, 157; Still, *Conflict*, 267.

[59] Barclay, 'Conflict', 515; see also his 'Thessalonica and Corinth: Social Contrasts in Pauline Christianity', in *Pauline Churches and Diaspora Jews*, WUNT 275 (Tübingen: Mohr, 2011), 53. For an extensive discussion see Still, *Conflict*, 232–55.

[60] See de Vos, *Conflicts*, 156–7; Barclay, 'Conflict', 514; and especially Still, *Conflict*, 260–6. On the relationship between Rome and Thessalonica, and the favoured political status that Thessalonica enjoyed, see Weima, *Thessalonians*, 3–7.

[61] Still, *Conflict*, 255–60. See also Barclay, 'Conflict', 515; Barclay also notes here (citing Christian and non-Christian sources) that if anything went wrong the Christians could get the blame.

in Thessalonica arose because the latter 'viewed the church to be subversive to the foundational institutions of Greco-Roman society, namely family, religion, and government'.[62]

4.3. Grief in 1 Thessalonians 4.13-18

4.3.1. Extent of the Passage

We turn our attention now to the specific issue of grief in 1 Thessalonians. At 4.13, Paul marks the start of a fresh topic in his letter – the fate of deceased believers at the return of Christ – with his mention of 'those who have died' (περὶ τῶν κοιμωμένων). The shift in topic at 4.13 is confirmed by the combined use of three distinct transitional devices: the disclosure formula at 4.13 ('I do not want you not to know', οὐ θέλομεν δὲ ὑμᾶς ἀγνοεῖν) – the double negative form of which contrasts with, and also functions as an emphatic equivalent to, the positive form found elsewhere in the letter ('you know that', see 2.1; 4.2; 5.2),[63] the vocative ἀδελφοί,[64] and the περὶ δέ formula[65] – together with the presence of several literary and thematic features that signal the end of the previous section at 4.12.[66]

Despite some similarities in content and structure between 4.13-18 and 5.1-11,[67] it is clear that the present section ends at 4.18 and not at 5.11. At 4.18, the particle ὥστε introduces a concluding clause[68] – παρακαλεῖτε ἀλλήλους ἐν τοῖς λόγοις τούτοις – which looks back on the preceding material in 4.13-17 and draws it to a close, while simultaneously forming a thematic *inclusio* with the passage's opening injunction to 'not grieve' (4.13). The coherence of 4.13-18 is further supported by a number of lexical and conceptual recurrences: κοιμωμένων/κοιμηθέντας (4.13, 14, 15) and its semantic equivalent οἱ νεκροὶ ἐν Χριστῷ (4.16); the double occurrence of the phrase ἡμεῖς οἱ ζῶντες οἱ περιλειπόμενοι (4.15, 17); and the conceptual parallels between ἄξει σὺν αὐτῷ (4.14) and σὺν κυρίῳ ἐσόμεθα (4.17), and also between Ἰησοῦς ... ἀνέστη (4.14) and οἱ νεκροὶ ἐν Χριστῷ ἀναστήσονται (4.16).[69] Moreover, it is also clearly apparent that at 5.1 a new section has begun: Paul uses two familiar transitional devices (the περὶ δέ formula and the vocative ἀδελφοί) and a paralipsis (οὐ χρείαν ἔχετε ὑμῖν γράφεσθαι) to flag the beginning of a new topic of discussion.

---

[62] Still, *Conflict*, 267.
[63] For details see Weima, *Thessalonians*, 307.
[64] See See n.41 of this chapter.
[65] Occurring in the letter also at 4.9 and 5.1, and elsewhere in the undisputed Paulines at 1 Cor. 7.1, 25; 8.1, 4; 12.1; 16.1, 12. Here in 1 Thess. 4.13 the disclosure formula nudges the preposition περί further along the sentence, while the particle δέ retains its position.
[66] For further discussion see Weima, *Thessalonians*, 249-51.
[67] See Raymond F. Collins, *Studies on the First Letter to the Thessalonians*, BETL 66 (Leuven: Leuven University Press, 1984), 154-72; Luckensmeyer, *Eschatology*, 181.
[68] ὥστε is used similarly to conclude a discussion in 1 Cor. 7.38; 11.27, 33; 14.39; 15.58.
[69] Weima, *Thessalonians*, 305-6.

4.3.2. The Disclosure Formula

In his opening assertion of 4.13, does Paul with his use of the disclosure formula οὐ θέλομεν δὲ ὑμᾶς ἀγνοεῖν introduce not only a change of topic but also one that is *completely new* to the Thessalonians? While there are some scholars who caution against reaching such a conclusion,[70] there are others who maintain that Paul is indeed presenting something that was previously unknown to his converts.[71] It seems to me that the matter is far from clear; from Paul's phraseology we cannot be sure whether he is providing totally new information to the Thessalonian believers or merely supplementing certain points in his earlier apocalyptic teaching. However, what seems certain is that Paul wants to give the Thessalonians instruction by emphasizing the material that immediately follows: he wants them to know περὶ τῶν κοιμωμένων.[72]

4.3.3. The Circumstances of the Thessalonians' Grief

From the evidence, we may reasonably surmise – based on the plural construction περὶ τῶν κοιμωμένων – that a number of the Thessalonian believers had died in the period between Paul's hurried escape from Thessalonica and the penning of this letter to them. Paul (understandably) in his response does not see any need to indicate who these individuals are or how they have died, since the Thessalonians must already be in full possession of the facts. The second half of 4.13 contains a purpose clause that sets out the thesis that Paul will establish in the verses that follow: ἵνα μὴ λυπῆσθε καθὼς καὶ οἱ λοιποὶ οἱ μὴ ἔχοντες ἐλπίδα. Quite clearly, the Thessalonians were grieving – and with some degree of intensity – over the deaths of some among them.[73] What is

---

[70] Perhaps most notably Malherbe, *Thessalonians*, 262, who opines that Paul's varied use of both the positive and negative forms of the disclosure formula 'makes it impossible to draw rigid conclusions about their significance' (see also the broader discussion in 262–3); cf. John M. G. Barclay, '"That You May Not Grieve, Like the Rest Who Have No Hope" (1 Thess 4.13): Death and Early Christian Identity', in *Pauline Churches and Diaspora Jews*, Wissenschaftliche Untersuchungen zum Neuen Testament 275 (Tübingen: Mohr Siebeck, 2011), 218. See also Luckensmeyer, *Eschatology*, 212–13, who makes the persuasive suggestion that 'Paul's repeated references to eschatological motifs increase the probability that he spoke at length on such subjects during his founding visit'.

[71] So e.g. Karl P. Donfried, 'The Cults of Thessalonica and the Thessalonian Correspondence', in *Paul, Thessalonica, and Early Christianity* (London: T&T Clark, 2002), 40; Colin R. Nicholl, *From Hope to Despair in Thessalonica: Situating 1 and 2 Thessalonians*, SNTSMS 126 (Cambridge: Cambridge University Press, 2004), 20–2; Weima, *Thessalonians*, 307–8.

[72] Terms relating to sleep were commonly employed as euphemisms for death in antiquity: see Wanamaker, *Thessalonians*, 167; and Weima, *Thessalonians*, 309, for examples from Greek, Jewish, and Christian writings. Indeed, the conceptual link between sleep and death was by no means distinctively Jewish or Christian, probably because their association was so intuitive (so Gene L. Green, *The Letters to the Thessalonians*, PilNTC (Grand Rapids, MI: Eerdmans, 2002), 217). The figurative extension of the meaning of 'sleep' as 'death' is the only way in which Paul uses κοιμάω (BDAG 551). A number of scholars suggest that Paul's metaphorical use of sleep for death may connote something about the individual's post-mortem state, e.g. a waiting for a future resurrection, or an interim, so-called intermediate state of existence; however, such arguments are overly speculative, especially in the absence of any clear semantic implications associated with the term that might support either conclusion (see the helpful discussion in Luckensmeyer, *Eschatology*, 214).

[73] The present passive of λυπέω means 'be sad, distressed, grieve' (BDAG 604); and as Weima, *Thessalonians*, 310, notes, 'The use of the present tense highlights the ongoing nature of the action and so hints at the great depth of the Thessalonians' grief.'

not made clear is *why* they should be grieving in such a manner. But before we try to ascertain in more precise terms the reason why the Thessalonian believers were in such grief, it is pertinent to consider if martyrdom might lie behind the deaths that are alluded to here.

4.3.3.a. The Martyrdom of Fellow Believers?

A number of exegetes have put forward the argument that some in the Thessalonian church were martyred for their faith.[74] This view is generally arrived at through an attempt to read Paul's instructions here in 4.13-18 against his earlier statements concerning the Thessalonians' θλῖψις in 1.6, 3.3-4, and especially 2.14 (where Paul sets up a parallel between the sufferings faced by the Thessalonians with those experienced by the churches in Judea), and by taking support from references to the afflictions that they had endured in 2 Thess. 1.4-7, 2 Cor. 8.2, and Acts 17.5-9.[75]

However, these scattered references to affliction more likely have in view severe social harassment and ostracism rather than physical death and martyrdom.[76] Indeed, as Bruce rightly notes, 'The references in both 1 and 2 Thessalonians to the "afflictions" endured by the Christians of Thessalonica scarcely give the impression that positive martyrdom was involved.'[77] Further, the parallel that Paul describes in 2.14 rests not so much on any similarity in the specifics of the suffering that the two groups have endured as on the presence of a similar type of opponent: both the Thessalonian and Judean churches have suffered at the hands of their 'own fellow countrymen' (τῶν ἰδίων συμφυλετῶν).[78] Finally, as we have already noted, based on his actions elsewhere we may well argue that Paul would have paid tribute to any Thessalonians who had actually died for their faith.[79] Overall, the evidence seems to suggest that martyrdom is not in view here.[80]

---

[74] See e.g. John S. Pobee, *Persecution and Martyrdom in the Theology of Paul*, JSNTSup 6 (Sheffield: JSOT Press, 1985), 113–14; Karl P. Donfried, 'The Theology of 1 Thessalonians', in *The Theology of the Shorter Pauline Letters*, by Karl P. Donfried and I. Howard Marshall (Cambridge: Cambridge University Press, 1993), 21–3; Donfried, 'Cults', 41–3.

[75] Donfried, 'Cults', 41–2, also makes much of a supposed parallel between the use of κοιμάω in 4.13 and the account of the martyrdom of Stephen in Acts 7.60. However, this conceptual link is tenuous at best; as de Vos, *Conflicts*, 159–60, points out, both Paul and Luke use κοιμάω elsewhere to refer to death without any sense of martyrdom (Acts 13.36; 1 Cor. 7.39, 11.30, 15.51).

[76] See Weima, *Thessalonians*, 311–12, and as already noted, Barclay, 'Conflict', 514.

[77] F. F. Bruce, *1 & 2 Thessalonians*, WBC 45 (Waco, TX: Word, 1982), 98; cited in Weima, *Thessalonians*, 309–310.

[78] As Wanamaker, *Thessalonians*, 113, rightly argues, 'Obviously, the persecution undergone by the Thessalonian Christians cannot be linked directly to the crisis in Judea. Rather the point of comparison, as the καθὼς shows, was that both groups had suffered harassment at the hands of their own compatriots.' See similarly Weima, *Thessalonians*, 310; also 166–7.

[79] See n.51 of this chapter.

[80] Note however Still, *Conflict*, 216–17, who broadly demurs at the identification of the Christian dead of whom Paul speaks here as martyrs while not completely rejecting 'the possibility that some of Paul's converts were victims of physical violence and that perhaps on the rarest of occasions such opposition might have culminated in death' (216). Still's concession is based on an interpretation of 2.14 in which τὰ αὐτὰ ἐπάθετε is taken literally, i.e. that the Thessalonians suffered the same things as the Judean churches did; however, as we have noted above, this reading does not adequately elucidate the meaning of the parallel that Paul is setting up here. In a not dissimilar way, de Vos, *Conflicts*, 160, while concluding that 'there is no textual basis for the idea that some were executed',

4.3.3.b. Major Hypotheses Concerning the Thessalonians' Grief

We return now to the larger question of the circumstances surrounding the Thessalonians' emotional state here at 4.13. A number of proposals have been offered, and here I discuss those that are more significant.[81]

An older, minority line of interpretation is that Gnostic missionaries in Thessalonica had subverted Paul's kerygma by insisting that the resurrection of the dead was a present reality. The unexpected deaths of some of the believers therefore triggered shock and grief within the church.[82] However, there is no evidence for the presence of Gnostic influences in Thessalonica, and in any case it may be questioned whether Gnosticism existed as a developed movement (or group of movements) at this early date. Furthermore, Paul's response in his letter does not indicate that a denial of the resurrection was the problem.[83]

The mainstream interpretations of the reason for the Thessalonians' grief may be placed into one of two groups. One group comprises those views that are based broadly on the premise that the Thessalonians were confused and unable to synthesize the dual sets of eschatological expectations concerning the Parousia and the resurrection of dead believers into a coherent whole. Their grief therefore stemmed from uncertainty concerning the relationship between the living and the dead at Christ's coming, and was further fuelled by Jewish apocalyptic speculation that those deceased would be at some sort of *relative* disadvantage compared to people who were alive (see e.g. 4 Ezra 13.24; cf. 6.25; 7.26-44; 13.16-18; Pss. Sol. 17.44; 18.6).[84] However, these views fail to account for the severity of the Thessalonians' reactions: it is hard to understand why they would grieve with such hopelessness since they believed that their brethren would eventually be resurrected (albeit some time after the Parousia).[85]

In contrast, in the second group are those views which take the Thessalonians as being overwhelmed by grief because they regarded their dead as being at an *absolute*

---

opines also that if the repressive measures against the Thessalonians were in response to charges of atheism or breaches against the oath of loyalty to the Emperor, 'physical violence, and even death cannot be ruled out'. However, against both Still and de Vos it must be pointed out that Paul nowhere links the deaths that are implied in 4.13-18 with the afflictions that the Thessalonian believers are undergoing (Barclay, 'Conflict', 514; 'Thessalonica', 53).

[81] For further details see the useful table in Luckensmeyer, *Eschatology*, 192–211.
[82] Wilhelm Lütgert, *Die Volkommenen im Philipperbrief und die Enthusiasten in Thessalonich*, BFCT 13 (Gütersloh: Bertelsmann, 1909), 55–81; Walter Schmithals, *Paul and the Gnostics*, trans. John E. Steely (Nashville, TN: Abingdon, 1972), 160–4; Wolfgang Harnisch, *Eschatologische Existenz: Ein exegetischer Beitrag zum Sachanliegen von 1. Thessalonicher 4,13–5,11*, FRLANT 110 (Göttingen: Vandenhoeck & Ruprecht, 1973), 16–51.
[83] Weima, *Thessalonians*, 310.
[84] So Malherbe, *Thessalonians*, 284; see also Ulrich Luz, *Das Geschichtsverständnis des Paulus*, BEvT 49 (Munich: Kaiser, 1968), 318–31; Helmut Merklein, 'Der Theologe als Prophet: Zur Funktion prophetischen Redens im Theologischen Diskurs des Paulus', *NTS* 38 (1992): 407–8; Weima, *Thessalonians*, 312–13; cf. James Everett Frame, *A Critical and Exegetical Commentary on the Epistles of St. Paul to the Thessalonians*, ICC (Edinburgh: T&T Clark, 1912), 163–4.
[85] Weima, *Thessalonians*, 313, tries to counter this objection by contending that it 'underestimates the great anticipation and hope that the Thessalonians have about participating in the glory of the parousia event (1.3, 10; 2.19) – a time when their faith would be vindicated and they would enjoy eternal life with Christ (4.17; 5.10), while their fellow citizens who caused them so much affliction would be justly punished in the "coming wrath" (1.10; 5.9)'; but the argument is not sufficiently convincing.

disadvantage at the Parousia compared to themselves; in other words, the deceased were thought to have lost their salvation. We may distinguish between several views that fall within this group:

1. One proposal rests on the hypothesis that Paul had previously described the participation of the Thessalonian church in the Parousia in terms of an assumption – which, according to Jewish apocalyptic teachings, could occur only in connection with living persons. With the death of some of their members, the Thessalonian believers were plunged into grief, since they took it as axiomatic that the dead were not in a condition to be taken up at the Parousia.[86] However, there is no evidence that Paul's kerygma included teaching about such a motif.[87] Furthermore, Paul depicts Christ's return with the metaphor of the *Einholung* or Hellenistic formal reception (ἀπάντησις, 4.17)[88] – an image which does not portray an upward movement from earth to heaven (which an assumption would involve) but its very opposite, that is, the believers meet Christ in the air and usher him down to earth.[89]

2. Another theory is that Paul did not teach the Thessalonians about the resurrection of dead believers because he was convinced that the return of Christ was highly imminent. Indeed, Paul's thinking about the resurrection had not yet been fully formulated, and it would take time for him to develop his early position here to the more developed understanding of 1 Cor. 15. Consequently, when some among the Thessalonian believers died, great sorrow ensued; and, with Christ's return still only in prospect, Paul was now obliged to provide instruction concerning the resurrection of dead believers.[90] However, against this view, it seems rather improbable that in the decade[91] prior to his arrival in Thessalonica Paul had not encountered and dealt with the death of any believers – which means that by the time of the Thessalonian mission, teaching concerning such matters would have become integral to his regular programme of instruction. In addition, as we have noted earlier (see Section 4.1.4), the contents of the letter reveal that the

---

[86] Joseph Plevnik, 'The Parousia as Implication of Christ's Resurrection: An Exegesis of 1 Thess 4,13–18', in *Word and Spirit: Essays in Honor of David Michael Stanley on His 60th Birthday*, ed. Joseph Plevnik (Toronto: Regis College, 1975), 199–277; see also his other work e.g. 'The Taking Up of the Faithful and the Resurrection of the Dead in 1 Thessalonians 4:13–18', *CBQ* 46 (1984): 274–83.

[87] So Malherbe, *Thessalonians*, 276; Nicholl, *Thessalonica*, 46–7.

[88] Erik Peterson, 'Die Einholung des Kyrios', *ZST* 7 (1930): 682–702, especially 693–7.

[89] On the debates surrounding how Paul uses εἰς ἀπάντησιν in 4.17 see Luckensmeyer, *Eschatology*, 260–6; he concludes that 'an association of Paul's reference with Hellenistic formal receptions cannot be rejected' (265).

[90] So Willi Marxsen, 'Auslegung von 1 Thess 4,13–18', *ZTK* 66 (1969): 22–37; Jürgen Becker, *Auferstehung der Toten im Urchristentum* (Stuttgart: KBW Verlag, 1976), 46–54; Nicholl, *Thessalonica*, 35–8.

[91] If we follow Michael Gorman's general chronology of Paul's life (which is broad enough to be acceptable to many scholars), Paul's conversion dates to ca. 32–36 CE, and the period of major missionary activity begins ca. 46 CE with the first missionary journey; see Michael J. Gorman, *Apostle of the Crucified Lord: A Theological Introduction to Paul and His Letters*, 2nd ed. (Grand Rapids, MI: Eerdmans, 2017), 56–60. The Macedonian mission was part of Paul's second missionary journey, i.e. sometime after 46 CE, which means that by the time he reached Thessalonica, Paul would have been preaching and teaching for some ten years at least.

Thessalonians had received extensive eschatological instruction, at which time the question would surely have come up.
3. A third solution, which has certain points of affinity with the foregoing view, but involves less speculation, is that Paul may have 'emphasized the possibility of Jesus' imminent return so much that the expectation of being alive at its occurrence had swallowed up what little Paul had taught them about a future resurrection'.[92] Notwithstanding the fact that some of the objections to the foregoing theory may also be raised here, on balance this is likely to be the best of the possible explanations for Thessalonians' grief.
4. A fourth proposal grants that the Thessalonians did learn about the resurrection of believers from Paul; however, the actual occurrence of the death of their brethren provoked an outpouring of grief that blunted their apprehension of the doctrine. As Marshall thus suggests, 'It is, after all, one thing to have a theoretical belief in resurrection and quite another to maintain that belief in the actual presence of death and physical decay'.[93] The ways in which this proposal captures some of the existential realities of lived human experience is not without its merits, but it does not account for why Paul takes such pains not only to reaffirm the doctrine of the resurrection of believers but also to explain its connection with the Parousia.[94]

To conclude at this stage: what Paul has mentioned so far in the passage points to the fact that a number of the Thessalonian Christians have died, for reasons that are not known to us (however, the wider evidence suggests that martyrdom is very likely not in view here). The grief that overwhelms the Thessalonians is probably caused by a lack of knowledge concerning the eschatological destiny of the deceased; it was thought that they had 'slipped, through death, out of the current which was heading for salvation: they would not, and could not, be present when the much-anticipated parousia took place'.[95] Such an interpretation allows for aspects of the fourth causal hypothesis (as outlined above) to have a place at the table also: thus, it seems not unreasonable to grant that the Thessalonians, who did not have an adequate understanding of life after death, were simply unable to manage their grief when they were suddenly confronted by the deaths of people who mattered to them. Furthermore, as Barclay points out, the precise circumstances of these deaths – that is, perhaps whether they had led to increased derision from the Thessalonians' opponents, who attributed these deaths to the wrath of the gods – could have affected the degree of distress and grief which they occasioned.[96]

---

[92] Robert H. Gundry, 'The Hellenization of Dominical Tradition and the Christianization of Jewish Tradition in the Eschatology of 1–2 Thessalonians', *NTS* 33 (1987): 167; see also Todd D. Still, 'Eschatology in the Thessalonian Letters', *RevExp* 96 (1999): 196–7.
[93] I. Howard Marshall, *1 and 2 Thessalonians*, NCB (Grand Rapids, MI: Eerdmans, 1983), 120–1, following Peter Siber, *Mit Christus Leben: Eine Studie zur paulinischen Auferstehungshoffnung*, ATANT 61 (Zürich: Theologischer Verlag, 1971), 13–22. See also Gary Shogren, *1 & 2 Thessalonians*, ZECNT (Grand Rapids, MI: Zondervan, 2012), 188.
[94] Weima, *Thessalonians*, 311.
[95] Barclay, 'Death', 221; similarly Marshall, *Thessalonians*, 122.
[96] See Barclay, 'Conflict', 516; and also his 'Death', 219.

We now turn our attention to Paul's consolatory strategy, beginning with a consideration of whether or not 4.13b is in effect an absolute prohibition against grief.

4.3.4. A Prohibition against Grief?

The question of *how* Paul intends the Thessalonians to grieve – ἵνα μὴ λυπῆσθε καθὼς καὶ οἱ λοιποὶ οἱ μὴ ἔχοντες ἐλπίδα (4.13b) – has attracted not a little debate. Here, ἵνα μή expresses a negatived purpose clause that presents the problem that is to be overcome, ἵνα μὴ λυπῆσθε. The adverb καθώς introduces the comparative subclause καθὼς καὶ οἱ λοιποὶ οἱ μὴ ἔχοντες ἐλπίδα: καθώς thus indicates that Paul's readers are being compared to 'the rest', that is, those outside the Christian community, who are 'those who do not have hope'.[97] In broad terms, the scholarly opinions that have been offered may be located in one of two camps.

Several exegetes argue that Paul is calling for an absolute prohibition: the Thessalonians are not to grieve at all for their deceased brethren.[98] To a significant degree, this argument rests on the interpretation of καθὼς καί:[99] those who champion this line of thought typically take it to be setting up an absolute contrast, based on its similarity with the καθάπερ καί in 4.5 (which introduces a negative comparison that functions as an antithesis). So Frame, for example, insists that

> καθὼς καί here does not mean that the Christians are indeed to grieve, but not in the same manner or degree as the unbelievers ... Paul speaks absolutely, for death has a religious value to him, in that after a short interval the dead are brought to the goal of Christian hope, σὺν αὐτῷ. In view of this glorious consummation, present grief, however natural, is excluded.[100]

However, this view remains rather controversial, not least because it glosses over the anguish of bereavement and denigrates the natural psychological responses that come in its wake.[101]

The majority of commentators from Theodoret and the Antiochenes onwards have supported more moderate interpretations, wherein καθὼς καί is thought to specify

---

[97] Wanamaker, *Thessalonians*, 167.
[98] See e.g. J. B. Lightfoot, *Notes on the Epistles of St. Paul from Unpublished Commentaries*, 2nd ed. (London: Macmillan, 1904), 63; Frame, *Thessalonians*, 167; Best, *Thessalonians*, 186; Malherbe, *Thessalonians*, 264; Barclay, 'Death', 223–4. Thus Malherbe e.g. argues that since the cause of the Thessalonians' grief is an incomplete understanding of matters pertaining to Christians who had died, 'Paul's attitude towards this grief is equally straightforward: it is prohibited' (264).
[99] καθώς can be an adverb of comparison or of degree; see BDAG 493–4.
[100] Frame, *Thessalonians*, 167, cited with approval by Barclay, 'Death', 224, who argues (225 n.22) that linguistic parallels involving the use of καθὼς καί and equivalents, such as 1 Thess. 4.5, strongly suggest an absolute contrast.
[101] This problem has not been ignored by those within the 'prohibition' camp: thus Lightfoot e.g. concedes that 'here, as elsewhere, he [Paul] states his precept broadly, without caring to enter into the qualifications which will suggest themselves at once to thinking men' (*Notes*, 63); while Malherbe suggests that Paul's absolute prohibition must be understood in its context and thus does not forbid 'any grief at all in any circumstance surrounding the death of Christians', but only 'in reply to the specific question the Thessalonians had addressed to him' (*Thessalonians*, 264).

a difference between Christian and pagan attitudes to grieving.[102] Thus Paul is by no means saying that Christians are not to grieve, but that they must not do so to the same degree and with the same types of motives as do those who are without hope. Scholars advocating this position often cite certain verses from Paul's letters elsewhere and from the New Testament in general to demonstrate that there is no support for the view that he is balking at the legitimacy of grief for believers. These include, in particular: Phil. 2.27, where Paul refers to the mercy that God had showed both Epaphroditus and him, lest he should have 'grief upon grief' (ἵνα μὴ λύπην ἐπὶ λύπην σχῶ); Paul's general exhortation in Rom. 12.15 to 'mourn with those who mourn' (κλαίειν μετὰ κλαιόντων); his description of the Corinthians' grief unto repentance (ἐλυπήθητε εἰς μετάνοιαν, 2 Cor. 7.9) as a godly grief leading to salvation (ἡ γὰρ κατὰ θεὸν λύπη μετάνοιαν εἰς σωτηρίαν, 2 Cor. 7.10a) and not a worldly grief that brings death (ἡ δὲ τοῦ κόσμου λύπη θάνατον κατεργάζεται, 2 Cor. 7.10b); and the example of Jesus weeping at the tomb of Lazarus in Jn 11.35.[103]

Yet the use of texts like these and others to substantiate the view that Paul in 1 Thess. 4.13 is not issuing an absolute prohibition of grief has not gone unchallenged. Barclay, for example, notes that while several Pauline passages show that a kind of λύπη is necessary and even beneficial (Rom. 9.2; 2 Cor. 2.2-5; 6.10; 7.8-11), or give examples of permissible weeping (Rom. 12.15; 1 Cor. 7.30), none of these passages concern death. In Paul's letters, only in Phil. 2.27 is death possibly at issue; and even so, here Barclay reads Paul as saying that he is relieved that he was altogether spared the experience of grief. Further, Barclay suggests that in the gospels it is Mk 5.39 rather than Jn 11.35 that is the closest rhetorical and theological parallel to the situation in Thessalonica.[104]

On balance, however, it seems preferable to follow the majority view that Paul is in 1 Thess. 4.13 not telling the Thessalonians that they are to stop grieving per se, but rather that they are to stop grieving as unbelievers do;[105] 'their grief, no matter how deep, should be of the hopeful variety'.[106] Such a reading preserves the broad sense in which grief in its various forms seems to be understood by Paul as a natural, legitimate expression of the human experience. Furthermore, as Still suggests, if full weight is given to the fact that Paul here uses the passive (λυπῆσθε), then it seems improbable that he has in mind an absolute prohibition on an emotional reaction that he himself understands as being more or less beyond the Thessalonians' control.[107]

Whether one takes Paul to be reframing grief or prohibiting it altogether, it is apparent that he wants the Thessalonians believers to understand and handle their grief in a way that distinguishes them from the people around them. Paul has already outlined the distinction between Christians and non-Christians by using expressions such as 'the Gentiles who do not know God' (τὰ ἔθνη τὰ μὴ εἰδότα τὸν θεόν, 4.5) and

---

[102] See the discussion in Paul Hoffman, *Die Toten in Christus: Eine religionsgeschichtliche und exegetische Untersuchung zur paulinischen Eschatologie*, NTAbh 2 (Münster: Aschendorff, 1966), 210–11.
[103] See e.g. Weima, *Thessalonians*, 314; Luckensmeyer, *Eschatology*, 215.
[104] Barclay, 'Death', 225 n.22.
[105] So e.g. Nicholl, *Thessalonica*, 25, and most commentators.
[106] N. T. Wright, *The Resurrection of the Son of God* (Minneapolis, MN: Fortress, 2003), 229.
[107] Todd D. Still, 'Interpretive Ambiguities and Scholarly Proclivities in Pauline Studies: A Treatment of Three Texts from 1 Thessalonians 4 as a Test Case', *CBR* 5 (2007): 207–19.

'the outsiders' (οἱ ἔξω, 4.12) to describe the latter group. In 4.13, he continues to use such in-group language to cement this distinction: the Thessalonians are instructed not to grieve like 'the rest who have no hope' (οἱ λοιποὶ οἱ μὴ ἔχοντες ἐλπίδα).

That οἱ λοιποί refers to unbelievers can be readily inferred from Paul's contextual use of the phrase here in 4.13 and again in 5.6;[108] this is confirmed by how Paul here juxtaposes it with an adjectival phrase, οἱ μὴ ἔχοντες ἐλπίδα, that qualifies οἱ λοιποί in the same way that τὰ μὴ εἰδότα τὸν θεόν qualifies τὰ ἔθνη in 4.5.[109] Thus 'the rest' are characterized as having 'no hope' – which is not at all surprising given that Paul's understanding of ἐλπίς is so thoroughly shaped by his kerygma. This hope is a distinctively Christian hope that is focused on the eschaton, as Pauline usage generally, and in 1 Thessalonians specifically (1.3; 2.19; 5.8), demonstrates.[110] The circle is thus clearly drawn: outside its boundary are found all who do not accept the gospel and who therefore do not share in the Christian hope of salvation, while inside are the Thessalonian (and other) believers, who know this eschatological hope and are exhorted to hold on to it in the very face of grief and death.

At this point, however, as Barclay cautions, commentators are apt to stumble as they wrestle with the ramifications of what Paul seems to be saying.[111] Those who think (perhaps on the basis that he is addressing a predominantly Gentile congregation) that Paul excludes the Jews from οἱ λοιποί[112] are missing the thrust of his deliberately blunt rhetoric: all of humanity is theologically bifurcated into two streams – those with and those without the Christian hope. Other exegetes, mindful of the evidence that there were some in antiquity who held hopes for an afterlife, try to defend Paul against the charge of overgeneralization when he speaks of the hopelessness of the pagan world in the face of death, by claiming that there is at least a sense in which this was actually true.[113] Admittedly, Paul does overstate the case to some extent;[114] but again, the point of his rhetoric is to establish a distinction between believers and non-believers, based on a distinctively Christian conception of hope. Luckensmeyer is right to say that Paul's use of the phrase οἱ μὴ ἔχοντες ἐλπίδα must be understood against the background of 'the polarising effect of ἐλπίς/ἐλπίζειν on humanity'.[115] For Paul, the Christian hope of salvation, as it is understood and appropriated in relation to the deep pain of bereavement, must not only inform but also condition, and in that way also demarcate, the very expression of sorrow. Thus, believers do not need to grieve as others do who are without this hope. As we shall see next, as part of his consolatory strategy Paul goes on to explain how and why this should be so. And as we

---

[108] Contra Edwin D. Freed, *The Morality of Paul's Converts* (Abingdon: Routledge, 2014), 91, whose view that οἱ λοιποί refers 'to other members of the brotherhood who have not yet reached the status of "in Christ" (4.16)' fails to account for Paul's use of the phrase here and its parallels in 4.5, 12.
[109] See Luckensmeyer, *Eschatology*, 216.
[110] See Luckensmeyer, *Eschatology*, 215–16, for a helpful précis of Paul's use of the word group ἐλπίς/ἐλπίζειν; Nicholl, *Thessalonica*, 25–6.
[111] Here I largely follow Barclay's incisive argumentation in his 'Death', 223–4.
[112] E.g. Lightfoot, *Notes*, 64; Nicholl, *Thessalonica*, 23; Ernst von Dobschütz, *Die Thessalonicher-Briefe*, 7th ed., KEK 10 (Göttingen: Vandenhoeck & Ruprecht, 1909), 188.
[113] Barclay, 'Death', 224, citing Bruce, *Thessalonians*, 104.
[114] So Wanamaker, *Thessalonians*, 167 (cited by Barclay, 'Death', 224); cf. Best, *Thessalonians*, 185–6.
[115] Luckensmeyer, *Eschatology*, 217–18.

4.4. Consolation in 1 Thessalonians

4.4.1. The Theological Basis of Consolation

From the evidence so far, it would seem that the believers at Thessalonica are deeply anguished by the sudden demise of some within their midst, because they fear that their deceased brethren would miss out on the eschatological blessings that were associated with the imminent return of Christ. In response, Paul tells his readers not to grieve like the unbelievers around them, who do not have the hope that they have (4.13). In the verses that follow, he spells out the two fundamental reasons for this hope.[116]

4.4.1.a. The Confession of the Church (1 Thess. 4.14)

First, Paul writes εἰ γὰρ πιστεύομεν ὅτι Ἰησοῦς ἀπέθανεν καὶ ἀνέστη (4.14a) – which most likely encapsulates an early Christian, that is, pre-Pauline, credal formula concerning the death and resurrection of Christ.[117] By doing so, Paul reminds the Thessalonians about what he had previously taught them about Christ's death and resurrection, which he assumes that they have accepted and embraced; this is indicated by the grammatical construction εἰ γὰρ πιστεύομεν and by his earlier thanksgiving that they were waiting for the return of God's son, ὃν ἤγειρεν ἐκ [τῶν] νεκρῶν (1.10). Moreover, Paul's citing of the credal formula rhetorically reinforces the authority of what he is saying: the death and resurrection of Christ are not merely a matter of his own privately held beliefs, nor even those held by the Thessalonian congregation, but something continually affirmed by the wider church to which they all belong.[118]

In the second half of the verse, Paul draws out the implications of this belief as it relates to the deceased believers over whom the Thessalonians grieve: οὕτως καὶ ὁ θεὸς τοὺς κοιμηθέντας διὰ τοῦ Ἰησοῦ ἄξει σὺν αὐτῷ (4.14b). The authoritative confession of the church concerning the resurrection of Jesus effectively guarantees the resurrection of believers who have died, such that they will be alive and with him at the Parousia.[119] Putting it another way, Paul anchors the assurance that he gives to the Thessalonians concerning the fate of dead believers to their shared belief in the resurrection of Christ.

---

[116] The γάρ of 4.14 functions as a marker of cause or reason.

[117] So many commentators, typically on the basis of (1) the confession-like introduction; (2) the presence of the rare Pauline designation Ἰησοῦς without qualification; (3) the use of the verb ἀνίστημι instead of Paul's favoured verb ἐγείρω (all the more striking because the other New Testament writers employ ἀνίστημι to speak of the resurrection); (4) the reference to Jesus rising instead of God's activity in raising Jesus (which Paul always refers to); and (5) the sheer economy of words. See e.g. Weima, *Thessalonians*, 316–17; Luckensmeyer, *Eschatology*, 220–1; for a contrary view see Malherbe, *Thessalonians*, 265.

[118] Weima, *Thessalonians*, 317.

[119] See Weima, *Thessalonians*, 317. Paul also draws a paradigmatic connection between Christ's resurrection and that of believers in Rom. 8.11-12; 1 Cor. 6.14; 15.20-3; 2 Cor. 4.14.

However, even though the broad thought flow of the verse is indisputably logical, Paul's words are elliptical, largely because the protasis and apodosis do not correspond as one might expect: (1) the protasis introduced by the formally conditional εἰ (4.14a) is completed clumsily with the formally comparative οὕτως καί (4.14b); (2) the verb πιστεύομεν disappears; (3) the expected subject, Ἰησοῦς or οἱ κοιμηθέντες, is replaced with ὁ θεός; and (4) instead of the anticipated ἀνίστημι there is ἄγω; closely related to this is the question of whether the prepositional phrase διὰ τοῦ Ἰησοῦ modifies the preceding substantival participle (τοὺς κοιμηθέντας) or the main verb (ἄξει).[120]

With regard to (1) and (2), Nicholl's suggestion that Paul's assertive apodosis might be a concerted attempt on his part to avoid any uncertainty that might be inferred from εἰ seems quite plausible;[121] certainly, its grammatical awkwardness heightens its effect, and the καί strengthens what is being stated.[122] Change (4) is the most significant, and much hinges on the interpretation of διὰ τοῦ Ἰησοῦ, the result of which has a bearing on change (3). The more common of the two views is to take διὰ τοῦ Ἰησοῦ with τοὺς κοιμηθέντας, in which case it qualifies the object of the clause and is virtually equivalent in meaning to ἐν Χριστῷ.[123] Yet the decision to do so rests mainly on arguments of word order and parallelism in the pericope, but these are not so compelling as to rule out any other option.[124] I follow instead the majority of German and an increasing minority of Anglo-American scholars who opt for taking διὰ τοῦ Ἰησοῦ with ἄξει.[125] On this view, God acts through Jesus, his intermediary agent of salvation – a reading which makes good sense of Paul's thought here, and is also in keeping with his use of διά elsewhere to express Christ's agency.[126] In addition, this reading smooths the link between the two halves of the verse, by making God-through-Jesus the subject of the apodosis, that is, change (3).[127] Thus 4.14 would run: 'For since we believe that Jesus died and rose again, even so, God, through Jesus, will gather with him those who have died.'

The first option (διὰ τοῦ Ἰησοῦ with τοὺς κοιμηθέντας) has the advantage of making explicit an implicit fact – that those believers who have died are 'in Christ'. But the second option (διὰ τοῦ Ἰησοῦ with ἄξει) affords a different and perhaps more helpful nuance: the risen Jesus is the one through whom God will act to effect the resurrection likewise of those believers who have died, and so bring them to himself. Ultimately, however, both options do not affect the overall thrust of the verse, which is to emphasize the presence of deceased believers with Christ at his return (ὁ θεὸς ... ἄξει σὺν αὐτῷ, 4.14b).

4.4.1.b. The 'Word of the Lord' (1 Thess. 4.15-17)

The second reason Paul furnishes to explain why the Thessalonians have hope as they grieve involves a striking appeal to a 'word of the Lord', that is, to some kind

---

[120] See in particular the detailed discussion in Nicholl, *Thessalonica*, 26–32.
[121] Nicholl, *Thessalonica*, 26 (appealing to Lightfoot, *Notes*, 64; Dobschütz, *Thessalonicher-Briefe*, 190).
[122] Malherbe, *Thessalonians*, 264.
[123] So e.g. Wanamaker, *Thessalonians*, 168–9; Joseph Plevnik, *Paul and the Parousia: An Exegetical and Theological Investigation* (Peabody, MA: Hendrickson, 1997), 211.
[124] Nicholl, *Thessalonica*, 28; Luckensmeyer, *Eschatology*, 222 (see also 181–2).
[125] So e.g. among German scholars, Hoffman, *Die Toten*, 213–16; others taking this view include Malherbe, *Thessalonians*, 266; Nicholl, *Thessalonica*, 28; Luckensmeyer, *Eschatology*, 223.
[126] See e.g. Luckensmeyer, *Eschatology*, 223, for references.
[127] Nicholl, *Thessalonica*, 28.

of authoritative saying or teaching of Jesus: Τοῦτο γὰρ ὑμῖν λέγομεν ἐν λόγῳ κυρίου (4.15a).[128] Scholars are divided over all three major issues that emerge from the interpretation of these verses: where the precise placement of this 'word' is, its source, and Paul's aim in citing it. However, it is unnecessary for the purposes of my study to examine the first two issues in any detail.

Following an increasing number of scholars,[129] I take the logion to be located at 4.16-17a.[130] On this reading, it is preceded by an anticipatory statement that relates the logion to the Thessalonians' specific concern, ὅτι ἡμεῖς οἱ ζῶντες οἱ περιλειπόμενοι εἰς τὴν παρουσίαν τοῦ κυρίου οὐ μὴ φθάσωμεν τοὺς κοιμηθέντας (4.15b), and followed by a comment that reinforces its importance to their situation, καὶ οὕτως πάντοτε σὺν κυρίῳ ἐσόμεθα (4.17b).[131] As to the source of the 'word', it seems likely that Paul is citing a dominical saying within the Jesus tradition represented in the canonical gospels, but does not do so exactly, in keeping with his practice elsewhere (1 Cor. 7.10, 25; 9.14; 11.23-5).[132]

The third question, concerning *why* Paul quotes this logion, is far more important for our understanding of the pericope. Earlier, in 4.14, Paul had looked to a credal

---

[128] The conjunction γάρ parallels its use in the previous verse (so most commentators); however, recently a number of scholars have countered that it is explanatory, i.e. that it identifies 4.15 as an explication of 4.14 instead of providing a second ground for Paul's instructions in 4.13 (so e.g. Malherbe, *Thessalonians*, 267; Nicholl, *Thessalonica*, 35; Luckensmeyer, *Eschatology*, 177). The demonstrative pronoun τοῦτο looks ahead to the material that follows as the site of this logion (so virtually all commentators; *pace* Richard, *Thessalonians*, 226, 240, who takes it to refer to the preceding argument).

[129] E.g. Hoffman, *Die Toten*, 219-20; Harnisch, *Eschatologische*, 40-42; Plevnik, 'Parousia', 230-1; and more recently, Nicholl, *Thessalonica*, 32-3; Weima, *Thessalonians*, 320-1.

[130] 4.16: ὅτι αὐτὸς ὁ κύριος ἐν κελεύσματι, ἐν φωνῇ ἀρχαγγέλου καὶ ἐν σάλπιγγι θεοῦ, καταβήσεται ἀπ' οὐρανοῦ καὶ οἱ νεκροὶ ἐν Χριστῷ ἀναστήσονται πρῶτον, 4.17a: ἔπειτα ἡμεῖς οἱ ζῶντες οἱ περιλειπόμενοι ἅμα σὺν αὐτοῖς ἁρπαγησόμεθα ἐν νεφέλαις εἰς ἀπάντησιν τοῦ κυρίου εἰς ἀέρα·

[131] Some scholars argue that the converse is true, i.e. that 4.15b is the 'word' and 4.16-17 an explication of it; see e.g. Dobschütz, *Thessalonicher-Briefe*, 193-4; Holtz, *Thessalonicher*, 184-5; Merklein, 'Der Theologe', 410-11; Donfried, 'Theology', 39-41. Thus Merklein, e.g. (followed by Donfried), finds several parallels between 1 Thess. 4.13-18 and 1 Cor. 15.50-8 that, for him, limit the logion to 1 Thess. 4.15b. However, apart from the fact that there are also other New Testament passages that are cited as parallels by various scholars, Merklein's solution discounts the important matter of stylistic features and vocabulary. As Nicholl, *Thessalonica*, 32-3, persuasively argues, 4.15b is mostly consistent with Paul, while parts of 4.16-17a are not; the few particularly Pauline elements in 4.16-17a may be readily explained by Paul's redaction to suit the epistolary context. All this strongly suggests that the λόγος κυρίου is located at 4.16-17a (introduced by a recitative ὅτι), with 4.15b functioning as an anticipatory summary (introduced by an epexegetical ὅτι).

That 4.17b does not lie within the logion is clearly indicated by its thoroughly Pauline vocabulary; furthermore, the adverb οὕτως is 'summarizing a thought expressed in what precedes' (BDAG 742).

[132] So Weima, *Thessalonians*, 321; see also e.g. Wanamaker, *Thessalonians*, 171. This is one of five major possibilities that commentators have identified as the possible source of the logion; there is no consensus: (1) a Pauline revelation; (2) a non-Pauline prophecy which Paul has accepted as originating from Jesus; (3) an agraphon; (4) a general reference to Jesus's eschatological teachings; (5) a saying of Jesus as found in the gospels (i.e. my preference). Combinations of the above solutions are possible; e.g. Ben Witherington, *1 and 2 Thessalonians: A Socio-Rhetorical Commentary* (Grand Rapids, MI: Eerdmans, 2006), 135-6, who thinks it plausible that Paul saw himself both as an interpreter of the sayings of the historical Jesus and as a prophet who received direct messages from the risen Lord. The precise provenance of the logion is not important for my study; for a concise summary of the scholarly debates see Malherbe, *Thessalonians*, 267-70; Nicholl, *Thessalonica*, 38-41.

formulation about the death and resurrection of Jesus to lend authority to his argument that Christians, like their Lord, would rise from the dead. Now in 4.15-17 Paul solidifies this argument by not only providing further information concerning the fate of dead believers at the Parousia but also locating these details in nothing less than a dominical warrant – in something that Jesus had actually taught or said. As Wanamaker notes, 'By placing his assurance that the living would not have precedence over the dead at the coming under the rubric "a word of the Lord," Paul attributed the highest possible authority to his assertion in v. 15b.'[133] The fact that Paul finds it necessary to appeal to such weighty sources of Christian authority in relation to both his arguments certainly suggests that he sees the Thessalonians' grieving as no small matter.[134]

In his argument Paul emphasizes in the strongest terms that at the Parousia, believers who are alive 'will by no means precede' (οὐ μὴ φθάσωμεν, 4.15b)[135] those who are dead. The temporal character of the verb φθάνω is reinforced by the use of the adverbs πρῶτον and ἔπειτα in the following verses (4.16-17) to underscore the notion that deceased believers would rise 'first', and 'then' they, together with living believers, would be taken up to meet the Lord. Paul's obvious concern throughout is with the faithful who have died before the Parousia; and clearly his point is that they will not suffer any disadvantage whatsoever. In fact, as the first order of things at Christ's return, they will be raised from the dead.

In 4.16-17 Paul rehearses, using the most explicit descriptions anywhere in his writings, the events surrounding the return of Christ. These verses have received a great deal of scholarly attention, but we do not need to be bogged down by the debates;[136] it is sufficient for our purposes to remember that Paul is redacting, from diverse sources, traditional material rich in symbol and metaphor to paint a complex apocalyptic scenario – but always with his stated consolatory intention in mind (4.18). He paints a picture of the three events that would occur in sequence at the Parousia: the Lord would descend from heaven, dead Christians would be resurrected, and these resurrected Christians, together with those still living, would be joined with the Lord (4.16-17a). Thus the result, as Paul makes crystal clear, is that all believers – whether presently alive or dead – would be in the Lord's presence for eternity: καὶ οὕτως πάντοτε σὺν κυρίῳ ἐσόμεθα (4.17b).[137] This brief, climaxing summary seems to reinforce the likelihood that Paul's intention lies neither in documenting in precise terms the events surrounding the return of Christ nor in elaborating in any detail the

---

[133] Wanamaker, *Thessalonians*, 171.
[134] Weima, *Thessalonians*, 322.
[135] The construction οὐ μὴ with aorist subjunctive expresses the strongest form of negation possible (BDF §365). Excluding his quotations from the LXX, Paul employs this construction only three times elsewhere: 1 Cor. 8.13; Gal. 5.16; 1 Thess. 5.3. His highly emphatic response lends further credence to the view that the concerns being addressed are of actual and not merely theoretical import; so e.g. Malherbe, *Thessalonians*, 272, who thinks that the use of the construction here 'is so strong that it sounds like a denial of an opinion actually held by some people in Thessalonica', especially in view of the parallel in 5.3, οὐ μὴ ἐκφύγωσιν ('they will by no means escape'), which is directed at those who propound erroneous teachings because of a misplaced confidence in Roman 'peace and security'.
[136] For a recent and instructive discussion, see Luckensmeyer, *Eschatology*, 237–68.
[137] As we have already noted, this is almost certainly not part of the logion.

nature of the eternal life that believers would enjoy with the Lord. Rather, his concern is to provide pastoral comfort to the Thessalonian Christians who are grieving over their deceased brethren.

4.4.1.c. Comfort One Another with These Words (1 Thess. 4.18)

This aim is made explicit in the exhortation with which Paul brings this pericope to a close: Ὥστε παρακαλεῖτε ἀλλήλους ἐν τοῖς λόγοις τούτοις (4.18). The particle ὥστε, when introducing an independent clause, means 'for this reason, therefore, so';[138] accordingly, here it serves to draw out Paul's conclusion from what he has written earlier in 4.13-17.[139] The verb παρακαλέω – a favourite of his[140] – carries a range of meanings[141] which can be grouped into two main nuances: either command ('appeal, exhort, request, implore'), as in 2.12; 4.1, 10; 5.14, or comfort ('encourage, comfort, cheer up, console'), as in 3.2, 7; 4.18; 5.11.[142] From the context, here in 4.18 the latter nuance is undoubtedly in view: Paul writes to console his readers; moreover, they are to share this comfort with others within the Thessalonians church.

Stowers notes that ancient letter writers who wrote on the theme of grief often urged their bereaved readers to use their words of consolation to exhort both themselves and others. He cites the example of a second-century papyrus letter, P.Oxy. 115, where a woman named Irene writes to a couple who have lost a son. After expressing her own grief and reasoning that 'nothing can be done in the face of such things [i.e. death]', Irene concludes, 'Therefore comfort one another'.[143] Stylistically, Paul's closing exhortation in this pericope seems to parallel this. However, his ground of consolation is ideologically completely different.

The consolation that Paul speaks of has its basis in τοῖς λόγοις τούτοις (4.18); it is immediately apparent from the context that he is referring back to the two arguments that he has just outlined: first, the ecclesiastical confession that Christ has risen from the dead, which serves to guarantee the resurrection of Christians and their presence at the Parousia (4.14), and second, the authoritative 'word of the Lord' which specifies that the faithful dead would suffer no disadvantage compared to those who remain alive but would participate with them on equal terms at that great eschatological event (4.15-17). It is these two factors that enable Paul to tell the Thessalonians with confidence that they need not grieve like others who do not share in the Christian hope.

The ground of Paul's consolatory instruction is therefore resolutely theological: it rests squarely on the Christian belief in the resurrection of Jesus, which in turn renders certain the future resurrection of dead believers upon his return. As with Paul's

---

[138] BDAG 1107.
[139] Paul uses the particle in a similar manner in e.g. 1 Cor. 7.38; 14.39; 15.58 (see see n.68 of this chapter).
[140] The verb appears forty times in the undisputed Paulines: most frequently in 2 Cor. (eighteen times) and in 1 Thess. (eight times: 2.12; 3.2, 7; 4.1, 10, 18; 5.11, 14).
[141] See e.g. BDAG 764–5, which lists five meanings.
[142] Weima, *Thessalonians*, 336.
[143] Stowers, *Letter Writing*, 145–6 (translations his). See similarly e.g. Malherbe, *Thessalonians*, 280.

strategy for the inculcation of joy in the Philippian church, here in his letter to the Thessalonians he attempts to draw the attention of the believers to the eschatological realities on which Christian life (and life after death) is premised – dimensions of thinking and belief that the Thessalonians may perhaps have either not fully understood, or forgotten as a result of the emotional trauma that they are undergoing. Again, as with joy, a comprehensive re-evaluation and transfiguration of the believer's mental and emotional engagement with the world lie at the heart of Paul's teachings. He wants the Thessalonians to know that a hopeless sorrow because of the death of their believing brethren is both baseless and unnecessary. Paul does not completely prohibit the expression of grief when it comes to the death of believers. Rather, he contrasts Christian grief with the grief of those outside the faith, and emphasizes that the expression of the former must be different from that of the latter, because death does not have the last word in the kingdom of God. For Paul, this is comfort indeed – comfort that is to be shared within the church.

4.4.2. The Social Character and Function of Consolation

As we have seen earlier, Paul's adjuration to the Thessalonians to bring comfort to one another in their grief – παρακαλεῖτε ἀλλήλους (4.18) – is not something new, at least not from the standpoint of literary style. Paul is apparently following the letter-writing conventions of the day, which in turn reflected social norms and practices. Consolation in antiquity was a matter of sociality and social performance: one was expected to give comfort and support to one's bereaved friends and relatives. However, the eschatological ideas that Paul injects into the consolatory tradition make it his own. And as I hope also to demonstrate, the Thessalonians' consolatory praxis now becomes imbued with new sociological significance, because it carries with it the powerful potential to enhance and structure corporate sensibility and self-definition, as the believers begin to reckon fully with the profound implications of Paul's teachings.

4.4.2.a. The Social Regulation of Grief

Both private grief and its public expression in mourning were matters that were of much concern to the peoples of the Roman Empire.[144] This concern manifested itself in feeling rules that regulated the social display of grief and mourning.[145] Stephen Barton helpfully highlights several noteworthy aspects of these feeling rules as they operated within the emotional regimes of Greco-Roman society in general.[146] First, grief and mourning were subject to sanction and control in such things as the manner and intensity of mourning, and its duration. Second, it is evident from the rich

---

[144] For a sociological analysis of grief and mourning in relation to the political and social order of the time, see Keith Hopkins, *Death and Renewal*, Sociological Studies in Roman History 2 (Cambridge: Cambridge University Press, 1983), especially 201–55.
[145] See generally Valerie M. Hope, *Roman Death: The Dying and the Dead in Ancient Rome* (London: Continuum, 2009), especially 121–49.
[146] Stephen C. Barton, 'Eschatology and the Emotions in Early Christianity', *Journal of Biblical Literature* 130 (2011): 582–6; here I summarize his main points, modifying slightly their sequence.

textual-rhetorical tradition of consolatory discourses, laments, treatises, and the like, and also non-literary material in the form of funerary inscriptions, that attitudes to grief and mourning generated widespread public comment and philosophical scrutiny. Third, underlying these feeling rules was a gendered ordering of behaviour in both the private and public spheres of daily life; this was seen particularly vividly in how inordinate grief was disapproved of and thought to be something to which women were especially prone.

Fourth, and perhaps most important for our purposes, since mourning customs were governed by considerations that related emotions to larger questions of ontology and world view, the differences in these behavioural conventions served to distinguish one group from another and thereby contributed to corporate self-definition. As Barton rightly concludes, 'Given the plurality of philosophical and societal views, a distinctive stance on grief and mourning was a likely indication of group identity and moral ethos.'[147] All this is most helpful, because it gives us a firm basis on which we may build an account of consolation in 1 Thessalonians that is at once sympathetic to the historical context of contemporaneous attitudes to grief and mindful of the ways in which grief and its therapy can express belief and identity.[148]

4.4.2.b. The Thessalonians' Grief

Earlier, on the basis of on the evidence in 1 Thessalonians, we had surmised that the Thessalonian believers' grief was most likely brought on by their underdeveloped understanding of the fate of the faithful dead at the return of Christ. Up to now, we have not said very much about the *effect* of these apparently unexpected deaths on the Christian community at Thessalonica. This aspect is important because it forms part of the background against which we seek to interpret why Paul says what he does to the Thessalonians by way of consolation.

Again, our evidence shows that the nascent church in Thessalonica had found itself mired in an ongoing situation of social conflict; indeed, such was its severity that Paul, apparently worried that the believers' Christian confidence was under threat, had despatched Timothy to Thessalonica to strengthen and encourage them (1 Thess. 3.2-5). In all probability, the Thessalonians' deliberate repudiation of traditional religious Greco-Roman beliefs and practices (1.9) had sparked a virulent backlash against them in the form of opprobrium, discrimination, ostracism, and perhaps even physical harassment and abuse; their behaviour was denounced as being not just socially offensive but also religiously and politically subversive.

It is in this situation of considerable suffering (e.g. 1.6; 2.14) that the already vulnerable Thessalonians now find themselves having to cope also with the shock caused by the sudden demise of some of their members. The community was very likely a small one, and certainly tight-knit and characterized by deep bonds of mutual

---

[147] Barton, 'Eschatology', 586.
[148] In what follows I am indebted to Stephen Barton's insightful proposals in his 'Eschatology', 586–91, and also to John Barclay's succinct reading of the social factors behind the Thessalonians' grief in his 'Death', 221–3.

affection and support; after all, their exemplary φιλαδελφία was highlighted and commended by Paul (4.9-10). It is not unreasonable therefore to suppose that the feelings of grief that the Thessalonians were registering emotionally were particularly acute. They had probably already been dispossessed of many of their kinship and friendship ties through rejection and ostracism; that sense of loss was now compounded by further separation and emotional pain, this time due to bereavement.[149] It therefore seems fair to make the observation that at both personal and group levels, the deaths of their much-loved brethren represented a severe crisis of loss for the Thessalonian Christians.[150]

There is also another sense in which these deaths very likely occasioned a severe crisis for the believers. It seems that they did not understand what was happening: what was the fate of those who had died? Had they missed out on the future blessings that were supposed to accrue to Christ's followers? Were they really God's beloved (1.4)? It is wholly plausible that the Thessalonians were wrestling with difficult existential and teleological questions concerning their Christian identity. Barton is therefore right to say that for the believers the deaths of their brethren represented also 'a tear in the delicate fabric of their intensely eschatological faith ... and, if of their faith, then of their self-understanding, sense of identity, and sense of future destiny'.[151] In other words, the crisis that the Thessalonians were facing had as much to do with their faith as it had to do with the loss of people who mattered to them.[152]

This is, I think, confirmed by the way in which Paul deals with these matters. His consolatory strategy has a firmly theological basis, as has been earlier discussed in some detail – but its character and function are in many ways social. It is to the sociological dimensions of consolation that we now turn.

4.4.2.c. The Social Character of Consolation

We note, first of all, that the dominant social metaphor that Paul employs to address his recipients is thoroughly familial,[153] not only here in 4.13-18 but also in the rest of the letter: in the Lord, the Thessalonian believers are ἀδελφοί to one another and to him (4.13; for other occurrences see n.41 earlier in this chapter). Paul uses also the

---

[149] Barclay, 'Death', 221–2, referring to the classic study of Arnold van Gennep, *The Rites of Passage*, trans. Monika Vizedom and Gabrielle L. Caffee (Chicago: University of Chicago Press, 1960), notes that all mourners are in a 'liminal state', but the Thessalonian Christians now suffered a 'double liminality'.

[150] Barclay, 'Death', 222, offers the intriguing suggestion that for the Thessalonians, the normal mourning processes were disrupted by the social tensions that their faith had engendered. He does not elaborate further at this juncture, but one can well imagine a situation where the embattled believers find it difficult to grieve for their brethren as they might wish to (perhaps because they face continued mockery from others who attribute these deaths to the anger of the gods against the impiety of the Christians; on this see Barclay, 'Conflict', 516; 'Death', 219; and earlier in this chapter of my study at the end of Section 4.3.3.b), or where any distinctively Christian funerary proceedings become the target of derision or vitriol.

[151] Barton, 'Eschatology', 587.

[152] This is however not to say that the Thessalonians were discouraged to the point that their sense of hope had become 'disengaged from their faith'; *pace* Donfried, 'Theology', 27.

[153] Barton, 'Eschatology', 590.

imagery of loving parental nurture to describe the nature of his relationship with the Thessalonians (2.7, 11). In the consolatory material here, as in his letter generally, a distinctive form of sociality is clearly presupposed: one that is characterized by the mutual affection, devotion, and care that characterize, and indeed enhance, the best familial relationships.

That this type of sociality is important, even crucial, for the proper ordering and functioning of the Thessalonian church is seen in how Paul repeatedly draws the believers' attention to the life in common which they inhabit and of which they are to be fully engaged stakeholders. This common life includes such aspects as the Thessalonians' shared experiences of suffering (2.14; 3.7-8) as well as of hope (5.8); a decided emphasis on corporate holiness, which includes being careful not to wrong each other (4.1-8); a proactive and vigorous φιλαδελφία (4.9-10); and the keeping of ethical instructions that foster social cohesiveness (5.12-15) and strengthen their corporate witness to outsiders (4.11-12). Even everyday rituals could acquire new layers of meaning in Paul's conception of an ideal Christian community. The giving of a kiss as part of a greeting was widespread practice in the ancient Near East, but the behest Paul issues at 5.26 regarding the exchanging of a kiss greeting is far from being a merely perfunctory concluding exhortation, because this kiss is to be a 'holy kiss' (φίλημα ἅγιον).[154] It is perhaps no coincidence that Paul draws his letter to the Thessalonians to a close with a call to what is in effect a powerful somatic-symbolic enactment of the unique spiritual oneness and social solidarity to which they are to aspire.

However, for our purposes, the aspect of the Thessalonians' sociality that concerns us most has to do with their practice of consolation. Paul's exhortation to 'comfort one another' (4.18) on this occasion of immense grief places the responsibility for a ministry of consolation not on any single individual or group of people, but squarely within the believing community as a whole.[155] He reinforces this in no uncertain terms by repeating and further fleshing out the exhortation at 5.11 ('comfort one another and build up each other') and commends the Thessalonians for already doing this; thus it is clear that in the church at Thessalonica, consolation – and specifically, consolation that is grounded in Christian teachings about life beyond death – is to be a *shared* responsibility.

I venture to suggest three possible reasons as to why this is so. First, since the believers' grief is due to ignorance on their part concerning the fate of the faithful dead (4.13), it is precisely the studied, corporately reinforced articulation and rearticulation of the theological realities underlying Christian consolation – for as we have seen earlier, the phrase ἐν τοῖς λόγοις τούτοις within Paul's consolatory instructions (4.18)

---

[154] For a useful study of the Pauline 'holy kiss', and also the ancient kiss greeting generally, see the discussion and further references in Jeffrey A. D. Weima, *Neglected Endings: The Significance of the Pauline Letter Closings*, JSNTSup 101 (Sheffield: JSOT Press, 1994), 112–14; see also Jeffrey A. D. Weima, 'Sincerely, Paul: The Significance of the Pauline Letter Closings', in *Paul and the Ancient Letter Form*, ed. Stanley E. Porter and Sean A. Adams (Leiden: Brill, 2010), 330–2.

[155] Beverly R. Gaventa, *First and Second Thessalonians*, Interpretation (Louisville, KY: John Knox Press, 1998), 68.

relates to his antecedent arguments (4.14-17) – which provide the best corrective to the problem of inordinate grief.

Second, given Paul's painstaking efforts to highlight to the Thessalonians the exceptional sociality that is to mark and shape their common life, it stands to reason that he should locate the responsibility of consolation within the ambit of this sociality, providing as it does further concrete opportunities to demonstrate brotherly love and upbuild social solidarity. The type of community that Paul seems to want to develop within the Thessalonian church is one that is characterized by unity, mutuality, interdependence, and a loving concern for one another – and all this to a superlative degree. Indeed, the bonds of relationship among the believers are to be so close that they approximate those that one might find in ideal family relationships; thus, for example, Paul applauds their exemplary φιλαδελφία, yet expresses a desire to see this love for the brethren intensify further (4.10; cf. 3.12). It seems reasonable to imagine that in Paul's mind one way this would happen is if they were more intentional about their responsibility to bring encouragement and consolation to one another especially in difficult times, like grief; indeed, as we shall later see, such an attitude builds each other up (5.11).

There is a third possible reason why Paul sees consolation as a shared responsibility within the church. It is intriguing that for him consolation has its basis in a specific theological construal of a future, glorious sociality in which living believers are united with (σύν) deceased believers and both groups united with (σύν) their Lord for eternity (4.17; cf. 4.14; 5.10). It seems most fitting that the ministry of consolation – which, after all, announces and celebrates the eschatological warrant for such a perfected sociality – should be embedded within an earthly sociality that serves as a harbinger of that heavenly one.

We turn now to the closely related question of the relationship between consolation and mutual upbuilding. At 5.1-11, Paul concerns himself with the matter of the fate of living believers at the return of Christ, rather than the fate of deceased believers (4.13-18). That the Thessalonian believers are anxious about the timing of this event and its consequences is indicated by the way Paul treats the subject and carefully reassures them of their eschatological destiny. It is particularly noteworthy that he brings his argument to a close by returning to the theme of being with the Lord, which was already so prominent (see 4.13, 17): ἵνα εἴτε γρηγορῶμεν εἴτε καθεύδωμεν ἅμα σὺν αὐτῷ ζήσωμεν (5.10). Not only will all believers, deceased or living, be found in the company of Christ at his Parousia, but they 'will live' with him – the ἐσόμεθα of 4.17 being modified to ζήσωμεν to underscore the certainty of eternal life as the existential reality in which eschatological salvation consists.

Paul concludes the section with the injunction Διὸ παρακαλεῖτε ἀλλήλους καὶ οἰκοδομεῖτε εἰς τὸν ἕνα, καθὼς καὶ ποιεῖτε (5.11), in which the παρακαλεῖτε ἀλλήλους of 4.18 is repeated verbatim. Appended to it is a second command, οἰκοδομεῖτε εἰς τὸν ἕνα, which speaks unequivocally of the believers' obligation to build each other up: the verb οἰκοδομέω is always figuratively in Paul's letters to connote some aspect of spiritual edification,[156] while the elliptical phrase εἰς τὸν ἕνα (literally, 'one on one')

---

[156] BDAG 696: 'strengthen, build up, make more able'; likewise, its cognate noun is almost always used

seems to stress here the personal and intimate nature of such a mutual ministry.[157] He does not specify the precise teachings that form the basis for this individual, reciprocal upbuilding, but the flow of his argument shows that at the very least he has in view both the immediately preceding discussion (5.1-10) and the subsequent exhortations that conclude the letter (5.12-22). The inferential conjunction διό with which he introduces the double commands of 5.10 links them to the preceding material in 5.1-10 (the διό thus functions similarly to the particle ὥστε in 4.18, in relation to 4.13-17), while the call to mutual edification has also a transitional function in the way it sets the stage for the explicit exhortations that follow, especially regarding attitudes and behaviour towards church leaders and fellow members of the Christian community (5.12-15).[158]

Yet one may with some justification argue that Paul in 5.11 has in mind a more expansive picture of mutual encouragement than he has earlier at 4.18. Certainly, as we have seen, with its parallel syntax the παρακαλεῖτε ἀλλήλους in 5.11 picks up the note of comfort that is advocated in 4.18. However, it is noteworthy that here in 5.11 the ἐν τοῖς λόγοις τούτοις of 4.18 is omitted, and that the παρακαλεῖτε is now instead deliberately juxtaposed with οἰκοδομεῖτε – which thereby interprets it and nuances its import. For Paul, then, exhortation has to do with mutual spiritual edification. Yet since it is in consequence of being the eschatological community that the Thessalonians are to edify and upbuild one another, the διό παρακαλεῖτε ἀλλήλους, with its concomitant οἰκοδομεῖτε, must relate not only to 5.1-10 but also to the entire section, 4.13-5.10.[159] As such, the consolation of 4.18 is an integral aspect of the broader ministry of mutual edification that Paul speaks of and calls the believers to in 5.11.

This emphasis on mutuality is all the more striking when we compare Paul's thinking to the type of sociality that his Stoic contemporaries like Epictetus were advocating. At first blush, the two frameworks seem broadly comparable: Epictetus affirms the social nature of humankind, and also teaches that one should fulfil one's duties to others.[160] However, any apparent similarities very quickly vanish, because absent entirely from Epictetus's scheme is any notion of the corporate mutuality that is so central to Paul's programme. For Epictetus, as for the Stoics generally, happiness emerges through the deliberate limiting of one's desires to those things that are located within the sphere of one's volitional autonomy, and which are therefore reasonable for one to possess.[161] As such, a proper relationship consists only in what one can do for someone else; one is never dependent on that other person for anything, least of all one's own happiness and well-being. Long explains it well:

figuratively of 'spiritual strengthening' and thus connotes 'edifying, edification, building up' (BDAG 696-7). Paul uses the verb especially in 1 Corinthians (8.1, 10; 10.23; 14.4 (2x), 17).

[157] So Weima, *Thessalonians*, 372-3; Malherbe, *Thessalonians*, 300-1, 307-8; Witherington, *Thessalonians*, 153-4, who all argue that as in 2.11 ('how we dealt with each one of you') Paul is stressing here in 5.11 the individualistic nature of this ministry. In other words, Paul had claimed in 2.11 that he had treated his converts as individuals; now, he expects them, as individuals, to build up other individuals just as he has done.
[158] See Weima, *Thessalonians*, 373, for further discussion.
[159] On this see Malherbe, *Thessalonians*, 300.
[160] Epictetus, *Diatr.* 3.2.4. See also the discussion in Section 2.5.1.c above.
[161] Anthony A. Long, *Epictetus: A Stoic and Socratic Guide to Life* (Oxford: Clarendon, 2002), 191; see also Section 2.2.1 above.

The correct performance of one's social roles … is both outwardly and inwardly oriented. It is outward in what it requires by way of sensitivity to the dignity and claims of other persons, but *what it is about other persons that should concern us is not how they treat us … but only how we dispose ourselves in relation to them.* The relevant relationship is entirely one-sided: us in relation to them, not them in relation to us. That is because, as Epictetus views the basis of proper relationships, they should be entirely translated, like everything we deal with, into the domain of our volition and integrity.[162]

Thus, while the fulfilment of one's duties to others is integral to Epictetus's thought, one's first responsibility is to maintain the integrity of one's own volition – the result of which is properly dutiful behaviour that reveals a remarkably high level of relational self-sufficiency. Paul's emphasis on unity, mutual love, and reciprocity in the carrying out of responsibilities, such as the ministry of consolation and the upbuilding of one another, takes the Thessalonian church in a completely different direction. There is no trace of Stoic self-sufficiency in Paul's scheme; instead, what he promotes within the Thessalonians is a purposeful interdependence that is expressed through mutual ministry among them. Each person is to assume thoughtful responsibility for the spiritual nurture and upbuilding of others within the community of faith. In fact, we may go so far as to suggest that there is a sense in which Paul is saying that each member of the church *needs* the faithful, attentive ministry of other members so that together they can more fully become the community that God has called them to be. As we have seen, this ministry, as Paul construes it, is both deeply individual and warmly reciprocal in nature; and in good paraenetic style he concludes this section by complimenting the Thessalonian for already demonstrating it in their relationships with each other (καθὼς καὶ ποιεῖτε, 5.11). The believers are apparently already actively engaged in ministry to one another – ministry that is to include the bringing of consolation and comfort to the bereaved among them.

4.4.2.d. The Function of Consolation

We turn, finally, to a consideration of the function of consolation in the letter. To be sure, Paul's provision of feeling rules to the Thessalonians to manage their grief puts him in the company of many others in his day who sought to bring comfort to the bereaved. Whether one takes what Paul says to be an absolute prohibition against grief or otherwise, the fact remains that he prescribes strict qualitative limits on the extent of grief as it pertains to the death of other Christians. Why, however, is Paul so concerned about inordinate grief? Or, to ask a more pointed question: what would happen if the Thessalonians failed to console one another at this time of mourning?

As Barton notes, the instructions issued by Paul place him at or near one end of the spectrum of the philosophical (and general) debate as to whether grief and its social representation in mourning were reasonable responses to death for those who thought themselves to be truly wise and virtuous. He goes on to suggest that Paul's

---

[162] Long, *Epictetus*, 237 (emphasis mine). See Epictetus, *Diatr.* 2.22.20.

consolatory approach very likely carried moral and rhetorical weight with its recipients at least in part because it accorded with the strong emphasis on the control of the emotions within Stoic therapeutic paraenesis.[163] Certainly, there are some interesting parallels – at least at a superficial level – between Paul's teachings and that of his Stoic contemporaries on the subjugation of grief. In different ways, both Paul and the Stoics locate the possibility of consolation within a thoroughgoing rational dismantling of the usefulness and appositeness of grief in the face of death. A recapitulation of Stoic thinking about grief and its cure is helpful at this point.

In Stoicism, grief (λύπη) is the opinion that some present thing is an evil of such a sort that one should be downcast about it (see Section 2.3.3.a). More specifically, grief is the result of the combination of two related value judgements: an evaluation of an external object as being injurious to oneself and a belief in the appropriateness of a predicative reaction to it. However, since it is irrational to think that external objects are of any significance to one's state of well-being, both sets of judgements are systematically misguided. Therefore on the Stoic account, grief – being the consequence of fallacious reasoning – is a passion to be extirpated. As such, integral to Stoic philosophical teaching and therapeutic intervention is the insistence that the judgements with which the passions are identified are erroneous, since all externals do not carry any intrinsic value whatsoever.

Thus, as we have seen earlier (see Section 2.5.1.b), Seneca freely harnesses several stock philosophical arguments in his efforts to attenuate the grief that the addressees of his letters are experiencing: for instance, that death is inevitable for all, that it delivers those who have died from both present and future misfortunes, and that grief is of no use whatsoever – benefitting neither oneself nor the person for whom one mourns. Outwardly, his consolatory strategies share many similarities with Greco-Roman consolation in general, especially in regard to their ideological neutrality and highly practical bent. Embedded within Seneca's thought, however, is also some quintessentially Stoic thinking, at the heart of which is the conclusion that grief is inherently irrational because it is fuelled by a false opinion about the state of matters in which the individual finds himself. Yet, as I have argued, Seneca's view of grief and its expression is a multifaceted one. On the one hand, though he acknowledges that grief is a naturally reflexive and therefore unavoidable response to the tragedies that inevitably encroach on human life, he calls for a carefully deliberate application of reason to curb any grief that becomes uncontrollably excessive.[164] Seneca apparently champions, at least in relation to grief, a form of *metriopatheia*. On the other hand, he also seems to want to uncover within the boundaries of Stoicism the possibility of the presence of a specific type of grief that is not incompatible with virtuous thinking and living, or, in other words, the wise person's grief – one that emerges not because of some involuntary emotional reflex but because of positive, voluntary feelings that are based on fully veridical assessments of one's circumstances.[165] As we have noted, such a 'proper' grief might be considered a eupathic antithesis to pathological grief.

---

[163] Barton, 'Eschatology', 587–8.
[164] See especially Seneca, *Polyb.* 18.4-7.
[165] See Seneca, *Ep.* 99.18-21.

Seneca's multivalent understanding of grief stands in contrast to that of Epictetus, whose perhaps more straightforwardly Stoic reading of the passions construes grief as the result of the wholly mistaken judgement that death is something dreadful for the human person (see Section 2.5.1.c). Simply put, then, the Stoic wise person would not experience or exhibit grief of the kind that would compromise his state of rational equanimity. Yet even though Epictetus, unlike Seneca, does not show much interest in how one might bring consolation in practical ways to someone who was grieving, it is noteworthy that he mentions that one should not hesitate to show sympathy to such a person. However, any demonstration of affective solidarity must not result in sorrow that causes a disruption in one's control over one's own mind and thinking.[166] For Epictetus, the maintaining of the integrity of one's self-autonomy and volition is of the utmost importance.[167] Thus we see that both Seneca and Epictetus are seeking to work out and promote, within the Stoic philosophical framework, a rational basis for the management of grief. Since death is a natural phenomenon that lies beyond the ability of humans to control, it is to be accepted dispassionately. What is important is the manner in which one chooses to live.

That Paul has an equally reasoned interest in what makes consolation efficacious in the constraint of grief is hinted at in his choice of words relating to knowledge, belief, and the mind – οὐ θέλομεν δὲ ὑμᾶς ἀγνοεῖν (4.13), εἰ γὰρ πιστεύομεν (4.14) – and immediately confirmed when he discloses the theological rationale for his approach. The Stoics located their solution wholly within the human person's own internal resources or, more specifically, within his or her powers of right reason, but Paul has cast his gaze elsewhere – to God's action in human history in the past, present, and future. As Paul sees it, for the Christian to grieve in the manner of unbelievers is wholly irrational: not because death is an external good that is devoid of any intrinsic value but because death will give way to life with other believers and with Christ at the eschaton. At its core, then, Paul's consolatory strategy is rooted in his theological world view – in the hope of a cosmic union at the Parousia, one so powerful that it overcomes both physical and mortal separation and thereby reinterprets, and indeed relativizes, death itself.[168] Thus, for believers to grieve καθὼς καὶ οἱ λοιποὶ οἱ μὴ ἔχοντες ἐλπίδα (4.13b) would be to misrepresent the overarching eschatological narrative which encompasses their individual life histories, and thus misunderstand the true nature of their Christian identity. For as Christians, their destinies are eternally secure: the dislocation that death produces is only temporary, because Christ will return to bring to himself those who are his.

This, I suggest, points us towards the answer as to why Paul is so concerned about inordinate grief in the Thessalonian church. Simply put, for Paul, *how* one grieves is inextricably related to what one truly believes about death and therefore also to the entire system of Christian theological understanding that underpins and sustains these beliefs. The Stoics, too, thought that grief, like other passions, could be assuaged through a process of corrected cognitive evaluation. However, though both frameworks

---

[166] Epictetus, *Ench.* 16.
[167] See also Section 2.5.1.c above.
[168] Smith, *Comfort*, 57.

evince a rigorously reasoned approach to the therapy of grief, there are fundamentally different ideological bases for the consolation that they each offer. Furthermore, *why* such consolation is important is also not the same. Paul does not share the Stoics' overriding concern for inner serenity and rational imperturbability; instead, he is interested in the creation and maintenance of a robust Christian self-identity which will thereby foster the stability of the community of believers as a whole. Hence, for Paul, excessive grief is highly problematic not only because it betrays in the individual an inadequate understanding of Christian death but also because it threatens the ethos of the young church at Thessalonica. In fact, as Paul might see it, any failure of the Thessalonians to bring consolation to each other could be potentially disastrous; for if they were to waver in their Christian faith because of despairing grief, they would surely find it increasingly difficult to bear up under the social conflict in which they were embroiled – social conflict which had arisen precisely because of their allegiance to this faith.[169]

Given Paul's interest in safeguarding the health of the church at large, it is not surprising that while the feeling rules concerning grief that he gives to the Thessalonians are certainly premised on the specifics of his eschatological vision, these rules have also a distinctively sociological cast in that they reveal a powerful potential to establish clear group boundaries, thereby helping to structure both individual and corporate self-definition along distinctively Christian lines.

As we have noted earlier, in Paul's theological framework, all of humanity may be located in one of two categories: those who have eschatological hope, because they follow Christ, and everyone else – somewhat unceremoniously dismissed as 'the rest' (οἱ λοιποί, 4.13) – that is, those who are without this hope. There are no exceptions to the complete polarizing of humanity on this basis. Perhaps because he wishes to drive home the point, in several places but especially in chapter 5, Paul contrasts these two categories of humanity in starkly antithetical terms, often using metaphorical language. On the one side are the believers, ἀδελφοί[170] loved and chosen by God (1.4), to whom knowledge of 'the times and seasons' – a stock phrase relating to the timing of apocalyptic events[171] – has been disclosed (5.1-2).[172] In Paul's eschatological drama, they are cast in approving terms as 'children of light' (5.5) and 'children of the day' (5.5; cf. 5.8) who remain awake and sober (5.6); ultimately, they obtain salvation through Christ (5.9). On the other side lies the rest of humanity: they are 'outsiders' (4.12) who do not know God (4.5) or anything of his eschatological agendum (5.3). Depicted as a negative foil to believers, such people are 'of the night and of darkness' (5.5; cf.

---

[169] Barclay, 'Conflict', 516–18, argues convincingly that the Thessalonians' apocalyptic world view and their experience of social alienation reinforced each other in a complex dialectic: their apocalyptic perspective helped them to see their sufferings as something that was to be expected but also temporary; conversely, every experience of social conflict only reinforced the truth of the apocalyptic teachings that they had adopted.

[170] See n.41 in this chapter for the other occurrences in 1 Thess.

[171] See e.g. Wanamaker, *Thessalonians*, 177–8.

[172] Whether οὐ χρείαν ἔχετε ὑμῖν γράφεσθαι (5.1) is indeed a case of paralipsis (Weima, *Thessalonians*, 345) or not (Malherbe, *Thessalonians*, 289) does not affect the interpretation of 5.1-2: Paul is saying that the Thessalonians already know that the coming of the Parousia is certain but that it will be unexpected.

5.4), being drunk and asleep (5.7). In the end, lacking sober vigilance, they, unlike the believers, are unable to escape God's wrath (5.3, 9).[173]

One cannot fail to notice the care with which Paul distinguishes the believing community from the rest of humanity on the basis of their wholly different eschatological destinies. Barclay argues rightly that 'the crucial move that Paul makes here is to adjust this differentiation so as to take account of death, indeed to direct believers into making death itself – how they mark it and how they view it – a symbol of their distinction'.[174] In other words, the manner in which a Christian grieves can reveal a great deal about what he or she truly believes concerning the eternal destiny of the believer. On this view, eschatological confidence (or its lack thereof) becomes an important Pauline boundary marker of identity and self-definition on both the personal and corporate planes of Christian self-understanding. Putting it another way: for Paul, attitudes towards grief function to differentiate believers from the people around them, and thereby become intrinsic to the proper formation of Christian identity.

We may therefore conclude that for Paul consolation plays a highly distinctive role in the upbuilding of the Thessalonian church. Since consolation has to do with having a right knowledge of eschatological reality, Paul carefully summarizes the teachings of the church concerning the events at the Parousia. That which is certain to happen in the future has momentous ontological and ethical implications for the present state of bereavement in which the believers find themselves, in relation to their self-identity and to how they are to grieve. As Beverly Gaventa writes,

> What Paul affirms regarding the relationship of believers with one another and with their Lord reaches well beyond a social relationship confined to this place and time. Those who are bound together remain so, even after death. The boundary Paul has drawn around the church is a boundary that extends into the future. Although a boundary separates believers from non-believers, it does not separate the living from the dead. The social world created in the church runs in two directions – believers' association with the Lord and their association with one another.[175]

For Paul, consolation both expresses and is itself embedded within this extraordinary multidimensional sociality. It simultaneously brings comfort and assurance, because it occurs within and speaks of relationships that do not end with death, and because this felicitous state of affairs is grounded in a hope that is certain. It is interesting that this hope is directed towards an ultimate goal that is thoroughly social: eternal life lived with Christ, in the company of other believers.

---

[173] See further Barclay, 'Death', 225–7.
[174] Barclay, 'Death', 227. Though I am not persuaded by Barclay's interpretation of 1 Thess. 4.13 as an absolute prohibition against grief (see Section 4.3.4), in the main his thesis about a Pauline 'christianizing' of death is highly compelling; on this see in particular 227–8, 234.
[175] Gaventa, *Thessalonians*, 68.

4.5. Conclusion

In 1 Thessalonians, Paul responds to a beleaguered church that has also recently been thrown into grief because of the unforeseen deaths of some of its members. Several factors contributed to the opprobrium that the Thessalonians have had to endure, including, most notably, their rejection of traditional Greco-Roman religious beliefs, the social disruption resulting from their conversion experience, and the political overtones of the Christian message – all of which led to their being stigmatized as socially and ideologically deviant. These sufferings are now exacerbated by the heartache of bereavement; and there is a sense in which the deaths of their members represented a double crisis – of loss as well as faith – because the already emotionally fragile Thessalonians have been hit by deaths that they could not reconcile with what they knew of the Christian's identity and destiny. Unable to return to Thessalonica in person, Paul writes this letter to encourage them in their convictions and also to comfort them in their grief, which he presupposes is symptomatic of a confused or incomplete eschatology.

The painstaking care with which Paul addresses the Thessalonians' grief indicates how serious the matter is to him. At one level, there is the searing pain of personal loss – perhaps all the more acute given the close bonds of affection among the believers, and the fact that relationships within the church were probably particularly valued because of the social dislocation that scarred their lives. However, at another level, at stake is nothing less than the long-term stability of the Thessalonian church, because protracted and untreated sorrow that stemmed from an inadequate understanding of death would surely undermine the believers' confidence in the future and hope in God.

Like others in his day, Paul therefore imposes feeling rules to control grief; and like much of contemporaneous philosophical thought, these consolatory principles take their cue from some form of cognitive evaluation as to what death actually is. However, the ideological roots of Paul's injunctions are entirely unique: thus, where, for example, the Stoics reject grief because they see it as a completely misjudged and therefore wholly irrational affective response to death, which lies beyond one's ability to control, Paul instead grounds his consolatory instructions in a theological rehearsal of the events surrounding the Parousia. The death of fellow Christians is not an occasion for inordinate grief, because their eternal destiny is secure: the resurrection of Jesus is a guarantee of the resurrection of dead believers. Thus, as Paul seems to see it, a forward-looking confidence that is based on sound eschatological expectation can help to immunize believers against excessive grief, thereby making their response to death itself a powerful symbol of Christian distinctiveness.

At the same time, Paul charges the Thessalonians with the task of bringing comfort to one another in their grief, thus deliberately situating this shared responsibility for consolation within the locus of the remarkable sociality that their common life is to embody and manifest. The effect of all this is to foreground the distinctiveness of their faith, and with it the distinctiveness of their eschatological identity and corporate ethos, in two important ways.

First, the profoundly relational nature of the Christian life is emphasized. While a believer's identity certainly derives primarily from his or her relationship with Christ, it is reinforced and even vivified in community as individuals take seriously their responsibility to nurture and upbuild one another. Paul's summons to the Thessalonians to continue their ministry of mutual spiritual edification seems to imply that they require each other's ministry in order to develop and live out their Christian identity. Such a network of interdependent relationships would be unimaginable for a Stoic, in whose eyes the presence of others might possibly be instrumentally necessary for the exercise of virtue, but is never constitutive of it. For Paul, however, there is an intrinsically social dimension to the Christian's proper flourishing: it is in relationship with Christ and with other believers that one reaches one's fullest potential.

Second, and related to the foregoing, the permanence of these sets of relationships is highlighted. It is precisely because death results in only a temporary disruption of these bonds that consolation makes any sense at all. The Christian hope is that at the return of Christ, death will give way to life with him and with other believers. Therefore consolation, for Paul, has to do with believers reminding one another during times of grief – no matter how severe – that this beatific vision of consummate sociality is also an eschatological reality that awaits them.

5

The Pauline Emotional Regime

5.1. Introduction

Our study of two key emotional stances in Paul's writings – joy, and the assuaging of grief – has shown that emotion, far from being related only to the individual's inner states, has also a distinctively social cast: there are fundamental ways in which emotion is both socially constructed and socially promulgated. Moreover, an emotion is not a subjective, paroxysmal response to an external trigger, but is connected deeply to, and in fact generated from, fundamental dispositions of thought and belief. To the extent that all this is so, specific emotional states can therefore be commanded, and hence also be learnt and regularly practised. For the believer, emotions such as joy are to be actively encouraged, while other emotional patterns such as inordinate grief are to be jettisoned. Paul takes pains to promote certain means of affective response; in a highly pragmatic sense he is teaching his followers *how they should feel* – just as he constantly teaches them how they should think and act. All this suggests that in his overarching scheme, emotion plays a substantial role in helping to shape and stabilize key aspects of Christian identity at both the individual and corporate level. Right emotion can embody, and thereby reinforce, modes of cognition and thinking that are consonant with what it means to be a believer amidst other believers; conversely, uncontrolled displays of affect can severely compromise or even destroy the believer's self-identity and witness.

What I am therefore proposing is that for Paul, patterns of feeling are to go hand in hand with patterns of belief; and that these patterns of feeling, like the patterns of belief with which they are intertwined, have a social context and function. To use a term that we shall explain fully in due course, through what he is doing (i.e. encouraging certain emotions and discounting others) Paul is in effect inculcating in his churches a religious 'emotional regime' – an ordering of emotion, closely bound up with the social world of which it is a part and informed by the system of religious symbols to which it is intricately connected, that simultaneously structures and regulates the emotional responses of its members in accordance with the reality framework that is deemed as normative for them. Since this deliberate control of emotion has a set of functions or effects that are targeted at the upbuilding of the community of believers, there is ample justification to regard emotion as a key dimension of the social formation of the early Church – a dimension that has yet to be fully explored in current New Testament scholarship. Far from being only incidental in the effort to understand the lives of the first believers, a rigorous engagement with emotion – which encodes and communicates theological beliefs and moral judgements, and thus expresses individual and group identity in the everyday context of social relationships and cultural engagement – can only contribute to a fuller appreciation of Pauline Christianity.

In 1983, Wayne Meeks published his *The First Urban Christians* – an innovative, wide-ranging reconstruction of the social realities of the Pauline assemblies that placed early Christianity squarely in its sociocultural setting and signalled the fact that social-scientific approaches to the study of the New Testament had come to substantial maturity. Meeks's landmark work (now in its second edition[1]) arguably heralded a new era in scholarship on Paul, and numerous subsequent studies reveal its enduring influence. Of particular relevance to my study is Meeks's correlating of the beliefs and doctrines of the early Church with the social structures within which the early Christians operated and with certain aspects of their social experience. However, highly influential though his proposals have been, next to nothing is said about the emotional life of the believers. I suggest that the inclusion of the role of emotion would flesh out more fully Meeks's account of the socialization of Paul's converts in line with their newfound faith, and thereby help to move us towards an even more robust and full-orbed understanding of early Christianity.

In very broad terms, this chapter is laid out in the following manner. First, I will discuss Meeks's ideas concerning the two-way relationship between what a typical member of a Pauline congregation believed in regard to doctrine, and the social force of that belief. I will then outline and offer the sociological concept of the emotional regime as a heuristic tool for our investigation of Paul and emotion. Next, using precisely this tool to open up the question of the construction of emotion, I will explore key aspects of Paul's emotional regime in order to try to understand its potency and longevity. Finally, I will provide an account of the function of emotion in Paul's churches. I will argue that for Paul, how the believer is to feel is intimately related to what he or she thinks about crucially important matters of faith, life, and death. As such, a certain set of prescribed, right feelings must therefore be placed within that larger set of prescribed, right beliefs and behaviours that distinguish those who pledge their allegiance to Christ from others who do not belong to the community of faith. As with the right beliefs that constitute and animate them, right emotions have both a socially integrating and a differentiating function: a set of endorsed, taught, learnt, and mutually experienced emotions strengthens a group's solidarity while at the same time demarcating its boundaries. Thus, for Paul, emotion is an important aspect of the complex composite of Christian belief and sociality, and an integral aspect of what it means for a believer to be in community with other believers, and for that community to be in the world.

---

[1] Wayne A. Meeks, *The First Urban Christians: The Social World of the Apostle Paul*, 2nd ed. (New Haven, CT: Yale University Press, 2003).

5.2. The Early Christians and Emotion

5.2.1. Wayne Meeks's *The First Urban Christians*

In his study of the social world of the Pauline congregations, Meeks draws on a range of anthropological and sociological insights, on Roman social history, and on New Testament studies, to elucidate what life was like for ordinary Christians. Certainly, his study was part of a burgeoning body of scholarly work which, beginning in the 1970s, had incorporated social-scientific criticism in the study of early Christianity. Yet the creative ways in which Meeks consolidated much of the early scholarship on the Pauline churches (perhaps most notably Gerd Theissen's work on social stratification in Corinth) and also championed important new ideas (e.g. concerning the purpose of ritual and the role of 'status inconsistency' in attracting would-be converts) led to the widespread recognition that his study represented a milestone in New Testament scholarship, a mature flourishing of studies in this area.

Methodologically, Meeks regards himself as a social historian of early Christianity whose general approach is aimed at producing what is in effect a Geertzian 'thick description' or interpretative ethnography of the social world of the Pauline congregations.[2] Adopting what he takes to be an increasingly shared view among social scientists and historians of religion, for Meeks, 'society is viewed as a process, in which personal identity and social forms are mutually and continually created by interactions that occur by means of symbols'.[3] Hence, social and symbolic structures are related in a real but complex way, and religion is an integral part of the sociocultural web.[4] Within this general context, Meeks styles himself a 'moderate functionalist'; in his own words, the comprehensive question guiding the reading of his primary sources has to do with 'not only what each one says, but what it does'. For him, such a theoretical stance sidesteps the reductionism that would result from a purely functionalist, Durkheimian, reading of the function of religion.[5] Meeks's avowedly eclectic and piecemeal use of the social sciences parades a deliberate pragmatism in which a theory is employed as needed when it can help to shed light on some aspect of the social lives of the early Christians.[6] Accordingly, he borrows and carefully applies insights from a wide assortment of approaches.[7]

Especially germane to my study is Meeks's exploration (in chapter 6 of his book) of the relationship between the systems of doctrine reflected in the Pauline letters and the systems of social relations experienced by those to whom these letters are addressed. In Meeks's view, there are discernible correlations between these 'patterns of belief'

---

[2] Meeks, *Christians*, 5–6.
[3] Meeks, *Christians*, 6.
[4] Meeks, *Christians*, 6.
[5] Meeks, *Christians*, 6–7.
[6] Meeks, *Christians*, 6.
[7] E.g. Victor Turner (Meeks, *Christians*, 88–9, 157), Mary Douglas (97, 141), and Melford E. Spiro (140–1) on aspects of ritual; Tony Reekmans (22–3), P. R. C. Weaver (22–3), and Seymour Martin Lipset (54) on questions of social status and social mobility; Leon Festinger (85) on social cohesion; and Brian Wilson (85) on sects.

and 'patterns of life': the term 'correlation' is specifically chosen to indicate that one can speak of how belief structures match social forms without needing to assume that there is a direct causal relationship in either direction.[8] Meeks concludes his discussion by outlining four areas where the correlations between symbolization and socialization seem particularly apparent. First, the unity of the one God of Pauline Christianity is correlated with the unity that is to mark the entire body of believers, that is, in each local congregation and in the connections between them. Second, the belief that God is personal and active is correlated with the nature of the relationships within the local assembly of believers, which are to be marked by intimacy, mutual commitment, and interpersonal engagement. Third, Pauline eschatology is matched with, and thus helps the Christians to make sense of, the social experiences that have come in the wake of conversion. Fourth, the social contradictions experienced by the group and embodied personally by its members find their correlate in the contradictions experienced and embodied by Christ.[9] Meeks then reiterates his earlier proposal (in chapter 2 of his book) concerning how the new converts' status inconsistency – the lack of correlation between diverse social and economic indicators of status, such as ethnic origin, *ordo*, citizenship, wealth, occupation, and others – would have drawn them deeper into Christianity, with its powerful symbols of a divine ordering of the world and of personal and communal transformation, and its enticing promises of a sense of belonging and of relational intimacy.[10]

In summary, then: for Meeks, belief structures and sacred symbols (patterns of belief) affect social reality and socialization (patterns of life) in profound ways, and vice versa. Moreover, it is precisely this complex dialectic that helps to explain why typical converts to Pauline Christianity were attracted to it in the first place; matters concerning the societal status of the individual play directly into the question of how Christianity was viewed and accepted and its teachings legitimated. All this has led to the widespread acknowledgement that one of the most significant contributions that Meeks's work has made to the study of the New Testament is in its consideration of the extent to which the growth of first-century Christianity in its urban setting was assisted by socio-economic factors.[11]

Not unexpectedly, Meeks's proposals have also aroused much debate, perhaps especially in regard to his methodological stance on the social-scientific study of the New Testament and his use of status inconsistency to explain in socio-economic terms the allure of early urban Christianity.[12] Nonetheless, Meeks's legacy is immense, and

---

[8] Meeks, *Christians*, 164.
[9] Meeks, *Christians*, 190–1.
[10] Meeks, *Christians*, 191; on status inconsistency see 22–3, 54–5, 72–3.
[11] So e.g. Bruce W. Longenecker, 'Socio-Economic Profiling of the First Urban Christians', in *After the First Urban Christians: The Social-Scientific Study of Pauline Christianity Twenty-Five Years Later*, ed. Todd D. Still and David G. Horrell (London: T&T Clark, 2009), 36–7.
[12] For a summary of the reactions to Meeks insofar as they relate to methodological considerations, see David G. Horrell, 'Whither Social-Scientific Approaches to New Testament Interpretation? Reflections on Contested Methodologies and the Future', in *After the First Urban Christians: The Social-Scientific Study of Pauline Christianity Twenty-Five Years Later*, ed. Todd D. Still and David G. Horrell (London: T&T Clark, 2009), 7–8. On the debate over Meeks's approach to social profiling, see Longenecker, 'Socio-Economic Profiling', 38–45.

his work has hugely influenced subsequent generations of scholars and galvanized numerous studies.[13] Of course, all this scholarly activity must be placed in its broader context: in the three decades since the publication of *The First Urban Christians*, there has been a continued diversification in both the range of approaches and types of concerns associated with efforts to engage with the New Testament in social-scientific terms – and to such a diffuse degree that it is impossible to speak today of any kind of common approach, method, or focus to define the field.[14] Nonetheless, Meeks's work has in many ways remained highly seminal.

5.2.2. Moving beyond Meeks: The Social Function of Emotion

As mentioned, the aspect of Meeks's work that I want to focus on has to do with how he correlates the social experiences of the Pauline Christians with the structures of belief that were integral to their resocialization as members of a new social organization. The dialectical relationship that Meeks identifies between patterns of belief and patterns of life is extremely helpful in opening up the question of the social force of doctrine in relation to the formation of a distinctively Christian identity at both the individual and group level. Yet I wish to suggest that Meeks's account would be enriched, and perhaps to no small degree, if it incorporated an explicit consideration of the function of emotion in the socialization of these new converts, especially given what recent developments in cognitive science and in social-scientific research suggest about the nature and construction of emotion (see Section 1.3 above).

To be sure, at a number of points Meeks seems to acknowledge that emotion has some sort of role in this process, at least in connection with the use of language. For example, in his discussion of the formation of the Pauline communities, Meeks stresses that boundaries were drawn to help the groups identify themselves as groups and as a broader movement. These boundaries included 'aspects of language, practice, and expressed sentiments and attitudes that gave the group internal cohesion';[15] and among the aspects of language that Meeks highlights is the emotionally charged, fictive use of kinship terms within the group – which he understands to play a role in cementing a believer's new identity and thus in reinforcing the *communitas* of the Christian groups, especially when such use is accompanied by special terms for 'the outsiders' and 'the world'.[16] Noting the extremely unusual frequency and intensity of affective phrases in the Pauline corpus when compared to other ancient letters, Meeks cites several examples from 1 Thessalonians and Philippians and concludes that 'the Pauline letters are unusually rich in emotional language – joy and rejoicing, anxiety, longing'.[17]

---

[13] See especially the essays in Todd D. Still and David G. Horrell, eds, *After the First Urban Christians: The Social-Scientific Study of Pauline Christianity Twenty-Five Years Later* (London: T&T Clark, 2009).
[14] Horrell, 'Whither Social-Scientific Approaches', 8. See 8–11 for an overview of key developments in social-scientific approaches to the New Testament since the 1980s.
[15] Meeks, *Christians*, 85.
[16] Meeks, *Christians*, 85–6, 94–5; see also 88–9.
[17] Meeks, *Christians*, 86–7 (quote from 86).

Nowhere, however, does Meeks treat emotion independently of language as a separate aspect of the resocialization of the new believers.

Thus, later in his study (and still with reference to the function of language) Meeks makes the observation that

> not just the shared contents of beliefs but also shared forms by which the beliefs are expressed are important in promoting cohesiveness. Every close-knit group develops its own argot, and the use of that argot in speech among members knits them more closely still.[18]

In his discussion, Meeks has in mind such things as in-group jargon and special nuances, syntactical patterns of speech, slogans, and ritual language.[19] But while his wide-ranging focus on the function of language as a repository of belief is salutary, one wonders if his conclusions might be reinforced by an exploration of emotion itself as a site for the expression – linguistic or otherwise – of shared beliefs. Elsewhere, Meeks concludes in his analysis of 1 Thess. 4.13–5.11 that the function of Paul's apocalyptic language here and in the letter as a whole is to reinforce the sense of uniqueness and cohesion of the community, which in turn produces a disposition to act in a way appropriate to its well-being. Meeks sets out what such appropriate behaviour is: it 'includes internal discipline and obedience of leaders (5.13-22), a quiet life that will seem benign to outsiders (4.11-12)'.[20] While it seems right to think that it is not Meeks's intention to be exhaustive here, it is still rather surprising that a properly Christian response to the untimely death of believers is omitted from this rehearsal of appropriate behaviour patterns – after all, inordinate grief is a key matter addressed in the letter. Furthermore, as we have seen earlier, Paul takes painstaking care to bring consolation to the Thessalonians because, left untreated, such grief – which stemmed from a deficient understanding of eschatology – would surely rupture their self-identity and thus their well-being as a believing community. Again, it seems to me that attention to the function of emotion would further strengthen Meeks's fine arguments concerning the socialization of Paul's new converts.

My point, however, is not so much to try to identify gaps in Meeks's approach as to use it as a kind of launch pad for my proposal that there is much to be gained in placing emotion alongside belief when asking questions about the ways in which the early Christians were formed into communities and into a movement, and about how these social structures acquired such stability and longevity. What can be added to what we already know about the socialization of new believers in the first-century milieu of Pauline Christianity through a considered exploration of the role of emotion? I suggest that like the beliefs with which they are associated (and like the structures of language and ritual within which such beliefs are encoded), emotions as Paul sees them play a crucial role in staking the boundaries, personal as well as corporate, between believers and the world around them, and therefore in reinforcing the internal social cohesion

---

[18] Meeks, *Christians*, 93.
[19] Meeks, *Christians*, 93–4.
[20] Meeks, *Christians*, 174–5 (quote from 175).

of the Christian groups. Emotions are able to perform this role because, as we shall see, they can have a socially integrating or a socially differentiating function. The patterns of feeling that Paul seems to want to promote are related closely to the patterns of belief that mark out what it means to be a Christian.

It is at this point that I wish to introduce, from recent social-scientific thinking, the notion of the 'emotional regime' as an analytical framework for our heuristic engagement with emotion in Paul. Our reading of what he says about joy and grief and consolation in two of his letters has demonstrated that there is very clearly a social dimension to these states of emotion: they are socially generated and socially expressed, and they also influence and shape Christian sociality itself. As such, a tool that can help us to investigate in comprehensive terms the social dimensions of emotion, without losing sight of the fact that emotion is at the same time something intrinsic to the individual, will be very useful; and in what is to follow I will describe the sociological concept of the emotional regime (first introduced at Section 1.3.2) in some detail.

5.3. The Sociological Concept of the 'Emotional Regime'

5.3.1. The Emotional Regime

In their multidimensional account, Riis and Woodhead posit emotion as being produced in the interactions between (1) self and society, (2) self and symbol, and (3) symbol and society. Each of these three sets of relationships are dynamic, two-way, dialectical processes in which the *relata* are themselves shaped by the relationship. At the same time, these three sets of relationships are inherently interdependent and therefore mutually constitutive.[21] These three sets of dialectical relationships come together to form an entity that is more than the sum of its parts, because novel processes emerge from the interaction of the parts that are irreducible to those parts.[22] Conceptually, this entity – which Riis and Woodhead term an 'emotional regime' – captures how these dialectical processes come together in the construction of emotion. It therefore brings together the personal, symbolic, and social aspects of emotion, and in so doing discloses how emotions are integral to the structured social and material relations that constitute a particular social context.[23]

An emotional regime characteristically 'holds together a repertoire of different emotions, and specifies their rhythm, significance, mode of expression, and combination'.[24] Emotional regimes 'persist over time, and transcend individuals, shaping what they feel and how they feel it, and the way they can express their feelings, and hence the form of social relationship and course of action that are open to them'.[25] For Riis and Woodhead, the way their tripartite scheme conceives of the relationships

---

[21] Ole Riis and Linda Woodhead, *A Sociology of Religious Emotion* (Oxford: Oxford University Press, 2010), 7–9, 95.
[22] Riis and Woodhead, *Sociology*, 95.
[23] Riis and Woodhead, *Sociology*, 10.
[24] Riis and Woodhead, *Sociology*, 10.
[25] Riis and Woodhead, *Sociology*, 10.

between self, symbol, and society serves to prise apart processes that are in reality closely bound up with one another. By isolating these dialectical exchanges while also respecting their interwoven nature, a richly textured analysis of the cultivation of emotion becomes possible.[26]

5.3.2. Religious Emotional Regimes

Riis and Woodhead further propose that *religious* emotional regimes – which have their basis in an ideal ordering of reality – confront the everyday empirical world with this ostensibly perfected social and material order, and interpret the one in relation to the other. All aspects of personal and social life and interaction are viewed and evaluated in the light of this ideal ordering. Hence a religious emotional regime embodies and regulates the standards by which certain emotions are promoted and others are abased, so that the emotional lives of the adherents of the religion are formed according to an approved pattern of coherence.[27] Such training of the emotions occurs through both formal and informal mechanisms: emotional standards may be imposed through hierarchical structures, the promotion of authoritative, prescriptive teaching, and the meting out of punishment for disobedience; they can also be established through less formal means such as observation and imitation, and the use of more subtle obstacles to non-compliance. An emotional regime therefore subjugates errant unauthorized emotions, while at the same offering rewards for following emotional conventions.[28]

By promulgating and enforcing a unique emotional programme that guides how its adherents are to feel about themselves and their circumstances, a religious emotional regime educates and structures sensibility in profound ways. The reconfiguring of emotional response according to the ordering that is embodied by a religious group, its members, and its symbols, helps those within the group not only to cope with the everyday demands of life but also to navigate its transitions and crises. Religious emotional regimes can therefore inculcate long-lasting moods and motivations, and provide anchorage for meaning, moral identity, and choice-making.[29]

A religious emotional regime, then, may be described as a framework which conditions the way in which emotion is produced, amplified, or modified in the context of the dialectical relations between self, society, and symbol, leading to a structuring of the emotional life of participants and the social whole in accordance with the ordering of reality that the religion prescribes as normative for its adherents.

5.3.3. Key Characteristics of Religious Emotion

Riis and Woodhead outline three main features that they see as being particularly characteristic of religious emotion: 'emotional ordering', 'emotional transcendence-transition', and 'inspiration-orientation'.

---

[26] Riis and Woodhead, *Sociology*, 8–9.
[27] Riis and Woodhead, *Sociology*, 10–11, 69–73.
[28] Riis and Woodhead, *Sociology*, 48–9, 71.
[29] Riis and Woodhead, *Sociology*, 10–11, 69–70, 209–10.

5.3.3.a. Emotional Ordering

Religious emotions are structured according to a symbolically mediated ideal framework, or 'alternate ordering'. Such an ordering 'shapes an emotional template that may extend over the whole of life, and override other emotional programmes'.[30] Emotional ordering occurs at the individual, group, or societal level, or all three. It implies offering a coherent programme – involving components such as guidance, inspiration, ritual, symbolism, and living example – in which emotions embody normative patterns of feeling and relating that shape both personal and collective life. This means that over time, and with appropriate religious disciplines, discordant emotional notes can be removed in favour of the dominant ones that should sound within the religious emotional regime. Moreover, because religion has a reference point beyond the here and now, religious emotional orderings also integrate and reorient feelings related to death and bereavement. In addition, religious emotions serve also as markers of identity: those who respond emotionally in ways that are in line with a group's emotional orderings are taken as genuinely belonging to that group, while those who do not are decried as outsiders.[31]

5.3.3.b. Emotional Transcendence-Transition

Religious emotional regimes enable transcendence over everyday emotional states, at both personal and collective levels. As Riis and Woodhead put it, 'By multifarious means, religions offer some distance from everyday emotions, some critical purchase over them, some ability to review, alter, or selectively confirm them.'[32] Emotional transcendence has to do with the bringing of emotions into relation with alternate orderings and their structures and symbols in a ways that enhance order, control, and change.[33] Related to transcendence is 'emotional transition': a significant shift in the structure of personal sensibility that involves a de-patterning and re-patterning of emotion. Emotional transition is thus a dramatic form of transcendence that occurs over a much shorter time and involves more intense emotions. The authors posit that most religions combine routine, ritualized means of patterning religious sensibility with dramatic rites and techniques to make and mark more dramatic shifts. They use the term 'emotional transcendence-transition' in order to hold these two aspects together, though they can be distinguished from each other.[34]

5.3.3.c. Inspiration-Orientation

Riis and Woodhead observe that although religions can produce short-lived moments of emotional intensity, it is their ability to shape long-term emotional dispositions and thus influence both human character and relational stances that is more notable.

---

[30] Riis and Woodhead, *Sociology*, 76–7 (quote from 77).
[31] Riis and Woodhead, *Sociology*, 77–9.
[32] Riis and Woodhead, *Sociology*, 81–2.
[33] Riis and Woodhead, *Sociology*, 82.
[34] Riis and Woodhead, *Sociology*, 82.

Religious emotional regimes have an active and inspiring quality through the way that they promote certain specific feelings and spur the actions that correspond to them. At the same time,

> Since emotions are what orient us within our life worlds, and since religions claim to reveal what is truly sacred, valuable, and meaningful, the emotional orientation they provide often has a particularly strong bearing on how adherents live out their lives, and what inspires their ultimate loyalty.[35]

In addition to providing fundamental inspiration, religious emotions also play an important role in value direction, for example, by training emotions of love to become attached to their proper objects and detached from inappropriate ones. They provide orientation by providing a focus not only of devotion but also of such things as fear, anxiety, and aversion. Rogue emotions within a religious emotional regime are abjured, and internal deviants are castigated or stigmatized.[36]

5.3.4. Dialectical Relationships within an Emotional Regime

As we have seen, Riis and Woodhead's model involves three *relata* – agent, symbol, and community – which are shaped by the dialectical relationships between them. The authors depict their concept diagrammatically as follows (see Figure 1):

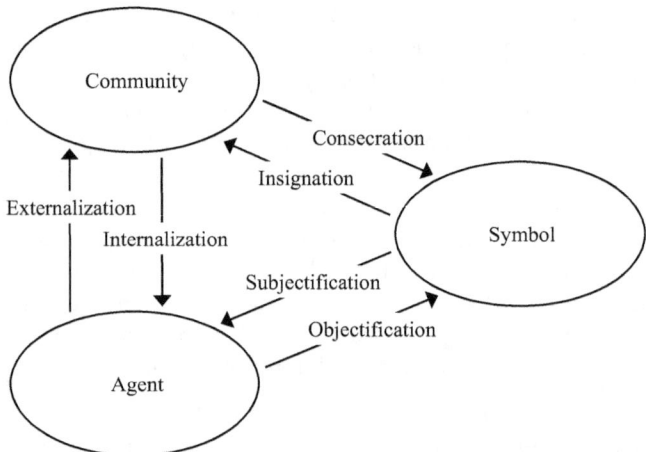

Figure 1 Dialectical Relationships within an Emotional Regime.

Source: This is my reproduction of the figure in Ole Riis and Linda Woodhead, *A Sociology of Religious Emotion* (Oxford: Oxford University Press, 2010), 118. © Ole Riis and Linda Woodhead 2010. Reproduced with permission of the licensor through PLSclear.

Located between agent and symbol are the processes of 'objectification' and 'subjectification'. In religious objectification, a symbolic object is created that produces

---

[35] Riis and Woodhead, *Sociology*, 89.
[36] Riis and Woodhead, *Sociology*, 89–90.

personal emotions that relate to the emotional regime's religious ordering. Examples of objectified expressions of religious emotion include sacred art, buildings, rituals, stories, and songs. On the other side of the relation, religious 'subjectification' occurs when a symbol provokes in an individual an emotion that is considered religious. In many religious contexts, the ability to feel emotions sanctioned by the wider regime when in the presence of its sacred objects is proof of piety.[37]

These processes have their parallels in the dialectic between community and symbol. 'Consecration' refers to the process in which a religious community legitimates an object as a religious sign that binds the community and helps define its identity; examples include the harnessing of a group's stories or rituals as focal points in its emotional programme. 'Insignation', on the other hand, is the process whereby a community is moved emotionally by a religious symbol.[38] Finally, 'internalization' refers to the ways in which a community influences the emotional lives of individuals. Its opposite, 'externalization', occurs when an individual's felt emotions are noticed. To externalize emotion by creating a communal sentiment involves the encouraging of appropriate emotions and the curtailing of deviant ones.[39]

In an emotional regime characterized by balanced dialectical connections, the relations between agents, symbols, and the community are mutually constitutive, and there is a correspondence between the emotional symbols, the community's emotional programme, and the emotions of individuals. As Riis and Woodhead express it,

> The power of the symbols is strengthened as they are venerated by the community and subjectified by individuals, the power of the community to move its members is enhanced as it refers to accepted symbols and as members participate in it, and religious emotions among participants are intensified as they participate in collective rituals or relate to established symbols.[40]

Using the same framework, *imbalances* in emotional regimes may also be analysed. If a human agent is emotionally unaffected by a symbol, the dialectical relation weakens to 'ultra-objectification'; on the other hand 'ultra-subjectification' occurs when the individual is overcome by emotion. Similarly, between a community and its symbols, 'ultra-consecration' is when its symbols do not emotionally affect it, while 'ultra-insignification' takes place when collective symbols overwhelm individuals. Finally, in the relationship between a community and its members, 'ultra-internalization' occurs when a regime considers that the only normative emotions are those that it sanctions; in contrast, 'ultra-externalization' happens when members freely express their emotions.[41]

---

[37] Riis and Woodhead, *Sociology*, 99–100.
[38] Riis and Woodhead, *Sociology*, 102–4.
[39] Riis and Woodhead, *Sociology*, 109, acknowledging the influence of Peter Berger and Thomas Luckmann's cognitive theory (*The Social Construction of Reality: A Treatise in the Sociology of Knowledge* (Garden City, NY: Anchor Books, 1966), see especially 78–9, 121–2, 149–93).
[40] Riis and Woodhead, *Sociology*, 121.
[41] Riis and Woodhead, *Sociology*, 124–40.

5.3.5. The Power of Religious Emotion

For Riis and Woodhead, the concept of an emotional regime is a helpful way of understanding the relationship between emotion and power, since the idea of emotional norms sanctioned and enforced by social and symbolic means is integral to an emotional regime.[42] The power of a religious group is heightened when emotional dialectics are in balance. In such a situation, individuals are in solidarity with one another and with the group; personal emotions find their resonance in the feelings of others, and these feelings are experienced as authentic. This experience is structured also by consecrated symbols that provide the focus of devotion and action. By being united by common inspiration and commitment, the sense of kinship among participants is strengthened. The experiences of individuals vivify the collective experience, reinforce it, and feed its emotional energy.[43] As such, religion can flourish even in competitive, pluralistic situations; its power then resides in its ability to nurture feelings such as solidarity and hope in the midst of grindingly hard conditions.[44] In fact, it is the power of a religion to focus, contain, and transform powerful emotions that lends that religion wider social power.[45]

Riis and Woodhead draw attention to the vital role of symbols: 'Symbols have power by representing an agenda in concentrated form and focusing feeling towards it.'[46] The power of symbols is related to how people feel about them, and to the number of people who feel this way. Religious symbols are especially significant in relation to power because they represent a higher, other-worldly power; more importantly, they are experienced as placing those who give assent to them in a direct relation with such power.[47] In other words, once consecrated, religious symbols bind the emotional regime of a group and cannot easily be separated from it; they accrue enormous power over the group and its members. The authors argue that

> in the right context, the most powerful of sacred symbols are the monotheistic Gods. Their power is related to the emotions of terror, awe, and surrender that they may evoke, and the counterbalancing feelings of joy, assurance, security, and power that come from knowledge of their protection and blessing.[48]

Accordingly, such symbols help individuals, groups, and nations gain a sense of control, meaning, and power, in life, while helping them to sacralize their agendas.[49]

---

[42] Riis and Woodhead, *Sociology*, 151.
[43] Riis and Woodhead, *Sociology*, 157–8.
[44] Riis and Woodhead, *Sociology*, 169.
[45] Riis and Woodhead, *Sociology*, 158.
[46] Riis and Woodhead, *Sociology*, 154.
[47] Riis and Woodhead, *Sociology*, 155–6.
[48] Riis and Woodhead, *Sociology*, 159.
[49] Riis and Woodhead, *Sociology*, 159.

5.3.6. Conclusion

Riis and Woodhead's account is a multidimensional, far-reaching, yet supple approach to the construction of emotion. Rather than privileging the self as the site of emotional life, their approach contextualizes feeling within a framework of dialectical interrelations between the individual, society, and religious and cultural symbols. Every social unit has a unique emotional programme in which certain emotional notes are encouraged and others repudiated; and when these patterns of affect are enforced, an emotional regime comes into being. Religious emotional regimes embody to an alternate ordering of reality that is seen to be foundational to life, and thereby offer transcendence over everyday emotional states, as well as long-term emotional inspiration.

5.4. The Function of Emotion in the Pauline Congregations

5.4.1. Introduction

In what follows we shall elucidate how, for Paul, right emotions help to forge and cement a distinctive and robust Christian identity in the individual believer as well as in the community of faith to which he or she belongs. As I shall suggest, in the way they embody structures of belief and promote patterns of sociality, emotions take on crucial integrating and differentiating roles in both the personal and corporate spheres of the believer's life. Clearly, Paul's therapeutic engagement with the emotions – his careful efforts to put into place an emotional regime – is aimed at the upbuilding of the congregations that he has established.

5.4.2. The Integrating and Differentiating Functions of Emotion

For Paul, how the believer is to feel is correlated at a fundamental level with the beliefs that form the basis for the Christian faith. Putting this another way, one might say that sanctioned emotions, such as joy in the midst of suffering, align the believer's experiences of life with the reasoned evaluation of those experiences in the light of the various interlocking theological convictions that together frame a portrayal of true reality. For the individual believer, right emotion therefore expresses the squaring of felt experience with belief; in this way it is a uniquely tangible, psychosomatic reification of sometimes abstract, and certainly slippery, Christian ideals concerning affect and its relation to belief and behaviour. At the same time, the theologically informed and socially structured reading of these personal felt experiences – resulting as they do in the promotion of emotional dispositions that are held in common as being normative – serves to integrate the believer with other believers by reinforcing individual and corporate notions of what it truly means to be a follower of Christ. Hence, through the bringing together of the experiential with the cognitive, there is a powerful, *integrating* dimension to emotions: at the level of the individual, right emotions embody the integration of felt experience with cognitive belief, while at the societal level they simultaneously signal the integration of personal subjectivity with group norms in regard to authorized patterns of feeling; and in both cases, the result is a strengthening of Christian identity and community.

Emotions have also a corresponding *differentiating* function; thus, when right emotions are given expression or when inappropriate ones are rejected, a similar result ensues. A clear example is found in relation to Paul's order to the Thessalonians not to grieve as those around them do. It is noteworthy that Paul here makes explicit his efforts to engineer a type of behavioural differentiation, that, for the Thessalonians, requires on their part a profound relativization of grief that is more than a little counterintuitive, especially given the already very challenging circumstances in which they seek to live out their faith. Yet it is precisely the counterintuitive, and indeed, countercultural, nature of such an emotional response that marks the divide between the believing community and the people around them, and showcases both the uniqueness of the Christian way of life and the audaciousness of its claims to truth.

It is important to note, however, that it is not as if such authorized emotional dispositions carry only either an integrating or differentiating function. In my view, these functions are actually the two sides of the same coin, and as such, right emotion incorporates facets of both functions. It is likely though that with a particular emotion the working of one of the two functions is more evident. To illustrate, using the example in the preceding paragraph: as we have seen, the prohibition against uncontrolled grief embodies a marked differentiating function in how it stakes the boundaries, both social and theological, between believers and others. Yet at the same time the imposition of such a feeling rule helps to bolster the believers' sense of group belonging by specifying and reinforcing the possibility of a specific form of normative affective behaviour for Christians in a particular context (the death of a fellow believer) and locating the warrant for such a stance in eschatological reality; as such, it incorporates also a possibly less obvious socially integrating function.

My contention, then, is that emotion in Paul's letters – at least based on the evidence of joy in Philippians and grief and consolation in 1 Thessalonians – plays an important role in the social formation of the believers in the congregations that he had planted. By issuing specific feeling rules to his followers, Paul is in fact creating an emotional regime in which cognition, reason, and emotion commingle to produce a distinctive Christian sociality that has its basis in his understanding of God's work in the past, present, and future – or, in other words, in an alternate, and explicitly theological, conception of reality. For Paul, right emotions are related to, and are to be in sync with, right beliefs; and such emotions – which, as we have seen, exhibit a mix of socially integrating and differentiating functions – are therefore integral to the socialization of his converts and to the development and safeguarding of their Christian identity. However, how exactly are these right emotions produced? What sustains their ongoing activity and functional potency? An exploration of the Pauline emotional regime, in which we combine our findings thus far with careful sociological analysis, will shed further light on how authorized emotions are generated and maintain their vigour, and also help us to answer in a fuller way the question of the role of such emotions in the early Church.

5.5. Exploring the Pauline Emotional Regime

To recap, in Riis and Woodhead's account of religious emotion that was outlined earlier, emotions are seen to be generated within a framework of mutually shaping interactions between (1) individual agents, and the communities to which they belong; (2) agents, and the cultural and material symbols that are attached to religious life; and (3) communities, and these sacred symbols. The interplay of these three sets of dialectical relationships forms a religious emotional regime, which, since it takes as normative a certain ordering of reality, shapes emotion in line with this reality and so plays a decisive role in the inculcation of long-term affective moods and motivations. Furthermore, through the way in which emotional norms are promoted and maintained, an emotional regime provides a mooring for abstract things such as meaning and morality, and also plays a key role in shaping sociality and structures of power.

It almost goes without saying that Riis and Woodhead's ideas seem extremely useful as a way into our inquiry into the function of emotion in the Pauline churches. Our exegetical exploration of joy in Philippians and grief and consolation in 1 Thessalonians has highlighted that emotion does not merely involve personal, inner states, but is also generated in a social context. Riis and Woodhead's theories are particularly helpful for our purposes because they propose a social basis for emotion without discounting the importance of the individual agent's decisions. To adopt Riis and Woodhead's conceptual tool: the *Pauline* emotional regime, then, is the framework within which emotion is generated, shaped, or transfigured in the context of the tripartite interrelationships between the individual believer (i.e. 'self'), the church to which he or she belongs ('society'), and such things as the Christian concepts of God, Christ, the Spirit, and the gospel ('symbol'). Rooted deeply in, and therefore comprehensively informed by, Paul's understanding of reality, the emotional regime prescribes and reinforces specific modes of feeling, and so profoundly influences such things as Christian self-understanding and corporate identity formation. In what is to follow, we shall examine several key aspects of the Pauline emotional regime.

5.5.1. Emotional Ordering

Central to the concept of a religious emotional regime is the premise that a symbolically mediated ideal ordering is at work to structure the emotional lives of participants in accordance with what the religion in question holds to be true reality. In Paul's missive to the Philippian believers, such an ordering is foregrounded whenever he makes mention of matters that relate to eschatological reality. Throughout the letter we find references to the Parousia and the events surrounding it (1.6, 10; 2.16; 3.10-11, 14); to the ultimate lordship of Christ (2.9-11; 3.20-1); to God's ongoing ministry in the lives of believers to achieve his purposes (2.13); and to the fact that the Philippians are citizens of heaven who are destined for eternal glory (3.20-1) – an eschatological fate that stands in stark contrast to that of those whom Paul lambastes as 'enemies of the cross of Christ', whose sure end is destruction (3.18-19). It is apparent that Paul is repeatedly reminding the Philippians that life is more than what they experience with their physical senses, for behind all that is happening to them is the providential hand of God, who is bringing to eschatological completion the work that he has begun in their lives (1.6).

If Philippians is rich with eschatological ideas and allusions, 1 Thessalonians – where these motifs are writ especially large – is at least equally so. Quite apart from the major apocalyptic pericopes of 4.13-18 and 5.1-11, in which he deals with the question of how the return of Christ will correlate with the eternal destinies of believers dead and living, Paul elsewhere also makes mention of the certainty of the Parousia (2.19; 3.13; 5.23) and assures the Thessalonian believers that on that day, they would be judged to be blameless in holiness before God (3.13; cf. 2.19-20 where Paul describes them as being his hope or joy or crown of boasting at that event) and thus be spared God's wrath (1.10), since they had been called to his kingdom and glory (2.12). By threading eschatological motifs right through the letter and tying them together, Paul obviously wants to highlight to his readers the presence of another reality in their lives – one that reveals the true contours of human history, and in fact governs its very course.

In the light of this alternate understanding of reality, Paul puts into place an emotional programme through which he seeks to educate the sensibility of his converts and to instil feeling patterns that legitimate this ideal ordering of life. As far as we may ascertain from the evidence in our two Pauline letters, the emotional programme includes such elements as the use of religious symbols, exhortation and instruction, the offering of exemplars, and participation in ritual action – all of which combine to shape an emotional template that extends over the whole of life. An investigation of these major elements will, as we shall see, reap ample dividends in terms of helping us to understand how Paul's emotional programme is effected, and maintains its efficacy and longevity.

5.5.2. Symbols and Emotional Ordering

We turn now to a consideration of the role of symbols in the cultivation of joy in Philippians and in the appeal against excessive grief in 1 Thessalonians.

In our exegetical analysis of joy in Philippians, we concluded that the joy about which Paul writes has three main dimensions. The first is the co-participation of Paul and his converts in the gospel mission. As he begins his letter, Paul speaks of the prayers of joy that constantly occur together with his thankful remembrances to God for the profound partnership in evangelism that he shares with them (Phil. 1.3-5). This is certainly a partnership that is based on shared convictions, but it is also a partnership that is disclosed in concrete ways, one of which – as Paul expresses great joy over – has to do with how the church in Philippi has renewed its concern for him through a recent monetary gift (4.10). Thus, for Paul, joy emerges from the ongoing partnership that he and the Philippians have in the advancement of the gospel – a deep and mutual participation that reveals both a spiritual and a material commitment to God's work.

The second main dimension of joy in the letter is related to the actual advancement of the gospel itself. This itself has several sub-dimensions. That the gospel is being preached in Rome – even if by those who are his rivals and who are taking advantage of the fact that he is in prison – is for Paul a cause for joy (1.15-18). Yet, despite his present circumstances, Paul remains joyfully confident that his deliverance is at hand, and that his ministry will continue to bear fruit in the lives of the Philippians, as will be evidenced by their continued growth in the faith and by the joy that accompanies it (1.18-26). These notions anticipate the emphatically mutual joy in serving the gospel that Paul speaks of in 2.17-18. It is clear that in Paul's mind the advancement of the gospel itself forms the basis for joy – joy that is also to be reflected to, and shared with, other believers.

The third dimension of joy concerns its eschatological origin and object. For Paul, as he makes clear at several points in his letter, joy is 'in the Lord' (3.1; 4.4; see also 4.10). Such joy should emerge in the life of the believer no matter how adverse his or her circumstances may presently be, because it has its basis in God's ongoing work, through Christ, of redemption and renewal in the world. That work will reach its final fruition on the day of Christ's return, when all who follow Christ will receive eschatological vindication and share in his glory. For Paul, present suffering must be read in the light of this perspective of true reality. Thus Paul summons the Philippians to joy 'in the Lord', because Christ is very much the ground and occasion for the believer's joy in the here and now.

Turning now to consolation in 1 Thessalonians, our findings earlier led us to see that Paul's instructions are premised firmly on the eschatological realities which he is calling his grieving readers to understand and fully embrace. At the centre of these realities is the work of Christ, in consequence of which a hopeless sorrow is not only unnecessary but also entirely baseless, because the resurrection of Christ serves as a sure guarantee of the resurrection of Christians and their presence at the Parousia, and because is it clear that at that great event those believers who are dead will not be at any disadvantage compared to those who remain alive.

To summarize at this point: we observe that the three dimensions of joy that we identified are coordinated with two basic symbols – the gospel and 'the Lord' (i.e. Christ). The possibility of consolation, meanwhile, is mediated by the symbolic content associated with Christ and his resurrection. Hence, taking Philippians and 1 Thessalonians together, it would seem that the two major symbols that we need to concern ourselves with in our discussion here are the gospel and Christ. It is pertinent to note also that these two symbols are, of course, related intrinsically to each other: the former chronicles the story of the latter, that is, the gospel is the story of the good news that Christ has come, and that he is coming again in eschatological glory.

Riis and Woodhead's conceptual framework offers us some helpful ways to understand the importance of these symbols in emotional life and their role in emotional ordering. Several observations can, I think, be put forward with profit.

First, and perhaps rather obviously, the emotions that Paul is promoting are directly inspired by, and related to, these symbols. The extent and quality of a believer's joy is commensurate with the degree to which the believer is influenced by, and participates in, the story of Christ – by seeking to understand, live according to, and make known to others the truths that he or she believes as a follower of Christ. Similarly, the believer's attitude to grief is also connected intimately to, and therefore reflective of, his or her theological understanding and intellectual appropriation of the work of Christ at the eschaton. In both scenarios we observe something about the connective role of symbols in emotional cultivation. Symbols seem to serve as means through which individual states of feeling are brought into relation with collective sentiments and memories, thereby connecting believers to a living tradition or way of looking at the world.[50] Thus we see that the sufferings of a believer in Philippi and the grief of a bereaved Christian in Thessalonica are both brought to a symbolic focus and articulated with some corporately held Christian ordering of reality. The results are joy, in the former instance, and the expulsion of inordinate sorrow in the latter one.

Second, and related to the above, these authorized emotions act back upon the symbolic structures from which they are generated. In other words, a particular dialectic is at play: as Riis and Woodhead express it,

> The conviction and power of a symbolic system are tied up with the emotions it inspires, while the emotions it inspires give it power and conviction. Indeed, the process is dialectical: our feelings shape our reality, and what we take to be real shapes our feelings.[51]

Thus, for example, in the case of joy: the believer whose perspective on suffering is framed by a thoroughgoing appreciation of the eschatological reality that is mediated through God's actions in Christ is imbued with the necessary inner resources to relativize his or her suffering in the light of this ultimate reality. This engenders joy; and the felt experience of this joy works in turn to validate and even cement the believer's perspective on what he or she takes to be the true state of affairs here on earth.

Third, we note that the symbols of the gospel and of Christ express and influence the course of social relations and can thus be said to be integral to them. A particularly clear instance of this is found when Paul tells the Philippians that his joy will be enlarged through their growth in like-minded unity and unselfish concern for one another – a mindset that is modelled for them by Christ (see Phil. 2.1-8). As we concluded earlier, the social basis of joy is depicted here: there is a sense in which joy is directly correlated to the quality of the relationships among the believers. Hence the symbolic paradigm of Christ helps to establish and consolidate new solidarities and shape social relations and even take them in new directions, all the while also contributing to the promotion of joy within the church. Noteworthy also for our purposes is how an emotional norm is articulated through a particular socio-symbolic structure.

Fourth, for the believer, the symbols of Christ and his gospel are freighted with associations to divinity and transcendence, and represent a higher power that surpasses all earthly ones. Furthermore, these symbols are experienced as placing those who give assent to them in a direct relation with this transcendent power – a power that is able to

---

[50] See further Riis and Woodhead, *Sociology*, 90–3.

[51] Riis and Woodhead, *Sociology*, 67, basing their argument on Clifford Geertz's famous definition of religion in his 'Religion as a Cultural System', in *Anthropological Approaches to the Study of Religion*, ed. Michael Banton (London: Tavistock, 1971), 1–43 (at 4): religion is '(1) a system of symbols (2) which acts to establish powerful, pervasive and long-lasting moods and motivations in men (3) by formulating conceptions of a general order of existence and (4) clothing these conceptions with such an aura of factuality that (5) the moods and motivations seem uniquely realistic'.

command a level of fealty and commitment that can trump all other personal interests and loyalties.[52] And because they shape social relations and act as a focus for feeling, these symbols potentially exert enormous influence and power over a church and its members, especially as the symbols acquire ever-increasing power by being repeatedly consecrated and objectified[53] in various settings such as, for example, ritualized gatherings involving acts of worship, teaching, corporate prayer, and the receiving of communion, or informal, personal moments of reflective meditation and devotional prayer. Such power can profoundly inspire not only shared patterns of emotion but also collective action.

5.5.3. Instruction, Imitation, and Emotional Ordering

It is not only religious symbols that help to determine patterns of feeling in an emotional regime. What we might term generally as human authorities also play decisive roles in setting emotional standards, and in training and enforcing emotional norms. These human authorities include formal means such as hierarchical structures within which figures of influence such as community leaders, religious teachers, or even parents prescribe what emotions should be felt (and proscribe what cannot be felt), and less formal mechanisms such as personal guidance, advice, and the pervasive presence of subtle societal sanctions against non-conforming patterns of affect and behaviour.[54] In addition, as Riis and Woodhead also note, 'much emotional training occurs through observation and imitation rather than through overt instruction'.[55]

In both Philippians and 1 Thessalonians some of the above-mentioned elements of an emotional programme are clearly in evidence. We have already seen how the theme of joy pervades Philippians and lies at the heart of much of its hortatory material – so much so that one may well say that Paul is offering his readers 'a pedagogy in joy'.[56] And as we have also seen, through careful teaching Paul sets emotional standards for the Thessalonian believers in relation to grief. Certainly, it seems clear that what Paul says carries significant weight; he is not only the founder of the churches that he is now writing to, but also one who claims apostolic authority from none other than the Lord.[57] He therefore wields considerable influence over his churches through his teaching as well as through his personal example, which he calls his converts to imitate.[58]

Paul makes specific laudatory mention of the fact that the Thessalonians have become imitators of both him and the Lord, in how they had accepted the gospel with

---

[52] On this see Riis and Woodhead, *Sociology*, 155–6.
[53] Using Riis and Woodhead's terminology; see Section 5.3.4 above.
[54] See Riis and Woodhead, *Sociology*, 48–9, 71; and Section 5.3.2 above.
[55] Riis and Woodhead, *Sociology*, 48.
[56] Barton, 'Spirituality and the Emotions in Early Christianity: The Case of Joy', in *The Bible and Spirituality: Exploratory Essays in Reading Scripture Spiritually*, ed. Andrew T. Lincoln, J. Gordon McConville, and Lloyd K. Pietersen (Eugene, OR: Cascade Books, 2013), 185. See also Section 3.4 above.
[57] On Paul's apostolic authority see John Howard Schütz, *Paul and the Anatomy of Apostolic Authority*, SNTSMS 26 (Cambridge: Cambridge University Press, 1975), in which the sociology of charismatic authority is brought into conversation with a theologically informed reading of the relevant Pauline texts.
[58] The express language of mimesis occurs several times in Paul: in the undisputed letters 1 Cor. 4.16; 11.1; Phil. 3.17; 1 Thess. 1.6; 2.14; cf. also Eph. 5.1; 2 Thess. 3.7, 9. On its use, see especially Brian J. Dodd, *Paul's Paradigmatic 'I': Personal Example as Literary Strategy*, JSNTSup 177

joy in the face of considerable affliction (Καὶ ὑμεῖς μιμηταὶ ἡμῶν ἐγενήθητε καὶ τοῦ κυρίου, δεξάμενοι τὸν λόγον ἐν θλίψει πολλῇ μετὰ χαρᾶς πνεύματος ἁγίου, 1 Thess. 1.6).[59] In fact, their conduct has been so exemplary that they, in turn, are now a model (τύπος) for other believers (1.7) – which says a great deal about the powerful, far-reaching influence of Paul's example and witness.[60] However, it is in Philippians that the motif of imitation comes into its own; and here it becomes readily apparent how central the use of imitation is for Paul, especially when it is combined with instruction – which suggests that Riis and Woodhead may perhaps be driving a little too sharp a wedge between these practices in terms of their relative importance in influencing emotional ordering. At least from what we observe in Paul's letter, they seem to go hand in hand and may even be said to reinforce each other. The two key texts that we shall look at in closer detail are Phil. 3.15-17 and 4.8-9; to understand the full import of these texts we need to see how Paul sets the stage for what he wishes to say.

Earlier, at 1.12-26, Paul has spoken paradigmatically of his own experiences, which includes joy in how the gospel is being advanced in spite of his incarceration (1.12-18), and the possessing of a joyful confidence that divine deliverance lies on the horizon and that he would be able to resume his ministry among the Philippians (1.18-26).[61] A showcasing of several exempla follows: superlatively, Christ (2.5-8),[62] and next, Timothy and Epaphroditus (2.19-30), who both illustrate in their lives a Christ-like mindset.[63] Then, at 3.4-14, Paul gives a heartfelt testimony of how Christ has shaped his own mindset; Paul is 'one who not only rejected his Jewish privileges for the gospel but also lives in the present totally orientated to the future'.[64]

Now, in Phil. 3.15-17 Paul enjoins his readers to follow his example and thus to grow in their personal appropriation of the life of Christ. At 3.15, Paul invites those who are mature to adopt his mindset (Ὅσοι οὖν τέλειοι, τοῦτο φρονῶμεν); here τέλειοι is best taken in its normal Pauline sense to refer to spiritual maturity, rather than to connote some use of the language of the Mystery cults.[65] Several commentators rightly note that Paul's use of τέλειοι is a play on Οὐχ ὅτι ἤδη ἔλαβον ἢ ἤδη τετελείωμαι (3.12), that is, those who are mature recognize that they have not yet been brought to completion in an eschatological sense.[66] In essence, Paul is therefore saying, 'let ὅσοι τέλειοι recognize that οὐ τετελειώμεθα'.[67] For a number of reasons – not least because

---

(Sheffield: Sheffield Academic Press, 1999); and also the survey in Andrew D. Clarke, '"Be Imitators of Me": Paul's Model of Leadership', *TynBul* 49 (1998): 329–60.

[59] It is noteworthy that Paul here singles out joy as that affective posture that has characterized the Thessalonians' reception of the gospel; this confirms our finding in Philippians that Paul correlates joy with the advancement of the gospel, among other things.

[60] Cf. 1 Thess. 2.14 where Paul commends the Thessalonians for imitating the churches in Judea in suffering for the sake of the gospel.

[61] See Sections 3.3.2.a and 3.3.2.b.

[62] See Section 3.2.3.

[63] See Section 3.2.4.

[64] Gordon D. Fee, *Paul's Letter to the Philippians*, New International Commentary on the New Testament (Grand Rapids. MI: Eerdmans, 1995), 351.

[65] See the discussion and references in Joseph H. Hellerman, *Philippians*, Exegetical Guide to the Greek New Testament (Nashville, TN: Broadman and Holman, 2015), 206; Fee, *Philippians*, 343 n.23; cf. Paul's similar use of the term in 1 Cor. 2.6 and 14.20.

[66] So e.g. Fee, *Philippians*, 355.

[67] Similarly, Friedel Selter and Colin Brown, 'Other', *NIDNTT* 2: 739–42, at 741. As Fee rather nicely puts it, 'Thus *teleioi* probably means "mature" in the sense outlined in v. 16; those who live in

Paul's language is inclusive and non-polemical (note his use of the first-person plural hortatory subjunctive φρονῶμεν, which places himself among the τέλειοι,[68] and the correlative conjunction ὅσοι, which tends to be used inclusively[69]) – it is improbable that any irony or polemic is intended.[70] The τοῦτο likely refers to 3.12-14 rather than to the entirety of Paul's autobiographical narrative in 3.4-14:[71] 'this' mindset, which Paul wants the Philippians to adopt, has to do with the eschatological orientation that he is modelling; not yet having been made perfect, he is pressing on to win the promised prize that awaits all believers (3.12-14).

After a qualification (καὶ εἴ τι ἑτέρως φρονεῖτε, καὶ τοῦτο ὁ θεὸς ὑμῖν ἀποκαλύψει, 3.15), which is best understood as Paul's allowing that some within the church might see things differently from himself but expecting that God will redirect their thinking,[72] Paul reaffirms the exhortation of 3.15: Christians are to keep in step with what they have already attained (πλὴν εἰς ὃ ἐφθάσαμεν, τῷ αὐτῷ στοιχεῖν, 3.16).[73] Then, at 3.17, using the express language of *imitatio*, Paul reiterates his call to the Philippians to embody the way of thinking and living that he exemplifies: Συμμιμηταί μου γίνεσθε, ἀδελφοί, καὶ σκοπεῖτε τοὺς οὕτω περιπατοῦντας καθὼς ἔχετε τύπον ἡμᾶς (3.17). They are to 'be fellow imitators of him'[74] – Paul's innovative terminology likely stresses his desire that there be a community effort in following his example[75] – and also to take note of others who are walking according to his pattern of life. To drive the point home, Paul goes on to warn the Philippians about others who live contrary to this pattern (3.18-19). It is important to note that Paul's charge to the Philippian believers to imitate him is based squarely on his own imitation of Christ as one who gave up privilege and power for the sake of others; thus, to assert that what Paul says is a defence of his own apostleship[76] or a way to shore up power via the 'hierarchy Christ-Paul-Christians'[77] is to misread him.[78]

---

keeping with what they have already attained are thus 'complete' to that degree, even though the final completion, when all are fully conformed into the likeness of the Christ whom they desire to know above all else, still remains' (*Philippians*, 355).

[68] So e.g. Fee, *Philippians*, 355, and in particular n.17 where he notes also the presence of the first-person plural verb ἐφθάσαμεν at 3.16.

[69] Markus Bockmuehl, *A Commentary on the Epistle to the Philippians*, Black's New Testament Commentaries (London: A & C Black, 1997), 225–6, citing BAGD 586.

[70] See further Bockmuehl, *Philippians*, 225–6. To be sure, however, the question is not at all settled: Fee, *Philippians*, 353 n.10, lists scholars holding contrary views.

[71] So many commentators, e.g. recently Hellerman, *Philippians*, 207, who argues that the τετελείωμαι/ τέλειοι shows that τοῦτο refers primarily to what Paul has emphasized in 3.12-14; *pace* Fee, *Philippians*, 356–7.

[72] See the discussion in Hellerman, *Philippians*, 208–10.

[73] Bockmuehl, *Philippians*, 228.

[74] The compound verb συμμιμηταί is found only here in the New Testament, and indeed only here in all of Greek literature; on its precise meaning see the discussion in Hellerman, *Philippians*, 212–14.

[75] Gerald F. Hawthorne and Ralph P. Martin, *Philippians*, revised ed., Word Biblical Commentary 43 (Nashville, TN: Thomas Nelson, 2004), 217, citing among others Willis Peter De Boer, *The Imitation of Paul: An Exegetical Study* (Kampen: Kok, 1962), 169–88.

[76] Adele Reinhartz, 'On the Meaning of the Pauline Exhortation: "*mimētai mou ginesthe*" – Become Imitators of Me', *SR* 16 (1987): 393–404.

[77] Elizabeth A. Castelli, *Imitating Paul: A Discourse of Power* (Louisville, KY: Westminster John Knox, 1991), 96.

[78] Walter G. Hansen, *The Letter to the Philippians*, Pillar New Testament Commentary (Grand Rapids, MI: Eerdmans, 2009), 261–2.

In chapter 4 of the letter, Paul again sets himself up as a model for imitation. He tells the Philippians in explicit terms that they are to put into practice those things that they have learnt from his teaching and observed in his conduct (ἃ καὶ ἐμάθετε καὶ παρελάβετε καὶ ἠκούσατε καὶ εἴδετε ἐν ἐμοί, ταῦτα πράσσετε, 4.9).[79] Paul is doubtless relating their mimetic practice to the morally excellent and praiseworthy mindset that he has just described and instructed them to take account of (Τὸ λοιπόν, ἀδελφοί, ὅσα ἐστὶν ἀληθῆ, ὅσα σεμνά, ὅσα δίκαια, ὅσα ἁγνά, ὅσα προσφιλῆ, ὅσα εὔφημα, εἴ τις ἀρετὴ καὶ εἴ τις ἔπαινος, ταῦτα λογίζεσθε, 4.8), but there is some debate over how 4.8 and 4.9 are linked syntactically,[80] as well as disagreement concerning the background of the virtues that Paul lists in 4.8.[81] On balance, a mediating view seems best: following Reumann, I see 4.8 as a call to reflection over 'norms in the world of the day that Christians too can practice'; and in this, the apostolic tradition and Paul himself serve as criteria (4.9).[82]

From the foregoing discussion it is clear that Paul's call to the Philippians to follow his example is closely linked to his pedagogical aims. As Bockmuehl notes,

> While the invitation to imitate one's teacher or rabbi was of course standard Graeco-Roman as well as Jewish didactic procedure, in Paul's case that invitation derives both its authority and its limitations from his own faithfulness to the prior example of Christ, who is himself the prototype and measure of all Christian discipleship (2.5ff. and *passim*). Paul's own ministry is merely the apostolic illustration and exemplification of that mind in Christ: it 'makes the truth visible' (cf. 2 Cor. 4.2).[83]

The mind of Christ – that remarkable, selfless, and self-giving φρόνησις that Paul patterns his own example after – is something that Paul delineates throughout the letter, along with

---

[79] The four verbs are variously grouped together, producing slightly different nuances in the resultant meaning. Hansen, for example, takes the first two to refer primarily to Paul's teaching of the gospel and the remaining two to refer to the paradigmatic value of his life (*Philippians*, 300). See the discussion in Hellerman, *Philippians*, 249; I follow Hellerman who suggests that it may be best however to leave the issue open by simply stringing the verbs together, as most English translations do, which preserves the staccato effect of the repeated καί (*Philippians*, 249, quoting BDF §460(3): 'polysyndeton produces the impression of extensiveness and abundance by means of an exhausting summary').

[80] Chiefly over whether the definite relative pronoun ἃ in 4.9 relates to (a) the antecedent ταῦτα of 4.8 (so Hansen, *Philippians*, 300, referencing Bockmuehl, *Philippians*, 254, who notes that sentences beginning with ἃ καί usually 'introduce a further and specific elaboration of the preceding subject at hand') – which means that 4.9 is an elaboration of 4.8, i.e. that Paul's teachings and way of life exemplify these things that are excellent and praiseworthy; or to (b) the subsequent ταῦτα within the same verse (so Fee, *Philippians*, 413 n.5) – in which case the ideas of 4.8 are put into perspective in 4.9; i.e. that the list of virtues is to be understood and practised in light of Paul's instructions and example.

[81] Attempts to read 4.8 as emerging from Jewish moral thinking have generally been criticized; many scholars now argue that Paul's language affirms virtues that are commonly seen in Greco-Roman, especially Stoic, moral discourse. See the discussion in Hellerman, *Philippians*, 244–5.

[82] John Reumann, *Philippians: A New Translation with Introduction and Commentary*, Anchor Bible 33B (New Haven, CT: Yale University Press, 2008), 640.

[83] Bockmuehl, *Philippians*, 254.

an interest in cognition and a focus on right thinking in general.[84] As his use of the verb φρονέω in connection with Christian maturity (Phil. 3.15) makes clear, what is at stake for Paul is 'a basic frame of mind, a way of looking at everything, which in turn leads to a way of behaving'.[85] Indeed, the frequency with which φρονέω occurs in the letter, and the way it is used, supports Meeks's proposal 'that this letter's most comprehensive purpose is the shaping of a Christian *phrōnesis*, a practical moral reasoning that is "conformed to [Christ's] death" in hope of his resurrection'.[86] As the Philippians conform their character and practice to the moral exemplar of Christ (and to others who take Christ as their model), they cultivate the virtues that are embodied in him and given expression in his life, such as humility, other-regard, confidence, and joy in suffering.[87]

We therefore observe that in Philippians and 1 Thessalonians, Paul combines careful theological instruction with explicit appeals to imitate exemplars in the faith in order to fashion the Christian mindset that he wants to see in his converts. And it seems readily apparent that with its inculcation comes, among other things, the fostering of an emotional programme that promotes emotional dispositions that reflect the beliefs upon which such a mindset is formed.

5.5.4. Ritual and Emotional Ordering

Another potentially far-reaching influence on emotional ordering is ritual.[88] As Riis and Woodhead observe,

> Ritual engages individuals in orchestrated and formalized social performances, and serves to coordinate bodily movements in synchronized and harmonious ways that can often reinforce and intensify certain feelings, and banish others. Emotion may, thereby, be focused more effectively by and upon certain symbols and myths.[89]

Citing the work of Jonathan Z. Smith, they argue that ritual creates a controlled environment that can simplify and concentrate the confusion of everyday experience, by focusing attention on what really matters and how one should feel about it.[90] In this

---

[84] As noted earlier; see Section 3.1.4.b and the end of Section 3.3.1.
[85] Fee, *Philippians*, 356.
[86] Meeks, 'Man from Heaven in Paul's Letter to the Philippians', in *In Search of the Early Christians: Selected Essays*, ed. Allen R. Hilton and H. Gregory Snyder (New Haven, CT: Yale University Press, 2002), 110. For an analysis of the appearances of φρονέω in Philippians together with a comparison of how the verb features in Greco-Roman thought, see Craig S. Keener, *The Mind of the Spirit: Paul's Approach to Transformed Thinking* (Grand Rapids, MI: Basic Books, 2016), 217–36.
[87] David G. Horrell, *Solidarity and Difference: A Contemporary Reading of Paul's Ethics*, 2nd ed. (London: T&T Clark, 2016), 235.
[88] For a helpful survey of scholarly discussion on the application of ritual theory to emotion, see Dorothea Lüddeckens, 'Emotion', in *Theorizing Rituals: Issues, Topics, Approaches, Concepts*, ed. Jens Kreinath, Jan Snoek, and Michael Stausberg (Leiden: Brill, 2006), 545–70.
[89] Riis and Woodhead, *Sociology*, 92.
[90] Riis and Woodhead, *Sociology*, 92, referencing Jonathan Z. Smith, *Imagining Religion: From Babylon to Jonestown* (Chicago: University of Chicago Press, 1988).

way, 'ritual brings an alternate ordering to life'.[91] Noting that the category of ritual is not clear-cut, Riis and Woodhead follow Catherine Bell in suggesting that is useful to think in terms of 'ritualization' instead of taking ritual as a fixed category involving a special place in social life; for them, this also helps to avoid isolating ritual from the other aspects of religious life in relation to which it makes sense.[92] Understood this way, the category of ritual can be broadened to include not only orchestrated public ritual practices but also domestic practices that may have profound emotional significance for participants.[93] Thus, in ritual, 'emotional cultivation has to do with not only crowds and intensity and authorized orchestration, but also with duration, repetition, and reinforcement'.[94]

All this is most helpful when we turn to Paul's letters and ask questions about the role of ritual in the ordering of emotion within his churches.[95] David Horrell has suggested that the Pauline material should be seen as the development of a body of tradition based on a specific narrative myth which, when enacted in ritual performance, gives meaning to, and shapes, the lives of its adherents. Attention to ritual activity reminds us that early Christian faith was not just 'believed' but also performed; and indeed, it is not least through such ritual performance that myth exercises its community-forming power.[96] Following Meeks, Horrell argues that questions should be asked not only of what each Pauline text 'says, but what it does',[97] since the Pauline texts 'are intended not only to inform, or to convey content, but quite clearly to persuade, and to shape the social practice of those to whom they are directed'.[98] Such a practice-based approach

---

[91] Riis and Woodhead, *Sociology*, 92.
[92] Riis and Woodhead, *Sociology*, 92, referencing Catherine Bell, *Ritual: Perspectives and Dimensions* (New York: Oxford University Press, 1997). On 'ritualization', see further Catherine Bell, *Ritual Theory, Ritual Practice* (Oxford: Oxford University Press, 1992), especially 74, 88–93; Bell uses the term to highlight how certain social actions differentiate themselves from others. Thus,

> ritualization is a way of acting that is designed and orchestrated to distinguish and privilege what is being done in comparison to other, usually more quotidian, activities. As such, ritualization is a matter of various culturally specific strategies for setting some activities off from others, for creating and privileging a qualitative distinction between the 'sacred' and the 'profane', and for ascribing such distinctions to realities thought to transcend the powers of human actors. (74)

[93] Riis and Woodhead, *Sociology*, 92–3, referencing Meredith B. McGuire, *Lived Religion, Faith and Practice in Everyday Life* (Oxford: Oxford University Press, 2008).
[94] Riis and Woodhead, *Sociology*, 93.
[95] New Testament scholarship is only just beginning to embrace the field of ritual studies, which has come into its own in recent years due to a recognition that ritual plays a central role in human societies. For overviews of scholarly work on key ritual themes in the New Testament, see Richard E. DeMaris, *The New Testament in Its Ritual World* (Abingdon: Routledge, 2008), 1–10; and Louise J. Lawrence, 'Ritual and the First Urban Christians: Boundary Crossings of Life and Death', in *After the First Urban Christians: The Social-Scientific Study of Pauline Christianity Twenty-Five Years Later*, ed. Todd D. Still and David G. Horrell (London: T&T Clark, 2009), 99–115.
[96] See Horrell, *Solidarity*, 99–100. Horrell's notion of 'myth' follows the use of the term in the study of religion in general, i.e. to refer to a means by which truth is conveyed (93–4). For Horrell, 'the centre of the myth which Paul's letters reflect is undoubtedly the Christ-event, that is the descending, dying and rising of Jesus Christ, which represents the saving action of God in which believers participate' (95).
[97] Horrell, *Solidarity*, 100, quoting Meeks, *Christians*, 7. See also Meeks, *Christians*, 142.
[98] Horrell, *Solidarity*, 100.

to understanding ritual[99] dovetails very neatly with Riis and Woodhead's proposals concerning how ritual practices can help to mould and reinforce an emotional programme, especially if over time such practices become increasingly entrenched, habituated patterns of behaviour.[100]

It is beyond the scope of this study to examine every occurrence of ritual activity in Philippians and 1 Thessalonians; such an effort would, in any case, be stymied at the onset because of the lack of a coherent taxonomy of ritual in Paul's letters, given the embryonic state of ritual criticism of the New Testament (see note 95 of this chapter). For my purposes, it is sufficient to draw attention to representative examples of ritual practices.

In Philippians and 1 Thessalonians, perhaps the most common mention of what we may term as 'ritualization' has to do with prayer. Paul speaks of his own impassioned prayers for the believers (Phil. 1.3-6, 9-11; 1 Thess. 1.2-3; 3.10), reminds them of the importance of prayer concerning all things (Phil. 4.6) and at all times (1 Thess. 5.17), and solicits their prayers for himself and his co-workers (1 Thess. 5.25).[101] Paul's repeated mentions of intercession are highly suggestive of a sustained effort to highlight its central importance in the life of the Christian. Certainly, in his own life and practice Paul exemplifies the believer who prays – and one who does so regularly (1 Thess. 1.2-3; 3.10; implied strongly in Phil. 1.3-4); and, having set an example for his readers, he mandates that they too adopt this attitude of constant prayer (1 Thess. 5.17). The fact that Paul does not urge prayer without also stressing the need for its regular practice suggests that he is intimately familiar with the danger of diminished enthusiasm and the eventual abandonment of prayer, whether from weariness, apathy, cynicism, or creeping unbelief; for him, persistent prayer characterizes the faithful.[102]

Drawing insights from cultural anthropology, Bruce Malina offers a useful definition of prayer that weaves together certain key emphases:

> Prayer is a socially meaningful symbolic act of communication, bearing directly upon persons perceived as somehow supporting, maintaining, and controlling the order of existence of the one praying, and performed with the purpose of getting results from or in the interaction of communication.[103]

Since prayer involves communication with a divine being who is thought to be able to shape one's 'order of existence', it presupposes the presence of certain attitudes related

---

[99] On this see Bell, *Ritual Theory*, 81–8.

[100] See also Douglas J. Davies, *Emotion, Identity, and Religion: Hope, Reciprocity, and Otherness* (Oxford: Oxford University Press, 2011), 37–67. Davies shows that the meanings and values that are inherent in ritual practice help to generate and sustain an identity that is replete with emotion.

[101] The same thoughts are found frequently in Paul's other letters too; for references see Jeffrey A. D. Weima, *1–2 Thessalonians*, Baker Exegetical Commentary on the New Testament (Grand Rapids, MI: Baker, 2014), 400.

[102] David Crump, *Knocking on Heaven's Door: A New Testament Theology of Petitionary Prayer* (Grand Rapids, MI: Baker, 2006), 215.

[103] Bruce J. Malina, 'What Is Prayer?', *The Bible Today* 18 (1980): 215; quoted in Jerome H. Neyrey, 'Prayer, in Other Words: New Testament Prayers in Social-Science Perspective', in *Social Scientific Models for Interpreting the Bible: Essays by the Context Group in Honor of Bruce J. Malina*, ed. John J. Pilch (Leiden: Brill, 2001), 351.

to dependence on, and trust in, that being, as well as the belief that some kind of tangible change can be truly effected within the ordering of reality that the one praying believes to be in force in the world. Applied to our context here, for Paul, prayer represents a renewed trust in God and in his ability to work in the world to achieve his divine will. Expressing this thought a little differently: prayer entails the believer's deliberate reorientation of himself or herself towards God, in the light of the symbolic structure that frames and gives shape to his or her conception of true reality. The result is a reaffirmation of one's identity and status, and with this, a recalibration of one's role, within this theological ordering of life.[104]

Malina's succinct definition also alerts our attention to the social dynamics surrounding the practice of prayer. To be sure, Malina's focus on prayer as communication between someone from a lower social standing and someone with a higher social power comes from how societal structures provide models for the language and ideology of prayer.[105] But there is another social aspect of prayer that has to do with its effect on relationships: it may be argued that intercessory prayer for others predisposes the one praying to experiencing heightened feelings of mutuality, affection, and solidarity of purpose towards those being prayed for (so Paul in Phil. 1.3-8 and in 1 Thess. 1.2-3, 9-10),[106] which would surely help to affirm and fortify social ties and thus strengthen the community as a whole.

We shall take 1 Thess. 5.16-18 by way of illustration. Here Paul instructs the believers to pray constantly (ἀδιαλείπτως προσεύχεσθε, 5.17),[107] sandwiching this command between two other commands, to rejoice always (Πάντοτε χαίρετε, 5.16),[108] and to give thanks in all circumstances (ἐν παντὶ εὐχαριστεῖτε, 5.18a).[109] These three commands are so general and terse, and form such a brief unit, that it is difficult to relate them to a specific situation in the Thessalonian church that Paul might want to address. Yet the

---

[104] Neyrey refers to the ritual 'status transformation' that petitionary prayers are associated with; 'Prayer', 376.

[105] See Rodney A. Werline, *Pray Like This: Understanding Prayer in the Bible* (New York: T&T Clark, 2007), 10.

[106] As John Koenig, *Rediscovering New Testament Prayer: Boldness and Blessing in the Name of Jesus* (New York: HarperCollins, 1992), 91, observes, 'Intercession creates a deep connection with others and a mutual caring that often leads to active ministry.'

[107] Paul has earlier in the letter repeatedly demonstrated the centrality of constant prayer in his own life, using different verbs for prayer and qualifying them with different adverbs: Εὐχαριστοῦμεν τῷ θεῷ πάντοτε … ἀδιαλείπτως μνημονεύοντες (1.2-3); εὐχαριστοῦμεν τῷ θεῷ ἀδιαλείπτως (2.13); νυκτὸς καὶ ἡμέρας ὑπερεκπερισσοῦ δεόμενοι (3.10) (Abraham J. Malherbe, *The Letters to the Thessalonians*, AB 32B (New Haven, CT: Yale University Press, 2000), 329). In several other letters in addition to this one, he likewise instructs his readers to devote themselves to prayer (2 Thess. 3.1; Phil. 4.6; Rom. 12.12). It should be obvious that here in 1 Thess. 5.17 (and elsewhere) Paul does not expect ἀδιαλείπτως to be taken literally; as Weima (*Thessalonians*, 400) notes, the adverb is formulaic and somewhat hyperbolic. Nonetheless it is clear that Paul expects the believers to take prayer seriously and to pray frequently for themselves and others, presumably whether in private or corporately.

[108] This echoes Paul's earlier mentions of joy in the letter (1 Thess. 1.6; 2.19-20).

[109] I take ἐν παντί (5.18) to mean 'in everything', i.e. in every situation, rather than the temporal idea of 'always'; for an outline of the debate see Weima, *Thessalonians*, 401. However, as Howard I. Marshall, *1 and 2 Thessalonians*, New Century Bible (Grand Rapids, MI: Eerdmans), 155, rightly points out, this is 'surely a pointless controversy, since either translation is virtually equivalent to the other. Believers are to find reason to praise and thank God in whatever situation they may find themselves and thus at all times' (quoted by Weima, *Thessalonians*, 401).

contextual locale of these injunctions indicates that he continues to cast his gaze on the Christian community as a whole, though his instructions are certainly pertinent also to the devotional life of the individual believer. The surrounding sections of the letter all have to do with the ordering of various aspects of church life and the relations within it: proper attitudes towards leaders (5.12-13); ministry to troubled members (5.14-15); and living in the Spirit, which includes handling prophecy in the setting of worship (5.19-22).[110]

To be sure, this is not the only place in Paul's letters where prayer is placed alongside rejoicing and thanksgiving; see earlier in the letter at 1 Thess. 3.9-10, and also Phil. 1.3-4 and 4.4-6. In fact, their recurrent, deliberate juxtaposition surely implies that Paul considers it important that these practices flourish in tandem in the life of the believer. For Paul, to rejoice is to acknowledge God's sovereignty in all of life and to remain certain of God's eschatological salvation. Prayer is grounded in the Christian's relationship with God and communicates his or her trust in God to achieve his perfect and sovereign will. Thanksgiving is the proper response of believers to God's gracious work and saving action in their lives and in the world. That Paul considers these three related directives to be of crucial importance is made clear through how he anchors them in the very will of God for the believer, and thereby imbues what he says with the greatest authority (τοῦτο γὰρ θέλημα θεοῦ ἐν Χριστῷ Ἰησοῦ εἰς ὑμᾶς, 5.18b).[111]

In this, we have an explicit portrayal of how prayer is integral not only to the social ordering of the Christian community but to its emotional ordering as well. While we cannot be completely sure as to how prayer was actually carried out whether privately or in corporate worship,[112] on Paul's part there is certainly an intentional, sustained effort to lift up prayer as what is, in effect, a ritual practice that covers all of the Christian life and helps to sustain it. Here, François Berthomé and Michael Houseman's recent analysis of the connection between ritual and emotion may help to illuminate matters further.[113] In regard to prayer, they argue that it is precisely its performative and self-referential property that makes it so emotionally exceptional in devotional practice. As they see it, in prayer,

> the perfect relationship devotees aim for, and the sequence of actions and dispositions that are held to embody it, are maximally fused, in stark contrast with the constant negotiation characteristic of the daily emotional grind. In this

---

[110] Weima, *Thessalonians*, 381, 398; see also Wanamaker, *The Epistles to the Thessalonians*, New International Greek Testament Commentary (Grand Rapids, MI: Eerdmans, 1990), 190–1.

[111] With most commentators I take the phrase to look backwards to embrace all three commands. There are a few scholars who see it as referring to only the final directive (so e.g. Malherbe, *Thessalonians*, 330); however, the parallel structure of the three commands and their co-appearance elsewhere (see discussion earlier) suggests that the majority view is to be preferred (so e.g. Weima, *Thessalonians*, 402).

[112] See e.g. Koenig, *Prayer*, 129–34, for an attempt to elucidate the circumstances, times, and postures of corporate prayer in the early Church.

[113] François Berthomé and Michael Houseman, 'Ritual and Emotions: Moving Relations, Patterned Effusions', *Religion and Society: Advances in Research* 1 (2010): 57–75, doi: 10.3167/arrs.2010.010105 (especially 66–9).

light, what ritual episodes achieve is probably less an incorporation of enduring dispositions than a fragile instantiation of exemplary … relationships. Such compressed, rarefied moments, which act as benchmarks for what it is for God to be present, may subsequently be used as a sounding board to navigate through the everyday, as long as certain reminders are close at hand.[114]

If this is so, then we may have another way to understand why Paul emphasizes not only the need to pray but also the importance of doing so frequently. As Berthomé and Houseman seem to see it, episodic prayer may not bring about a thoroughgoing inculcation of preferred long-term emotional dispositions. Yet, on the basis of their analysis, it seems fair to infer that an intensification of prayer – that is, by practising it deliberately and frequently, until it becomes a habituated form of behaviour – would help to school an appropriate repertoire of affective states. Furthermore, Berthomé and Houseman's perspective on prayer helps us to be alert to the presence of those 'certain reminders' – other forms of ritual activity, or media rich in symbolic content – that help to strengthen its efficacy as a way of making sense of quotidian experience.

There are in Philippians at least two other possible allusions to practices of ritualization. One is the Christ poem of Phil. 2.6-11: while there is widespread agreement that 'exalted, lyrical, quasi-credal language' is found here,[115] the matter of genre and whether the passage constitutes a 'hymn' is contentious.[116] Yet even if we take the passage to *not* be a hymn, its distinctively credal qualities surely suggest a connection to liturgical practice[117] and thus also to its function within some kind of ritual process.[118]

Another allusion to ritualization comes from a reference that Paul makes in Phil. 3.3 to the service of God as one of the defining characteristics of those who have faith in Christ, within his scathing indictment against his Judaizing adversaries (3.2-4a). The use of the verb λατρεύω in 3.3 (ἡμεῖς γάρ ἐσμεν ἡ περιτομή, οἱ πνεύματι θεοῦ λατρεύοντες) comes from the LXX, where it is widely used as a cultic term; and in both the Old and New Testaments the verb signifies divine service either to God or to pagan deities.[119] Fee observes that Paul's usage stands in ironical contrast to 3.2, where he decries the illegitimate service rendered by those whom he pejoratively labels as the 'mutilation' – the 'workers of evil' who are engaged in doing the very thing that was forbidden in the temple cultus. It is the believers who are the true circumcision, who 'serve' by the Spirit, over against serving by the flesh. Hence the verb refers not to the

---

[114] Berthomé and Houseman, 'Ritual and Emotions', 68.
[115] Bockmuehl, *Philippians*, 116.
[116] See the succinct discussion in Paul A. Holloway, *Philippians: A Commentary*, Hermeneia (Minneapolis, MN: Fortress, 2017), 116–17.
[117] Perhaps as an encomium that the Philippians had worked out to use in mission proclamation (so e.g. Reumann, *Philippians*, 333, 365–6; see also Hellerman, *Philippians*, 106).
[118] Meeks, *Christians*, 144–5.
[119] Hellerman, *Philippians*, 173–4, noting also that in the LXX λατρεύω is applied to the cultic service of the people as a whole, versus λειτουργέω, which is restricted to priestly functions. See also BDAG 587: 'in our lit. only of the carrying out of religious duties, esp. of a cultic nature, by human beings'.

worship offered to God as a gathered people, but rather represents 'the "service" of God's people in terms of their devotion to him as evidenced in the way they live before him'. As Fee summarizes: Paul is contrasting 'not external rite over against internal "spiritual" service', but rather life in the flesh against life 'as the eschatological people of God, evidenced to be so by the Spirit of God, through whom all life in the present is now service and devotion to God'.[120] Here we are perhaps on less firm ground when it comes to identifying *obvious* ritual activity; but if we take what Paul says to be an emphasis that for the believer every activity in every sphere of life is to be an act of worship, consecration, and service to God (Rom. 12.1), then what we have here is tantamount to a view of life itself as a deliberate, wholehearted, and also 'ritualistic' offering of oneself to God, in so far as devotion and duty are brought together in both the privately expressed and publicly performed contexts of a vital, ongoing relationship with God.

Furthermore, on the basis of the evidence of passages such as Acts 2.42-7 (a vignette of life in the early church that highlights, among other things, the importance of the Lord's Supper, prayer, and worship for the first Christians) and Acts 16.13-15 (which narrates the story of the baptisms of Lydia and the members of her household at Philippi) and parts of Paul's letters in addition to Philippians and 1 Thessalonians that relate to these same patterns of activity, that is, baptism (e.g. Rom. 6.4), the Lord's Supper (e.g. 1 Cor. 11.17-34), prayer (e.g. Rom. 12.12), and worship (e.g. 1 Cor. 14.26-40), it seems entirely reasonable to suppose that all these practices were regarded as being integral to the proper functioning of each of Paul's churches. As such, there is in place in the Pauline churches a regular and highly variegated ritual embodiment and expression of the beliefs that arise in relation to the Christ story.[121] From an anthropological perspective, one might say that these practices of ritualization are in fact 'bodily and collective means of meaning making' that 'allow actions to become part of the very essence of people's identities'.[122] All these practices help to schematize an emotional programme and thereby instil and manage appropriate emotional repertoires; and there is a profound resultant impact on individual and corporate identity formation. As Davies maintains, 'Ritual, by bonding a group's core values with its preferred emotions in response to life's reciprocal obligations and opportunities, fosters identity by giving meaning and hope to life.'[123]

---

[120] Fee, *Philippians*, 299–300 (all quotes are from 300); see also Bockmuehl, *Philippians*, 192. Similarly Hellerman, Philippians, 174, notes that λατρεύοντες functions here in a broadly metaphorical sense to denote the entirety of Christian existence, i.e. the 'cultic concept is now spiritualized' (quoting Hermann Strathmann, 'λατρεύω, λατρεία', *TDNT* 58–65, at 65).

[121] See the still useful discussion in Meeks, *Christians*, 140–63. However, Meeks's influential schematic classification of rituals as major (baptism and the Lord's Supper), minor (most other ritualized actions), and unknown and controverted (e.g. funeral rites and baptism for the dead) has been questioned by certain scholars; for discussion see Lawrence, 'Ritual', 102–5.

[122] Louise J. Lawrence, *Reading with Anthropology: Exhibiting Aspects of New Testament Religion* (Bletchley: Paternoster, 2005), xvi, drawing on the work of Ronald Grimes, *Deeply into the Bone: Re-Inventing Rites of Passage* (Berkeley: University of California Press, 2000).

[123] Davies, *Emotion, Identity, and Religion*, 37.

5.5.5. Language and Emotional Ordering

Riis and Woodhead argue also that 'just as emotions can be stabilized, objectified, communicated, and shaped by symbolic-material objects, so they can be by language'.[124] Further, they emphasize that there is no need to make a sharp distinction between linguistic and non-linguistic forms of communication, since both arise from the 'felt sense' of a situation which is associated with the 'continent of feeling' that underlies all meaning, thought, and symbolically mediated expression.[125] As Riis and Woodhead see it, this felt sense of life – the elemental form of engagement with the world – is full of protolinguistic possibilities relating to the patterned, recurring relations between oneself and one's social and material settings, which take shape as structures of meaning through which one's world acquires coherence and intelligibility. While visual images may be the most basic means by which such patterns are brought to consciousness, they can also be articulated by way of words; in fact, as already noted the two are closely linked, since language works through metaphor by articulating felt, embodied, understandings of the world through words. Thus it becomes apparent that one's felt sense of life is shaped significantly by language. Furthermore, there is a profound connection between language and emotion. When personal feelings are expressed using a common language, these feelings are interpreted and presented within the shared framework of emotional language. As Riis and Woodhead observe, 'Just as meaning can be concentrated material symbolization, so sets of words can become cultural objects with the same power to move and motivate.'[126]

Riis and Woodhead go on to make the important point that

> this discussion of emotions, cultural symbols, and language reminds us that human lives are characterized by emotional indeterminacy, which articulation in words and images helps us to control. In reality we are uncertain about how we feel, and need help to work it out. Even when we have some grasp on how we feel, we may struggle to clarify our emotions and their consequences … We have no clear touchstones by which to identify our feelings; the causes of those feelings are often mixed or unclear, and our language for expressing them is inadequate. (*Sociology*, 46)

For them, it is precisely this emotional indeterminacy that explains why the tendency of many theorists to treat emotions 'like stones or ponds or static objects that are given labels' is so misleading.[127] Moreover, it is also mistaken to think that the general field of

---

[124] Riis and Woodhead, *Sociology*, 44.
[125] Riis and Woodhead, *Sociology*, 44–5, citing the work of Eugene T. Gendlin, *Experiencing and the Creation of Meaning: A Philosophical and Psychological Approach to the Subjective* (Evanston, IL: Northwestern University Press, 1997).
[126] Riis and Woodhead, *Sociology*, 44–5 (quote from 45).
[127] Riis and Woodhead, *Sociology*, 46, quoting Norman K. Denzin, *On Understanding Emotion* (San Francisco, CA: Jossey-Bass, 1984), 26. As Denzin notes here, those who take this view locate the explanation of emotion in the development and appearance of the emotion as that development is shaped by factors external to the person, instead of treating emotions as processes lived by self-reflective individuals in interactional experiences.

emotion can be subdivided into ever more complex general classifications of emotions, because emotions such as fear, shame, and so on 'are culturally contingent words with which we try, with varying degrees of inadequacy, to capture aspects of shifting social and material relationships and associated image-schema that always exceed the capacity of our words'.[128]

Riis and Woodhead's ideas regarding the connection between language and emotion are helpful for our exploration of the Pauline emotional regime in at least two ways. First, the importance of language in articulating and even concretizing an emotional stance is highlighted. So, for instance, by referring to his own joy and stressing to the Philippian believers the basis for this joy (1.3-5, 15-19; 2.1-4, 17-18; 4.10-19), or by issuing to the Thessalonians a prohibition against inordinate grief and explaining why such grief is not appropriate (1 Thess. 4.13-17), the literary formulations with which he communicates with them become the media through which theologically rich symbolic content that helps one to make sense of one's felt reality is shared and given expression. As discussed earlier (see in particular Sections 3.4.1 and 4.4.1), Paul seems to expect this material to influence strongly his readers' ways of thinking and thereby shape the concomitant emotional dispositions that emerge as a result of their excogitations concerning their new terms of engagement with their surroundings. Thus, he is able to confidently adjure the Thessalonians to bring encouragement to one another in the very words with which he has just emphasized the theological ground for consolation (1 Thess. 4.18); in this we see further reinforcement of Riis and Woodhead's idea that language functions as a repository of symbolic meaning that, through articulation, can motivate emotional change.

Second, and related to the above, it may be that we perhaps underestimate the importance of Paul's use of language in fostering greater emotional determinacy. Taking the example of joy: throughout the letter, as we have seen, Paul makes much of his joy and correlates it to the new ordering of reality that is to govern the lives of those who follow Christ. Then, at 3.1 and 4.4, he expressly commands joy from the Philippians. While the use of the imperative recalls its earlier appearance at 2.18, where Paul calls the believers to mutual joy in the face of suffering, here at 3.1 and again (twice) at 4.4, the joy that the Philippians are told to show forth is ἐν κυρίῳ. It seems likely that Paul's language comes from the Psalms;[129] and if so, this imperative refers not only to an inward feeling but also to an outward display or action – 'to verbalize with praise and singing'.[130] In both these cases (i.e. in Paul's descriptions of his own joy and in his explicit behests concerning the social display of joy) it seems apparent that there is in place a deliberate effort – through the use of symbol-laden written language and rhetorical formulations – to achieve a heightened, fuller sense of emotional determinacy in regard to the precise nature of joy (and its expression) that should characterize the life of the believer.

---

[128] Riis and Woodhead, *Sociology*, 46.
[129] See earlier Section 3.3.3.
[130] Fee, *Philippians*, 291; cf. Hansen, *Philippians*, 288, who relates Paul's language to the joyful corporate worship of the Lord in the Psalms.

5.5.6. Letters and Emotional Ordering

It is helpful at this juncture to make some remarks concerning the nature of Paul's own role in the ordering of his churches. One of his major concerns was that they would not just survive in what was often a belligerent social environment but also thrive as unified, Spirit-filled communities of love, grace, goodness, and joy (so e.g. Phil. 1.9-11; 2.1-4; 1 Thess. 5.14-24). However, Paul has a great many things to do as a community organizer: he has to acquaint himself with the particular problems faced by each congregation, solve conflicts, deal with false teachings and troublemakers, build unity between the believers, strengthen them in their faith, and comfort the afflicted and the grieving – in short, to do everything necessary to upbuild the fledgling churches. That for the most part all these things have to be accomplished from a very great distance only multiplies the challenges that are involved in what are already complex tasks. To accomplish his plans, Paul seems to depend on three main instruments: prayer to God concerning the believers, letters that he pens to his churches, and emissaries such as Timothy and Epaphroditus who are sent to them on his behalf. It is in his letters that these elements come together: in addition to the encouragement and instructions that Paul gives to the believers, he makes mention of them in his prayers, thereby further revealing his deep concern and enduring affection for his converts (Phil. 1.3-11; 1 Thess. 1.2-3), and refers to the previous or impending pastoral visits of his co-workers, which again signals to them his anxiety over their well-being (Phil. 2.19-30; 1 Thess. 3.1-10).

In antiquity, letters were regarded as a means of mediating one's actual physical presence,[131] and scholars have sought to apply findings from the study of ancient epistolography to Paul's epistles.[132] In particular, Robert Funk's form-critical study of Paul's 'apostolic parousia' remains influential:[133] as Funk sees it, Paul's presence by letter is a manifestation of the apostolic parousia in and of itself, even though it is not as powerful an expression of it when compared to Paul's personal presence. There is in the apostolic parousia a hierarchy of authoritative communication: the weakest is the letter; stronger than this is the emissary; while the most powerful is the personal

---

[131] The topos of parousia in ancient epistolography was identified several decades ago by Heikki Koskenniemi (*Studien zur Idee und Phraseologie des griechischen Briefes bis 400 n. Chr.*, AASF, Series B, vol. 102.2 (Helsinki: Finnish Academy, 1956), 38–42). For examples of ancient letters which functioned as a mode of personal presence see Hans-Josef Klauck, *Ancient Letters and the New Testament: A Guide to Context and Exegesis* (Waco, TX: Baylor University Press, 2006), 192–3; Stanley K. Stowers, *Letter Writing in Greco-Roman Antiquity*, Library of Early Christianity 5 (Philadelphia, PA: Westminster Press, 1986), 59–60.

[132] E.g. Abraham J. Malherbe (*Paul and the Thessalonians: The Philosophic Tradition of Pastoral Care* (Philadelphia, PA: Fortress, 1987), 72–3) has argued that the theme of bodily absence but spiritual presence is a standard feature of epistolographic theory, and that Paul consciously uses the literary conventions of his day to communicate his anxiety about the Thessalonians and to guide their religious and moral development; cf. Stanley K. Stowers, 'Friends and Enemies in the Politics of Heaven: Reading Theology in Philippians', in *Pauline Theology 1: Thessalonians, Philippians, Galatians*, ed. Jouette M. Bassler (Minneapolis, MN: Fortress, 1991), 109.

[133] Robert W. Funk, 'The Apostolic *Parousia*: Form and Significance', in *Christian History and Interpretation: Studies Presented to John Knox*, ed. W. R. Farmer, C. F. D. Moule, and R. R. Niebuhr (Cambridge: Cambridge University Press, 1967), 249–69.

visit.¹³⁴ While not all scholars have accepted Funk's precise conclusions,¹³⁵ the tendency to relate Paul's sensitivity to the effects of personal presence to matters of epistolary form has persisted;¹³⁶ and certainly, the evidence of passages such as 1 Cor. 5.3-4 seems to demonstrate that Paul himself sees a consistency between his letters and his personal presence.¹³⁷

Jane Heath has helpfully nuanced the debate over the relevance of the epistolary topos of personal presence by exploring the literary and rhetorical concept of *enargeia* in 1 Thess. 1.2–2.16.¹³⁸ Heath argues that the effect of Paul's prompting of the believers' memories of his missionary visit 'is likely to have been experienced as *making* that *absent* past experience *present* and vivid to the senses and emotions'.¹³⁹ For the Thessalonians, this past event had to do with their experience of God's saving love as it was made known to them through the teachings of Paul and his co-workers; their experience also pointed to and anticipated the Parousia of Christ, since this was the focus of the gospel proclamation. Now that Paul is absent, this experience has to be supplied by memory – which makes vivid the truth of the gospel while also arousing a desire for renewed personal contact.¹⁴⁰ Heath concludes that

> Paul's purpose is understood to be a making present of the absent apostles with cognitive and emotional intent, directed essentially not on their relationship to him and the other missionaries, so much as on their relationship to God and anticipation of the *parousia* as it was experienced through the missionaries. The effect is to strengthen faith and Christian love … Remembering Paul effects and strengthens a relationship to God and to Christ, as well as to Paul and his companions themselves, as the visible, perceptible link to that divine Other.¹⁴¹

As we have seen, there is broad agreement that Paul in his letters seems to believe, and even assume, that he is making his presence felt in ways that reveal a certain

---

[134] Funk, 'Apostolic *Parousia*', 258–9, following the conclusions of Koskenniemi, *Studien*, 38–42, 172–80.
[135] See especially Margaret M. Mitchell, 'New Testament Envoys in the Context of Greco-Roman Diplomatic and Epistolary Conventions: The Example of Timothy and Titus', *JBL* 111 (1992): 641–62, especially 642–3. Mitchell contests Funk's conclusions, noting that Paul's own comments (2 Cor. 10.10) reveal that he privileges his letters over his personal presence, and she suggests that Paul in each situation chooses which one of the three modes of communication (letter, envoy, and personal presence) would best suit his purposes.
[136] See Jane M. F. Heath, 'Absent Presences of Paul and Christ: *Enargeia* in 1 Thessalonians 1–3', *JSNT* 32 (2009): 6.
[137] See Peter Orr, *Christ Absent and Present: A Study in Pauline Christology*, WUNT 2.354 (Tübingen: Mohr Siebeck, 2014), 132.
[138] Heath, 'Absent Presences', 3–38.
[139] Heath, 'Absent Presences', 28 (emphases original).
[140] Heath, 'Absent Presences', 28, see also 20. As Heath notes, 'To the ancient mind, *enargeia* was achieved through memory even when the subject portrayed was something beyond the previous experience of the audience. This was because the ancient understanding of imagination was not creative but mimetic: it drew on preconceived notions of reality and values concerning it, lying within a common cultural experience' (11, referencing Ruth Webb, 'Imagination and the Arousal of Emotions in Greco-Roman Rhetoric', in *The Passions in Roman Thought and Literature*, ed. Susanna Morton Braund and Christopher Gill (Cambridge: Cambridge University Press, 1997), 123–4).
[141] Heath, 'Absent Presences', 29.

continuity with his personal presence. The view that Paul's presence via the written word is but a weak substitute for a personal visit has not gone unchallenged; and it must be noted in any case that scholarly discussions of 'absent-presences' in Paul have taken place in the light of epistolary conventions – a premise which itself has been called into question by those who define the apostolic parousia as a literary rather than an epistolary topos.[142]

Heath's insightful analysis of *enargeia* in 1 Thessalonians helps to move the discussion forward: by focusing on a significant phenomenon in the social discourse and experience of the day and judiciously sidestepping the debates over such matters as the literary or rhetorical categories that can be applied appropriately to the study of the letter, a rich and potentially highly fruitful hermeneutic emerges with which one can examine Paul's power of drawing significance from absent presences. Paul's words make vivid the apostolic presence and thus also God's past work and Christ's Parousia, which in turn prompts both awareness of the immediacy of the divine and longing for its fuller realization.[143] If this is so, it then seems entirely reasonable to conjecture that these cognitive and emotional associations would have been taken up along with Paul's instructions later in the letter concerning such matters as community ethics (1 Thess. 4.1-12; 5.12-15) and eschatology, along with the proper handling of grief (4.13–5.11), and helped to form the 'lived' context in which these teachings were appropriated through belief, praxis, and feeling.

All this interfaces rather nicely with what Judith Lieu has recently highlighted about the symbolic significance of early Christian letters: while they were grounded in the letter-writing conventions of the day, these letters – which instantiated and gave expression to new, Christian, modes of being and relating – were powerful cultural symbols that were instrumental in shaping an alternate world view.[144] In the very articulation of standard epistolary *topoi* such as matters concerning distance, relationality, and intimacy, letters were actually cultural strategies that had to do with performance and ritual, and with these, the ritualization of relationships.[145] It seems evident that in 1 Thessalonians these social and ritual dynamics come into play, and in a rather pronounced way. Paul describes a new world view – a Christian symbolic universe in which new patterns of thinking, feeling, and relating are to hold sway; and his letter is thus itself a 'performed', symbolic expression of this alternate reality.

At the same time, if Heath is correct, Paul's presence with the Thessalonians is supplied not only by means of what he writes but also through vivid memory – which, in turn, triggers for the believers cognitive and emotional associations related to God's continuing dealings with them. Furthermore, in the foregoing we might see some vindication of Riis and Woodhead's understanding of the interplay between symbols

---

[142] So Terence Y. Mullins, 'Visit Talk in New Testament Letters', *CBQ* 35 (1973): 350–8; David E. Aune, *The New Testament in Its Literary Environment*, LEC 8 (Philadelphia, PA: Westminster, 1987), 190.
[143] Heath, 'Absent Presences', 26.
[144] Judith M. Lieu, 'Letters and the Topography of Early Christianity', *NTS* 62 (2016): 167–82.
[145] Lieu, 'Letters', 181. Lieu observes also that even the materiality of letters has its own intrinsic power: 'Like a bundle of love-letters tied with a ribbon, the letter almost embodies the affective dimensions of its contents, even beyond those whom it initially bound together' (182).

and collective memory in the formulation of the framework of a religious emotional regime: bringing together the work of Durkheim and Halbwachs, they propose that present-day concerns and the remembered past (both of which are mediated by sacred symbols and stories) shape social action and emotion.[146] All this goes some way towards helping us to understand how Paul is able in his churches to play the role of community organizer with such effectiveness, even to the extent of being able to pull the emotional strings of his converts from a great distance.[147]

5.5.7. Conclusion

It remains for us to pull together the different but closely related strands of our investigation into how authorized emotions are constructed and shored up in the Pauline communities. Key to Paul's strategy is the putting in place of an emotional programme in which a symbolically mediated emotional ordering operates to guide and also reinforce the emotional notes that are to be sounded, in line with the eschatological reality framework that is seen to govern all of life and human existence. Emotional ordering involves aspects such as inspiration and instruction, personal exemplification, ritual practice, language, and most of all the pervasive use of symbols. And as we have seen, the harmonized interplay of the symbolic, material, and social elements within an emotional regime has a profound effect on feeling and sensibility.[148] A particularly striking example of this comes from Paul's delimiting of the grief of the Thessalonian believers in 1 Thess. 4.13-18 in the light of the eschatological ordering of reality: it would seem that here there is every possibility that the Thessalonian believers can achieve an unusually high degree of emotional transcendence[149] through a deliberate cauterization of excessive grief.

The application to the above of Riis and Woodhead's understanding of balanced dialectics within an emotional regime makes this even clearer.[150] Based on the evidence in the letter, we may well imagine the following (not unlikely) scenario taking place. The believers in Thessalonica – reeling from the shock of the unexpected deaths of a number of their brethren, and plunged into grief – receive and read Paul's letter. They are confronted anew and deeply encouraged by the symbol-charged theological realities that he espouses and which they remember as being integral to the Christian vision of life after death. Processes of objectification and consecration begin to gain momentum as individuals, along with the wider body of believers to which they belong, look afresh to Christ to fashion their mindsets – through prayer, worship,

---

[146] Riis and Woodhead, *Sociology*, 38–9, referencing Émile Durkheim, *The Elementary Forms of Religious Life*, trans. Carol Cosman (Oxford: Oxford University Press, 2001), and Maurice Halbwachs, *On Collective Memory*, trans. Lewis A. Coser (Chicago: University of Chicago Press, 1992).

[147] Our conclusions here emerge primarily from an investigation of 1 Thessalonians. Given the presence of thematically parallel (and similarly interlocking) motifs in Philippians, an investigation of it along the same lines is very likely to only bolster our findings, and will therefore be foregone in the interest of space.

[148] Riis and Woodhead, *Sociology*, 71.

[149] See Section 5.3.3.b.

[150] See Section 5.3.4.

and other ritual enactments; the recollection of memories and their articulation through shared language; a readiness to follow Paul's directives; and the adoption of exemplars as models for imitation. As objectification (in individuals) and consecration (in the church) occur, the corresponding dialectical processes of subjectification and insignation come into play as individual believers and the church as a whole, respectively, are inspired and moved by symbols that are the very objects of devotion and reverence (here, in the main, Christ), and by the eschatological realities that these symbols reference (principally, the resurrection of believers at the Parousia of Christ and the promise of eternal life with him). The remaining pair of dialectical relationships, internalization and externalization, is simultaneously given expression as the renewed emotional stance of the individual – characterized in particular by the excision of inordinate grief and the repristination of true joy – influences and vivifies the affective experiences of the collective whole, which in turn acts back upon and further enlivens the individual believer's experiences.

This illustration of balanced dialectics within the emotional regime of the church at Thessalonica demonstrates clearly a situation in which authorized emotions acquire great stability and power. Our reconstruction coheres remarkably well with, and is amplified further by, Riis and Woodhead's description of balanced emotional dialectics that reinforce one another:

> Individual participants are in solidarity with one another and with the group as a whole. Their feelings are amplified by being reflected in the feelings of other participants. Whether metaphorically or literally, everyone is dancing to the same tune, their bodies, thoughts, and feelings echoing and reinforcing one another. Feelings are experienced as authentically personal, not as externally imposed. There is harmony between the group and its leaders: they are all parts of the same whole, participating in the same experience. The experience is not amorphous, but structured by consecrated symbols that provide the focus of attention, devotion, feeling, and action. Because participants feel equally about their focus of devotion, their sense of harmony and kinship with their fellows is heightened; they are united by common inspiration and commitment. (*Sociology*, 157–8)

To conclude our discussion at this point, the conceptual apparatus of the emotional regime allows us to explore emotion in Paul's letters in dialogue with the increasingly widespread argument that emotion is as much a social and relational construct as it is a private, inner state. Furthermore, careful attention is paid also to the effect of symbolic relations, since an emotional regime presupposes the presence of a symbolically charged alternate ordering of reality that embraces all of existence and helps individual believers and the churches to which they belong gain a deeper sense of meaning and purpose in life. Such an ordering implies the offering of an emotional programme that regulates affect, promoting sanctioned emotions such as joy and stigmatizing rogue ones like uncontrolled grief. As we have seen, when balanced dialectics are at work within an emotional regime, its emotional programme is given full sway to establish and police normative patterns of feeling.

5.6. Comparing the Pauline and Stoic Emotional Regimes

As we conclude our study, it is helpful to place the Pauline emotional regime alongside our earlier findings concerning Stoic thinking on emotion, and to identify their major points of similarity and contrast. By doing so we are able to see especially clearly the sharp edges, as it were, of Paul's account of emotion, since Stoic ethics offers a powerful alternative to it. We begin by briefly summarizing Paul's, and then the Stoics', attitude to joy and grief.

5.6.1. Paul on Joy and Grief

For Paul, the basis of joy is irreducibly theological: it is premised entirely upon God's work – past, present, and future – of radically renewing all of creation in the light of the death, resurrection, and coming again of Christ, and the sending of the Spirit. It is of course the gospel that announces these realities; and as such, joy is correlated in profound ways to the believer's understanding of and involvement in the kerygma, in the sense of how its truths come to authentic, 'lived' expression within the life of the believer. Indeed, as Fee expresses it, 'joy is the distinctive mark of the believer in Christ Jesus'.[151] Putting it another way: to the degree that the Christian is able not only to discern but also to participate in, this all-encompassing metanarrative that envelopes and gives meaning to all of life, and which is thus that overarching story within which all other life stories are to be located and made sense of, joy – 'the felt form of Christian hope'[152] – may be found.

However, as Paul repeatedly demonstrates, far from being only a private experience for the individual, Christian joy is simultaneously also very much a social phenomenon: it emerges and flourishes within the context of active participation with others in the advancement of the gospel. For Paul, there is thus an important sense in which joy is understood to be both socially generated in relationship with fellow believers and also socially embodied through expressions of mutual joy. This decidedly social dimension to joy seems to reinforce the fact that the Christian life is not to be lived alone, but in community – a community whose raison d'être is centred squarely on the gospel of Christ and whose mission is fully bound up with its faithful proclamation in word and deed.

Turning now to grief: in the light of the above, it is perhaps not at all surprising that inordinate, runaway grief over the death of other believers has no place in Paul's thinking concerning the believer's proper emotional constitution. For as he sees it, such excessive grief exposes a serious lack of understanding as to what death actually is for Christians, and thus also a grossly inadequate eschatology. To counter the problem, Paul issues loving yet firm instructions: he does not expect his converts to stop grieving entirely, but asks that they temper their sorrow in the light of the true, eschatological state of affairs. The demise of another believer should not, and

---

[151] Fee, *Philippians*, 53.
[152] Nicholas Lash, *Seeing in the Dark* (London: Darton, Longman & Todd, 2005), 201 (see also n.176 of Chapter 3 of my book).

indeed must not, trigger uncontrolled outpourings of grief, because the resurrection of Christ renders certain the resurrection at the Parousia of the dead who have put their trust in him.

Paul's consolatory strategy, like his attitude towards the promotion of joy, reveals a perceptive awareness and appreciation of the inherently social nature of the Christian life. The onus for bringing comfort, perspective, and encouragement to the bereaved rests not on his shoulders alone, but jointly on those of each member of the community of faith. As Paul understands it, then, the task of consolation is undeniably a shared responsibility, one that falls within the broad sweep of the ever-growing, protean ministry of mutual upbuilding that is both to mark and to vivify the common life of the believing community.

5.6.2. The Stoics on Joy and Grief

In Stoicism, joy is understood as an elevation of the material *psychē* that occurs in the wise person in response to present goods.[153] It is one of the *eupatheiai*: that select trio of normative versions of emotions that are evoked through veridical judgements of value, and which are therefore the consistent experience of the wise person, since such a person's behaviour is always wholly in keeping with the proper exercise of virtue. For the wise, virtue and the actions emanating from it are the only true goods towards which their perfected rational impulses are directed.

In contrast, grief, the mistaken opinion that there is something in the present that is evil and therefore to be avoided, is classified as one of the passions: the group of rogue emotions that arise from erroneous evaluations of the value of external goods. Since grief, along with all the other passions, was the product of deficient processes of rationality and their concomitant false beliefs, it was to be not only repudiated but also extirpated. The solution, as the Stoics saw it, was the treatment of the mind, because the passions were the direct result of faulty thinking. Their therapeutic arsenal comprised the careful application of philosophical teaching on the one hand, and cognitive tools such as psychagogy and the imitation of exemplar figures on the other; acting in concert, both approaches comprehensively targeted the person's rational core in an effort to perfect it.

5.6.3. Similarities

To be sure, there are some apparent parallels, at least prima facie, between Paul's and the Stoics' approaches to emotion. First, they share a deep concern with the importance of right thinking as the basis for appropriate affective response. For the Stoics, the only thing that can bring mastery over the passions, and indeed over oneself in general, is the proper exercise of reason:

---

[153] Margaret R. Graver, 'Anatomies of Joy: Seneca and the Gaudium Tradition', in *Hope, Joy, and Affection in the Classical World*, ed. Ruth R. Caston and Robert A. Kaster (Oxford: Oxford University Press, 2016), 125. See also Section 2.3.3.b earlier.

> These passions, which are heavy taskmasters, sometimes ruling by turns, and sometimes together, can be banished by you by wisdom, which is the only true freedom. There is but one path leading thither, and it is a straight path; you will not go astray. Proceed with steady step, and if you would have all things under your control, put yourself under the control of reason; if reason becomes your ruler, you will become ruler over many. (Seneca, *Ep.* 37.4)

Paul, too, shows a not dissimilar interest in the key role of cognition in emotion and in living life well. He stresses to the believers at Philippi that it is the adoption of a Christ-like mindset, coupled with a right understanding of Christian truths, that would enable them to joyfully overcome their sufferings and trials. Likewise, the grieving Thessalonians are offered a thoroughly reasoned theological basis for consolation, and instructed to use this to encourage one another.

Second, and related to the above, both the Stoics and Paul try to effect an active, comprehensive management of emotion so that transcendence over the emotional vicissitudes of day-to-day life is achieved.[154] With both, emotion is brought into relation with an ideal, overarching ordering of life, and reordered accordingly; certain emotional dispositions or types of emotion are encouraged, and even prescribed or commanded, while others are censured and repudiated. Thus, the Stoics, and Paul, go to great lengths to establish and fortify their respective emotional regimes. The Stoics, as we have seen, utilized a wide battery of complementary philosophical, paraenetic, cognitive, and practical apparatus to reorient and then consolidate their students' conceptual frames; the Stoic philosophers understood that repeated, systematic exhortation, and the judicious application of philosophical instruction, was needed to radically overhaul a person's thought processes. The parallels with Paul's general approach and methodology are apparent – Paul, too, employs similar types of tools to fashion in his converts the type of mindset that he wants to see in them. Both the Stoics and Paul seem to have fully appreciated the fact that a wide-ranging and yet carefully targeted approach was necessary precisely because it was aimed at bringing about a fundamental, and in many ways also counterintuitive, reconfiguration of a person's value system.

A third parallel is found in how the Stoics and Paul seem to assign a broadly similar place to the role of affect in their respective conceptions of human flourishing: both do not regard the achievement of complete emotional equanimity as a goal in and of itself, but instead see right feeling as the natural corollary of right thinking. To be sure, specific emotions were encouraged and others rejected in accordance with the emotional ordering that was at work; and it is clear that the possession of prescribed emotional dispositions was something that was aimed at. Yet this was so largely because emotion was seen to be a telling reflection of one's innermost beliefs and values. In Stoicism, as Christopher Gill notes, emotions are not typically presented as aspirations in their own right.[155] Furthermore,

---

[154] On the concept of emotional transcendence, see Section 5.3.3.b earlier.
[155] Christopher Gill, 'Positive Emotions in Stoicism', in *Hope, Joy, and Affection in the Classical World*, ed. Ruth R. Caston and Robert A. Kaster (Oxford: Oxford University Press, 2016), 149.

The appropriate target for aspiration is the development of the virtues, through ongoing transformation of one's understanding, character, interpersonal relationships, and way of life, that is, through *oikeiōsis*, in its various strands. This transformation naturally or necessarily, on Stoic psychological assumptions, brings about the change of emotional inclinations, from foolish to wise, that forms part of developmental process.[156]

To use joy as a specific example: for Seneca, the advent of joy is not the purpose of moral progress; instead, virtuous wisdom continues to be the aim of existence, and joy is, on Stoic principles, a further characteristic of the virtuous life.[157] Paul, too, does not see the possession of joy as the chief aim of believers. For him, gaining Christ and being transformed into his likeness is the goal of life (Phil. 3.21), and Christians are to think and act with this goal always before them.[158] That such a goal (and its attainment) is at all possible in the first place is because of God's work in the world through Christ and the Spirit; and therefore, as Paul sees it, joy flourishes to the degree that the believer is able to discern and participate in this work, even in the face of great adversity. Thus, for both the Stoics and Paul, regulation over the emotions is important, not as an end to itself, but because a person's emotional repertoire – in particular, the presence in it of those dispositions that are encouraged and the absence from it of those that are rejected – is a clear indication of the extent to which any claimed allegiance to a system of beliefs has translated to actual, lived reality.

5.6.4. Differences

Though there are certain parallels between Stoic and Pauline thinking on emotion, a closer examination soon discloses, as in fact we have already begun to see, that the two traditions diverge in fundamental ways at the very places where they seem to exhibit some agreement. While there are what we might perhaps term, albeit inadequately, 'structural' affinities in how they each conceive of emotion vis-à-vis their construal of reality and how it is schematized, the content of that reality in the two accounts is entirely different.

In more specific terms: while the Stoics and Paul both demonstrate an interest in the cognitive dimension of emotion, locate emotion within a systematic ordering of life, and commandeer a broad range of philosophical, cognitive, and practical approaches to help their respective adherents to develop new ways of thinking and feeling that reflect and in turn validate such an ordering of reality, their arguments stem from intrinsically disparate ideological commitments. Taking centre stage in Stoic philosophical thought is, of course, reason: and it is reason, consistently and

---

[156] Gill, 'Positive Emotions', 150.
[157] Graver, 'Anatomies', 140; see also 131–2 and references there.
[158] See Bradley Arnold, *Christ as the Telos of Life: Moral Philosophy, Athletic Imagery, and the Aim of Philippians*, WUNT 2.371 (Tübingen: Mohr Siebeck, 2014), 219–21 and *passim*. Arnold argues persuasively that in Philippians Paul exhorts the believers to pursue Christ as the ultimate goal in life, by structuring his argument using the thought pattern in ancient moral philosophy which posits that there is one τέλος of life that all choices and actions are to be directed towards.

perfectly exercised in accordance with nature, or the order of the cosmos, that leads to a life of virtue and thus of *eudaimonia*. It is highly noteworthy that there is in Stoicism an unwavering confidence in the ability of humans to repair their own thinking and transfigure themselves in accordance with Stoic principles. As Rowe rather nicely describes it,

> The Stoic story of human reparation has at its heart the claim that the human being is its own resource and the resolution of its problem. As we progress further and further in the Stoic disciplines, we discover a deeper and more profound ability to rely on ourselves.[159]

However, for Paul, nothing could be further from the truth: we human beings simply do not have the power ourselves to escape from the never-ending cycles of self-defeating damage that we are tethered to because of sin. Such is the utter helplessness of the human condition that Christ was sent into the world to set humanity on a radically recreated foundation through his life, death, and resurrection. Again, quoting Rowe,

> In the Christian story, human reason is not capable of self-repair, indeed, left on its own, it will even lead one astray, mistaking foolishness for wisdom and wisdom for folly. Reason's repair occurs only through knowing God in Christ – or, rather, being known by him – and the communal norms that inculcate reason's right workings in a pattern of church life and public witness. The re-creation of reason is simultaneously the participation in the ecclesial form of life that matches the future's arrival in the present – to be a people of the meantime is to learn how to know truth and love wisdom.[160]

At the heart of Paul's thinking, then, is the importance of an eschatological faith in God who is still at work to remake humanity and society. Completely absent from his account is the remarkable confidence that Stoic anthropology invests in the human ability to find within oneself the resources necessary to transform one's reason. Yet Paul's interest in the mind and in correct thinking is just as deep-seated as it is for his Stoic contemporaries; both would certainly argue that what one believes is not only integral to emotion but actually controls it. However, cognition itself is differently conceived in the two accounts: for the Stoics, right thinking stems from the exercise of reason in accordance with nature, while for Paul, right thinking has everything to do with the development of a wholly renewed mindset that is patterned after that of Christ – a process in which reason itself becomes recreated.

A further key difference between Paul and the Stoics emerges in regard to how the two traditions relate emotion to social life. Paul firmly locates emotion in the context of the relationships within the believing community. As we have seen, for him, there is an unalienable mutuality and sociality in Christian joy, because it comes from the

---

[159] Kavin C. Rowe, *One True Life: The Stoics and Early Christians as Rival Traditions* (New Haven, CT: Yale University Press, 2016), 214.
[160] Rowe, *One True Life*, 221.

believers' shared engagement with God's ongoing redemptive work in the world. Similarly, consolation in grief, too, is located squarely within the ambit of the mutual responsibilities that believers have towards one another. Paul is very much aware of the communal dimension of emotion – that it is in community that right emotions are formed and expressed. All of this emphasizes the profoundly social nature of the Christian life: it is in relationship with one another that believers flourish both as individuals and as a community.

Contrary to the popular but caricatured view of them that often gets bad press, the Stoics were not self-absorbed and unfeeling automata who cared nothing about the people around them. In fact, they understood that living according to nature's design meant that each person should recognize that he or she had been given one or more roles to play in society, for example, son, brother, father, town councillor,[161] and that it was the person's responsibility to 'play admirably the role assigned you', since 'the selection of that role is Another's'.[162] However, the acknowledgement and carrying out of such natural duties was to be completely independent of how others might behave towards you. In other words, the Stoic's conduct was to always emerge from, and be circumscribed by, his or her *prohairesis*, the sphere of one's volition. Discharging one's familial and societal obligations in a fitting manner entailed making correct evaluations concerning whether happenings were under one's control or not, and acting in accordance with these decisions, thereby fulfilling one's natural duties to others while also preserving the integrity of one's security and self-sufficiency.[163] Thus, for example, the Stoics taught that it was entirely proper to come alongside a grieving person to offer solidarity and support. However, in showing sympathy, one must not be overwhelmed by the person's grief – which, after all, came from his or her judgement about an event rather than from the occurrence of the event itself. For the Stoics, one's inner imperturbability was never to be troubled or compromised.[164] Hence, while a Stoic would not shirk from his or her responsibilities towards other people, in relating to them the Stoic would never allow false judgements to derail his or her self-sufficiency and emotional tranquillity.

We see therefore that both the Stoics and Paul presuppose a certain relational embeddedness, and with it, the presence of a network of social duties towards others, which characterizes and dignifies human existence. Even so, the Stoics are able, through their craft of reason, to maintain and even entrench the self-sufficiency and serenity that have been hard won by their philosophy. Paul, too, through the consistent exercise of right thinking, achieves a kind of self-sufficiency – but it is entirely different from Stoic *autarkeia*, because he derives it from his relationship to Christ. One might argue that it is precisely because Paul's inner security is so firmly anchored in Christ's sufficiency in all things that he is able to allow his relational dealings with his converts to be shot through with a pronounced vulnerability that a Stoic would find decidedly alarming. So, for example, and as we have discussed earlier, the quality of Paul's own

---

[161] Epictetus, *Diatr.* 2.10.7-23.
[162] Epictetus, *Ench.* 17; the designation is a reverent one for divinity.
[163] Epictetus, *Ench.* 30.
[164] Epictetus, *Ench.* 16.

joy is intentionally bound up with the progress of the Philippians in the faith and with their growth in like-minded unity, and indeed, with their joy as well. Paul sees Christian joy as being generated in relationship with other believers, because joy is a felt corollary of their shared commitment to the hope that they hold to be true reality.

This brings us to the third key difference between the Stoic and Pauline emotional regimes. Each regards the right ordering of emotion as coming from, and in turn also validating, a particular conceptual framework that encompasses and seeks to make sense of all of life. However, the frameworks that the two traditions espouse, reflecting as they do mutually exclusive ideological interests, paint very different pictures of cosmological reality, not least in how it relates to humans and emotion.

As Seneca explains it, the Stoics see the world as being beset by incursions of fortune (*fortuna*) – the myriad miscellaneous happenings, freakish or more ordinary, baneful or salubrious, that bear upon humankind. Fortune thus represents 'all that which touches and shapes our lives for good or for ill from somewhere beyond the reach of our control'.[165] However, the Stoics are confident that humans possess within themselves the requisite resources to triumph over fortune. For the Stoics, there is an overarching governing principle over the entire universe, and this is nature, or divinity, which is constituted by reason; and since humanity is imbued with this same reason – for reason is, as Seneca variously defines it, 'nothing else than a portion of the divine spirit set in a human body'[166] and 'copying nature'[167] – the natural goal of the human person is to exercise his or her reason in a life of virtue. It is precisely the following of this goal that produces in that person a rightly formed soul, one that will flourish in the very face of fortune's capriciousness by forming correct judgements at all times.

Yet it is important to note that as the Stoics see it – and notwithstanding the mercurial vagaries of fortune's forays into the lives of people – the world, ultimately ordered as it is by divine rationality, is exactly as it should be. As Epictetus proclaims, there is every occasion for humankind to recognize the divine character of the providential ordering of the universe.[168] As such, each human being's path to happiness lies in internally reconfiguring his or her way of being in the world; and thus, the person who is wise 'takes Nature for his teacher, conforming to her laws and living as she commands'.[169] By doing so, that is, by training the soul's rational capacities and practising virtue in line with nature's dictums, one frees oneself from the destructive power of the passions by submitting them to reason,[170] and experiences instead their corrected versions, the *eupatheiai*.

The Stoic view of the world and of humanity is manifestly out of kilter with Pauline eschatology, which describes instead how a thoroughly sick world and its inhabitants, who are marred by sin, mired in its deleterious effects, and rendered completely unable to help themselves, will one day be wholly and radically repristinated. God's act of renewing creation was inaugurated at the first coming of Christ, and it will come to a

---

[165] See Rowe, *One True Life*, 22–4 (quote from 22).
[166] Seneca, *Ep.* 66.12; see also *Ep.* 92.1
[167] Seneca, *Ep.* 66.39.
[168] Epictetus, *Diatr.* 1.6.1.
[169] Seneca, *Ep.* 45.9.
[170] Seneca, *Ep.* 37.4.

glorious culmination at his return. This transcendent metanarrative of God's ongoing work in the world should form the backdrop against which believers locate their own life stories, if they are to make sense of what they believe to be true about their faith in Christ. Thus, even in present suffering the believing community can still experience joy: not because things are fine now, but because of the certain hope that things will be fine in the future. And even though some among them have unexpectedly died, they need not give rein to helpless grief: again, not because things are fine now, but because of the certain hope that things will be fine in the future. Joy celebrates the believer's participation with other believers in the story of God's recreation of the cosmos – a story that reaches its zenith at the Parousia, where death itself is finally and conclusively vanquished. We thus observe that layered deeply within Pauline Christianity are several distinctively forward-looking, storied, and social registers that have no echo in Stoicism. For the Stoics, the world is as it should be, and life is what one makes of it. For Paul, the world is not yet as it should be, but the time will come when the world is remade; and on that day, all who know Christ as Lord, who have allowed his life to map the course of theirs, will be united with him and with one another for all eternity.

5.7. Conclusion

This study has argued that as Paul sees it, emotions are intrinsic to the proper formation and stabilizing of identity and community, because they emerge from and encode structures of belief, and also influence patterns of sociality. Right emotions have an important integrating function: for the individual, they bolster Christian identity through the squaring of felt experience with held beliefs; while for the believing community, they help to cement group belonging by reinforcing the shared eschatological realities upon which authorized norms of affect are based. At the same time, right emotions have an important differentiating function: the social expression of sanctioned emotional dispositions (particularly if they are countercultural) demarcates the social and theological boundaries between Christians and others, which further strengthens group solidarity within the church by accentuating the insider status of its members.

For Paul, the management of emotion is therefore a crucial aspect of his efforts to establish his churches and resocialize his new converts. This explains why in his congregations he assiduously imposes feeling rules that specify not only which emotions are approved and which ones rejected, but also how those emotions that are approved are to come to expression within the community. The upshot of Paul's efforts is the crystallization of what is in effect an emotional regime: a framework of dialectical interactions between the self, society, and symbol, which produces and shapes emotion in accordance with a transcendent ordering of reality. Using the concept of the emotional regime as a heuristic tool, we discovered that the interplay of symbolic, ritual, and social elements within the eschatological ordering of reality has a remarkably profound influence on the construction and reinforcement of authorized emotions in the Pauline communities. All this helps also to explain how such emotions maintain their longevity and power.

To be sure, Paul was not the only person of his time to establish feeling rules; his Stoic contemporaries, too, thought deeply about emotion and came up with a far more systematic way to approach the whole subject, particularly in regard to the passions – those unruly, damaging patterns of affect that had no place in the life of the wise person. Throughout our study we have allowed both traditions to speak for themselves, and on their own terms; but we also made comparisons between them whenever appropriate so that the distinctiveness of their respective views of emotion would come into sharp focus. Even though both the Stoics and Paul emphasize the centrality of right thinking as the means to control emotion, it is exactly at this point of similarity that the Stoics and Paul diverge, and fundamentally so, because their accounts are premised on completely different conceptions of reality.

For Paul, as with the Stoics, right patterns of feeling come from right patterns of belief, and their social expression validates the truth-claims of these beliefs. However, as Paul sees it, these patterns of belief are rooted not in the workings of some cosmic rationality, but in nothing less than the epic narrative of how God is renewing his creation on the basis of Christ's work – a story in which Paul's converts are invited to anchor their own life stories. And it is indubitably because Paul himself has done just so, that he can instruct them, with untrammelled confidence and, perhaps, a certain exultation of spirit: Χαίρετε ἐν κυρίῳ πάντοτε· πάλιν ἐρῶ, χαίρετε (Phil. 4.4).

5.7.1. Suggestions for Further Research

It is hoped that this study has helped to open up, in a fuller way than hitherto, the question of the social function of emotion in Paul's letters, and also demonstrated one way in which a methodologically robust inquiry into this neglected aspect of early Christianity life might be conceptualized and conducted. It is hoped too that the findings from this study show that there are useful gains to be had from such an approach. Yet I hasten to emphasize that this study represents only an exploratory effort in terms of mining emotion within the Pauline corpus, and that there is potential for much more work to be done. For example, one might explore the nature and function of joy or grief in Paul's other letters (e.g. in 2 Corinthians, where grief is inflected in a variety of ways throughout the letter) to see how our account of emotion could be more finely nuanced. Alternatively, the scope of this study could be extended to include other affective dispositions as specific subjects for analysis, in order to build up a richer and more comprehensive understanding of emotion in Paul's letters. Another worthwhile direction for research might be to investigate in a more systematic fashion how certain complexes of symbolic and social meaning are connected to the ordering and expression of emotion in Paul's writings: particularly fruitful aspects of study might be the relationships between ritual and emotion (using ongoing research in ritual studies and the New Testament), or language and emotion (drawing on work in sociolinguistics and related fields). It will be interesting to see how New Testament scholars develop this necessarily interdisciplinary field of study in the future.

Bibliography

Primary sources

Alexander of Aphrodisias. *On Fate.* Translated by Robert W. Sharples. In *Alexander of Aphrodisias on Fate: Text, Translation, and Commentary.* London: Duckworth, 1983.
Aristotle. *Nicomachean Ethics.* Translated by H. Rackham. Loeb Classical Library. Cambridge, MA: Harvard University Press, 1926.
Aristotle. *On the Soul. Parva Naturalia. On Breath.* Translated by W. S. Hett. Loeb Classical Library. Cambridge, MA: Harvard University Press, 1957.
Aristotle. *Parts of Animals. Movement of Animals. Progression of Animals.* Translated by A. L. Peck and E. S. Forster. Loeb Classical Library. Cambridge, MA: Harvard University Press, 1937.
Cicero. *Letters to Atticus.* 4 vols. Edited and translated by D. R. Shackleton Bailey. Loeb Classical Library. Cambridge, MA: Harvard University Press, 1999.
Cicero. *Letters to Friends.* 3 vols. Edited and translated by D. R. Shackleton Bailey. Loeb Classical Library. Cambridge, MA: Harvard University Press, 2001.
Cicero. *Letters to Quintus and Brutus. Letter Fragments. Letter to Octavian. Invectives. Handbook of Electioneering.* Edited and translated by D. R. Shackleton Bailey. Loeb Classical Library. Cambridge, MA: Harvard University Press, 2002.
Cicero. *On Ends.* Translated by H. Rackham. Loeb Classical Library. Cambridge, MA: Harvard University Press, 1914.
Cicero. *On Old Age. On Friendship. On Divination.* Translated by W. A. Falconer. Loeb Classical Library. Cambridge, MA: Harvard University Press, 1923.
Cicero. *On the Nature of the Gods. Academics.* Translated by H. Rackham. Loeb Classical Library. Cambridge, MA: Harvard University Press, 1933.
Cicero. *On the Orator: Book 3. On Fate. Stoic Paradoxes. Divisions of Oratory.* Translated by H. Rackham. Loeb Classical Library. Cambridge, MA: Harvard University Press, 1942.
Cicero. *Tusculan Disputations.* Translated by J. E. King. Loeb Classical Library. Cambridge, MA: Harvard University Press, 1927.
Cicero. *Tusculan Disputations.* Translated by Margaret R. Graver. In *Cicero on the Emotions: Tusculan Disputations 3-4.* Chicago: University of Chicago Press, 2002.
Diogenes Laertius. *Lives of the Eminent Philosophers.* 2 vols. Translated by R. D. Hicks. Loeb Classical Library. Cambridge, MA: Harvard University Press, 1925.
Doxographi Graeci. Edited by H. Diels. Berlin: Reimer, 1879.
Epictetus. *Discourses, Books 1-2.* Translated by W. A. Oldfather. Loeb Classical Library. Cambridge, MA: Harvard University Press, 1925.
Epictetus. *Discourses, Books 3-4. Fragments. The Encheiridion.* Translated by W. A. Oldfather. Loeb Classical Library. Cambridge, MA: Harvard University Press, 1928.

Galen. *On the Doctrines of Hippocrates and Plato*. 3 vols. Translated by Philip De Lacy. Berlin: Akademie-Verlag, 1978–80.

Homer. *Iliad*. 2 vols. Translated by A. T. Murray. Revised by William F. Wyatt. Loeb Classical Library. Cambridge, MA: Harvard University Press, 1924–5.

Long, Anthony A., and David N. Sedley. *The Hellenistic Philosophers*. 2 vols. Cambridge: Cambridge University Press, 1987.

Marcus Aurelius. *Marcus Aurelius*. Edited and translated by C. R. Haines. Loeb Classical Library. Cambridge, MA: Harvard University Press, 1916.

Novum Testamentum Graece. Edited by Barbara Aland, Kurt Aland, Johannes Karavidopoulos, Carlo M. Martini, and Bruce M. Metzger. 28th revised ed. Stuttgart: Deutsche Bibelgesellschaft, 2012.

Philo. *On the Confusion of Tongues. On the Migration of Abraham. Who Is the Heir of Divine Things? On Mating with the Preliminary Studies*. Translated by F. H. Colson and G. H. Whitaker. Loeb Classical Library. Cambridge, MA: Harvard University Press, 1932.

Philo. *On the Creation. Allegorical Interpretation of Genesis 2 and 3*. Translated by F. H. Colson and G. H. Whitaker. Loeb Classical Library. Cambridge, MA: Harvard University Press, 1929.

Philo. *Questions on Genesis*. Translated by Ralph Marcus. Loeb Classical Library. Cambridge, MA: Harvard University Press, 1953.

Philostratus. *Apollonius of Tyana, Volume III: Letters of Apollonius. Ancient Testimonia. Eusebius's Reply to Hierocles*. Edited and translated by Christopher P. Jones. Loeb Classical Library. Cambridge, MA: Harvard University Press, 2006.

Plato. *Charmides. Alcibiades I and II. Hipparchus. The Lovers. Theages. Minos. Epinomis*. Translated by W. R. M. Lamb. Loeb Classical Library. Cambridge, MA: Harvard University Press, 1927.

Plato. *Lysis. Symposium. Gorgias*. Translated by W. R. M. Lamb. Loeb Classical Library. Cambridge, MA: Harvard University Press, 1925.

Plato. *Phaedo*. Translated by Reginald Hackforth. Cambridge: Cambridge University Press, 1955.

Pliny the Younger. *Letters*. 2 vols. Translated by Betty Radice. Loeb Classical Library. Cambridge, MA: Harvard University Press, 1969.

Plutarch. *Lives*. 11 vols. Translated by Bernadotte Perrin. Loeb Classical Library. Cambridge, MA: Harvard University Press, 1914–26.

Plutarch. *Moralia*. 16 vols. Translated by Frank Cole Babbitt et al. Loeb Classical Library. Cambridge, MA: Harvard University Press, 1936–86.

Seneca. *Epistles*. 3 vols. Translated by Richard M. Gummere. Loeb Classical Library. Cambridge, MA: Harvard University Press, 1917–25.

Seneca. *Moral Essays*. 3 vols. Translated by John W. Basore. Loeb Classical Library. Cambridge, MA: Harvard University Press, 1928–35.

Septuaginta: Id est Vetus Testamentum Graece iuxta LXX interpretes. Edited by Alfred Rahlfs and Robert Hanhart. Revised ed. Stuttgart: Deutsche Bibelgesellschaft, 2006.

Sextus Empiricus. *Against Professors*. Translated by R. G. Bury. Loeb Classical Library. Cambridge, MA: Harvard University Press, 1949.

Stobaeus. *Arius Didymus: Epitome of Stoic Ethics*. Edited by Arthur J. Pomeroy. Atlanta, GA: Society of Biblical Literature, 1999.

Stobaeus. *Ioannis Stobaei Anthologium*. 4 vols. Edited by C. Wachsmuth and O. Hense. Berlin: Weidmann, 1884–1912.

Stoicorum Veterum Fragmenta. 4 vols. Edited by H. von Arnim. Leipzig: Teubner, 1903–24.

Tacitus. *Annals: Books 13–16*. Translated by John Jackson. Loeb Classical Library. Cambridge, MA: Harvard University Press, 1937.

Secondary sources

Aasgaard, Reidar. *'My Beloved Brothers and Sisters!': Christian Siblingship in Paul*. Journal for the Study of the New Testament Supplement Series 265. London: T&T Clark, 2004.

Abu-Lughod, Lila. *Veiled Sentiments: Honor and Poetry in a Bedouin Society*. Berkeley: University of California Press, 1986.

Alexander, Loveday. 'Hellenistic Letter-Forms and the Structure of Philippians'. *Journal for the Study of the New Testament* 37 (1989): 87–101.

Annas, Julia. *Hellenistic Philosophy of Mind*. Berkeley: University of California Press, 1992.

Annas, Julia. *The Morality of Happiness*. New York: Oxford University Press, 1993.

Arnold, Bradley. *Christ as the Telos of Life: Moral Philosophy, Athletic Imagery, and the Aim of Philippians*. Wissenschaftliche Untersuchungen zum Neuen Testament 2.371. Tübingen: Mohr Siebeck, 2014.

Aune, David Charles. 'Passions in the Pauline Epistles: The Current State of Research'. In *Passions and Moral Progress in Greco-Roman Thought*, edited by John T. Fitzgerald, 221–37. Abingdon: Routledge, 2008.

Aune, David E. *The New Testament in Its Literary Environment*. Library of Early Christianity 8. Philadelphia, PA: Westminster, 1987.

Barclay, John M. G. 'Conflict in Thessalonica'. *Catholic Biblical Quarterly* 55 (1993): 512–30.

Barclay, John M. G. 'Security and Self-Sufficiency: A Comparison of Paul and Epictetus'. *Ex Auditu* 24 (2008): 60–72.

Barclay, John M. G. '"That You May Not Grieve, Like the Rest Who Have No Hope" (1 Thess 4.13): Death and Early Christian Identity'. In *Pauline Churches and Diaspora Jews*, 217–35. Wissenschaftliche Untersuchungen zum Neuen Testament 275. Tübingen: Mohr Siebeck, 2011.

Barclay, John M. G. 'Thessalonica and Corinth: Social Contrasts in Pauline Christianity'. In *Pauline Churches and Diaspora Jews*, 181–203. Wissenschaftliche Untersuchungen zum Neuen Testament 275. Tübingen: Mohr, 2011.

Barth, Karl. *The Epistle to the Philippians*. Translated by James W. Leitch. Louisville, KY: Westminster John Knox, 2002.

Barton, Stephen C. '"Be Angry But Do Not Sin" (Ephesians 4.26a): Sin and the Emotions in the New Testament with Special Reference to Anger'. *Studies in Christian Ethics* 28 (2015): 21–34.

Barton, Stephen C. 'Eschatology and the Emotions in Early Christianity'. *Journal of Biblical Literature* 130 (2011): 571–91.

Barton, Stephen C. 'Spirituality and the Emotions in Early Christianity: The Case of Joy'. In *The Bible and Spirituality: Exploratory Essays in Reading Scripture Spiritually*, edited by Andrew T. Lincoln, J. Gordon McConville, and Lloyd K. Pietersen, 171–93. Eugene, OR: Cascade Books, 2013.

Barton, Stephen C. 'Why Do Things Move People?: The Jerusalem Temple as Emotional Repository'. *Journal for the Study of the New Testament* 37 (2015): 351–80.

Bauer, Walter, Frederick W. Danker, William F. Arndt, and F. Wilbur Gingrich. *Greek-English Lexicon of the New Testament and Other Early Christian Literature*. 3rd ed. Chicago: University of Chicago Press, 2000.
Becker, Jürgen. *Auferstehung der Toten im Urchristentum*. Stuttgart: KBW Verlag, 1976.
Bell, Catherine. *Ritual: Perspectives and Dimensions*. New York: Oxford University Press, 1997.
Bell, Catherine. *Ritual Theory, Ritual Practice*. Oxford: Oxford University Press, 1992.
Berger, Peter, and Thomas Luckmann. *The Social Construction of Reality: A Treatise in the Sociology of Knowledge*. Garden City, NY: Anchor Books, 1966.
Berthomé, François, and Michael Houseman. 'Ritual and Emotions: Moving Relations, Patterned Effusions'. *Religion and Society: Advances in Research* 1 (2010): 57–75. doi:10.3167/arrs.2010.010105.
Bertschmann, Dorothea H. *Bowing before Christ – Nodding to the State?: Reading Paul Politically with Oliver O'Donovan and John Howard Yoder*. The Library of New Testament Studies 502. London: T&T Clark, 2014.
Best, Ernest. *A Commentary on the First and Second Epistles to the Thessalonians*. Black's New Testament Commentaries. London: A & C Black, 1972.
Betz, Hans Dieter. *Studies in Paul's Letter to the Philippians*. Wissenschaftliche Untersuchungen zum Neuen Testament 343. Tübingen: Mohr Siebeck, 2015.
Blass, Friedrich, Albert Debrunner, and Robert W. Funk. *A Greek Grammar of the New Testament and Other Early Christian Literature*. Chicago: University of Chicago Press, 1961.
Bloomquist, L. Gregory. *The Function of Suffering in Philippians*. Journal for the Study of the New Testament Supplement Series 78. Sheffield: Sheffield Academic Press, 1993.
Bockmuehl, Markus. *A Commentary on the Epistle to the Philippians*. Black's New Testament Commentaries. London: A & C Black, 1997.
Bormann, Lukas. *Philippi: Stadt und Christengemeinde zur Zeit des Paulus*. Supplements to Novum Testamentum 78. Leiden: Brill, 1995.
Braund, Susanna Morton, and Christopher Gill, eds. *The Passions in Roman Thought and Literature*. Cambridge: Cambridge University Press, 1997.
Brennan, Tad. 'The Old Stoic Theory of Emotions'. In *The Emotions in Hellenistic Philosophy*, edited by Juha Sihvola and Troels Engberg-Pedersen, 21–70. Dordrecht: Kluwer Academic, 1998.
Briones, David E. *Paul's Financial Policy: A Socio-Theological Approach*. The Library of New Testament Studies 494. London: T&T Clark, 2013.
Brown, Colin, ed. *New International Dictionary of New Testament Theology*. 4 vols. Grand Rapids, MI: Zondervan, 1975–8.
Bruce, F. F. *1 & 2 Thessalonians*. Word Biblical Commentary 45. Waco, TX: Word, 1982.
Bruce, F. F. *Philippians*. New International Biblical Commentary on the New Testament. Peabody, MA: Hendrickson, 1989.
Bruce, F. F. 'St. Paul in Macedonia. 3. The Philippian Correspondence'. *Bulletin of the John Rylands University Library of Manchester* 63 (1980–1): 260–84.
Bultmann, Rudolf. *Primitive Christianity in Its Contemporary Setting*. Cleveland, OH: Collins, 1956.
Burke, Trevor J. *Family Matters: A Socio-Historical Study of Kinship Metaphors in 1 Thessalonians*. Journal for the Study of the New Testament Supplement Series 247. London: T&T Clark, 2003.
Caird, G. B. *Paul's Letters from Prison*. New Clarendon Bible. Oxford: Oxford University Press, 1976.

Castelli, Elizabeth A. *Imitating Paul: A Discourse of Power*. Louisville, KY: Westminster John Knox, 1991.
Chapa, Juan. 'Is First Thessalonians a Letter of Consolation?' *New Testament Studies* 40 (1994): 150–60.
Clarke, Andrew D. '"Be Imitators of Me": Paul's Model of Leadership'. *Tyndale Bulletin* 49 (1998): 329–60.
Clough, Patricia Ticineto, and Jean O'Malley Halley, eds. *The Affective Turn: Theorizing the Social*. Durham, NC: Duke University Press, 2007.
Cohick, Lynn H. *Philippians*. The Story of God Biblical Commentary. Grand Rapids, MI: Zondervan, 2013.
Collange, Jean-François. *The Epistle of Saint Paul to the Philippians*. Translated by A. W. Heathcote. London: Epworth, 1979.
Collins, Raymond F. *Studies on the First Letter to the Thessalonians*. Bibliotheca ephemeridum theologicarum lovaniensium 66. Leuven: Leuven University Press, 1984.
Cooper, John M. 'Eudaimonism, the Appeal to Nature, and "Moral Duty" in Stoicism'. In *Reason and Emotion: Essays on Ancient Moral Psychology and Ethical Theory*, 427–48. Princeton, NJ: Princeton University Press, 1999.
Cooper, John M. 'The Emotional Life of the Wise'. In *Ancient Ethics and Political Philosophy: Proceedings of the Spindel Conference 2004*, 176–218. Southern Journal of Philosophy Supplement 43. Memphis, TN: University of Memphis, 2005.
Corrigan, John. 'Introduction: Emotions Research and the Academic Study of Religion'. In *Religion and Emotion: Approaches and Interpretations*, edited by John Corrigan, 3–31. Oxford: Oxford University Press, 2004.
Cousar, Charles B. *Philippians and Philemon: A Commentary*. New Testament Library. Louisville, KY: Westminster John Knox, 2009.
Crump, David. *Knocking on Heaven's Door: A New Testament Theology of Petitionary Prayer*. Grand Rapids, MI: Baker, 2006.
Davies, Douglas J. *Emotion, Identity, and Religion: Hope, Reciprocity, and Otherness*. Oxford: Oxford University Press, 2011.
De Boer, Willis Peter. *The Imitation of Paul: An Exegetical Study*. Kampen: Kok, 1962.
de Vos, Craig Steven. *Church and Community Conflicts: The Relationship of the Thessalonian, Corinthian, and Philippian Churches with Their Wider Civic Communities*. Society of Biblical Literature Dissertation Series 168. Atlanta, GA: Scholars, 1999.
DeMaris, Richard E. *The New Testament in Its Ritual World*. Abingdon: Routledge, 2008.
Denis, A. M. 'La fonction apostolique et la liturgie en Esprit. Étude thématique des métaphores paulinieres du culte nouveau'. *Revue des sciences philosophiques et théologiques* 42 (1958): 617–56.
Denzin, Norman K. *On Understanding Emotion*. San Francisco, CA: Jossey-Bass, 1984.
Dixon, Thomas. '"Emotion": The History of a Keyword in Crisis'. *Emotion Review* 4 (2012): 338–44.
Dixon, Thomas. *From Passions to Emotions: The Creation of a Secular Psychological Category*. Cambridge: Cambridge University Press, 2003.
Dobschütz, Ernst von. *Die Thessalonicher-Briefe*. 7th ed. Kritisch-exegetischer Kommentar über das Neue Testament 10. Göttingen: Vandenhoeck & Ruprecht, 1909.
Dodd, Brian J. *Paul's Paradigmatic 'I': Personal Example as Literary Strategy*. Journal for the Study of the New Testament Supplement Series 177. Sheffield: Sheffield Academic Press, 1999.
Donfried, Karl P. 'The Cults of Thessalonica and the Thessalonian Correspondence'. In *Paul, Thessalonica, and Early Christianity*, 21–48. London: T&T Clark, 2002.

Donfried, Karl P. 'The Theology of 1 Thessalonians'. In *The Theology of the Shorter Pauline Letters*, edited by Karl P. Donfried and I. Howard Marshall, 1–79. Cambridge: Cambridge University Press, 1993.

Donfried, Karl P. 'The Theology of 1 Thessalonians as a Reflection of Its Purpose'. In *Paul, Thessalonica, and Early Christianity*, 119–38. London: T&T Clark, 2002.

Durkheim, Émile. *The Elementary Forms of Religious Life*. Translated by Carol Cosman. Oxford: Oxford University Press, 2001.

Edart, Jean-Baptiste. *L'Épître aux Philippiens, Rhétorique et Composition Stylistique*. Etudes Bibliques 45. Paris: Gabalda, 2002.

Elliott, Matthew. *Faithful Feelings: Emotion in the New Testament*. Leicester: Inter-Varsity, 2005.

Engberg-Pedersen, Troels. 'Discovering the Good: Oikeiōsis and Kathēkonta in Stoic Ethics'. In *The Norms of Nature: Studies in Hellenistic Ethics*, edited by Malcolm Schofield and Gisela Striker, 145–83. Cambridge: Cambridge University Press, 1986.

Engberg-Pedersen, Troels. *Paul and the Stoics*. Edinburgh: T&T Clark, 2000.

Engberg-Pedersen, Troels. 'Self-Sufficiency and Power: Divine and Human Agency in Epictetus and Paul'. In *Divine and Human Agency in Paul and His Cultural Environment*, edited by John M. G. Barclay and Simon J. Gathercole, 117–39. London: T&T Clark, 2006.

Engberg-Pedersen, Troels. 'Stoicism in Philippians'. In *Paul in His Hellenistic Context*, edited by Troels Engberg-Pedersen, 256–90. Edinburgh: T&T Clark, 1994.

Engberg-Pedersen, Troels. *The Stoic Theory of Oikeiosis: Moral Development and Social Interaction in Early Stoic Philosophy*. Aarhus: Aarhus University Press, 1990.

Ernst, Josef. *Die Briefe an die Philipper, an Philemon, an die Kolossser, an die Epheser*. Regensburger Neues Testament. Regensburg: Pustet, 1974.

Faulkenberry Miller, John B. 'Infants and Orphans in 1 Thessalonians: A Discussion of Ἀπορφανίζω and the Text-Critical Problem in 1 Thess. 2:7'. Paper presented at the Annual Meeting of the Society of Biblical Literature. Boston, 20 March 1999.

Fee, Gordon D. *Paul's Letter to the Philippians*. New International Commentary on the New Testament. Grand Rapids, MI: Eerdmans, 1995.

Fehr, Beverly, and James A. Russell. 'Concept of Emotion Viewed from a Prototype Perspective'. *Journal of Experimental Psychology: General* 113 (1984): 464–86.

Fitzgerald, John T., ed. *Passions and Moral Progress in Greco-Roman Thought*. Abingdon: Routledge, 2008.

Fitzgerald, John T. 'Paul and Friendship'. In *Paul in the Greco-Roman World: A Handbook*, edited by J. Paul Sampley, 319–43. Harrisburg, PA: Trinity Press International, 2003.

Fitzgerald, John T. 'The Passions and Moral Progress: An Introduction'. In *Passions and Moral Progress in Greco-Roman Thought*, edited by John T. Fitzgerald, 1–25. Abingdon: Routledge, 2008.

Fortna, Robert T. 'Philippians: Paul's Most Egocentric Letter'. In *The Conversation Continues: Studies in Paul and John in Honor of J. Louis Martyn*, edited by Robert T. Fortna and Beverly R. Gaventa, 220–34. Nashville, TN: Abingdon, 1990.

Fowl, Stephen E. 'Christology and Ethics in Philippians 2:5–11'. In *Where Christology Began: Essays on Philippians 2*, edited by Ralph P. Martin and Brian J. Dodd, 140–53. Louisville, KY: Westminster John Knox, 1998.

Frame, James Everett. *A Critical and Exegetical Commentary on the Epistles of St. Paul to the Thessalonians*. International Critical Commentary. Edinburgh: T&T Clark, 1912.

Frederickson, David E. 'When Enough Is Never Enough: Philosophers, Poets, Peter, and Paul on Insatiable Desire'. In *Mixed Feelings and Vexed Emotions: Exploring Emotions in Biblical Literature*, edited by F. Scott Spencer, 311-30. Atlanta, GA: SBL Press, 2017.
Freed, Edwin D. *The Morality of Paul's Converts*. Abingdon: Routledge, 2014.
Funk, Robert W. 'The Apostolic Parousia: Form and Significance'. In *Christian History and Interpretation: Studies Presented to John Knox*, edited by W. R. Farmer, C. F. D. Moule, and R. R. Niebuhr, 249-69. Cambridge: Cambridge University Press, 1967.
Garland, David E. 'The Composition and Unity of Philippians: Some Neglected Literary Factors'. *Novum Testamentum* 27 (1985): 141-73.
Gaventa, Beverly R. *First and Second Thessalonians*. Interpretation. Louisville, KY: John Knox Press, 1998.
Geertz, Clifford. 'Religion as a Cultural System'. In *Anthropological Approaches to the Study of Religion*, edited by Michael Banton, 1-43. London: Tavistock, 1971.
Gendlin, Eugene T. *Experiencing and the Creation of Meaning: A Philosophical and Psychological Approach to the Subjective*. Evanston, IL: Northwestern University Press, 1997.
Gill, Christopher. 'Competing Readings of Stoic Emotions'. In *Metaphysics, Soul, and Ethics in Ancient Thought: Themes from the Work of Richard Sorabji*, edited by Ricardo Salles, 445-70. Oxford: Clarendon, 2005.
Gill, Christopher. 'Positive Emotions in Stoicism'. In *Hope, Joy, and Affection in the Classical World*, edited by Ruth R. Caston and Robert A. Kaster, 143-60. Oxford: Oxford University Press, 2016.
Gnilka, Joachim. *Der Philipperbrief*. Herders theologischer Kommentar zum Neuen Testament 10.3. Freiburg: Herder, 1976.
Gorman, Michael J. *Apostle of the Crucified Lord: A Theological Introduction to Paul and His Letters*. 2nd ed. Grand Rapids, MI: Eerdmans, 2017.
Graver, Margaret R. 'Anatomies of Joy: Seneca and the Gaudium Tradition'. In *Hope, Joy, and Affection in the Classical World*, edited by Ruth R. Caston and Robert A. Kaster, 123-42. Oxford: Oxford University Press, 2016.
Graver, Margaret R. *Cicero on the Emotions: Tusculan Disputations 3-4*. Chicago: University of Chicago Press, 2002.
Graver, Margaret R. 'Philo of Alexandria and the Origins of the Stoic Προπάθειαι'. *Phronesis* 44 (1999): 300-25.
Graver, Margaret R. *Stoicism and Emotion*. Chicago: University of Chicago Press, 2007.
Graver, Margaret R. 'The Weeping Wise: Stoic and Epicurean Consolations in Seneca's 99th Epistle'. In *Tears in the Graeco-Roman World*, edited by Thorsten Fögen, 235-52. Berlin: Walter de Gruyter, 2009.
Green, Gene L. *The Letters to the Thessalonians*. Pillar New Testament Commentary. Grand Rapids, MI: Eerdmans, 2002.
Gregg, Robert C. *Consolation Philosophy: Greek and Christian Paideia in Basil and the Two Gregories*. Patristic Monograph Series 3. Cambridge: Philadelphia Patristic Foundation, 1975.
Griffin, Miriam T. *Seneca: A Philosopher in Politics*. Oxford: Clarendon, 1976.
Grimes, Ronald. *Deeply into the Bone: Re-Inventing Rites of Passage*. Berkeley: University of California Press, 2000.
Gundry, Robert H. 'The Hellenization of Dominical Tradition and the Christianization of Jewish Tradition in the Eschatology of 1-2 Thessalonians'. *New Testament Studies* 33 (1987): 161-78.

Gupta, Nijay K. *1 & 2 Thessalonians*. Zondervan Critical Introductions to the New Testament. Grand Rapids, MI: Zondervan, 2019.
Hadot, Pierre. *Philosophy as a Way of Life: Spiritual Exercises from Socrates to Foucault*. Edited by Arnold I. Davidson. Translated by Michael Chase. Oxford: Blackwell, 1995.
Hahm, David E. *The Origins of Stoic Cosmology*. Columbus: Ohio State University Press, 1977.
Halbwachs, Maurice. *On Collective Memory*. Translated by Lewis A. Coser. Chicago: University of Chicago Press, 1992.
Hansen, G. Walter. *The Letter to the Philippians*. Pillar New Testament Commentary. Grand Rapids, MI: Eerdmans, 2009.
Harnisch, Wolfgang. *Eschatologische Existenz: Ein exegetischer Beitrag zum Sachanliegen von 1. Thessalonicher 4,13–5,11*. Forschungen zur Religion und Literatur des Alten und Neuen Testaments 110. Göttingen: Vandenhoeck & Ruprecht, 1973.
Hawthorne, Gerald F., and Ralph P. Martin. *Philippians*. Revised ed. Word Biblical Commentary 43. Nashville, TN: Thomas Nelson, 2004.
Heath, Jane M. F. 'Absent Presences of Paul and Christ: Enargeia in 1 Thessalonians 1–3'. *Journal for the Study of the New Testament* 32 (2009): 3–38.
Hellerman, Joseph H. *Philippians*. Exegetical Guide to the Greek New Testament. Nashville, TN: Broadman and Holman, 2015.
Hochschild, Arlie Russell. 'Emotion Work, Feeling Rules, and Social Structure'. *American Journal of Sociology* 85 (1979): 551–75.
Hochschild, Arlie Russell. *The Managed Heart: Commercialization of Human Feeling*. Berkeley: University of California Press, 1983.
Hockey, Katherine M. 'The Missing Emotion: The Absence of Anger and the Promotion of Nonretaliation in 1 Peter'. In *Mixed Feelings and Vexed Emotions: Exploring Emotions in Biblical Literature*, edited by F. Scott Spencer, 331–53. Atlanta, GA: SBL Press, 2017.
Hockey, Katherine M. *The Role of Emotion in 1 Peter*. Society for New Testament Studies Monograph Series 173. Cambridge: Cambridge University Press, 2019.
Hoffman, *Paul. Die Toten in Christus: Eine religionsgeschichtliche und exegetische Untersuchung zur paulinischen Eschatologie*. Neutestamentliche Abhandlungen 2. Münster: Aschendorff, 1966.
Holloway, Paul A. *Consolation in Philippians: Philosophical Sources and Rhetorical Strategy*. Society for New Testament Studies Monograph Series 112. Cambridge: Cambridge University Press, 2001.
Holloway, Paul A. *Philippians: A Commentary*. Hermeneia. Minneapolis, MN: Fortress, 2017.
Holtz, Traugott. *Der erste Brief an die Thessalonicher*. Evangelische-katholischer Kommentar zum Neuen Testament 13. Zürich: Benziger, 1986.
Hooker, Morna D. 'Philippians 2:6–11'. In *Jesus und Paulus: Festschrift für Werner Georg Kümmel zum 70. Geburtstag*, edited by E. E. Ellis and E. Grässer, 151–64. Göttingen: Vandenhoeck & Ruprecht, 1975.
Hope, Valerie M. *Roman Death: The Dying and the Dead in Ancient Rome*. London: Continuum, 2009.
Hopkins, Keith. *Death and Renewal*. Sociological Studies in Roman History 2. Cambridge: Cambridge University Press, 1983.
Horrell, David G. *Solidarity and Difference: A Contemporary Reading of Paul's Ethics*. 2nd ed. London: T&T Clark, 2016.
Horrell, David G. 'Whither Social-Scientific Approaches to New Testament Interpretation? Reflections on Contested Methodologies and the Future'. In *After the First Urban*

Christians: The Social-Scientific Study of Pauline Christianity Twenty-Five Years Later, edited by Todd D. Still and David G. Horrell, 6–20. London: T&T Clark, 2009.

Hossenfelder, Malte. 'Epicurus – Hedonist Malgré Lui'. In *The Norms of Nature: Studies in Hellenistic Ethics*, edited by Malcolm Schofield and Gisela Striker, 245–63. Cambridge: Cambridge University Press, 1986.

Inwood, Brad. 'Comments on Professor Görgemanns' Paper: The Two Forms of Oikeiōsis in Arius and the Stoa'. In *On Stoic and Peripatetic Ethics: The Work of Arius Didymus*, edited by W. W. Fortenbaugh, 190–201. New Brunswick, NJ: Transaction Books, 1983.

Inwood, Brad. *Ethics and Human Action in Early Stoicism*. Oxford: Clarendon, 1985.

Izard, Carroll E. 'The Many Meanings/Aspects of Emotion: Definitions, Functions, Activation, and Regulation'. *Emotion Review* 2 (2010): 363–70.

Jennings, Mark A. *The Price of Partnership in the Letter of Paul to the Philippians: 'Make My Joy Complete'*. The Library of New Testament Studies 578. London: T&T Clark, 2018.

Jewett, Robert. *The Thessalonian Correspondence: Pauline Rhetoric and Millenarian Piety*. Philadelphia, PA: Fortress, 1986.

Johanson, Bruce C. *To All the Brethren: A Text-Linguistic and Rhetorical Approach to 1 Thessalonians*. Coniectanea Biblica: New Testament Series 16. Stockholm: Almqvist & Wiksell, 1987.

Kagan, Jerome. 'Once More into the Breach'. *Emotion Review* 2 (2010): 91–9.

Kagan, Jerome. *What Is Emotion? History, Measures, and Meanings*. New Haven, CT: Yale University Press, 2007.

Kaster, Robert A. *Emotion, Restraint, and Community in Ancient Rome*. New York: Oxford University Press, 2005.

Keener, Craig S. *The Mind of the Spirit: Paul's Approach to Transformed Thinking*. Grand Rapids, MI: Basic Books, 2016.

Kennedy, George A. *New Testament Interpretation through Rhetorical Criticism*. Chapel Hill: University of North Carolina Press, 1984.

Kilpatrick, George D. 'ΒΛΕΠΕΤΕ, Philippians 3:2'. In *In Memoriam Paul Kahle*, edited by Matthew Black and G. Fohrer. Berlin: Töpelmann, 1968.

Kittel, Gerhard, and Gerhard Friedrich, eds. *Theological Dictionary of the New Testament*. 10 vols. Translated by Geoffrey W. Bromiley. Grand Rapids, MI: Eerdmans, 1964–76.

Klauck, Hans-Josef. *Ancient Letters and the New Testament: A Guide to Context and Exegesis*. Waco, TX: Baylor University Press, 2006.

Knuuttila, Simo. *Emotions in Ancient and Medieval Philosophy*. Oxford: Clarendon, 2004.

Koenig, John. *Rediscovering New Testament Prayer: Boldness and Blessing in the Name of Jesus*. New York: HarperCollins, 1992.

Konstan, David. *Friendship in the Classical World*. New York: Cambridge University Press, 1997.

Konstan, David. *The Emotions of the Ancient Greeks: Studies in Aristotle and Classical Literature*. Toronto: University of Toronto Press, 2006.

Koskenniemi, Heikki. *Studien zur Idee und Phraseologie des griechischen Briefes bis 400 n. Chr*. Annales Academiae Scientarum Fennicae, Series B, Vol. 102.2. Helsinki: Finnish Academy, 1956.

Kraftchick, Steven J. 'Πάθη in Paul: The Emotional Logic of "Original Argument"'. In *Paul and Pathos*, edited by Thomas H. Olbricht and Jerry L. Sumney, 39–68. Society of Biblical Literature Symposium Series 16. Atlanta, GA: Society of Biblical Literature, 2001.

Krentz, Edgar M. '1 Thessalonians: Rhetorical Flourishes and Formal Constraints'. In *The Thessalonians Debate: Methodological Discord or Methodological Synthesis?*, edited by Karl P. Donfried and Johannes Beutler, 287–318. Grand Rapids, MI: Eerdmans, 2000.

Krentz, Edgar M. 'ΠΑΘΗ and ΑΠΑΘΕΙΑ in Early Roman Empire Stoics'. In *Passions and Moral Progress in Greco-Roman Thought*, edited by John T. Fitzgerald, 122–35. Abingdon: Routledge, 2008.

LaBarge, Scott. 'How (and Maybe Why) to Grieve Like an Ancient Philosopher'. In *Virtue and Happiness: Essays in Honour of Julia Annas*, edited by Rachana Kamtekar, 321–42. Oxford Studies in Ancient Philosophy, Supplementary Vol. 2012. Oxford: Oxford University Press, 2012.

Lambrecht, Jan. 'A Structural Analysis of 1 Thessalonians 4–5'. In *The Thessalonians Debate: Methodological Discord or Methodological Synthesis?*, edited by Karl P. Donfried and Johannes Beutler, 163–78. Grand Rapids, MI: Eerdmans, 2000.

Lash, Nicholas. *Seeing in the Dark*. London: Darton, Longman & Todd, 2005.

Lawrence, Louise J. *Reading with Anthropology: Exhibiting Aspects of New Testament Religion*. Bletchley: Paternoster, 2005.

Lawrence, Louise J. 'Ritual and the First Urban Christians: Boundary Crossings of Life and Death'. In *After the First Urban Christians: The Social-Scientific Study of Pauline Christianity Twenty-Five Years Later*, edited by Todd D. Still and David G. Horrell, 99–115. London: T&T Clark, 2009.

LeDoux, Joseph. 'A Neuroscientist's Perspective on Debates about the Nature of Emotion'. *Emotion Review* 4 (2012): 375–9.

Lieu, Judith M. 'Letters and the Topography of Early Christianity'. *New Testament Studies* 62 (2016): 167–82.

Lievestad, Ragnar. '"The Meekness and Gentleness of Christ" II Cor. X.1'. *New Testament Studies* 13 (1965–6): 156–64.

Lightfoot, J. B. *Notes on the Epistles of St. Paul from Unpublished Commentaries*. 2nd ed. London: Macmillan, 1904.

Lightfoot, J. B. *Saint Paul's Epistle to the Philippians*. 6th ed. London: Macmillan, 1881.

Lohmeyer, Ernst. *Die Briefe an die Philipper, an die Kolosser und an Philemon*. 14th ed. Kritisch-exegetischer Kommentar über das Neue Testament 9. Göttingen: Vandenhoeck & Ruprecht, 1974.

Lohmeyer, Ernst. *Kyrios Jesus: Eine Untersuchung zu Phil 2.5–11*. Sitzungsberichte der Heidelberger Akademie der Wissenschaften. Philosophisch-historische Klasse, Jahrgang 1927–8, 4. Abhandlung, 18. Heidelberg: Carl Winter, 1928.

Long, Anthony A. *Epictetus: A Stoic and Socratic Guide to Life*. Oxford: Clarendon, 2002.

Long, Anthony A. 'Epictetus on Understanding and Managing Emotions'. In *From Epicurus to Epictetus: Studies in Hellenistic and Roman Philosophy*, 377–94. Oxford: Clarendon, 2006.

Long, Anthony A. *Hellenistic Philosophy*. 2nd ed. Berkeley: University of California Press, 1986.

Long, Anthony A. 'Soul and Body in Stoicism'. *Phronesis* 27 (1992): 34–57.

Long, Anthony A. 'Stoic Eudaimonism'. In *Stoic Studies*, 179–201. Cambridge: Cambridge University Press, 1996.

Long, Anthony A. 'The Logical Basis of Stoic Ethics'. In *Stoic Studies*, 134–55. Cambridge: Cambridge University Press, 1996.

Longenecker, Bruce W. 'Socio-Economic Profiling of the First Urban Christians'. In *After the First Urban Christians: The Social-Scientific Study of Pauline Christianity*

Twenty-Five Years Later, edited by Todd D. Still and David G. Horrell, 36–59. London: T&T Clark, 2009.

Luckensmeyer, David. *The Eschatology of First Thessalonians*. Novum Testamentum et orbis antiquus / Studien zur Umwelt des Neuen Testaments 71. Göttingen: Vandenhoeck & Ruprecht, 2009.

Luckensmeyer, David, and Bronwen Neil. 'Reading First Thessalonians as a Consolatory Letter in Light of Seneca and Ancient Handbooks on Letter-Writing'. *New Testament Studies* 62 (2016): 31–48.

Lüddeckens, Dorothea. 'Emotion'. In *Theorizing Rituals: Issues, Topics, Approaches, Concepts*, edited by Jens Kreinath, Jan Snoek, and Michael Stausberg, 545–70. Leiden: Brill, 2006.

Lupton, Deborah. *The Emotional Self: A Sociocultural Exploration*. London: Sage, 1998.

Lütgert, Wilhelm. *Die Volkommenen im Philipperbrief und die Enthusiasten in Thessalonich*. Beiträge zur Förderung christlicher Theologie 13. Gütersloh: Bertelsmann, 1909.

Lutz, Catherine A. *Unnatural Emotions: Everyday Sentiments on a Micronesian Atoll & Their Challenge to Western Theory*. Chicago: University of Chicago Press, 1988.

Luz, Ulrich. *Das Geschichtsverständnis des Paulus*. Beiträge zur evangelischen Theologie 49. Munich: Kaiser, 1968.

Lyons, George. *Pauline Autobiography: Towards a New Understanding*. Society of Biblical Literature Dissertation Series 73. Atlanta, GA: Scholars, 1985.

Malherbe, Abraham J. *Ancient Epistolary Theorists*. Society of Biblical Literature Sources for Biblical Study 19. Atlanta: Scholars, 1988.

Malherbe, Abraham J. 'Exhortation in 1 Thessalonians'. In *Paul and the Popular Philosophers*, 49–66. Minneapolis, MN: Fortress, 1989.

Malherbe, Abraham J. 'Hellenistic Moralists and the New Testament'. *Aufstieg und Niedergang der römischen Welt* 2.26.1 (1992): 267–333.

Malherbe, Abraham J. *Moral Exhortation: A Greco-Roman Sourcebook*. Philadelphia, PA: Westminster, 1986.

Malherbe, Abraham J. *Paul and the Thessalonians: The Philosophic Tradition of Pastoral Care*. Philadelphia, PA: Fortress, 1987.

Malherbe, Abraham J. 'Paul's Self-Sufficiency (Philippians 4.11)'. In *Friendship, Flattery, and Frankness of Speech: Studies in Friendship in the New Testament World*, 125–39. Supplements to Novum Testamentum 82. Leiden: Brill, 1996.

Malherbe, Abraham J. *The Letters to the Thessalonians*. Anchor Bible 32B. New Haven, CT: Yale University Press, 2000.

Malina, Bruce J. 'What Is Prayer?' *The Bible Today* 18 (1980): 214–20.

Manning, C. E. *On Seneca's 'Ad Marciam'*. Mnemosyne Supplement 69. Leiden: E. J. Brill, 1981.

Manning, C. E. 'The Consolatory Tradition and Seneca's Attitude to the Emotions'. *Greece and Rome* 21 (1974): 71–81.

Marshall, I. Howard. *1 and 2 Thessalonians*. New Century Bible. Grand Rapids, MI: Eerdmans, 1983.

Marshall, I. Howard. *The Epistle to the Philippians*. Epworth Commentaries. London: Epworth, 1991.

Marshall, I. Howard. 'The Theology of Philippians'. In *The Theology of the Shorter Pauline Letters*, edited by Karl P. Donfried and I. Howard Marshall, 115–66. Cambridge: Cambridge University Press, 1993.

Marshall, Peter. *Enmity in Corinth: Social Conventions in Paul's Relations with the Corinthians*. Wissenschaftliche Untersuchungen zum Neuen Testament 2.23. Tübingen: Mohr, 1987.

Martin, Ralph P. *Carmen Christi: Philippians 2.5–11 in Recent Interpretation and in the Setting of Early Christian Worship*. 2nd ed. Grand Rapids, MI: Eerdmans, 1983.

Martin, Ralph P. *Philippians*. New Century Bible. London: Oliphants, 1976.

Marxsen, Willi. 'Auslegung von 1 Thess 4,13–18'. *Zeitschrift für Theologie und Kirche* 66 (1969): 22–37.

McGuire, Meredith B. *Lived Religion, Faith and Practice in Everyday Life*. Oxford: Oxford University Press, 2008.

Meeks, Wayne A. *The First Urban Christians: The Social World of the Apostle Paul*. 2nd ed. New Haven, CT: Yale University Press, 2003.

Meeks, Wayne A. 'The Man from Heaven in Paul's Letter to the Philippians'. In In *Search of the Early Christians: Selected Essays*, edited by Allen R. Hilton and H. Gregory Snyder, 106–14. New Haven, CT: Yale University Press, 2002.

Merklein, Helmut. 'Der Theologe als Prophet: Zur Funktion prophetischen Redens im Theologischen Diskurs des Paulus'. *New Testament Studies* 38 (1992): 402–29.

Mesquita, Batja, and Michael Boiger. 'Emotions in Context: A Sociodynamic Model of Emotions'. *Emotion Review* 6 (2014): 298–302.

Mitchell, Margaret M. 'New Testament Envoys in the Context of Greco-Roman Diplomatic and Epistolary Conventions: The Example of Timothy and Titus'. *Journal of Biblical Literature* 111 (1992): 641–62.

Moffatt, James. *Love in the New Testament*. London: Hodder and Stoughton, 1929.

Moors, Agnes. 'Theories of Emotion Causation: A Review'. *Cognition and Emotion* 23 (2009): 625–62.

Moors, Agnes, Phoebe C. Ellsworth, Klaus R. Scherer, and Nico H. Frijda. 'Appraisal Theories of Emotion: State of the Art and Future Development'. *Emotion Review* 5 (2013): 119–24.

Morrice, William G. 'Joy'. In *Dictionary of Paul and His Letters*, edited by Gerald F. Hawthorne and Ralph P. Martin, 511–12. Downers Grove, IL: Intervarsity, 1993.

Morrice, William G. *Joy in the New Testament*. Exeter: Paternoster, 1984.

Müller, Ulrich B. *Der Brief des Paulus an die Philipper*. Theologisher Handkommentar zum Neuen Testament 11.1. Leipzig: Evangelische Verlagsanstalt, 1993.

Mulligan, Kevin, and Klaus R. Scherer. 'Toward a Working Definition of Emotion'. *Emotion Review* 4 (2012): 345–57.

Mullins, Terence Y. 'Visit Talk in New Testament Letters'. *Catholic Biblical Quarterly* 35 (1973): 350–8.

Neugebauer, Fritz. *In Christus: Eine Untersuchung zum Paulinischen Glaubensverständnis*. Göttingen: Vandenhoeck & Ruprecht, 1961.

Neyrey, Jerome H. 'Prayer, in Other Words: New Testament Prayers in Social-Science Perspective'. In *Social Scientific Models for Interpreting the Bible: Essays by the Context Group in Honor of Bruce J. Malina*, edited by John J. Pilch, 349–80. Leiden: Brill, 2001.

Nicholl, Colin R. *From Hope to Despair in Thessalonica: Situating 1 and 2 Thessalonians*. Society for New Testament Studies Monograph Series 126. Cambridge: Cambridge University Press, 2004.

Nussbaum, Martha C. 'Aristotle on Emotions and Rational Persuasion'. In *Essays on Aristotle's Rhetoric*, edited by Amélie O. Rorty, 303–23. Berkeley: University of California Press, 1996.

Nussbaum, Martha C. *The Therapy of Desire: Theory and Practice in Hellenistic Ethics*. Princeton, NJ: Princeton University Press, 1994.
Nussbaum, Martha C. *Upheavals of Thought: The Intelligence of Emotions*. Cambridge: Cambridge University Press, 2001.
Oakes, Peter. *Philippians: From People to Letter*. Society for New Testament Studies Monograph Series 110. Cambridge: Cambridge University Press, 2001.
Oatley, Keith, and P. N. Johnson-Laird. 'Cognitive Approaches to Emotions'. *Trends in Cognitive Science* 18 (2014): 134–40.
Oatley, Keith, W. Gerrod Parrott, Craig Smith, and Fraser Watts. '*Cognition and Emotion* over Twenty-Five Years'. *Cognition and Emotion* 25 (2011): 1341–8.
Ogereau, Julien M. *Paul's Koinonia with the Philippians: A Socio-Historical Investigation of a Pauline Economic Partnership*. Wissenschaftliche Untersuchungen zum Neuen Testament 2.377. Tübingen: Mohr Siebeck, 2014.
Olbricht, Thomas H. 'An Aristotelian Rhetorical Analysis of 1 Thessalonians'. In *Greeks, Romans, and Christians: Essays in Honor of Abraham J. Malherbe*, edited by David J. Balch, Everett Ferguson, and Wayne A. Meeks, 216–36. Minneapolis, MN: Fortress, 1990.
Olbricht, Thomas H. 'Introduction'. In *Paul and Pathos*, edited by Thomas H. Olbricht and Jerry L. Sumney, 1–4. Society of Biblical Literature Symposium Series 16. Atlanta, GA: Society of Biblical Literature, 2001.
Olbricht, Thomas H., and Jerry L. Sumney, eds. *Paul and Pathos*. Society of Biblical Literature Symposium Series 16. Atlanta, GA: Society of Biblical Literature, 2001.
Orr, Peter. *Christ Absent and Present: A Study in Pauline Christology*. Wissenschaftliche Untersuchungen zum Neuen Testament 2.354. Tübingen: Mohr Siebeck, 2014.
Osiek, Carolyn. *Philippians, Philemon*. Abingdon New Testament Commentaries. Nashville, TN: Abingdon, 2000.
Pearson, Birger A. '1 Thessalonians 2.13–16: A Deutero-Pauline Interpolation'. *Harvard Theological Review* 64 (1971): 79–94.
Peterlin, Davorin. *Paul's Letter to the Philippians in the Light of Disunity in the Church*. Supplements to Novum Testamentum 79. Leiden: Brill, 1995.
Peterman, Gerald W. *Paul's Gift from Philippi: Conventions of Gift-Exchange and Christian Giving*. Society for New Testament Studies Monograph Series 92. Cambridge: Cambridge University Press, 1997.
Peterson, Erik. 'Die Einholung des Kyrios'. *Zeitschrift für systematische Theologie* 7 (1930): 682–702.
Plamper, Jan. *The History of Emotions: An Introduction*. Translated by Keith Tribe. Oxford: Oxford University Press, 2015.
Plevnik, Joseph. *Paul and the Parousia: An Exegetical and Theological Investigation*. Peabody, MA: Hendrickson, 1997.
Plevnik, Joseph. 'The Parousia as Implication of Christ's Resurrection: An Exegesis of 1 Thes 4,13–18'. In *Word and Spirit: Essays in Honor of David Michael Stanley on His 60th Birthday*, edited by Joseph Plevnik, 199–277. Toronto: Regis College, 1975.
Plevnik, Joseph. 'The Taking Up of the Faithful and the Resurrection of the Dead in 1 Thessalonians 4:13–18'. *Catholic Biblical Quarterly* 46 (1984): 274–83.
Pobee, John S. *Persecution and Martyrdom in the Theology of Paul*. Journal for the Study of the New Testament Supplement Series 6. Sheffield: JSOT Press, 1985.
Pohlenz, Max. *Die Stoa: Geschichte einer geistigen Bewegung*. 2 vols. Göttingen: Vandenhoeck & Ruprecht, 1947.

Pomeroy, Arthur J., ed. *Arius Didymus: Epitome of Stoic Ethics*. Atlanta, GA: Society of Biblical Literature, 1999.

Rapske, Brian. *The Book of Acts and Paul in Roman Custody*. The Book of Acts in Its First Century Setting 3. Grand Rapids, MI: Eerdmans, 1994.

Reddy, William M. *The Navigation of Feeling: A Framework for the History of Emotions*. Cambridge: Cambridge University Press, 2001.

Reinhartz, Adele. 'On the Meaning of the Pauline Exhortation: "Mimētai Mou Ginesthe" – Become Imitators of Me'. *Studies in Religion* 16 (1987): 393–404.

Reumann, John. *Philippians: A New Translation with Introduction and Commentary*. Anchor Bible 33B. New Haven, CT: Yale University Press, 2008.

Reumann, John. 'Philippians, Especially Chapter 4, as a "Letter of Friendship": Observations on a Checkered History of Friendship'. In *Friendship, Flattery, and Frankness of Speech: Studies in Friendship in the New Testament World*, edited by John T. Fitzgerald, 83–106. Supplements to Novum Testamentum 82. Leiden: Brill, 1996.

Reydams-Schils, Gretchen. 'Human Bonding and Oikeiōsis in Roman Stoicism'. *Oxford Studies in Ancient Philosophy* 22 (2002): 221–51.

Reydams-Schils, Gretchen. *The Roman Stoics: Self, Responsibility, and Affection*. Chicago: University of Chicago Press, 2005.

Richard, Earl J. *First and Second Thessalonians*. Sacra Pagina 11. Collegeville, PA: Liturgical, 1995.

Riis, Ole, and Linda Woodhead. *A Sociology of Religious Emotion*. Oxford: Oxford University Press, 2010.

Rosaldo, Michelle Z. *Knowledge and Passion: Ilongot Notions of Self and Social Life*. Cambridge: Cambridge University Press, 1980.

Rosaldo, Michelle Z. 'Towards an Anthropology of Self and Feeling'. In *Culture Theory: Essays on Mind, Self, and Emotion*, edited by Richard A. Schweder and Robert A. LeVine, 137–57. Cambridge: Cambridge University Press, 1984.

Rosenwein, Barbara H. *Emotional Communities in the Early Middle Ages*. Ithaca, NY: Cornell University Press, 2006.

Rowe, C. Kavin. *One True Life: The Stoics and Early Christians as Rival Traditions*. New Haven, CT: Yale University Press, 2016.

Russell, James A. 'Introduction to Special Section: On Defining Emotion'. *Emotion Review* 4 (2012): 337.

Sampley, J. Paul. *Pauline Partnership in Christ: Christian Community and Commitment in Light of Roman Law*. Philadelphia, PA: Fortress, 1980.

Sandbach, F. H. *The Stoics*. 2nd ed. Indianapolis, IN: Hackett, 1989.

Schenk, Wolfgang. *Die Philipperbriefe des Paulus*. Stuttgart: Kohlhammer, 1984.

Schmithals, Walter. *Paul and the Gnostics*. Translated by John E. Steely. Nashville, TN: Abingdon, 1972.

Schütz, John Howard. *Paul and the Anatomy of Apostolic Authority*. Society for New Testament Studies Monograph Series 26. Cambridge: Cambridge University Press, 1975.

Scourfield, J. H. D. *Consoling Heliodorus: A Commentary on Jerome, Letter 60*. Oxford: Clarendon, 1993.

Scourfield, J. H. D. 'Towards a Genre of Consolation'. In *Greek and Roman Consolations: Eight Studies of a Tradition and Its Afterlife*, edited by Hans Baltussen, 1–36. Swansea: Classical Press of Wales, 2013.

Sellars, John. *The Art of Living: The Stoics on the Nature and Function of Philosophy*. 2nd ed. London: Bloomsbury, 2009.
Sevenster, Jan Nicolaas. *Paul and Seneca*. Supplements to Novum Testamentum 4. Leiden: Brill, 1961.
Shantz, Colleen. '"I Have Learned to Be Content?": Happiness According to St. Paul'. In *The Bible and the Pursuit of Happiness: What the Old and New Testaments Teach Us about the Good Life*, edited by Brent Strawn, 187–201. New York: Oxford University Press, 2012.
Shogren, Gary. *1 & 2 Thessalonians*. Zondervan Exegetical Commentary on the New Testament. Grand Rapids, MI: Zondervan, 2012.
Siber, Peter. *Mit Christus Leben: Eine Studie zur paulinischen Auferstehungshoffnung*. Abhandlungen zur Theologie des Alten und Neuen Testaments 61. Zürich: Theologischer Verlag, 1971.
Sihvola, Juha, and Troels Engberg-Pedersen, eds. *The Emotions in Hellenistic Philosophy*. Dordrecht: Kluwer Academic, 1998.
Silva, Moisés. *Philippians*. 2nd ed. Baker Exegetical Commentary on the New Testament. Grand Rapids, MI: Baker, 2005.
Smit, Peter-Ben. *Paradigms of Being in Christ: A Study of the Epistle to the Philippians*. The Library of New Testament Studies 476. London: T&T Clark, 2013.
Smith, Abraham. *Comfort One Another: Reconstructing the Rhetoric and Audience of 1 Thessalonians*. Louisville, KY: Westminster John Knox, 1995.
Smith, Jonathan Z. *Imagining Religion: From Babylon to Jonestown*. Chicago: University of Chicago Press, 1988.
Sorabji, Richard. *Emotion and Peace of Mind: From Stoic Agitation to Christian Temptation*. Oxford: Oxford University Press, 2000.
Spencer, F. Scott, ed. *Mixed Feelings and Vexed Emotions: Exploring Emotions in Biblical Literature*. Atlanta, GA: SBL Press, 2017.
Standhartinger, Angela. 'Letter from Prison as Hidden Transcript: What It Tells Us about the People at Philippi'. In *The People beside Paul: The Philippian Assembly and History from Below*, edited by Joseph A. Marchal, 107–40. Atlanta, GA: SBL Press, 2015.
Stets, Jan E., and Jonathan H. Turner, eds. *Handbook of the Sociology of Emotions*. New York: Springer, 2006.
Still, Todd D. *Conflict at Thessalonica: A Pauline Church and Its Neighbours*. Journal for the Study of the New Testament Supplement Series 183. Sheffield: Sheffield Academic Press, 1999.
Still, Todd D. 'Eschatology in the Thessalonian Letters'. *Review and Expositor* 96 (1999): 195–210.
Still, Todd D. 'Interpretive Ambiguities and Scholarly Proclivities in Pauline Studies: A Treatment of Three Texts from 1 Thessalonians 4 as a Test Case'. *Currents in Biblical Research* 5 (2007): 209–17.
Still, Todd D., and David G. Horrell, eds. *After the First Urban Christians: The Social-Scientific Study of Pauline Christianity Twenty-Five Years Later*. London: T&T Clark, 2009.
Stowers, Stanley K. 'Friends and Enemies in the Politics of Heaven: Reading Theology in Philippians'. In *Pauline Theology 1: Thessalonians, Philippians, Galatians*, edited by Jouette M. Bassler. Minneapolis, MN: Fortress, 1991.
Stowers, Stanley K. *Letter Writing in Greco-Roman Antiquity*. Library of Early Christianity 5. Philadelphia, PA: Westminster Press, 1986.

Striker, Gisela. 'The Role of Oikeiosis in Stoic Ethics'. *Oxford Studies in Ancient Philosophy* 1 (1983): 145–67.
Sumney, Jerry L. 'Paul's Use of Πάθος in His Argument against the Opponents of 2 Corinthians'. In *Paul and Pathos*, edited by Thomas H. Olbricht and Jerry L. Sumney, 147–60. Society of Biblical Literature Symposium Series 16. Atlanta, GA: Society of Biblical Literature, 2001.
Sumney, Jerry L. 'Studying Paul's Opponents: Advances and Challenges'. In *Paul and His Opponents*, edited by Stanley E. Porter, 7–58. Leiden: Brill, 2005.
Tangney, Julia Price, Jeff Stuewig, and Debra J. Mashek. 'Moral Emotions and Moral Behavior'. *Annual Review of Psychology* 58 (2007): 345–72.
Taylor, Gabriele. *Pride, Shame, and Guilt: Emotions of Self-Assessment*. Oxford: Clarendon, 1985.
Thompson, James W. 'Paul's Argument from Pathos in 2 Corinthians'. In *Paul and Pathos*, edited by Thomas H. Olbricht and Jerry L. Sumney, 127–45. Society of Biblical Literature Symposium Series 16. Atlanta, GA: Society of Biblical Literature, 2001.
Thrall, Margaret E. *Greek Particles in the New Testament: Linguistic and Exegetical Studies*. Leiden: Brill, 1962.
Thúren, Lauri. 'Was Paul Angry? Derhetorizing Galatians'. In *The Rhetorical Interpretation of Scripture: Essays from the 1996 Malibu Conference*, edited by Stanley E. Porter and Dennis L. Stamps, 302–20. Sheffield: Sheffield Academic Press, 1999.
Tieleman, Teun. *Chrysippus' On Affections: Reconstructions and Reinterpretations*. Leiden: Brill, 2003.
Turner, Jonathan H. 'The Sociology of Emotions: Basic Theoretical Arguments'. *Emotion Review* 1 (2009): 340–54.
van Gennep, Arnold. *The Rites of Passage*. Translated by Monika Vizedom and Gabrielle L. Caffee. Chicago: University of Chicago Press, 1960.
Vincent, M. R. *A Critical and Exegetical Commentary on the Epistles to the Philippians and to Philemon*. International Critical Commentary. Edinburgh: T&T Clark, 1897.
Voorwinde, Stephen. *Jesus' Emotions in the Fourth Gospel: Human or Divine?* The Library of New Testament Studies 284. London: T&T Clark, 2005.
Voorwinde, Stephen. *Jesus' Emotions in the Gospels*. London: T&T Clark, 2011.
Walton, Steve. 'What Has Aristotle to Do with Paul? Rhetorical Criticism and 1 Thessalonians'. *Tyndale Bulletin* 46 (1995): 229–50.
Wanamaker, Charles A. 'Epistolary vs. Rhetorical Analysis: Is a Synthesis Possible?' In *The Thessalonians Debate: Methodological Discord or Methodological Synthesis?*, edited by Karl P. Donfried and Johannes Beutler, 255–86. Grand Rapids, MI: Eerdmans, 2000.
Wanamaker, Charles A. *The Epistles to the Thessalonians*. New International Greek Testament Commentary. Grand Rapids: Eerdmans, 1990.
Wansink, Craig S. *Chained in Christ: The Experience and Rhetoric of Paul's Imprisonments*. Journal for the Study of the New Testament Supplement Series 130. Sheffield: Sheffield Academic Press, 1996.
Watson, Duane F. 'A Rhetorical Analysis of Philippians and Its Implications for the Unity Question'. *Novum Testamentum* 30 (1988): 57–88.
Watson, Francis B. 'Barth's Philippians as Theological Exegesis'. In *The Epistle to the Philippians*, translated by James W. Leitch, xxvi–li. Louisville, KY: Westminster John Knox, 2002.
Webb, Ruth. 'Imagination and the Arousal of Emotions in Greco-Roman Rhetoric'. In *The Passions in Roman Thought and Literature*, edited by Susanna Morton Braund and Christopher Gill. Cambridge: Cambridge University Press, 1997.

Weima, Jeffrey A. D. *1–2 Thessalonians*. Baker Exegetical Commentary on the New Testament. Grand Rapids, MI: Baker, 2014.
Weima, Jeffrey A. D. *Neglected Endings: The Significance of the Pauline Letter Closings*. Journal for the Study of the New Testament Supplement Series 101. Sheffield: JSOT Press, 1994.
Weima, Jeffrey A. D. 'Sincerely, Paul: The Significance of the Pauline Letter Closings'. In *Paul and the Ancient Letter Form*, edited by Stanley E. Porter and Sean A. Adams, 307–45. Leiden: Brill, 2010.
Welborn, Larry L. 'Paul and Pain: Paul's Emotional Therapy in 2 Corinthians 1.1–2.13; 7.5–16 in the Context of Ancient Psychagogic Literature'. *New Testament Studies* 57 (2011): 547–70.
Welborn, Larry L. 'Paul's Appeal to the Emotions in 2 Corinthians 1.1–2.13; 7.5–16'. *Journal for the Study of the New Testament* 82 (2001): 31–60.
Werline, Rodney A. *Pray Like This: Understanding Prayer in the Bible*. New York: T&T Clark, 2007.
White, L. Michael. 'Morality between Two Worlds: A Paradigm of Friendship in Philippians'. In *Greeks, Romans, and Christians: Essays in Honor of Abraham J. Malherbe*, edited by David J. Balch, Everett Ferguson, and Wayne A. Meeks, 201–15. Minneapolis, MN: Fortress, 1990.
Wick, Peter. *Der Philipperbrief: Der formale Aufbau des Briefs als Schlüssel zum Verständnis seines Inhalts*. Beiträge zur Wissenschaft vom Alten und Neuen Testament 135. Stuttgart: Kohlhammer, 1994.
Wiles, Gordon P. *Paul's Intercessory Prayers: The Significance of the Intercessory Prayer Passages in the Letters of St Paul*. Society for New Testament Studies Monograph Series 24. Cambridge: Cambridge University Press, 1974.
Wilson, Marcus. 'Seneca the Consoler? A New Reading of His Consolatory Writings'. In *Greek and Roman Consolations: Eight Studies of a Tradition and Its Afterlife*, edited by Hans Baltussen, 93–121. Swansea: Classical Press of Wales, 2013.
Wilson, Marcus. 'The Subjugation of Grief in Seneca's "Epistles"'. In *The Passions in Roman Thought and Literature*, edited by Susanna Morton Braund and Christopher Gill, 48–67. Cambridge: Cambridge University Press, 1997.
Winston, David. 'Philo of Alexandria on the Emotions'. In *Passions and Moral Progress in Greco-Roman Thought*, edited by John T. Fitzgerald, 201–20. Abingdon: Routledge, 2008.
Wischmeyer, Oda. '1Korinther 13. Das Hohelied der Liebe zwischen Emotion und Ethos'. In *Deuterocanonical and Cognate Literature Yearbook 2011*, edited by Renate Egger-Wenzel and Jeremy Corley, 343–59. Berlin: De Gruyter, 2012.
Wisse, Jakob. *Ethos and Pathos from Aristotle and Cicero*. Amsterdam: Hakkert, 1989.
Witherington, Ben. *1 and 2 Thessalonians: A Socio-Rhetorical Commentary*. Grand Rapids, MI: Eerdmans, 2006.
Witherington, Ben. *Paul's Letter to the Philippians: A Socio-Rhetorical Commentary*. Grand Rapids, MI: Eerdmans, 2011.
Wright, N. T. 'Joy: Some New Testament Perspectives and Questions'. In *Joy and Human Flourishing: Essays on Theology, Culture, and the Good Life*, edited by Miroslav Volf and Justin E. Crisp, 39–61. Minneapolis, MN: Fortress, 2015.
Wright, N. T. *Paul and the Faithfulness of God*. London: SPCK, 2013.
Wright, N. T. *The Resurrection of the Son of God*. Minneapolis, MN: Fortress, 2003.

Index of Ancient Sources

1. GRECO-ROMAN AUTHORS

Aetius

Doxographi Graeci
4.4.4	27
4.12.1	28
4.21.1–4	27, 28

Alexander of Aphrodisias

Fat.
183.5–10	31

Andronicus

De passionibus
1	34, 37
1–6	38
2–5	38
6	39, 61

Apollonius of Tyana

Ep.
55	52
58	52

Aristotle

De an.
1.1.403	26
3.9.432–3	40

Mot. an.
11.703	40

Aulus Gellius

Noct. att.
19.1.17–20	42

Calcidius

On the Timaeus of Plato
220	28

Cicero

Acad.
1.39	27
1.40–1	30
1.41–2	30
2.24–5	28
2.30–1	30
2.37–8	30
2.108	31
2.135	53

Acad. pr.
2.135	55

Att.
12.10	52, 53
15.1	52, 53

Ep. Brut.
1.9	52, 53

Fam.
4.5	52, 53
5.16	52, 53
5.18	52
6.3	52, 53

Fat.
41–2	28

Fin.
3.17–21	45
3.20	45
3.20–1	45
3.23–6	83
3.32	83
3.50–4	35
3.62–8	45
3.68	45
3.74	24

Nat. d.
1.39	24
2.37–9	25

Tusc.		4.60–2	43, 50
1.65	53	4.63	53
1.76	53	5.82	26
1.83	53		
3.5	47, 48	**Diogenes Laertius**	
3.6	48	2.84	52
3.13	48	4.11	52
3.19–20	49	4.27	53
3.22	55	5.23	22
3.25	36	5.42	52
3.28	54	5.45	22
3.33	54	6.15	52
3.52	54	6.80	52
3.61–2	36	7.4	53
3.61–6	50	7.49	28
3.66–7	55	7.51	28
3.70	53	7.54	29
3.74	36, 55	7.85–6	45
3.75	36	7.88	44
3.76	36, 43, 49, 53, 54	7.89	25
3.77	43	7.94	25
3.77–8	42	7.104–7	35
3.79	36, 49, 50	7.108–9	44
3.81	53	7.110	27, 32, 53
3.82–3	40	7.111	53
3.83	34, 48	7.111–14	34, 37, 38
4.11	32	7.116	38, 39, 61
4.11–14	38	7.117	48
4.12–14	39	7.127	25
4.13	61	7.130	25
4.14	36, 39	7.134	24
4.14–15	34, 37	7.135–6	27
4.15	34	7.166	53
4.16–21	38	7.178	53
4.23	47	9.20	52
4.29	25	9.46	52
4.31	48		
4.34	25	**Epictetus**	
4.34–5	25	*Diatr.*	
4.35	48	1.1.7	47
4.37	48	1.1.12	30
4.38–42	49	1.1.12–13	45
4.38–47	55	1.3.4	47
4.42	33	1.6.1	181
4.48	48	1.6.13	47
4.52	48	1.7.33	47
4.53	48	1.12.20–1	37
4.55	49	1.12.34	47
4.59	55	1.20.15	47
4.60	50		

2.2.1–7	50		4.2.10–18	33
2.10.1–2	45, 48		4.3.2	34
2.10.7–23	180		4.3.2–3	35
2.11.3–4	46		4.6.2–3	37
2.11.4–18	46		4.7.1–5	34
2.13	50		4.7.3–4	58
2.16	50		4.7.16–17	40
2.18.1–14	49		5.1.4	35
2.18.12–18	51		5.2.23–4	47
2.18.23–6	50		7.1.112	27
2.22.20	131			
3.2.4	60, 130		**Homer**	
3.3	50, 59		*Il.*	
3.3.1	59		6.486–9	52
3.3.14–16	59		24.522–51	52
3.3.17	59			
3.3.17–19	59–60		**Nemesius**	
3.8.1–6	50, 60		*De natura hominis*	
3.8.5	60		19.229–21.235	38
3.22.19–22	47		78.7–79.2	27
3.23.27–38	43			
3.24.23	60		**Philo**	
3.24.24	60		*Alleg. Interp.*	
3.24.58–9	60		3.18	51
4.7.14	83			
4.11.111–12	60		*Heir*	
4.12	51		253	51
4.12.6	51			
			Migration	
Ench.			156–7	58
1.5	50			
3	60		*QG*	
4–5	50		4.15–16	58
5	37, 60		4.19	58
9–10	50		4.73	42
16	60, 133, 180		4.101	58
17	180			
26	60		**Plato**	
30	180		*Alc.*	
33	51		118b–c	42
Eusebius			*Symp.*	
Praep. evang.			215e–216c	42
15.14.2	27			
			Pliny	
Galen			*Ep.*	
Intr.			1.12	52
14.726.7–11	27		3.21	52
			9.9	52
PHP				
4.2.4–6	34			

Plutarch

Alc.
4	42

Arist.
21.2–5	75

Cons. ux.
Generally	52, 53

Exil.
Generally	52

St. rep.
1037F–1038A	38
1046E–F	25
1053F–1054B	27
1057A	32
1057B	30

Virt. mor.
441B–C	25
441B–D	37
441C–D	25
441D	33
446F–447A	37
449A	40
449A–B	38

Ps-Plutarch

Cons. Apoll.
Generally	52, 53
102d	55

Seneca

Ep.
5.1	46
5.4	46
11.1–2	41
15	48
16.1	46
16.1–3	47
16.3	46
23	61–2
23.1–2	62
23.1–6	57
23.3	62, 94
23.4–6	62
27.1	56
27.2–3	57
37.4	177, 181
38.1	47
41.1–2	44
45.9	181
57.4–5	41
59.2	57, 62
59.16	62
63	52, 53, 56
63.1	56
63.3	56
63.4–7	56
63.12	53
63.14	56
63.15	56
63.15–16	56
66.12	63, 181
66.14	63
66.37	63
66.39	181
68.9	56
71.29	41
74.24–6	57
74.30–1	57
76.9–10	25
85.6–16	49
92.1	181
92.3	26
92.30	44
93	52
99	52, 53, 56–8
99.1	56, 57
99.1–2	55
99.3	56
99.3–4	58
99.4	55
99.4–5	54
99.7–9	53
99.7–13	57
99.15	57
99.16–17	57
99.18–19	57
99.18–21	132
99.20–1	58
113.2	31
121	45
124.13–14	24, 25

Helv.
Generally	52, 53

5.1–2	62	5.1–3	55
5.3	54	5.4–6.5	54
17.2–5	54	6.2	55
18–19	54	8	54
18.7–8	54	9.1–3	55
		9.4–5	54
Ira		10	54
1.7.4	33	12–13	54
1.12.1–13.5	48	14.1–16.3	54
1.13.5	48	17.1–6	54
2.1.3–5	40	18.1–2	54
2.1.4–5	40	18.4–5	55
2.2.1–3	41	18.4–7	132
2.2.1–2.3.3	40	18.6–7	55
2.3.1–2	40	18.7–8	54
2.3.1–2.4	37		
2.3.4–5	41	*Tranq.*	
2.4.1–2	42	1.1–17	43
3.36.2–3	51		
		Vit. beat.	
Marc.		3.1–3	63
Generally	52, 53	3.3–4	63
1	34	3.4	63, 94
1.1	55	4.2–5	57
2.1–4.4	54	4.4	63, 94
3.3	55	6.2	83
6.1–2	55	8.1–2	63
7	41	8.3–4	63
7.1	55	8.5	63
7.1–2	55		
7.3	55	**Sextus Empiricus**	
8.1–2	53	*Math.*	
9–10	54	7.157–7	30
10.2	54	7.234	27
11	53	7.242–6	29
12.1–3	54	7.247–52	29
17.1	53	8.263	27
19.1	55	8.70	28
19.4–5	54		
20.6	54	**Stobaeus**	
22.1–2	54	1.213.15–21	27
24.1–4	54	1.368.12–20	28
		2.66.14–67.4	25
Polyb.		2.75.11–76.8	25
Generally	52, 53	2.85.12–86.4	44
1.4	53	2.86.17–19	31
2.1	55	2.88.2–3	30
2.2	54	2.88.2–6	31, 32
4.1	54	2.88.8–10	32
4.3	55		

2.88.11–12	37
2.88.22–89.3	37
2.89.4–12	33
2.89.16–18	33
2.90.7–18	33–4, 37
2.90.19–92.20	38
2.102.23–5	43
2.102.25–6	43
2.111.18–112.8	30
2.155.5–17	33
4.44.81	52

Tacitus
Ann.
15.64	75
16.35	75

2. OLD TESTAMENT
Genesis
23.2	41

Numbers
28.7	75

Job
13.16	92

Psalms
32.11	89
33.21	89
35.9	89

3. APOCRYPHA
Sirach
41.21	84
42.7	84

Wisdom of Solomon
2.19	91

4. PSEUDEPIGRAPHA
4 Ezra
6.25	114
7.26-44	114
13.16-18	114
13.24	114

Psalms of Solomon
17.44	114
18.6	114

5. NEW TESTAMENT
Mark
5.39	118

John
11.35	118

Acts
2.42-7	167
7.60	113
13.36	113
16.13-15	167
16.19-39	76
17.1-10	101, 107, 109
17.5-6	110
17.5-9	113
17.10	106
24.4	91
28.30-1	73

Romans
5.3-4	77
6.4	167
8.11-12	120
8.17-18	77
9–11	102
9.2	118
11.1	109
11.7	85
12.1	167
12.12	164, 167
12.15	118
14.17	98
16.4	109

Galatians
2	110
5.16	123
5.22	98

1 Corinthians
4.16	157
5.3-4	171

6.14	120	13.11	66
7.1	111		
7.10	122	**Ephesians**	
7.25	111, 122	1.13	4
7.30	118	4.25	4
7.38	111, 124	4.26	4
7.39	113	5.1	157
8.1	111, 130	5.9	4
8.4	111	6.14	4
8.10	130		
8.13	123	**Philippians**	
9.14	122	1.1–3.1	67
10.23	130	1.3	81
11.1	157	1.3-4	90, 163, 165
11.17-34	167	1.3-5	154, 169
11.23-5	122	1.3-6	163
11.27	111	1.3-8	73, 164
11.30	113	1.3-11	67, 87, 88, 170
11.33	111	1.4	71, 81, 88
12.1	111	1.4-5	88
14.4	130	1.5	69, 81, 82, 84
14.17	130	1.6	82, 85, 88, 92, 94, 153
14.26-40	167	1.7	66, 69, 71, 72, 73, 74, 77, 81, 84
14.39	111, 124		
15	115	1.7-8	69
15.20-3	120	1.9-10	72
15.24-8	93	1.9-11	163, 170
15.50-8	122	1.10	70, 92, 94, 153
15.51	113	1.12	86, 87
15.58	111, 124	1.12-14	66
16.1	111	1.12-18	158
16.12	111	1.12-26	77, 158
		1.13	66
2 Corinthians		1.13-14	73, 74
2.2	90	1.14	66, 74
2.2-5	118	1.14-17	66
4.2	160	1.15	74, 87
4.14	120	1.15-18	155
4.17-18	77	1.15-19	169
6.10	118	1.16	74
7.8-11	118	1.17	66, 73, 74, 86, 87
7.9	118	1.18	71, 86, 88, 93
7.10	118	1.18-19	92
8.1-2	72, 85	1.18-26	9, 155, 158
8.2	113	1.19-20	76
9.8	83	1.19-26	69, 87
10.1	91	1.20-1	75
12.14	96		

1.23	76	2.27	118
1.24-6	76	2.28	71, 85
1.25	71, 87, 88, 89	2.28-9	96
1.27	72, 76, 78, 87, 88	2.29	71, 80
1.27-8	66, 72	2.29-30	69, 85
1.27-30	9, 67, 69, 76, 93	2.30	65, 79
1.27–2.4	69	3.1	66, 67, 71, 82, 89, 90, 92, 93, 96, 155, 169
1.27–2.18	66, 69		
1.27–4.3	67	3.1-2	67
1.28	76, 78	3.1–4.3	66, 69
1.29	77, 80	3.2	66, 67, 69, 76, 166
1.29-30	66	3.2-4	166
1.30	69, 72, 76, 77, 79	3.2–4.3	67
2.1	69, 81, 84	3.3	166
2.1-2	66	3.4-14	69, 158, 159
2.1-4	87, 88, 96, 169, 170	3.5	109
2.1-8	156	3.7	71
2.2	69, 71, 72, 86, 87, 88, 96	3.7-14	86
		3.8	71
2.2-4	78, 88	3.8-10	72
2.2-5	96	3.10	69, 75, 77, 81
2.3	71, 78	3.10-11	93, 153
2.3-4	78, 91	3.12	158
2.4	72, 78	3.12-14	72, 94, 159
2.5	69, 71, 72, 78, 80, 86, 160	3.13	72
		3.13-15	72
2.5-8	158	3.14	153
2.5-11	67, 78, 80, 90	3.15	71, 72, 158, 159, 161
2.6	71, 78	3.15-17	158
2.6-8	78, 79	3.16	159
2.6-11	69, 72, 78, 166	3.17	72, 86, 157, 159
2.7	78	3.17-19	69
2.9-11	72, 79, 153	3.18-19	66, 153, 159
2.11	94	3.19	71, 72
2.12	69	3.20	85
2.13	153	3.20-1	67, 72, 90, 92, 93, 94, 153
2.16	75, 85, 88, 92, 94, 153		
		3.21	178
2.17	71, 74, 88	4.1	65, 69, 71, 72, 85, 88, 96
2.17-18	69, 74, 88, 89, 93, 95, 96, 155, 169		
		4.1-2	65
2.18	71, 89, 169	4.1-3	66, 72
2.19-30	79, 158, 170	4.2	69, 71, 72
2.20	79	4.2-3	87
2.20-1	79, 87	4.4	71, 73, 82, 89, 90, 92, 93, 96, 155, 169, 183
2.20-2	69		
2.24	75, 76	4.4-5	9, 96
2.25	71	4.4-6	91, 92, 165
2.25-30	65, 79, 81, 109	4.4-7	67, 91

4.4-9	67, 90	2.8	106, 107
4.5	90, 91	2.9	106
4.6	91, 163, 164	2.11	107, 128, 130
4.7	91	2.11-12	102
4.8	67, 72, 160	2.12	107, 108, 124, 154
4.8-9	158	2.13	102, 103, 164
4.9	86, 160	2.13-16	102–3
4.10	65, 71, 72, 81, 84, 86, 88, 89, 93, 154, 155	2.14	102, 104, 106, 107, 108, 109, 110, 113, 126, 128, 157, 158
4.10-19	169		
4.10-20	67, 69, 81	2.14-16	101
4.11	82, 83, 84, 85	2.15	107, 108
4.11-13	84	2.15-16	102, 107, 108
4.12	83	2.16	102
4.13	83	2.17	101, 102, 106
4.14	69, 84, 86	2.17-20	106
4.14-16	81	2.18	101, 107, 108
4.14-18	84	2.19	88, 107, 114, 119, 154
4.15	69		
4.15-16	65, 84	2.19-20	107, 154, 164
4.15-18	84	2.20	107
4.17	85	3.1-5	101, 108
4.18	65, 81, 85	3.1-10	170
4.19	85	3.2	106, 107, 108, 124
4.21-3	67	3.2-3	77
		3.2-5	126
Colossians		3.3	107, 108, 109
1.9-12	90	3.3-4	101, 113
3.15	91	3.4	109
		3.5	101, 108
1 Thessalonians		3.6	101
		3.6-11	106
1.2-3	163, 164, 170	3.7	106, 107, 124
1.2–2.16	171	3.7-8	128
1.3	107, 114, 119	3.8	101
1.4	106, 127, 134	3.9-10	90, 165
1.6	72, 101, 104, 107, 108, 109, 113, 126, 157, 158, 164	3.10	101, 107, 163, 164
		3.10-11	106
		3.12	129
1.7	158	3.13	107, 154
1.9	108, 110, 126	4.1	104, 106, 107, 124
1.9-10	164	4.1-8	128
1.10	107, 108, 114, 120, 154	4.1-12	172
		4.1-18	106
2.1	106, 111	4.2	111
2.1-8	104	4.5	117, 118, 119, 134
2.1-12	106	4.6	106
2.2	107, 108	4.9	111
2.4	107	4.9-10	127, 128
2.7	19, 107, 128		

4.10	104, 106, 107, 124, 129	5.11	104, 107, 111, 124, 128, 129, 130, 131
4.11-12	128, 144	5.12	106
4.12	111, 119, 134	5.12-13	165
4.13	7–8, 111, 112, 113, 114, 117, 118, 119, 120, 122, 127, 128, 129, 133, 134, 135	5.12-15	108, 128, 130, 172
		5.12-22	130
		5.13-22	144
		5.14	106, 107, 124
4.13-17	111, 124, 130, 169	5.14-15	165
4.13-18	7, 104, 107, 108, 109, 111, 113, 114, 122, 127, 129, 154, 173	5.14-24	170
		5.16	164
		5.16-18	90, 164
4.13–5.10	130	5.17	163, 164
4.13–5.11	101, 144, 172	5.18	164, 165
4.14	111, 120, 121, 122, 124, 129, 133	5.19-22	165
		5.23	108, 154
4.14-17	129	5.25	106, 163
4.15	111, 122, 123	5.26	106, 128
4.15-17	123, 124	5.27	106
4.16	111, 119, 122		
4.16-17	122, 123	**2 Thessalonians**	
4.17	111, 114, 115, 122, 123, 129	1.4-7	113
		3.1	164
4.18	107, 111, 123, 124, 125, 128, 129, 130, 169	3.7	157
		3.9	157
5.1	106, 111, 134	**1 Timothy**	
5.1-2	134	3.3	91
5.1-10	130	6.6	83
5.1-11	107, 111, 129, 154		
5.1-22	106	**2 Timothy**	
5.2	107, 111	3.16	75
5.3	108, 123, 134	4.6	75
5.4	106, 135		
5.5	134	**Titus**	
5.6	119, 134	3.2	91
5.7	135, 163		
5.8	119, 128, 134	**1 Peter**	
5.9	114, 134, 135	2.1	91
5.10	114, 129		

Index of Subjects

Abraham 41–2
action
   Stoic psychology of 31–2
affect/affection
   as an emotion term 15–18, 28
affection
   in Paul's letters 8, 65, 69, 71, 106, 126–8,
      136, 164, 170
affective turn 10
afflictions, *see* suffering
Alcibiades 42–4
Alexander, Loveday 68
anger 3–4, 5, 40–1, 51
Apollonius of Tyana 52
Aquinas 15, 17
Aristotle
   and *eudaimonia* 26
   and involuntary movements 39
   on mental events 26
   and passions 6–7, 23
assent 28, 29–32
Augustine 15, 17
Aune, David Charles 5

Barclay, John M. G. 7–8, 60, 109–10,
   116–20, 126–7, 134–5
Barton, Stephen C. 3–4, 125–7, 131–2
Bell, Catherine 162
Berthomé, François, and Michael
   Houseman 165–6
Bockmuehl, Markus 68, 70, 71,
   76, 160

caution 38–9, 61, see also *eupatheiai*
χαρά/χαίρω, *see also* joy
   in Paul 66, 67, 70, 71, 73, 77, 81, 86, 87,
      88, 89, 90, 92, 107, 158, 164, 183
   in Stoicism 38
Christ hymn/poem 72, 78–9, 166
Chrysippus
   on excessive impulses 33–5

   on grief and consolation 43, 49–50, 53,
      54–5, 56
   on impressions 28
   on involuntary weeping 40
   on *oikeiōsis* 45
   on *pneuma* 27
Cicero
   on grief and consolation 36, 43,
      49–50, 52–3
   on joy 61
   on passions 48–9
   and philosophical therapy 47–9
cognition, *see under* emotion(s)
community, *see also* relationships
   of believers 4, 6, 7–8, 65, 76, 97, 99, 108,
      110, 117, 126, 128, 129, 130, 131, 134,
      135, 137, 139, 140, 144, 159, 172,
      175–6, 179–80, 182
   and emotional regimes 148–9, 151–2,
      162, 164–5, 179–81
conflict, *see* suffering
consolation
   1 Thessalonians as a letter of 104–5,
      120–5, 126–31, 155, 169
   in antiquity 7, 43, 49–50, 52–4, 104, 124,
      125, 132
   in Epictetus, *see under* Epictetus
   eschatological basis of 7–8, 101, 120–37,
      144, 152, 153, 155–6, 169, 173–4,
      175–6, 177, 180, 182
   Philippians as a letter of 70
   in Seneca, *see under* Seneca
   social character and function of 126–37,
      176–7, 180, 182
Crantor of Soli 53
Cyreniacs 54, 56

Davies, Douglas J. 163, 167
delight 34, 35, 36–8, 43, *see also* passions
desire 33, 34, 36–8, *see also* passions
desire for improvement, *see* moral emotions

de Vos, Craig Steven 110, 113–14
Dixon, Thomas 15–16
Donfried, Karl P. 105
Durkheim, Émile 141, 173

emotion(s), *see also* feeling(s); grief; joy; passions
  authorized/sanctioned emotions 139, 140, 146, 149, 150, 151–2, 156, 162, 173–4, 175–6, 177–8, 182
  and belief 3–4, 6, 139, 140, 144–5, 146–9, 150, 151, 152, 153, 155–7, 161, 162, 165, 169, 173–4, 175–6, 177–83, *see also under* passions
  and cognition 3–4, 7, 10–14, 17, 19–20, 139, 140, 143, 147, 151–2, 169, 172, 176–7, 179, 183
  conceptual history of 14–17
  as evaluative judgements 3–4, 17, 140, 176, 180, *see also under* passions
  and formation of the early believers 97–9, 134–7, 139–40, 144–5, 152, 153, 167, 174, 175–6, 179–80, 182
  and language 7, 89, 104, 119, 143–4, 168–9, 173, 174
  and power 150, 153, 156, 157, 168, 174, 183
  in research, *see* emotion studies
  social character and function of 3, 4, 7–14, 19–20, 139, 140, 143–7, 149, 150, 151–2, 153, 156, 169, 174, 175–6, 179–81, 182–3, *see also under* consolation; joy
  Stoic taxonomy of 37–44
  terminology of 14–18, 23–4
  trivializing of 16–17
emotional ordering 139, 147, 151, 153–74, 177–8, 181, 182–3; *see also* feeling rules
  and instruction and imitation 146, 157–61, 173, 175, 182–3
  and language 168–9, 173–4, 183
  and letters 170–3, 183
  and ritual 161–7, 173–4, 182, 183
  and symbols 139, 146, 147, 149, 151, 153–7, 161, 173–4, 182–3
emotional programme 146, 147, 149, 151, 154, 157, 161, 163, 167, 173, 174, 177, 182

emotional regime 13–14, 20–1, 139, 140, 145–52, 153, 157, 169, 173–4, 175, 177, 181–3
  alternate/ideal ordering of reality 146, 147, 151, 152, 153–4, 155, 156, 162, 164, 172, 174, 177, 182, *see also under* eschatology
  dialectical relationships within 145–9, 151, 153, 156, 173–4, 182
  emotional ordering, *see* emotional ordering
  emotional programme, *see* emotional programme
  emotional transcendence-transition 147, 151, 173, 177
  inspiration-orientation 147–8, 173
  in New Testament research 3, 4
  Pauline emotional regime 139, 140, 151–74, 182–3
  Pauline versus Stoic emotional regimes 175–83
  and power 149, 150, 153, 156, 157, 168, 174, 183
  religious emotional regime 146–51
  and symbols, *see under* symbols
emotion studies
  contemporary 11–18
  New Testament 1–10, 16–17, 19–20
emotional turn 10
Engberg-Pedersen, Troels 23, 29
Epaphroditus 65–6, 67, 69, 79–80, 81, 85, 89, 95, 96, 118, 158, 170
Epictetus
  on grief and consolation 52, 59–61, 133
  on impressions 30, 37, 47, 50, 59
  on joy 61
  on judgements 37, 50, 59, 60–1, 83
  and *oikeiōsis* 46
  and philosophical therapy 43, 47, 48, 50, 59, 60, 133
  on *prohairesis*, *see below* on volition
  on social roles 60, 130–1, 180
  on universe's ordering 181
  on volition 45, 59, 130–1, 133, 180
Epicurus 26, 49, 56
eschatology
  eschatological reality 8, 9, 73, 92–5, 97–9, 107–8, 119, 124–5, 128, 129, 130, 133–7, 151–2, 153–4, 155–6,

159, 164, 167, 169, 172, 173, 174, 175, 181, 182
eschatological vindication 72, 79, 80, 92, 98, 155
and grief and consolation 7–8, 101, 114–16, 119, 120–37, 144, 152, 153, 155–6, 169, 172, 173–4, 175–6, 177, 180, 182
and joy, *see under* joy
eudaimonia 24–6, 64, 179
eupatheiai
  versus moral emotions 43
  in Stoicism 38–9, 58, 61–4, 93–4, 176

fear 34, 35, 36–8, 40, 42, *see also* passions
fear of future error, *see* moral emotions
Fee, Gordon D. 66, 73, 74, 79, 83–4, 89, 166–7, 175
feeling rules 3, 13, 125–6, 131, 134, 136, 152, 182–3
feeling(s), *see also* emotion(s); feeling rules
  as an emotion term 15–16, 18
  involuntary 40–2
  patterns of 139, 145–7, 150–4, 157, 161, 172–4, 177–8, 183
formation of the early believers, *see under* emotion(s)
Frame, James Everett 117
friendship, *see also* relationships
  Greco-Roman notions of 68–70, 74, 83, 84, 85, 125
  loss of 127
  Paul and 86, 87–8, 96, 97
  Philippians as a letter of 68–70
  in Stoicism 56–8, 83
Funk, Robert W. 170–1

Garland, David E. 67
gift
  the Philippians' gift to Paul 65–7, 81–6, 95, 96, 154
Gill, Christopher 23, 177–8
gospel
  living worthy of 72, 78
  partnership in 65, 73, 81–6, 95–7, 154
  progress of 3, 66, 73, 77, 79, 80, 87–8, 85, 97, 98, 154–5, 158, 175
  suffering for 74, 76, 77, 80, 89, 93, 98, 107–9, 158

truth of 78, 98, 107, 119, 153, 155, 171, 175
Graver, Margaret R. 35, 38–9, 57–8, 63
grief, *see also* consolation; λύπη/λυπέω
  in New Testament scholarship 2, 3, 5, 7–8
  societal regulation of 125–6
  Stoic definitions of 34, 36–8, 40, 42, 43, 132, 176
  Stoic therapy of, *see under* Chrysippus; Cicero; Epictetus; Seneca
  the Thessalonians' 101, 111–20, 126–7, 128–9, 131–2, 133, 134, 136–7, 145, 152, 156, 157, 169, 172, 173–4, 175–6, 182

Halbwachs, Maurice 173
happiness, *see also* joy
  in Paul 9–10
  in Stoicism 26, 50, 62–3, 130, 181
Hawthorne, Gerald F., and Ralph P. Martin 75
Heath, Jane M. F. 171–2
hēgemonikon 27–8, 32, 33, 37, 59
ἡγέομαι 71, 72, 78, 93
Hochschild, Arlie Russell 13
Hockey, Katherine M. 4, 16–17
Holloway, Paul A. 70
Homer 52
Hooker, Morna D. 78
Horrell, David G. 143, 162–3

identity
  of believers 3, 4, 19, 93, 98, 126, 127, 133, 134, 135, 136–7, 139, 140, 143, 144, 151–2, 153, 164, 182
  and religious emotional regimes 146, 147, 148
imitation 41, 69, 72, 77, 78–80, 86, 104, 107, 109, 146, 154, 156, 157–61, 174, 176
  and emotional ordering, *see under* emotional ordering
exemplars in Stoicism 50, 54, 176
impression 28–31, 37, 40–2, 47, 50, 59–60, 97
  hormetic 31, 32
  kataleptic 29–30
  propositional content of 28–30, 35

impulse 28, 31–5
  and appropriate/proper function 31, 34
  excessive 32–5
instruction
  and emotional ordering, *see under*
    emotional ordering
involuntary feelings, see *propatheiai*
Inwood, Brad 23, 28, 38
Izard, Carroll E. 11

joy, *see also* χαρά/χαίρω
  eschatological basis of 3, 8–9, 72–3, 80,
    88, 90, 92–5, 97–9, 107, 125, 152, 154,
    155–6, 165, 169, 175, 178, 181, 182
  in the gospel's advancement 3, 86–9,
    95–6, 98, 154–5, 158, 175, 181
  in the Lord 66, 67, 81, 82, 86, 89–92, 93,
    96, 155, 169, 183
  mutual 8, 76, 87, 88–9, 95–7, 169, 175,
    179, 181, 182
  in New Testament scholarship 1–5, 8–10
  in partnership in the gospel 79–80, 81–6,
    95–7, 154, 175
  and right thinking 72–3, 86, 93–5, 98–9,
    175, 178
  and sacred symbols 150
  social character and function of 3, 9,
    95–7, 98–9, 145, 152, 153, 155, 156,
    175, 176, 179, 181, 182
  in Stoicism 38–9, 93–4, 96, 97, 99, 176,
    178, *see also under* Epictetus; Seneca
  and suffering 72–3, 88–9, 90, 92, 93,
    95–6, 98, 151, 155, 156, 158, 161, 169,
    177, 182

Kagan, Jerome 10, 14
Kennedy, George A. 105
knowledge
  Stoic psychology of 28–31
  and *eupatheiai* 38–9
κοινωνία, *see under* gospel
Kraftchick, Steven J. 6

language
  and emotional ordering, *see under*
    emotional ordering
  Paul's use of 5, 7, 74, 83, 84, 85, 89, 103,
    104, 108, 119, 134, 143–4, 159, 166,
    169, 173, 174,

terminology of emotions, *see under*
  emotion
letters
  of consolation, *see under* consolation
  and emotional ordering, *see under*
    emotional ordering
  and *enargeia* 171–2
  of friendship, *see under* friendship
  letter writing in antiquity 67, 68, 69, 70,
    125, 143, 170
  letter writing as paraenesis 7, 47, 54, 69,
    103–4, 131, 132, 177
  and personal presence 170–1, *see also*
    parousia, apostolic
  symbolic significance of 172
Lieu, Judith M. 172
Long, Anthony A. 25, 26, 59, 130–1
Long, Anthony A., and David N. Sedley 32
Luckensmeyer, David 114, 119
λύπη/λυπέω, *see also* grief
  in Paul 8, 112, 117, 118
  in Stoicism 34, 37–8, 132
Lutz, Catherine A. 12

Malherbe, Abraham J. 7, 83, 103–4,
  109, 112
Malina, Bruce J. 163–4
Manning, C. E. 53, 54
Marshall, I. Howard 116
Meeks, Wayne A. 72, 140–5, 161, 162, 167
metriopatheia, *see under* Seneca
moral emotions 42–4
  versus *eupatheiai* 43

nature
  living in accordance with 24–6, 30, 31,
    44–6, 47, 55, 57, 59, 62, 63, 64, 94,
    179, 180, 181
  living contrary to 32–3
Nicholl, Colin R. 121
non-wise/ordinary person 30, 31, 38, 43,
  44, 48–9, 57, 63, 64, 94
Nussbaum, Martha C. 14, 45, 48, 50–1

oikeiōsis 45–6, 178
opinion 30, 33–4, 37, 39, 55, 97, 132, 176
opponents, *see* opposition
opposition 66, 72, 76, 78, 79, 89, 101, 107,
  109, 113, 116, *see also* suffering

parousia, apostolic 102, 170–3
Parousia of Christ 7, 80, 88, 92, 107–8,
    114–16, 120–4, 129, 133–6, 153–5,
    171–6, 182
partnership in the gospel, *see under* gospel
passions
    as evaluative judgements 32, 35–7, 43,
        48–9, 59–60, 62, 64, 97, 132, 176
    as excessive impulses 32–5
    and false beliefs 24, 33, 36–7, 43, 48, 55,
        56–7, 59, 64, 132, 176
    Stoic definitions of 37–8
    terminology of 15–18, 23–24
pathos
    rhetorical use of 4, 5–7
    terminology of 23–4
patterns of feeling, *see under* feeling(s)
Pauline emotional regime, *see under*
    emotional regime
Pauline versus Stoic emotional regimes,
    see under emotional regime
Pearson, Birger A. 102–3
persecution 4, 73, 102, 105, 108–11, 113,
    126, 134, 138, *see also* suffering
Philo 41–2, 51, 58
φρονεῖν/φρονέω 71, 72, 78, 81–2, 86, 93,
    96, 158–9, 161, see also *phrōnesis/*
    φρόνησις
phrōnesis/φρόνησις
    of Christ 78–9, 80, 96, 160–1
    Christian 80, 86, 96, 160–1
Plamper, Jan 11–12, 14
Pliny 52
Plutarch 52
pneuma 27–8
prayer, *see under* ritual
pre-emotions/passions, see *propatheiai*
propatheiai 39–42, 57, 64
Ps.-Plutarch 52
psychē 27–8, 31, 34, 63, 176

rationality, *see* reason
reason
    Stoic understanding of 24–6, 27, 28–9,
        30, 32–9, 42, 44–6, 48, 50–1, 56, 58,
        59, 63, 64, 94, 97, 132, 133, 176–7,
        178–9, 180, 181
relationships, *see also* friendship;
    community

among believers 87–8, 96–9, 114–16,
    127–31, 135–7, 142, 151, 156, 164,
    171–2, 175, 179–181
with Christ/God 77, 83–4, 86, 96–9,
    135–7, 165–7, 171–2, 175, 179–181
partnership in the gospel, *see*
    under gospel
between Paul and his churches 65,
    69–70, 77, 81–2, 87–8, 96–9,
    127–8, 171–2
in Stoicism 60, 64, 97, 130–1, 178, 180
remorse, *see* moral emotions
Reydams-Schils, Gretchen 57, 58
Riis, Ole and Linda Woodhead 13–15,
    20–1, 145–51, 153, 155–6, 157, 158,
    161–3, 168–9, 172–3, 173–4
ritual 141, 144, 147, 154, 161–7, 172,
    173–4, 182, 183
    and emotional ordering, *see under*
        emotional ordering
    and prayer 163–7
Rosaldo, Michelle Z. 12
Rowe, Kavin C. 20, 179, 181

sage, *see* wise person
self-sufficiency 60, 83–4, 97, 131, 180
Seneca
    on anger 40–1, 51
    on fortune 181
    on grief and consolation 52–8,
        60–1, 132–3
    on joy 61–3, 94, 178
    on joy in non-integral goods 63
    on *metriopatheia* 55–6, 132
    and philosophical therapy 43, 46–7,
        51
    on reason 44, 177, 181
    on self-examination 51
    on unassented feelings 40–2
    on the wise person's weeping 58–9
Shantz, Colleen 9–10
Smith, Abraham 104
Smith, Jonathan Z. 161
social function of emotion, *see under*
    emotion(s); consolation; joy
soul 25, 27, see also *hēgemonikon*
    four powers of the rational soul 28
status inconsistency 141–2
Still, Todd D. 110–11, 113–14, 118, 143

Stoicism, *see also* Chrysippus; Cicero; Epictetus; Seneca
    dominance of 19–20
    philosophical background of emotion 24–32
    psychophysical nature of mental events in 26–32, 33–5, 39
    theory of emotion 32–44
    therapy of emotion 44–64
suffering, *see also* opposition; persecution
    believers' 4, 66, 72–3
    Christ's 6, 73, 77, 78–9, 80, 98
    for the gospel, *see under* gospel
    joy and, *see under* joy
    Paul's 5, 9, 73–6, 77, 80, 84, 86, 88, 89, 92, 95–6, 98, 107, 158
    the Philippians' 66, 72–3, 76–7, 80, 92, 93, 95–6, 98, 156, 161, 169, 177
    in Stoicism 36, 94
    the Thessalonians' 101, 102, 107, 108–11, 113, 126–7, 128, 136, 158
Stowers, Stanley K. 47, 124
Sumney, Jerry L. 6
symbols
    death as a symbol of Christian distinction 8, 135, 136
    and emotional regimes 3, 13–4, 139, 145–51, 153–7, 161, 173–4, 182
    and eschatology 8, 123, 135, 136, 155–6, 169, 173–4, 182
    and language 164, 166, 168–9
    and letters 172–3
    and ritual 128, 157, 161, 163, 164, 166, 172

Theodoret 103, 117
Thompson, James W. 6
Timothy 65–6, 79–80, 101, 108, 126, 158, 170

unwise person, *see* non-wise person

vice 25, 36, 39, 43, 94
virtue 24–6, 39, 41, 43, 44, 56–7, 61–4, 83, 94, 131, 137, 176, 179, 181
virtues, Christian 160, 161
volition, *see under* Epictetus

Watson, Duane F. 67
Weima, Jeffrey A. D. 102, 128
Welborn, Larry L. 8
Wiles, Gordon P. 67–8
Wilson, Marcus 53, 60–1
wise person 24, 26, 30–1, 38–9, 41–2, 43, 47–8, 56–8, 60, 61, 62–4, 70, 83, 94, 97, 131, 132, 133, 176, 181, 183
wish 38–9, 61, see also *eupatheiai*
Wright, N. T. 8–9

Zeno 27, 34–5, 37

www.ingramcontent.com/pod-product-compliance
Lightning Source LLC
Chambersburg PA
CBHW072108010526
44111CB00037B/2049